THE AGE OF DISAPPOINTMENT

The review of the year in Australian politics

The Age Of Disappointment: The review of the year in Australian politics
ISBN (paperback): 978-1-7635701-2-2
ISBN (Amazon):   979-8-3025811-6-7

©2024 Eddy Jokovich & David Lewis

All rights reserved. No part of this book may be reproduced in any form or by any electronic or mechanical means, including information storage and retrieval systems, without written permission from the authors, except for the use of brief quotations in book reviews and promotional material.

December 2024.
Published by New Politics, an imprint of ARMEDIA Pty. Ltd.

New Politics
PO Box 1265, Darlinghurst NSW 1300
www.newpolitics.com.au
Email: info@newpolitics.com.au

Production: ARMEDIA

Published and produced on the lands of the Wangal and Gadigal people.

EDITORIAL NOTE ON THE USE OF AI TECHNOLOGY
We employ artificial intelligence tools in the editing process of our articles. These tools assisted with transcriptions of audio recordings, grammar correction, refinement and formatting.

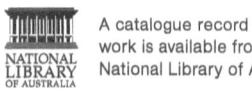

A catalogue record for this work is available from the National Library of Australia

CONTENTS

Introduction: The year in politics 6

FEBRUARY
1. The big Labor shift in fiscal policy 9
2. International condemnation while Israel's brutal actions in Gaza continue 17
3. The devil in Dutton's details 23
4. Australia's asylum seeker debate amidst media manipulation 29
5. The Coalition's fear and exaggeration campaign 35
6. Unveiling the imbalance in Australia's coverage of the Gaza conflict 40

MARCH
7. Labor triumphs in Dunkley 44
8. Nuclear ambition: A naked political power play masked as energy policy 50
9. Does the ABC have a future in the changing media landscape? 59
10. The great Australian silence in Gaza 66
11. The religious discrimination bill is a test of Australia's secular values 73
12. Sweeping campaign and donation reforms needed for democratic renewal ... 79

APRIL
13. The death of aid workers in Gaza sparks global outrage 85
14. Supermarket shake-up: A need for stronger regulation 90
15. Fixing Australia's housing affordability crisis 96
16. Lehrmann case exposes flaws in Australia's defamation practices 102
17. Navigating the complexities of the Gaza conflict and global diplomacy 107
18. Australia's rise in the global economic rankings downplayed by the media ... 112

MAY
19. Men, we have a problem: Australia's escalating domestic violence crisis 118
20. UN vote on Palestine exposes Australia's inconsistent foreign policy 124
21. A federal 2024 Budget to address fiscal priorities and political challenges 130
22. Justice denied: Deep flaws in whistleblower protection and accountability ... 136
23. Israel increasingly isolated over genocide in Gaza 142
24. Julian Assange: The government's inadequate and weak diplomacy 147

JUNE
25. The media's broken mirror exposes Australia's racial divides 151
26. A second term for Labor? A balance between governing and politics 157
27. Frydenberg's failed comeback reveals big problems in the Liberal Party 162
28. NACC ignores Robodebt corruption: Is accountability at risk? 168
29. Dutton's conservative stance and climate wars will isolate Australia 175
30. The wrecking ball of Australia politics: Nuclear not in the public interest 181
31. The struggle for press freedom and whistleblower advocacy continues 189

JULY

32. The slight on the hill: A schism within Labor's membership 195
33. Navigating Islamophobia in Australian media and politics 203
34. Religion in politics: Should we be wary or accept its influence? 210
35. The surreal state of American politics 217
36. ICJ ruling condemns Israel's occupation of Palestinian territories 224
37. Unpacking the Australian media's preoccupation with a U.S. election 232

AUGUST

38. Is the National Anti-Corruption Commission living up to expectations? 238
39. Australia's elevated terror alert: National security or politics as usual? 243
40. The ethical dilemma of using gambling to support the world's worst media ... 248
41. AUKUS is jeopardising Australia's independence and economic stability 253
42. Conservative race-baiting politics in the spotlight yet again 258
43. The struggle to define the government's vision and direction 264
44. Reclaiming the public interest and challenging the power of the super rich 273

SEPTEMBER

45. Will super-profits and wealth taxes unlock a fairer future? 280
46. Labor's fight for progressive reform in the face of Coalition sabotage 286
47. The sanitisation of war and the human cost of the Land Forces expo 294
48. The Labor–Greens infighting over housing leaves Australians in limbo 299
49. Israel's escalating war crimes in Lebanon and Australia's weak response 306

OCTOBER

50. Australia's unquestioning support for Israel and a deafening silence 312
51. The politics of protest: Double standards and undermining free speech 319
52. Albanese and the mistake of endlessly appeasing the Israel lobby 324
53. NACC fails to deliver, corruption wins again 331
54. Fuck the colony: The uncomfortable truths about colonisation 337
55. When will Australia embrace a republic of ideas? 344

NOVEMBER

56. A dark new era for U.S. democracy? 350
57. The unmasking of the West reveals an ugly face 358
58. The social media ban is just another political smokescreen 364
59. Democracy for sale: Donations reforms will protect the powerful 370
60. Labor's immigration retreat: Pandering to fear and loathing 376

DECEMBER

61. Netanyahu arrest warrant could see a rapid change in Palestine 382
62. Labor's legislative inertia could cost it at the next election 388
Epilogue 395

ABOUT THE AUTHORS

EDDY JOKOVICH is editor of *New Politics*, and co-presenter of the New Politics Australia podcast. He has worked as a journalist, publisher, author, political analyst, campaigner, war correspondent, and lecturer in media studies at the University of Technology, Sydney and the University of Sydney; has a wide range of experience working in editorial and media production work and is Director of ARMEDIA, an independent publishing and communications company specialising in public interest media.

DAVID LEWIS is co-presenter of the New Politics Australia podcast, historian, musicologist, musician and political scientist based in Sydney. His lecturing and research interests include roots music, popular music, Australian, U.K. and U.S. politics and crime fiction. He has published in *Music Forum Australia*, *Eureka Street*, *Quadrant*, *Crikey* and has edited several books.

NEW POLITICS AUSTRALIA is a weekly podcast, providing analysis and opinions on Australia politics. It can be found at Apple and Google podcasts, Amazon Audible and Spotify.

INTRODUCTION: THE YEAR IN POLITICS

The Age of Disappointment is a nod to Eric Hobsbawm's classic 'Age of...' series, a sprawling and excellent history of modern Europe from 1789 to 2000. This work, however, is a more modest appraisal of a strange year in Australian federal politics. As we explored in *Diary of an Election Victory* published in 2022, the Albanese government came to power on a wave of optimism, heralding hopes for real change and progress. Yet, high expectations can be a double-edged sword, and for some, the government has fallen short of these lofty aspirations.

Our next book—*Rising Phoenix, Falling Shadows*—examined the Albanese government's second year—2023—a period characterised by policy missteps, rookie errors, and significant stakeholder disappointment. While there were notable successes, the government's ongoing support for AUKUS, tacit support and complicity in atrocities and genocide committed by the state of Israel in Palestine (as well as unprovoked attacks by the Israel Defense Forces on Lebanon and Syria), has overshadowed much of its positive legacy.

A failed referendum to amend the Constitution to recognise Indigenous Australians and establish a Voice to Parliament was defeated by a vigorous and deceptive "No" campaign, compounded by a lacklustre and inflexible "Yes" campaign that alienated more people than it convinced. This is where the drift for the Albanese government commenced. As 2024 began, the government stumbled into its third year, seemingly adrift and with a purpose less clear than the electorate might have hoped.

First-term governments often face steep challenges—scandals, gaffes, policy overreach, and ministers testing the boundaries of propriety. Navigating which policy goals are achievable, which must be abandoned due to the previous government's legacy, and which risk alienating key stakeholders or failing in the Senate are all part of the growing pains. To its credit, the Albanese government has largely avoided major scandals or gaffes. However—and this is a *significant* caveat—there have been notable mistakes and what many would call disappointments.

Before launching into the criticisms, let us first acknowledge the government's successes.

The economy has been managed impressively, considering the unmanageable mess inherited from what many regard as the most corrupt and venal government in Australian history. While challenges remain, there have been significant advanced in taming this chaos. The government has fostered a renewed and more positive relationship with China and the Pacific region, which counts as a clear success. In addition, a strong cabinet has avoided major scandals, and some ministers have performed exceptionally well.

However, the government has faced considerable challenges. A recalcitrant Reserve Bank Board has kept interest rates fixed at levels many economists consider too high, with little justification beyond dubious comparisons to other governments. Negotiations with the crossbench have also proven difficult. Perhaps most egregiously, the government used its numbers, along with Opposition support, to push through new electoral funding laws without allowing independents and minor parties to review or amend the legislation. Meanwhile, the government's unwillingness or inability to negotiate effectively with the Australian Greens has delayed crucial housing crisis legislation.

The tertiary education sector has been an outright disaster. Overpaid vice-chancellors, mimicking the worst excesses of 1980s CEOs, have gutted universities. Although the government has promised to slash HECS debts in a potential second term, alarming developments such as the University of Adelaide's decision to cease face-to-face lectures—claiming it enhances the 'student experience'—have caused widespread concern. The University of Wollongong's decision to axe its history program is another devastating blow to intellectual rigour and critical thinking in Australia.

It is not only the government that has disappointed. Although it is marginally ahead in the opinion polls, the Peter Dutton-led Liberal Party has failed to gain credibility, despite its attempts to import U.S.-style culture wars and leverage a compliant mainstream media. The disastrous 2022 election left the party in an almost impossible position to win government outright. Dutton's awkward anti-intellectual leadership style, coupled with a shadow cabinet composed of remnants of the previous government, does not inspire confidence. Although the re-election of Donald Trump in the U.S. has emboldened some within the party, the path for the Liberal–National Coalition to forming even a minority government seems tenuous. The Coalition needs to win 22 seats at the next election—an enormous challenge even under favourable conditions and with a popular leader. Its purge of moderates has hardened its base but alienated the critical Australian 'centre', leaving blue-ribbon Liberal seats in teal-independent hands with little chance of recovery.

How did we get here? How did the government and the Opposition find themselves in these positions? The following chapters explore the many contributing factors. Were we to write this in the grand, sweeping style of Manning Clark, with heroes and villains etched in bold relief, the pages would overflow with villains, while true heroes would be harder to find: whistleblowers facing long-term imprisonment—such as David McBride and possibly Richard Boyle—for doing the right thing, might be among them. Despite the disheartening efforts of Attorney-General Mark Dreyfus—whose fine legal mind seems riddled with blind spots—the fight for their release continues and will hopefully persist until justice is served.

The chapters ahead dissect the dramas, intrigues, politics, and personalities of the strange and critical year that was 2024. Politically, Australia finds itself in an unusual and unsettling place. In these pages, we endeavour to make sense of it all.

***

FEBRUARY

THE BIG LABOR SHIFT IN FISCAL POLICY

3 February 2024

The recent adjustments to the Stage 3 tax cuts by the Labor government represent a significant shift in fiscal policy, one that diverges markedly from the course set by the previous Coalition government in 2019. Originally, these tax cuts were criticised for disproportionately benefiting high-income earners while providing minimal support to lower and middle-income individuals and this approach was seen as antithetical to the Labor Party's core principles, yet the party supported it with considerable reluctance in opposition, and then after they formed government after May 2022—up until last week. The question of why it took the Labor government such a long time to amend this policy is complex, involving strategic considerations and the timing of the announcement.

The Labor government's eventual decision to adjust the tax cuts so that almost 85 per cent of wage earners would benefit more equitably marks a critical departure from the policy's initial design. The original plan, which would have seen individuals on a $200,000 income receive a $9,000 tax cut, was halved to $4,500 under the revised scheme. This change aligns more closely with the Labor Party's ideological commitment to equity and social welfare, challenging the perception of inaction or reluctance to amend policies inherited from previous administrations.

The strategic timing of the announcement, made during a relatively quiet period in January, suggests a calculated move to ensure maximum visibility and impact, avoiding the risk of the message being lost amidst other news. This period was marked by minor controversies led by the Coalition, such as the debate over Australia Day merchandise at Woolworths, which ultimately did not overshadow the tax cut announcement. The Labor government's strategy appears to have been to wait for an opportune moment to introduce these changes, thereby maximising the political and social impact.

Criticism of the tax cuts' adjustment has emerged from the usual quarters—such as key elements of the media, including News Corporation—that reducing the amount high-income earners receive as a tax cut is somehow unjust. However, this perspective overlooks the broader aim of tax policy to achieve a fair distribution of tax burdens and benefits across all income brackets. The revision of the Stage 3 tax cuts has been welcomed by many economists, who argued that the original plan was regressive and would exacerbate income inequality. By making the tax system less regressive, Labor seeks to address these concerns, promoting a more equitable distribution of wealth.

The reluctance of the Labor government to amend the Stage 3 tax cuts earlier was attributed to fears of political fallout, including accusations of breaking promises and being fiscally irresponsible. However, the government's decision to proceed with the adjustments reflects a prioritisation of policy effectiveness and equity over political expediency. This move is consistent with the principles traditionally associated with Labor governments, which generally prioritise the welfare of low and medium-income earners.

The adjustment of the Stage 3 tax cuts is a significant policy shift that seeks to rectify the regressive nature of the original plan. By spreading the benefits of tax cuts more evenly across income groups, the government aims to promote fairness and reduce income inequality. This decision, while politically risky, highlights the government's commitment to its ideological foundations and its willingness to make tough decisions in the interest of promoting social welfare. The strategic timing and handling of the announcement demonstrate a nuanced understanding of the political landscape and the challenges of governing in a complex, often contentious, policy environment.

NAVIGATING BROKEN PROMISES AND POLICY SUBSTANCE

The critique of mainstream media's handling of the policy shift on Stage 3 tax cuts highlights a broader issue with political journalism and public discourse. The focus on the narrative of "broken promises", rather than the substance and implications of policy changes, reflects a pervasive challenge in how political news is covered and consumed. The media's anticipation of a policy reversal, followed by an immediate shift to accusations of "broken promises" upon the announcement of such a change, illustrates a dynamic where the complexity of governance is often overshadowed by the pursuit of controversy and conflict.

The historical context provided by referencing past leaders' unfulfilled promises—such as John Howard's introduction of the GST in 2000 and Tony Abbott's cuts to education, health, and public broadcasting in 2014—serves to highlight a perceived double standard in media and public reactions to policy shifts. The intense scrutiny faced by the Labor government over the adjustment of tax cuts, contrasted with the relatively muted response to previous administrations' policy reversals, suggests an inconsistency in how broken promises are judged and politicised.

The aggressive questioning faced by Prime Minister Anthony Albanese at the National Press Club, and his defence of the policy change as a necessary response to evolving economic circumstances, highlights the government's attempt to navigate the delicate balance between political accountability and pragmatic governance:

> **Michelle Grattan:** Prime Minister, can I take you up on this point about not adding to inflation?"
>
> **Phillip Coorey:** "Once the cost of living crisis is over, do something about bracket creep?"
>
> **Clare Armstrong:** "Why should Australians trust that you won't lie to them again?"
>
> **David Crowe:** "When you name those factors as reasons for this change, aren't you just looking for excuses here? Why didn't you level with voters at the election in May 2022?"

> **Melissa Clarke:** "You said that you asked Treasury for advice this summer—given families and many households have been feeling pain from those economic circumstances for more than a year. Why have changing Stage 3 tax cuts been off the table until this summer?
> **Olivia Caisley:** "You told Australians time and time again that there'd be no changes to the Stage 3 tax cuts, despite privately doing the exact opposite. Will you rule out bringing in a retirees tax or any changes to negative gearing?"
> **Joe Kelly:** "Labor MPs are concerned about rebuilding trust now, with the public following your decision. You promised to do politics differently, to bring integrity honesty back to politics. Isn't it important that you level with the Australian people today? And admit that you breached an election commitment? Is that something you can do?"

Albanese's emphasis on acting in the national interest, and the portrayal of the decision as a difficult but necessary deviation from previous commitments, aimed to reframe the narrative around responsible leadership rather than political expediency:

> **Anthony Albanese:** "This is the right decision done for all the right reasons. And as Prime Minister, I will always do what I believe is in the national interest. And good government is about being responsive is about doing what is necessary, not what is easy. And I want to be known as a prime minister, who had the ticker to say what was needed and to set about doing it."

The criticism of the mainstream media's focus on the "broken promise" narrative, to the exclusion of a more nuanced discussion on the merits of the policy change, reflects a broader dissatisfaction with the state of political journalism. The expectation that journalists should look deeper into the implications of policy decisions, rather than fixating on the political game of promises made and broken, suggests a desire for a more substantive and informative public discourse.

The analysis of the tax cut adjustments as a strategic move by Labor, driven by both economic necessity and a commitment to equitable policy, challenges the notion that the change constitutes a straightforward breach of trust. Instead, it is presented as an adaptation to changing economic conditions and a fulfillment of the party's broader ideological commitments to supporting lower and middle-income earners.

This discussion of the Stage 3 tax cuts adjustment reveals the complex interplay between political strategy, economic policy, and media narratives. The government's decision to prioritise economic equity and responsiveness over rigid adherence to previous commitments is defended as a reflection of responsible governance. Meanwhile, the critique of the media's focus on the broken promise narrative highlights a need for a more nuanced and informed approach to political reporting, one that better serves the public's understanding of the challenges and trade-offs inherent in policymaking.

DUTTON'S BROKEN PROMISE NARRATIVE CLASHES WITH LABOR'S TAX CUT REALIGNMENT FOR GREATER EQUITY

The opposition's strategy, spearheaded by leader of the Liberal Party, Peter Dutton, to frame the adjustment of Stage 3 tax cuts as "a breach of trust", with implications for other contentious issues like negative gearing and franking credits, represents a classic political manoeuvre aimed at capitalising on perceived inconsistencies in government policy.

However, this approach encounters a fundamental challenge when the policy change in question results in tangible benefits for the majority of wage earners. The decision to recalibrate the tax cuts, and providing greater relief to 85 per cent of wage earners than initially proposed under the Coalition, highlights a strategic realignment towards equity and fairness in fiscal policy. This realignment, while criticised by the opposition as a "broken promise", could instead be interpreted by the public as a responsive and adaptive measure to current economic conditions, enhancing the government's credibility with voters who prioritise substantive outcomes over strict adherence to campaign promises.

The National Party leader David Littleproud's comments regarding the financial pressures faced by people earning around

$190,000 annually illustrate a disconnect between political rhetoric and the economic realities of the average Australian. By positioning individuals in the top 5 per cent of income earners as representative of the broader electorate's financial challenges, the opposition risks alienating a significant portion of the population for whom such incomes are far beyond reach. This perspective highlights the disparity between the opposition's narrative and the lived experiences of the majority of Australians, potentially undermining the effectiveness of their critique.

The opposition's focus on high-income earners' reduced tax benefits neglects the progressive nature of taxation, where tax rates increase with income to ensure a fairer distribution of the tax burden. This principle ensures that while all income earners receive some form of tax relief, the system remains designed to benefit those at the lower end of the income spectrum more significantly. The misunderstanding or misrepresentation of how progressive taxation works, especially in the context of bracket creep and the structure of tax brackets, suggests a need for a more informed debate on tax policy that goes beyond the simplistic portrayal of tax cuts as universally beneficial or detrimental.

The contention that adjusting tax cuts to provide greater relief to the majority while still benefiting high-income earners—albeit to a lesser extent—constitutes a betrayal, fails to account for the complexity of governing in the public interest. Government decisions must balance a range of factors, including economic conditions, social equity, and fiscal sustainability. Labor's approach to modifying the Stage 3 tax cuts reflects an attempt to navigate these considerations, prioritising broad-based relief over adherence to previous commitments that no longer align with the current economic landscape or the principles of equity and fairness.

In this context, the debate over the Stage 3 tax cuts adjustment and the opposition's narrative of broken promises reveals deeper questions about the role of government, the nature of political promises, and the priorities that should guide policy decisions. As the government seeks to address the immediate and long-term needs of the Australian populace, the challenge lies in communicating the rationale behind policy shifts and ensuring that the benefits of such changes are widely understood and appreciated. This ongoing dialogue between the government, the opposition, and the electorate is essential for maintaining trust and ensuring that policy decisions reflect the evolving needs and values of society.

ALBANESE'S BOLD MOVE ON TAX CUTS: A TURNING POINT FOR GOVERNANCE AND POLICY REFORM

The potential legislative success—due to be debated in Parliament this week, but very likely to pass—of the amendments to the Stage Three tax cuts, is a significant moment for the Prime Minister and his administration. It highlights the strategic process of modern governance, where the interplay between political negotiation, public policy, and media narratives shapes the legislative process. The willingness of Labor to revise these tax cuts, despite potential media backlash and political opposition, may mark a critical juncture in its tenure, revealing a newfound assertiveness in pursuing its policy agenda in other areas. This moment could be reflective of a broader realisation within the Albanese government that, despite the inherent challenges and opposition, it possesses the mandate and capacity to enact significant and positive changes aligned with its ideological foundations.

The speculation about the government's future direction, including the consideration of reforms to negative gearing and franking credits, illustrates a potential shift towards more bold and transformative policy initiatives. Such a shift would not only address areas of economic inequality but also signal the government's commitment to leveraging its electoral mandate to challenge entrenched interests and promote a more equitable fiscal policy landscape. This approach, while likely to encounter resistance, represents a crucial step in redefining the government's relationship with both the media and the opposition.

The critique of the mainstream media and opposition figures such as Peter Dutton—who essentially engages on a purely negative and destructive basis—speaks to a broader challenge facing the government: navigating the complex and often adversarial political landscape without being unduly constrained by the fear of media criticism or opposition sabotage. The government's potential embrace of a more assertive and proactive policy stance may serve as a counterpoint to the strategy employed by the opposition, which has been characterised by attempts to exploit cultural and political divisions.

Labor's focus on inclusive and constructive policy-making, as opposed to the Liberal Party's tactics of engaging in or responding to culture war provocations, offers a path towards consolidating its position by appealing to the broader electorate's desire for stability, fairness, and progress.

For the opposition, there are new challenges faced by Dutton and the Liberal Party in repositioning themselves as a viable alternative to the government. The necessity of capturing the political centre, alongside the internal deliberations about the party's leadership and strategic direction, highlights the broader dynamics of political competition and the search for relevance in an evolving political landscape: electoral success is never found by searching for the extremes on the left or the right of the electorate—elections are always won by engaging people in the centre, not the extremists on the edge of society.

By potentially embracing a more courageous and policy-driven approach, the government may set a precedent for addressing longstanding issues of inequality and economic fairness. This development, while fraught with challenges, suggests a critical moment in Australian politics, where the pursuit of transformative change becomes a defining characteristic of governance.

***

INTERNATIONAL CONDEMNATION WHILE ISRAEL'S BRUTAL ACTIONS IN GAZA CONTINUE

12 February 2024

In the midst of escalating tensions and the ongoing humanitarian crisis in Gaza, recent actions by Israeli forces and the subsequent international response have drawn strong condemnation and raised questions about the principles guiding international relations and humanitarian aid. The suspension of funding for the United Nations Relief and Works Agency for Palestinian Refugees—based on unsubstantiated claims made by the Israel government—by countries such as the United States and Australia, has broader implications on international protocols and the plight of the Palestinian people.

Israeli forces have fired at crowds of Palestinians in Gaza for nine consecutive days, targeting individuals gathered to collect humanitarian aid and the severity of the situation is highlighted by the attack on trucks carrying humanitarian aid for northern Gaza. These actions have taken place against a backdrop of Israel blocking aid to the north of the Gaza Strip, exacerbating the dire humanitarian situation faced by the Palestinian population.

The suspension of funding for UNRWA by the United States and Australia marks a significant escalation in the international response to the conflict. This suspension, justified by unverified accusations from the Israeli government regarding UNRWA members' involvement in Hamas attacks against Israeli civilians, represents a worrying shift away from the established norms of evidence and investigation in international relations. The acknowledgment by U.S. Secretary of State Antony Blinken of the U.S. government's inability to independently verify the claims, while still considering them "highly credible," highlights the duplicity of Western governments. These governments have been all too willing to overlook the acts of genocide and ethnic cleansing carried out by the Israeli government.

This situation raises critical questions about the role of international aid organisations, the responsibilities of donor nations, and the impact of geopolitical considerations on the provision of humanitarian aid. The suspension of funding for UNRWA without a thorough investigation not only undermines the credibility of the international system but also deprives Palestinian refugees of essential services and support. The decision by Australia and other countries to follow suit, without concrete evidence, suggests a broader alignment with political pressures rather than an adherence to principles of justice and humanitarian need.

The implications of these developments are profound. Firstly, they underscore the vulnerability of international aid organisations to political manipulation and the potential for such actions to disrupt essential humanitarian services. Secondly, the lack of consistency and apparent double standards in the international community's response to the crisis in Gaza point to a broader erosion of trust in international norms and institutions. The immediate consequence of these actions is the further entrenchment of suffering among the Palestinian population, which finds itself caught between the violence of military actions and the political machinations that hinder the flow of aid.

The unfolding crisis in Gaza and the international response to it reveal deep-seated challenges in the realms of humanitarian aid, international law, and geopolitical strategy. The suspension of UNRWA funding on questionable grounds and the apparent impunity with which military actions are conducted against civilians highlight a troubling departure from the principles of evidence-based decision-making and respect for human rights. There is a critical need for a return to principled action that prioritises the wellbeing of vulnerable populations and the pursuit of peace over political expediency. This is not happening in Gaza.

NOT ALL POLITICIANS ARE LOOKING AWAY

The escalating humanitarian crisis in Gaza has not only drawn international condemnation but has also sparked significant debate within national governments, including Australia's. The Australian Greens have been vociferous in their criticism of the Australian Government's one-sided support for Israel, highlighting a broader discourse on the complexities of international alliances and the principles that should guide them. The Federal Labor member for Fremantle, Josh Wilson, provides a stark contrast within the Australian Labor government itself, offering a poignant insight into the devastating human toll of the conflict in Gaza:

> "The truth is that Gaza is being bombed into rubble, with 70 per cent of buildings damaged and the entire population being squeezed further and further south in starvation conditions, without basic medical services. In four months, 28,000 civilians have been killed, two thirds of whom are women and children. It is wrong, and it has to stop—history tells us that violence almost never solves anything, and state sponsored violence almost always causes enormous disproportionate harm to innocent people."

Wilson's statement highlights the severe situation in Gaza, characterised by extensive bombing that has led to widespread destruction and a significant humanitarian crisis. However, there appears to be a lack of collective voice within the Labor government. While there have been some instances of isolated commentary, notably from Senator Fatima Payman and Minister Ed Husic, the response from Prime Minister Anthony Albanese and Foreign Minister Penny Wong has been underwhelming.

There is an urgent need for a commitment to peace and the protection of human rights, as opposed to militaristic strategies that invariably harm innocent individuals. The question arises as to when the Labor government will confront the actions and influence of the Israel lobby in Australia. How many innocent civilians must be killed in Gaza before governments finally denounce Israel's actions as genocide and ethnic cleansing? Is the threshold 30,000? Or 50,000? Does it need to reach 100,000, or even one million?

The behaviour of the Israeli government and the Israel Defense Force in Gaza is reminiscent of those willing to inflict extensive torture, as evidenced by the Stanford University Prison Experiment in the early 1970s and the abuses at Abu Ghraib within the Guantánamo Bay Naval Base in the 2000s. Israel acts like the unhinged psychopath who does not know when to stop, primarily because no one is telling them to stop.

The situation in Gaza and the international response to it raise critical questions about the responsibility of governments to act in accordance with international human rights standards and the principles of justice and peace. The disparity in the global reaction to crises, as illustrated by the contrasting figures in Gaza and Ukraine, highlights a perceived inconsistency in the international community's commitment to these values. This inconsistency not only undermines the credibility of international law but also exacerbates suffering by allowing political considerations to override humanitarian needs.

For meaningful progress to be made, there must be a concerted effort to bridge the gap between rhetoric and action. The growing calls for a reassessment of the situation in Gaza, both within Australia and internationally, reflect a broader demand for policies that prioritise human dignity and the protection of civilians in conflict zones. As more voices within government and the international community advocate for change, the pressure mounts for a re-evaluation of support mechanisms and for holding accountable those who violate international norms.

THERE ARE NO SAFE ZONES IN GAZA

The escalation of hostilities in Gaza, particularly in the city of Rafah, marks a critical juncture in the ongoing conflict between Israel and Palestinian factions. The Israeli Defence Force's actions in Rafah, including bombings and a planned ground offensive, have intensified the humanitarian crisis and raised significant international concerns. The reported killing of at least 112 people in Israeli air and sea attacks on Rafah, as stated by the Ministry of Health in Gaza, highlights the dire consequences of military operations on civilian populations.

The strategic significance of Rafah, coupled with the Israeli Defence Force's justification of its actions as being for the "safety" of Palestinians, reveals a disturbing aspect of the conflict. The bombardment of areas into which Palestinians have been forced into raises profound questions about the efficacy and ethics of such military strategies. Furthermore, the potential derailment of captive exchange negotiations by a ground offensive in Rafah, as indicated by senior Hamas leaders, highlights the intricate interplay between military actions and diplomatic efforts in the region.

The international reaction to the situation in Rafah has been muted. The communication between U.S. President Joe Biden and Israeli Prime Minister Benjamin Netanyahu, which emphasised the need for a "safety" plan for the over one million people sheltering in Rafah, reflects global concern over the humanitarian implications of a ground assault. However, similar to Senator Wong's meaningless rhetoric of "deep concerns", it is clear that no one in the West is prepared to take action to defend Gaza and halt the daily massacre of innocent civilians, including women and children.

Similarly, the obstruction of vital supplies, as evidenced by the blocking of a shipment containing a month's supply of food for Gaza at Israel's Ashdod Port, further exacerbates the humanitarian crisis and highlights the urgent need for international intervention to ensure the provision of aid.

Senator Wong's expression of concern about the "potentially devastating consequences" for the civilians of Rafah is in stark contrast to the growing international sentiment that calls for an immediate cessation of hostilities and a re-evaluation of military strategies that risk civilian lives. The "potential" that Senator Wong refers to has already been reached: Rafah is already being devastated and the war against innocent civilians is continuing.

In light of these developments, the international community stands at a crossroads. Just as we discovered the effectiveness and value of their actions during the massacres in Rwanda and Bosnia in the 1990s, and in Darfur in the 2000s, it has become evident that the

United Nations functions as a "paper tiger"—incapable of responding to any international disaster or atrocity unless the permanent members of the Security Council are prepared to agree to act. Given their divergent fields of geopolitical interests, such consensus on Gaza is highly unlikely.

The events in Rafah demand a concerted and unified response that prioritises the protection of civilian lives, the facilitation of humanitarian aid, and the pursuit of peaceful resolutions to the conflict. The juxtaposition of military objectives with the humanitarian needs of the Palestinian population in Gaza necessitates a re-evaluation of the strategies employed in the conflict and a renewed commitment to peace, human rights, and international law.

The imperative to prevent further loss of life and address the humanitarian crisis in Gaza demands a recommitment to peace, non-violence, and the principles of international law. Only through such reorientation can the international community hope to resolve the conflict in Gaza and restore dignity and hope to its people. However, this goal is unlikely to be achieved as long as governments in the West lack courage and continue to acquiesce to and appease the genocidal behaviour of the Israeli government and the Israel Defense Forces.

***

THE DEVIL IN DUTTON'S DETAILS

17 February 2024

The management and oversight of contracts within the Home Affairs Department under the tenure of Peter Dutton as Minister up until 2022 have come under intense scrutiny, revealing significant lapses in due diligence and a concerning disregard for potential corruption and fraud risks. The internal audit concerning the Paladin contract, in which the company operated the Manus Island detention centre, uncovers a series of failures that raise serious questions about the department's commitment to transparency, accountability, and the efficient use of public funds, as well as Dutton's lack of competence in the management of this department.

At the heart of the controversy is Home Affairs' handling of the Paladin contract, worth $532 million, a critical component of Australia's offshore detention regime. The audit's findings that Paladin was selected without a proper assessment of its capability to manage detention centres are alarming and this lapse is compounded by the department's failure to evaluate the risks of engaging in contractual relationships in Papua New Guinea, a region known for its challenges with corruption and fraud. Such oversight suggests a systemic flaw in the department's procurement and risk management processes, directly implicating the leadership and oversight mechanisms in place under Dutton's watch.

The revelation that the financial strength assessment conducted by KPMG was directed at the wrong entity within Paladin's corporate structure further illustrates the depth of mismanagement. This critical error—if indeed it was an "error"—of evaluating Paladin

Solutions instead of Paladin Holdings indicates a fundamental breakdown in the due diligence process. That the assessment focused on a construction arm rather than the offshore-processing arm tasked with managing a complex and sensitive operation such as Manus Island detention centre is a stark illustration of the department's negligence and reflects upon a broader culture of complacency and a lack of accountability within the department.

The implications of these failures extend beyond administrative missteps. They touch on the integrity and effectiveness of Australia's immigration and border protection policies, particularly as they relate to the management of offshore detention centres. The investigations revealing credible allegations of corruption in both the Nauru and Manus contracts, coupled with the Australian Federal Police's initiation of foreign bribery investigations, underscore the potential for systemic abuse and exploitation within these contracts. Such developments not only tarnish the reputation of the Home Affairs Department—and that of Peter Dutton—but also raise profound ethical and legal concerns regarding Australia's treatment of asylum seekers and its commitment to upholding standards of governance and accountability.

In light of these findings, the response from then-Minister Dutton, as evidenced by his mere acknowledgment of the audit report without further action or inquiry, is particularly disconcerting. This response suggests a lack of engagement with the audit's critical findings and a missed opportunity to address and rectify the identified deficiencies. The lack of substantive reaction from the ministerial level highlights a concerning indifference to the principles of responsible governance and oversight, further compounding the gravity of the department's mismanagement under his tenure.

A DEEPLY CONCERNING LACK OF ACCOUNTABILITY

The unfolding narrative around the management of contracts within the Home Affairs Department, particularly under Dutton's ministerial responsibilities, intensifies as further details emerge about the extent of mismanagement and the lack of accountability. Labor Senator Deborah O'Neill's critique at Senate Estimates hearings highlights a fundamental issue at the core of this saga: the apparent indifference by Dutton to deeply concerning audit findings, encapsulated in his minimal response to the damning internal audit.

This attitude, where significant concerns over a half-billion-dollar contract were met with a mere acknowledgment, highlights a troubling disconnect between the responsibilities of high office and the actions (or lack thereof) of those tasked with such roles.

The report's indictment of senior officials for failing to leverage intelligence to prevent financial dealings with companies linked to alleged serious crimes over a decade further exacerbates concerns about systemic failures within the department, and the former minister. The current Home Affairs minister, Clare O'Neil, has characterised the findings as "extraordinary" and the investigation by prominent media outlets into suspect payments underscore the gravity and breadth of the mismanagement and corruption risks involved.

The Australian Greens' immigration spokesman, Senator Nick McKim's condemnation of the failure to identify responsible parties, captures the broader frustration and concern over the lack of accountability. The Senate committee's inquiries into investigations related to criminal activities, including attempts to circumvent U.S. sanctions against Iran and links to drugs and arms smuggling, further illuminate the scope of the department's challenges.

Why did Dutton exhibit such indifference to these issues during his tenure as Minister for Home Affairs? Was he so preoccupied with the leadership challenges to then-Prime Minister Malcolm Turnbull in 2018—and equally absorbed by the subsequent opportunity to contest during Scott Morrison's tenure—that any developments within the department became secondary concerns, with his role merely serving as a stepping stone to the prime ministership? Alternatively, is Dutton merely an incompetent leader who also ignored the persistent corruption within his department? Is he fit to be Prime Minister, if he were to ever win a federal election?

There needs to be a re-evaluation of the structures and practices that allowed such failings to occur, underscoring the imperative for systemic reforms to restore integrity and public trust in the department and its leadership.

DUTTON NEEDS TO TAKE RESPONSIBILITY FOR THE FAILINGS IN HOME AFFAIRS

The scrutiny of Dutton's tenure as Minister for Home Affairs deepens with considerations of the broader implications of his leadership decisions and the department's operational shifts. The transformation of the Australian Customs Service into the Australian Border Force under Dutton's watch in 2015 symbolises a significant change in the approach to border security, marked by an emphasis on a militarised perception and enforcement. This shift, colloquially known by its critics a "Border Farce," reflects a contentious rebranding that appeared to prioritise appearance over efficacy, particularly in addressing high-level smuggling and maintaining efficient border operations.

Dutton's defence in all of this has been to emphasise his lack of involvement in contract negotiations or the execution of agreements, but it does little to absolve the broader accountability issues that plague the Home Affairs Department. The Richardson report seems to shift the ministerial responsibilities in the regional processing contracts and procurement decisions towards the department's senior officials. However, under the conventions of the Westminster system, it *is* the minister who takes *all* responsibility for their portfolio, whether they caused the problem, or not.

This system predicates that ministers are ultimately accountable for the actions and failures of their departments, a convention that raises questions about Dutton's responsibility for the lapses and scandals that occurred on his watch. If the minister isn't responsible for failings with the system, who is? It's the fundamental basis of ministerial responsibility in all democracies: without it, democracies fail.

THE LACK OF INTEREST FROM THE MAINSTREAM MEDIA

There have been suggestions from conservative media—most notably, News Limited—that the current Labor government's focus on these scandals might serve as a diversion from its challenges but even if they were, it does not diminish the gravity of the allegations under Dutton's administration. The Paladin contract scandal, alongside other mismanagement issues, represents a significant concern that has not been adequately addressed by the media or political discourse. The lack of widespread outrage or accountability for these missteps highlights potential deficiencies in public and media scrutiny of government operations.

The limited scrutiny from both the media and the public, especially regarding immigration and asylum seeker issues, mirrors a wider societal and political dynamic. These subjects, often sensationalised and polarising, can be twisted into narratives of "fear and loathing," a strategy the Liberal Party has historically employed for political gain. A prime example occurred when 43 asylum seekers from Pakistan, Sri Lanka, and India arrived in the remote Western Australian town of Beagle Bay. This event triggered the typical irrational response from the Liberal Party and mainstream media, which described the situation as a "catastrophe" and proclaimed the "loss of control over our borders," framing it as a threat to the Australian community.

It is a clear indicator of the immaturity, racism, and bigotry within the Liberal Party and conservative media when the arrival of 43 individuals is portrayed as an existential threat to an Australian population of nearly 27 million people.

The current Labor government's strategic focus on Dutton's role, steering clear of directly invoking the contentious issues of immigration or asylum seekers, illustrates a nuanced approach to political critique and by concentrating on allegations of drug smuggling and weapons trafficking, the government's aims to construct a narrative that questions Dutton's competence and suitability for higher office without inflaming already divisive topics.

It's evident that the Labor government is intensifying its critique of Dutton ahead of a potential federal election and this indicates a strategic positioning meant to shape public opinion, as well as an increase in political pressure, with the intention of highlighting Dutton's perceived shortcomings to the electorate at a time when assessments of both the government's performance and any alternatives provided by the opposition will be coming to the fore. The essence of this strategy is not just to critique Dutton's past actions but to frame him as a liability for the future, particularly in the context of leadership and governance.

Dutton's role within the Home Affairs Department and the subsequent political ramifications offers a microcosm of the broader challenges facing contemporary Australian politics. Issues of governance, accountability, and political strategy converge, underscoring the importance of ethical leadership and the impact of political narratives on public discourse and trust, especially at a time when it was lacking from the Coalition government between 2013–22. As the political landscape evolves, the lessons drawn from this period will need to inform future debates on governance, policy, and the ethical responsibilities of those in public office.

***

AUSTRALIA'S ASYLUM SEEKER DEBATE AMIDST MEDIA MANIPULATION

24 February 2024

The narrative surrounding asylum seekers and border protection in Australia frequently oscillates between humanitarian concern and stringent national security measures, often influenced by political motives rather than pragmatic or ethical considerations. This dichotomy was starkly illuminated by recent events involving the arrival of 43 asylum seekers from India, Bangladesh, and Pakistan in the remote Western Australian town of Beagle Bay. The political rhetoric that ensued exemplifies how the issue of asylum seekers is exploited for political capital, highlighting a broader discourse that oscillates between fear-mongering and calls for empathy and international responsibility.

The leader of the opposition, Peter Dutton—a prime agitator of this fear mongering—leveraged this event to criticise the current Labor government, asserting a breakdown in Australia's border protection system under a "weak Prime Minister". Dutton's comments underscore a broader strategy employed by the Liberal Party to amplify the perceived threats associated with unauthorised arrivals, framing them as indicative of governmental incompetence and a lapse in national security.

This approach, however, is not without its contradictions. Dutton's critique of the current government's handling of border protection and asylum seekers starkly contrasts with the more reticent stance the Liberal Party adopted while in power, particularly regarding "on water matters," and this discrepancy suggests a selective engagement with the issue, contingent on its utility for political positioning rather than a consistent policy approach.

Prime Minister Anthony Albanese's response to Dutton's accusations highlights a defensive stance against what is baseless fear campaigns. "He's just wrong," said the Prime Minister. "You know what he does every day you see it. It's just fear campaigns every day, that don't have a basis in what is going on. And he's someone who is defined by being negative."

Albanese's remarks attempt to redirect the political discourse towards more pressing domestic issues, such as the cost of living, thereby challenging the opposition's focus on border protection as a primary concern. This interaction between Dutton and Albanese reflects a broader political dynamic where the issue of asylum seekers is ensnared in a cycle of accusation and counter-accusation, often detached from the substantive realities and challenges of managing asylum and refugee protection.

The politicisation of asylum seekers and border protection in Australia also reveals a disjunction between the scale of the challenge faced by Australia and that encountered by other countries. The arrival of a single boat in Beagle Bay is juxtaposed against the backdrop of the global refugee crisis, where millions are displaced, and many countries grapple with far greater numbers of asylum seekers and refugees. This context highlights the extent to which political discourse in Australia around asylum seekers is disproportionately amplified, often obscuring the legal and humanitarian obligations Australia holds as a signatory to the UN Refugee Convention.

The strategic timing of the leak to the media—which appears to have come from the Australian Federal Police—concerning the arrival of asylum seekers, potentially aimed at influencing the Dunkley by-election, points to a cynical use of such events for electoral advantage. This practice is indicative of a broader political strategy that seeks to capitalise on border protection as a polarising issue, irrespective of the broader implications for asylum seekers' rights and Australia's international reputation.

The recent political skirmishes over the arrival of asylum seekers in Beagle Bay sheds light on the complex interplay between national security concerns, political opportunism, and Australia's international obligations—which are usually given short shrift—a discourse characterised by hyperbolic rhetoric and political gamesmanship, which often serves to obscure the nuanced challenges of asylum and refugee protection. While this is unlikely to happen within the current structure of Australian politics, there is a need for a more measured, informed, and compassionate approach to asylum seekers and border protection.

MEDIA MANIPULATION AND THE POLITICISATION OF BORDER FORCE

The arrival of 43 asylum seekers in Beagle Bay not only reignited political debates but also highlighted the racial undertones often associated with discussions of asylum in Australia. The emphasis on the asylum seekers' countries of origin—India, Bangladesh and Pakistan—and implied racial characteristics speaks to a broader strategy of fear-mongering, which has been a staple in the political toolkit of certain conservative factions within the Australian political landscape.

The manipulation of media coverage and the suspected involvement of the Australian Federal Police in politicising the arrival of asylum seekers represent a significant departure from impartial governance and law enforcement. The suggestion that the Australian Federal Police might have been complicit in orchestrating media coverage to benefit the Liberal Party raises serious concerns about the independence and integrity of national security and law enforcement agencies. Such actions, if correct, not only undermine public trust in these institutions but also highlight the extent to which political agendas can infiltrate and influence the operations of entities that should remain apolitical.

The historical reluctance of former immigration ministers, such as Scott Morrison and Peter Dutton, to discuss "on water matters" while in government, juxtaposed with the eagerness to exploit these issues when politically convenient, illustrates a profound hypocrisy. This approach manipulates public perception of border security, transforming it into a political weapon rather than a matter of national or humanitarian interest. The selective transparency and strategic leaks to the media, particularly during sensitive political periods, such as elections or amidst scandals, reveal a calculated attempt to sway public opinion and electoral outcomes.

The role of the media and its relationship with law enforcement and political entities is also under scrutiny. The presence of media at sensitive operations before official actions are taken—as was the case with the anti-terror and union raids in 2017, even though no charges were ever laid—suggests a level of co-ordination between the Australian Federal Police and conservative politics that undermines the integrity of both the media and the police force. When media coverage is orchestrated to maximise political fallout for opponents, it ceases to be an independent fourth estate and becomes a tool in the political arsenal.

The call for a comprehensive reform of the Australian Federal Police, to purge it of perceived political biases and restore its credibility as an impartial law enforcement agency, is a monumental task. It highlights the need for transparency, accountability, and integrity within all branches of government and their associated agencies. Such reforms are not merely administrative but symbolic, representing a commitment to the principles of justice and impartiality that should underpin democratic institutions.

Reforming the Australian Federal Police and addressing the broader issues of media manipulation and the politicisation of asylum seekers require a concerted effort from all sectors of Australian society. It demands a re-evaluation of the values that Australia stands for on the international stage and a commitment to uphold these values. As the debate on asylum seekers continues, it is imperative that it is conducted with a focus on humanity, respect for international obligations, and a strong commitment to the principles of fairness and justice. Only through such a comprehensive approach can Australia navigate the complex interplay of national security, immigration policy, and human rights that defines the contemporary discourse on asylum seekers and border protection.

NAVIGATING FEAR, MEDIA, AND THE QUEST FOR HUMANITARIAN PRINCIPLES

The weaponisation of asylum seekers in Australian politics is a multifaceted issue, deeply entwined with the nation's political, media, and social landscapes. The portrayal of asylum seekers as a looming threat to national security, often amplified by media narratives, reflects a profound disconnect between the realities of asylum and the fear-driven rhetoric employed for political gain. This dissonance is particularly evident in the contrasting depictions of asylum seekers: on one hand, as individuals fleeing unimaginable hardships and seeking refuge, and on the other, as pawns in a broader political strategy designed to stoke public fear and secure electoral advantage.

The historical context provided by the discussions on past Australian Prime Ministers' stances towards refugees, from Gough Whitlam's initial hesitance to Malcolm Fraser's more welcoming approach, highlights the evolving nature of Australia's refugee policy. This evolution reflects broader global trends, where wealthier, predominantly Western nations exhibit increasing apprehension towards immigration and asylum seekers. The juxtaposition of Fraser's openness on the issue in late 1970s with the subsequent politicisation of the issue, initially by the Howard government from 1998 onwards, and ramped up by the Abbott and Morrison governments after 2013, highlights a shift towards using asylum seekers as tools in political opportunism rather than addressing their plight as a humanitarian concern.

The recurring theme of fear and xenophobia—evident in Australia since its racist imperialist project commenced in 1788—leveraged by political figures to consolidate power, undermines the potential for a rational and compassionate discourse on asylum. The suggestion that legislation could be introduced to prevent the politicisation of "on-water matters" highlights the need for structural changes to ensure that discussions around border security and asylum are conducted in a manner that prioritises human dignity and international obligations over political expediency, an expediency that is always exploited by conservatives.

In considering a path forward, it is essential to recognise the importance of depoliticising the asylum seeker issue and reframing it within a humanitarian, rather than a security-focused, context. This requires a concerted effort to dismantle the narratives of fear and threat that have been constructed around asylum seekers and to foster a more inclusive and empathetic understanding of their circumstances.

The Australian political landscape, particularly the Labor Party, faces a critical challenge in navigating these complex dynamics, balancing national security concerns with a commitment to humanitarian principles and international law.

The discussion surrounding asylum seekers in Australia should extend beyond mere policy considerations to touch upon fundamental questions about the nation's identity, values, and place in the global community. There needs to be a re-evaluation of the principles guiding Australia's approach to asylum and a renewed commitment to upholding the rights and dignity of those who seek refuge within its borders.

Only through such a re-evaluation can Australia hope to move beyond the divisive and dehumanising rhetoric that has characterised much of the debate on asylum seekers, towards a more compassionate and principled approach that recognises the shared humanity of all individuals, regardless of their origin or status.

***

THE COALITION'S FEAR AND EXAGGERATION CAMPAIGN

25 February 2024

In analyzing the Coalition's strategy within the Australian political landscape, one cannot overlook the instrumental use of fear campaigns and exaggeration as tools for political mobilisation and unfair electoral advantage. The essence of such a strategy is not new; it has roots in the annals of conservative political history where fear has often been leveraged as a potent catalyst for influencing public opinion and swaying electoral outcomes. Robert Menzies did it in the 1950s with the fear of communism; John Howard and the fear of asylum seekers and the "war on terror" in the late 1990s, and Tony Abbott with the outright fear of everything and anything. The Liberal Party and the National Party have demonstrated a proclivity for employing such tactics, particularly evident in their approach to various policy debates and election campaigns: Peter Dutton is the bookend of this Liberal tradition of vacuous negativity and ramping up the fear and loathing.

And so it was with the Coalition's response to the federal government's proposal for a national vehicle efficiency standard. This initiative, grounded in environmental and economic rationality, aimed to reduce emissions while offering financial savings to the average Australian car driver—estimated at around $1,000 per year and $17,000 over the life of the vehicle. However, the Coalition's counter-narrative framed this policy as a punitive measure, dubbing it a "car tax" and projecting it as a direct threat to a specific segment of the Australian populace: tradies.

This narrative was spearheaded by Senator Bridget McKenzie and Dutton, who criticised Labor's policy by claiming it would disproportionately impact tradies and get them to be "smashed between the eyes", suggesting an increase in the price of utes by an unsubstantiated $25,000. This claim, lacking in clarity, detail or evidence, was less about the factual inaccuracy and more about the emotional resonance with a demographic perceived as crucial to the Coalition's electoral base.

The rhetoric employed by the Coalition does not exist in a vacuum; it is a strategic choice aimed at replicating the success of past campaigns, notably the 2019 federal election victory under Scott Morrison. This approach seeks to galvanise support by appealing to the fears and economic concerns of tradies, projecting the Coalition as their protector against perceived Labor Party threats. However, this strategy simplifies the diverse political and economic perspectives within the tradie demographic, ignoring the nuances of their voting behaviours and priorities.

Tradies are the starting point: the Coalition's campaign strategy extends beyond targeting tradies to broader implications on gender and environmental policy. The opposition to the vehicle efficiency standard, coupled with derogatory rhetoric towards renewable energy and electric vehicles, positions the Coalition against progressive environmental initiatives, framing them as somehow antithetical to the interests of the "average Australian." This not only polarises the electorate along gender lines, appealing to a "blokey" identity while potentially alienating professional women, but also highlights a resistance to environmental sustainability.

The underlying issue with the Coalition's strategy is its reliance on fear and exaggeration without offering a constructive vision for Australia's future. This essentially was their strategy for their time in office between 2013–22, which turned out to be disaster for Australia—government lead by ego and personal ambitions, and hoping to maintain office without implementing any useful policy.

The reference to past tactics, such as "stopping the boats" and tax cuts under Tony Abbott's leadership, highlights a pattern of short-term electoral gains at the expense of long-term policy substance.

This approach, while historically effective in certain contexts, raises questions about its sustainability and the potential for alienating broader segments of the Australian electorate.

The Coalition's use of fear campaigns and exaggeration serves as a case study in the complexities of political strategy within a democratic society. While such tactics may mobilise specific voter bases in the short term—usually appealing to base instincts and getting these groups to vote against their own interests—they risk undermining the foundational principles of informed debate and constructive policy-making. The challenge for Australian politics, and indeed for democratic systems globally, is to navigate the delicate balance between electoral strategy and the imperative for visionary, inclusive, and sustainable governance.

BEYOND ENVIRONMENTAL POLICY: EXPANDING THE ARENA OF FEAR AND MISINFORMATION

The continuation of the Coalition's fearmongering and exaggeration campaign extends beyond the confines of environmental policy and vehicle standards, moving into a broader critique of their opposition to progressive initiatives. It's important to look deeper into the mechanisms of misinformation and the targeting of specific demographics and regional communities, as well as the implications for leadership and electoral prospects within the Australian political context.

The narratives promoted by the Coalition, particularly through figures such as leader of the National Party, David Littleproud, perpetuates a dichotomy between urban and rural Australia. Littleproud's assertion that fuel efficiency standards would "take away the country ute" and discriminate against regional people is a calculated move to stoke fears of disenfranchisement among rural voters. This narrative, unsupported by evidence, suggests that electric vehicles lack the capability for agricultural work, a claim directly contradicted by the advancements in EV technology, which include powerful electric farm utes and heavy roadside vehicles. The reluctance to acknowledge the capabilities of electric transportation, even in the face of electrically powered commuter trains across

Australia, highlights a deliberate choice to prioritise ideological opposition over practical and environmental considerations.

This strategy of misinformation is amplified by a media landscape that often fails to scrutinise these claims, allowing them to be presented as fact without counterargument. This lack of journalistic integrity and interrogation enables the Coalition to perpetuate myths about the impracticality and economic impact of transitioning to more sustainable practices, without addressing the long-term benefits of such a shift for both the environment and the economy.

The rhetoric utilised by Scott Morrison during the 2019 election campaign, warning of the "end of the weekend" and "see you later to the SUV" if Labor policies on electric cars were implemented, exemplifies the Coalition's approach to fearmongering. By framing the debate around the loss of freedom and leisure, the Coalition seeks to mobilise ignorant voters through emotional appeal rather than factual debate. This strategy, while effective in rallying a base resistant to change, fails to engage with the broader implications of climate change and technological innovation on Australian society.

The upcoming Dunkley by-election serves as a focal point for these tactics, with the Coalition ramping up its campaign in hopes of generating a protest vote against the perceived threats posed by electric vehicle policies and broader progressive agendas. However, the unpopularity of figures such Peter Dutton, especially a more progressive state such as Victoria, signals a potential miscalculation in the Coalition's strategy. Dutton's stance and rhetoric may resonate with certain segments of the Queensland electorate—which is where he is from—but it risks alienating voters in key battlegrounds such as Victoria and New South Wales, underscoring a broader issue of leadership and electoral viability for the Coalition.

The Dunkley by-election is a litmus test for Dutton's leadership and the Coalition's electoral strategy. The anticipation of Dutton's political vulnerability in Victoria, coupled with a broader dissatisfaction within the Liberal Party, suggests a moment of reckoning. The outcome of the by-election could either reinforce the Coalition's current trajectory or necessitate a re-evaluation of their approach to leadership, policy, and electoral strategy.

The Coalition's reliance on fear campaigns and exaggeration reflects a deeper struggle within Australian politics to reconcile the demands of progress with the preservation of traditional values and lifestyles. While such tactics may offer short-term electoral gains, they risk undermining the capacity for substantive policy debate and long-term planning, essential for addressing the complex challenges facing Australia in the 21st century.

***

UNVEILING THE IMBALANCE IN AUSTRALIA'S COVERAGE OF THE GAZA CONFLICT

26 February 2024

In examining the complex and emotive issue of media coverage concerning the conflict in Gaza, particularly from the perspective of Australian reporting, one cannot help but confront a deeply unsettling narrative of imbalance and, arguably, misrepresentation. The stark contrast in casualties, with around 1,200 Israeli civilians and almost 30,000 Palestinians killed since October the seventh, starkly highlights not just a disproportionate scale of loss but also a fundamental question of how such events are framed and understood through the lens of media. This disparity in numbers, which by any measure suggests a grave imbalance in the human cost of conflict, raises significant ethical questions about the role of media in shaping public perception and, by extension, political discourse.

The media landscape in Australia, characterised by major outlets such as News Corporation and Nine Media, has been critiqued for a perceived one-sidedness in its coverage of the conflict. This critique extends beyond the borders of Australia, touching upon a broader concern about Western media's portrayal of the Israeli–Palestinian conflict. The ramifications of such reporting are profound, affecting not just public opinion but also the political will and policy-making that directly impact the region's future. The cycle of violence, perpetuated in part by this skewed narrative, continues unabated, fueled by a lack of balanced reporting that might otherwise foster a more nuanced understanding and, potentially, a more concerted effort towards peace.

Social media, meanwhile, has emerged as a counterbalance to traditional media narratives, providing a platform for the dissemination of images and stories that often go unreported or underreported in mainstream channels. The poignant images of children and civilians caught in the crossfire serve as a powerful testament to the human cost of the conflict, challenging narratives that seek to minimize or ignore Palestinian suffering. However, the role of social media is double-edged, serving both as a space for critical discourse and as a battleground for ideological clashes, where accusations of anti-Semitism and racism can sometimes overshadow the urgent need for dialogue and understanding.

The call for balanced and ethical journalism is not merely a matter of professional integrity but a crucial step towards addressing the underlying issues that fuel the conflict. Quality journalism should strive to present diverse perspectives, seeking to understand the complexities of the conflict beyond simple binaries of victim and aggressor. The recent legislative developments in Australia, such as the anti-doxxing legislation, underscore the influence of media narratives on political decisions, raising questions about the timing and motivations behind such measures. The implications of media bias extend beyond the Israeli–Palestinian conflict, influencing a wide range of political and social issues, from international diplomacy to domestic policy.

As we look deeper into the intricacies of media representation and its impact on the Israeli–Palestinian conflict, it becomes increasingly clear that the challenge lies not only in reporting the facts but in navigating the delicate terrain of historical grievances, cultural sensitivities, and political aspirations. The path to a more balanced and informed public discourse is fraught with obstacles, from the fear of defamation to the risks of oversimplification. Yet, the pursuit of a more nuanced and empathetic understanding of the conflict is not only a journalistic imperative but a moral one, demanding courage, integrity, and a steadfast commitment to the principles of fairness and justice.

The role of media in shaping the narrative of the Israeli–Palestinian conflict, particularly within the Australian context, highlights a pressing need for a reevaluation of how stories are told and whose voices are amplified. As we move forward, the imperative for media outlets, journalists, and society at large is to engage in a more critical and reflective discourse, one that acknowledges the complexity of the conflict and the shared humanity of all those affected. Only through such a balanced and ethical approach can we hope to contribute to a more informed and, ultimately, more peaceful resolution to one of the most enduring and divisive conflicts of our time.

ECHOES OF SILENCE: THE STORY OF HIND RAJAB AND THE MEDIA'S ROLE IN SHAPING WAR NARRATIVES

The tragic story of Hind Rajab, a six-year-old Palestinian girl caught in the brutal crossfire of the conflict in Gaza, encapsulates the profound human cost of war and the critical role of media in bringing such narratives to light. Her desperate plea for help, broadcast by Al Jazeera, starkly contrasts the often sanitised and dehumanised portrayal of Palestinian suffering in parts of the Australian media landscape. This incident, where Hind and her family were allegedly lured to their deaths by the Israeli military, has been labeled by many as a war crime, yet its coverage—or the lack thereof—by major Australian news outlets highlights a disturbing disparity in the portrayal of victims based on their national or ethnic identities.

The relationship between media coverage and political influence is further exemplified by the response to Hind Rajab's story. Where international outlets and social media platforms provided a platform for her story to be shared and mourned, the silence or minimal coverage from certain Australian media entities raises questions about the impact of journalistic practices and affiliations on public perception and policy making. The fact that such a heart-wrenching narrative received limited attention in Australia, especially from outlets that have historically participated in state-sponsored educational tours provided by the Israeli government, highlights the intricate connections between media representation, political narratives, and the shaping of public opinion.

This imbalance in media coverage extends beyond individual tragedies, reflecting a broader trend of humanising Israeli victims while marginalising or ignoring Palestinian suffering. Such practices not only distort the reality of the conflict but also contribute to a skewed understanding of the dynamics at play, reinforcing stereotypes and entrenching biases. The criticism directed at public figures and entities that dare to challenge this narrative, including international dignitaries and members of the royal family, highlights the challenges faced by those seeking to promote a more balanced and equitable discourse.

The consequences of this media imbalance are far-reaching, influencing not only domestic policy in countries like Australia but also international responses to the conflict. The narrative that emerges from mainstream media coverage can shape the decisions made at the highest levels of government and international diplomacy, affecting the lives of millions and the prospects for peace. As the story of Hind Rajab and countless others fade from public consciousness, the imperative for a more ethical, balanced, and human-centred approach to journalism becomes ever more critical.

In addressing these challenges, the role of alternative media sources and social media platforms in providing a counter-narrative becomes increasingly important. As traditional media outlets face accusations of irrelevance and bias, the democratisation of information through digital platforms offers a glimmer of hope for a more nuanced and comprehensive understanding of the conflict. However, this shift also highlights the need for media literacy and critical engagement from the public, ensuring that the stories that shape our perceptions and policies are scrutinised and understood in all their complexity.

The narrative of the Israeli–Palestinian conflict, as presented in parts of the Australian media, serves as a poignant reminder of the power of media to shape our understanding of the world. It challenges us to seek out diverse perspectives, to question the narratives presented to us, and to strive for a more just and empathetic portrayal of those caught in the crosshairs of history. Only through such a collective effort can we hope to move towards a future where the stories of all victims are heard, where the cycles of violence are broken, and where peace is not just a distant dream but a tangible reality.

***

MARCH

LABOR TRIUMPHS IN DUNKLEY

2 March 2024

Within the ever-fluctuating political landscapes and the continuous emergence of national issues, the Dunkley by-election was not merely a critical local electoral contest in outer Melbourne but also served as a barometer for broader political sentiment across Australia. Despite pre-election polls indicating a tight race between the major political parties, the Labor Party's victory in the Dunkley by-election by Jodie Belyea offers a multifaceted lens through which to analyse current political dynamics, the effectiveness of the parties' strategies, and the electorate's response to both local and national issues.

At the heart of pre-election discussions were the Essential and Newspoll surveys—not specific to the Dunkley area but reflective of the overall electorate—which painted a picture of a potentially close contest. The Essential poll indicated a narrow lead for the Coalition, marking the first time it had edged ahead of the Labor government since the 2022 federal election, with figures of 48 percent for the Coalition and 47 percent for Labor in Essential's version of two-party preferred voting (Essential excludes undecided voters). However, the Newspoll results remained unchanged, showing a lead for Labor at 52 percent, compared to the Coalition's 48 percent. These conflicting signals highlighted the unpredictable nature of voter sentiment and the potential for the Dunkley by-election to swing in any direction.

The analysis prior to the election highlighted the impact that national issues often have on by-elections, suggesting that the outcome could reflect broader national sentiments rather than purely local concerns. This dynamic was further complicated by the sad passing of the former member for Dunkley, Labor's Peta Murphy, which introduced an element of emotional complexity to the electoral narrative. Speculation about a sympathy vote in favour of Labor to honour Murphy's legacy added another layer to the pre-election analysis.

Labor's eventual victory in Dunkley—52.6 percent of the vote, against the 47.4 percent recorded by the Liberal Party—despite the political challenges that it faced, signifies more than just a retention of their current number of 78 seats in the House of Representatives. It represents a validation of Labor's policies and political strategy in a contentious environment—not only was Labor facing a negative and hostile Liberal Party, but it was up against a negative, hostile and febrile conservative media landscape.

The victory also offers somewhat of a reprieve to the Albanese government, which had been portrayed as potentially becoming even more cautious in the face of an electoral loss. The outcome suggests that, despite the tight race and the swirling national issues, the electorate in Dunkley favoured continuity and endorsed the Labor Party's direction.

The Dunkley by-election served as a referendum on several key issues, mainly Labor's economic measures such as reworking the Stage 3 tax cuts, and the government's general competence since it assumed office in May 2022. The electorate's response, therefore, provides critical insights into the political priorities and concerns of the voters, particularly in terms of how these national issues influenced their decision-making at the ballot box.

The Labor Party's victory in the Dunkley by-election is a testament to the complex interplay of local sentiments, national issues, and the effectiveness of political strategies. This result not only reinforces the Labor Party's position within the Australian political landscape but also offers crucial lessons for both major parties as they recalibrate their approaches in anticipation of future electoral contests.

The Labor Party ran a very clear and effective campaign, despite the 3.9 percent swing against it in two-party preferred voting—Peta Murphy won the seat with a 6.3 percent margin at the 2022 federal election. While the two-party preferred vote is the measure that decides which candidate wins the seat, several factors were in play: Labor's primary vote actually increased; the Liberal Party's primary vote increased substantially, primarily due to the absence of the United Australia Party and One Nation; and the Australian Greens' primary vote plummeted from 10.3 percent to 6.2 percent.

YET ANOTHER FAILURE FOR THE LIBERAL PARTY

Regardless of how the media attempts to misrepresent the outcome—depicting it as a failure for the Labor government, despite their victory, and portraying it as some sort of triumph for the Liberal Party, despite their defeat—it was undeniably a significant loss for the opposition leader, Peter Dutton.

The by-election experienced a modest two-party swing against the government, which is within the typical range for such electoral contests. This result has led political analysts to question the effectiveness of the opposition's campaign strategies and their failure to capitalise on prevailing voter sentiments. The issue of cost of living, a topic heavily emphasised by the media since Labor's rise to power in May 2022, did not sway the electorate in Dunkley, an outer suburban seat crucial for the Liberal Party's efforts to bolster its position in anticipation of the 2025 general elections.

The Liberal Party, despite failing to make inroads into Labor's primary vote share, did witness a notable increase in their primary vote, rising by 6.8 percent to 39.3 percent, yet it still lagged behind Labor's primary vote of 41.1 percent. This increase occurred in the absence of candidates from One Nation and the United Australia Party, allowing the Liberals to reclaim a significant portion of their base. Nevertheless, their inability to diminish Labor's primary vote highlights a significant challenge for the party, pointing to the electorate's desire for more than just traditional party loyalties.

The Prime Minister's strategic revision of the Stage 3 tax cuts, aimed at providing greater financial relief to the majority of taxpayers by July 1, was well-received by the electorate. This policy shift, markedly different from the original proposals under Stage 3, was perceived as a tactical strategy to align government policy with the economic interests of the general public.

The outcome of the Dunkley by-election will amplify scrutiny on Dutton's leadership, particularly given the Liberal Party's electoral dynamics in Victoria. The party's internal discussions about the leadership of John Pesutto and the ongoing search for a new leader underscore the broader challenges the Liberals face in reasserting their electoral appeal within the state. If the Liberal Party cannot leverage 13 consecutive interest rate rises and cost of living pressures, and go to win a seat that a half-competent opposition party normally would, there have to be questions arising regarding the usefulness of Peter Dutton's leadership.

Dutton's predominantly negative campaign approach, highlighted by deputy leader Sussan Ley's controversial comments on public safety and immigration—where she stated, "if you do not want to see Australian women being assaulted by foreign criminals, vote against Labor"—failed to resonate with voters. This highlights a critical disconnect between the party's messaging and the electorate's expectations. Such tactics not only proved ineffective but also further alienated potential supporters, indicating a pressing need for the Liberal Party to reassess its strategic direction and adopt a more positive, forward-looking agenda.

SHOULD WE END BY-ELECTIONS?

In the aftermath of the Dunkley by-election, broader questions emerged regarding the mechanics of Australian democracy, particularly the role and process of by-elections. This victory, while reaffirming Labor's position in Parliament, also serves as an opportunity to reflect on the logistical and constitutional aspects of electoral processes in Australia, including debates on the necessity and cost of by-elections.

The current process for filling Senate vacancies, seen as a time and cost-saving measure, contrasts with the more expensive and logistically demanding process of conducting by-elections for the House of Representatives. The cost to taxpayers, ranging between $2 million and $5 million for a lower house by-election, though not massive, is still a significant consideration in discussions on electoral reform.

The suggestion to potentially eliminate by-elections and instead allow for a replacement mechanism, either through party selection or by elevating the second-place candidate, introduces a complex debate intertwined with constitutional requirements. Such a change would necessitate amending Section 24 of the Australian Constitution, which emphasises that members of Parliament must be "chosen by the people of the Commonwealth". Given Australia's historical reluctance toward constitutional amendments, this proposal faces a steep uphill battle.

The rarity of by-elections—with Dunkley being only the third in the current term—coupled with their potential to significantly alter the political landscape, highlights the importance of maintaining a mechanism that allows for direct voter input in representative changes. The possibility of by-elections to shift government control is a critical aspect of the democratic process, providing a direct avenue for public accountability and influence over the government's composition.

The debate over the necessity and format of by-elections is not merely administrative but touches on fundamental principles of democratic representation and governance. While the logistical challenges and costs associated with by-elections are valid concerns, the broader implications for democratic engagement and accountability must be the guiding factors in any discussion on electoral reform.

However, the future of by-elections can be discussed at a future point—it's unlikely to change, given the electorate's cynicism about any changes to the Constitution and the likelihood that the Coalition would oppose such changes, even if it might be to their own advantage.

The more immediate concern is the Labor Party's victory in the Dunkley by-election and its reflection of the broader political currents shaping Australian politics. The electorate's response highlights a desire for substantive policy discussions and a departure from negative campaigning, setting the stage for a potentially transformative period in the lead-up to the 2025 general elections.

The Labor Party won this by-election because they ran a positive campaign, focusing on issues that governments can address to improve people's lives. The Liberal Party lost this by-election because they ran a negative campaign, terrorised the electorate, and failed to make a case for change. Until the Liberal Party starts to recognise this formula for electoral success, they will continue to lose election after election. If only they could see what is so obviously evident to everyone else.

***

NUCLEAR AMBITION: A NAKED POLITICAL POWER PLAY MASKED AS ENERGY POLICY

9 March 2024

In exploring the propagandising of nuclear energy by the Liberal Party, it's critical to understand the context and rhetoric surrounding the issue. This latest round of announcements commenced in the final week of the recent Dunkley by-election campaign, with leader of the opposition Peter Dutton's assertion on the viability and necessity of considering nuclear power as an alternative energy source for Australia, an argument which centres on the supposed competitive disadvantage Australia faces in energy costs compared to the United States, where companies purportedly—according to Dutton, and *only* according to Dutton—enjoy significantly lower electricity expenses due to their embrace of nuclear energy. Dutton refuses to engage in a substantive debate on the matter, opting instead for a blanket promotion of assorted disinformation about nuclear energy without a detailed examination of its potential benefits and drawbacks.

This false narrative propagated by the Liberal Party hinges on a critique of renewable energy sources' limitations, with allegations about their inability to provide base load energy consistently (which again, is not correct), and a critique which extends to environmental and logistical concerns associated with renewable energy infrastructure, such as wind turbines. Dutton's remarks, however, encapsulate a broader political strategy employed by the Liberal Party, which oscillates between endorsing—when they're in opposition—or ignoring nuclear energy when they're actually in the government. This pattern reveals a tendency to leverage nuclear energy as a political tool rather than a genuine solution to Australia's energy challenges.

Critically, the Liberal Party's approach to nuclear energy reflects a broader issue of political posturing and media manipulation, where the discussion around nuclear power is reignited as a diversion from other pressing issues or as a means to rally support amidst political turmoil. The cyclic nature of this discussion, fueled by selective media coverage and vested interests—the Murdoch empire has substantial mineral and resources interests, including uranium, through its Cruden Investments company—highlights the manipulative tactics employed to shape public opinion and policy direction. This manipulation is further evidenced by the inconsistency in the party's actions regarding nuclear energy, marked by a lack of concrete steps towards its development when in power, and enthusiastic advocacy when in opposition. If the Liberal Party was serious about nuclear energy, by now Australia would have a nuclear reactor in every capital city: however, they are not; it's all about the political posturing and trouble making when they've got nothing else to talk about, and damaging the interests of the renewable energy sector.

The counter-narrative to the Liberal Party's position on nuclear energy is supported by the shifting dynamics of the global energy market and the growing consensus among major fuel companies and influential figures towards renewable energy. The transition towards renewables, exemplified by companies like Shell and Exxon Oil, and figures such as Fortescue's Andrew Forrest, signifies a broader recognition of the unsustainability of fossil fuels and the economic and environmental viability of renewable energy sources. This shift challenges the foundational arguments of the Liberal Party's nuclear advocacy, revealing it as a outdated and strategically flawed stance.

The practical challenges associated with nuclear energy, particularly the long-term environmental and logistical concerns of waste management and the lengthy timeline required for the development of nuclear facilities, highlight the complexity and potential impracticality of adopting nuclear energy as a primary solution to Australia's energy needs.

The Liberal Party's propagandising of nuclear energy emerges as a multifaceted political strategy, characterised by rhetorical and emotionally-charged appeals to the electorate, media manipulation, and a cyclic pattern of advocacy and inaction. This strategy not only reveals the party's approach to nuclear energy as politically motivated but also highlights the broader challenges and dynamics shaping Australia's energy policy discourse.

NUCLEAR IS UNVIABLE IN AUSTRALIA, ON ECONOMIC, ENVIRONMENTAL AND POLITICAL GROUNDS

The viability of nuclear energy in Australia requires an in-depth examination of various factors including economic, environmental, technological, and societal considerations. Despite the periodic advocacy from the Liberal and National parties, and other assorted conservative fringe political parties, a thorough analysis of published reports and research suggests that nuclear energy is unviable for Australia for several reasons.

Firstly, the economic challenges of nuclear power are formidable. The construction of nuclear power plants involves high initial capital costs, long development timelines, and complex regulatory and safety requirements. A report by the CSIRO, *GenCost 2018*, highlights that the levelised cost of electricity for nuclear power is significantly higher compared to renewable energy sources like wind and solar, even when considering the future cost reductions for small modular reactors, if they ever become feasible for domestic markets which, at this stage, is unlikely. The financial risks are exacerbated by global trends showing escalating costs for nuclear construction projects and decreasing costs for renewables.

Environmental concerns also play a critical role in assessing nuclear energy's viability. The management of radioactive waste poses a long-term challenge, with no universally accepted solution for its disposal. The Australian context, with its unique biodiversity and ecosystems, raises significant concerns over the potential consequences of nuclear accidents or waste leakage. Australia's abundant solar and wind resources offer a cleaner, more sustainable path towards meeting energy demands and climate targets, undermining the rationale for adopting nuclear energy with its associated environmental risks.

Technological advancements in renewable energy and storage solutions further challenge the case for nuclear power in Australia. Innovations in battery technology, pumped hydro, and other forms of energy storage are rapidly improving the reliability and stability of renewable energy sources, addressing the intermittency issues often cited as a drawback of renewables. These advancements diminish the appeal of nuclear power as a necessary component of Australia's energy mix.

Societal acceptance is another critical barrier to nuclear energy's viability. Public opposition to nuclear power in Australia is significant driven by concerns over safety, environmental impact, and nuclear proliferation. This resistance is not only a reflection of the potential risks associated with nuclear energy but also a response to the global history of nuclear accidents in the U.S., Soviet Union and Japan, which have left lasting impressions on public perception.

Finally, the regulatory and political landscape in Australia is not conducive to the development of nuclear energy. The current legal framework, which includes the *Environment Protection and Biodiversity Conservation Act* 1999, effectively prohibits the construction of nuclear power plants. Any attempt to introduce nuclear power into Australia's energy mix would require substantial legislative changes, a process likely to be contentious and protracted, given the deep-seated public and political opposition.

The evidence from published reports and research overwhelmingly suggests that it is unviable for Australia. The economic, environmental, technological, and societal challenges associated with nuclear power make it an impractical choice, especially in light of the rapidly evolving and increasingly competitive landscape of renewable energy technologies. Australia's energy future lies in harnessing its vast renewable resources, supported by innovative storage solutions, to achieve a sustainable, cost-effective, and socially acceptable energy system, and not in an unviable nuclear industry.

IF NUCLEAR IS UNVIABLE, WHY DOES THE LIBERAL PARTY SUPPORT IT?

The motivations behind the Liberal Party's persistent advocacy for nuclear energy, despite the overwhelming evidence against its viability in Australia, can be analysed through the prism of political strategy and financial donations from the resources industry.

The influence of financial contributions from the mining sector, including those involved in uranium extraction, on political parties and their policy agendas cannot be understated. Although the donations might seem modest relative to the overall funding political parties receive, the symbolic and practical impact of these contributions is significant. Such donations not only provide direct financial support to the Liberal Party but also establish a network of relationships and obligations between politicians and the mining sector. These connections are indicative of a broader pattern where policy positions may align more closely with the interests of benefactors than with the public good or empirical evidence regarding energy policy.

The presence of high-profile politicians at events hosted by influential figures in the mining industry further illustrates the cozy relationship between some political leaders and the mining sector. Attendance at these events is not merely a social engagement; it symbolises a mutual endorsement and a public display of alliance, as was evident when Dutton flew across to Perth for the 70th birthday celebration of mining magnate and doyen for the conservatives, Gina Rinehart. Certainly, it's not just the Liberal Party that frequents these types of events—the Prime Minister, Anthony Albanese, also attended a private function organised by the billionaire cardboard entrepreneur Anthony Pratt during the week—this proximity raises questions about the impartiality of political figures in matters where the interests of their benefactors are at stake, including energy policy.

The strategy of promoting nuclear energy, despite its documented drawbacks, serves multiple political objectives for the Liberal Party. Firstly, it creates a point of differentiation from the Labor Party, which advocates for renewable energy sources. By positioning nuclear energy as an alternative, the Liberal Party seeks to appeal to segments of the electorate and the energy sector that are skeptical of or resistant to the transition to renewables, or simply don't pay attention at all to politics. This differentiation is not rooted in a genuine belief in nuclear energy's feasibility but in the desire to carve out a distinct political identity and to challenge the prevailing narrative around energy policy.

Secondly, the emphasis on nuclear energy allows the Liberal Party to divert public and media attention from its lack of a coherent and sustainable energy policy. By proposing the development of nuclear energy infrastructure, including naming potential sites for reactors, the party engages in a form of speculative policy-making. This approach is characterised by the promotion of initiatives that are unlikely to be realised but serve to generate debate and controversy, thereby keeping the party relevant in public discourse.

The opposition to renewable energy initiatives can also be seen as a tactic to create political challenges and difficulties for the incumbent government, aiming to portray it as ineffective or out of touch with the needs of the energy sector. This opposition is aligned with the interests of resource and energy companies, as well as some media entities, which prefer the status quo or gradual changes that do not disrupt existing business models.

WHY DOES NEWS CORPORATION WANT A NUCLEAR INDUSTRY?

Firstly, it's essential to understand the broader context of Australia's energy market and its transition towards renewable sources. Australia has vast potential for solar and wind energy, making it an attractive option for meeting the country's energy needs sustainably. However, the shift to renewables poses a threat to traditional energy industries, which are more centralised and offer greater control over energy supplies. Nuclear power, despite its challenges, presents an opportunity for these vested interests to maintain a stronghold in the energy sector.

The Murdoch empire and similar conservative entities have historically demonstrated a preference for centralised power generation models. Nuclear power fits this model perfectly due to the large scale of plants, the complexity of technology involved, and the regulatory barriers to entry, which collectively create significant obstacles for new entrants. This environment is conducive to the formation of monopolies or oligopolies, where a few large firms have considerable control over the market.

By supporting the development of a nuclear power industry, these interests are essentially advocating for a future energy market in which they can dominate, and control the supply chain of energy generation: digging up uranium, enriching the uranium, controlling the energy supply through nuclear power generators, and having enough political clout and influence within government to keep other potential competitors at bay. This is not a *potential* goldmine for these oligarchs, it *is* a goldmine, ready-made and guaranteed.

This the goal of Rupert Murdoch, and all it needs is a compliant government to sign away the resources owned by the Commonwealth of Australia—*the people*—which would then be used against the interests of those citizens of the Commonwealth, in higher energy costs and long-term environmental damage.

This is the pure, naked ambition of oligarchs and an old-style, twentieth-century robber-baron mentality that is highly prevalent in the high-end Australian business community, and it needs to be resisted at every opportunity.

One of the critical arguments in favour of nuclear power is its potential to provide stable, low-carbon energy as part of the broader energy mix. However, the economics of nuclear power in Australia raise questions about its viability. The high upfront costs associated with building nuclear power plants and the long lead times before they become operational make them a risky investment, especially compared to the rapidly decreasing costs of renewable energy technologies. Yet, for vested interests such as the Murdoch empire, the justification for such an investment lies in the long-term returns of securing a dominant position in the energy market. Once established, a nuclear power industry would offer these entities the ability to control supply and influence pricing, potentially at the expense of consumers and businesses.

The prospect of increased electricity prices stems from the need to recover the substantial initial capital investments in nuclear technology. Unlike renewable sources, where costs continue to fall, nuclear power requires extensive ongoing expenditure in maintenance, fuel, and eventually decommissioning. These costs, combined with the monopolistic control over supply, would likely result in higher electricity prices for consumers. The argument that nuclear power would reduce electricity prices overlooks these economic dynamics and the lessons learned from other countries where nuclear energy has not always led to lower consumer prices.

THE PURPOSE OF CONSERVATIVE POLITICS IN AUSTRALIA IS TO DEFLECT AND DELAY

While we can never be certain of this hypothetical scenario, based on what we see in contemporary politics in Australia, if the Labor government somehow was a pro-nuclear entity with well-established proposals to establish a nuclear industry, the knee-jerk reaction from the Liberal Party would be to provided opposition for the sake of opposition, look for opportunities to halt progress and hitch onto the bandwagon of renewable energies. It's what the modern Liberal Party does: good or bad and irrespective of what it is or whatever is proposed, the Liberal Party needs to oppose and be on the opposite spectrum of the Labor government. It's a party of political terrorists and nihilists.

Such a strategy not only stymies constructive debate and collaboration but also impedes the development of comprehensive and forward-thinking policies that address the pressing challenges of energy sustainability and climate change.

Exploring other energy options is crucial for Australia's future. The emphasis on economic viability, cost efficiency, environmental sustainability, and the potential to reduce greenhouse gas emissions guides the evaluation of these options. In the global context, where the share of renewable energy is steadily increasing—30 per cent of global energy supplies—and nuclear power remains a smaller fraction—9 per cent—Australia's focus on renewable energy appears both pragmatic, forward-looking and economically sensible. The significant investments in renewable energy infrastructure, such as the Tesla battery in South Australia, demonstrate the potential for innovation and efficiency in the sector.

The mention of small modular reactors—untried unicorn technology—further highlights the speculative nature of some nuclear energy proposals. Despite the theoretical benefits of small modular reactors, such as scalability and reduced safety concerns, their practical application remains largely unproven, especially within the Australian context. Taking these issues into account, the preference for renewable energy sources over nuclear, is not only a matter of environmental and economic pragmatism but also a strategic choice to avoid the uncertainties and potential risks associated with nuclear technology.

The assertion that adopting a nuclear energy strategy could be financially and environmentally detrimental resonates with the broader argument against nuclear power in Australia. The notion that "if you go nuclear, you go broke" encapsulates the financial risks and the long-term liabilities associated with nuclear energy, including construction costs, waste management, and decommissioning. In contrast, renewable energy presents a more cost-effective and environmentally friendly alternative that aligns with global trends and Australia's unique advantages in solar and wind resources.

The political dynamics surrounding energy policy in Australia, characterised by oppositional stances and the pursuit of controversial energy options such as nuclear power, highlight the need for a more collaborative and evidence-based approach to policy-making. The focus should shift towards harnessing Australia's renewable energy potential, which offers a viable and sustainable pathway to meet the country's energy needs and environmental commitments. By prioritising renewables over nuclear energy, Australia can avoid the pitfalls of speculative technologies and align with global advancements in clean energy, ultimately fostering a more sustainable and economically viable energy future.

**

DOES THE ABC HAVE A FUTURE IN THE CHANGING MEDIA LANDSCAPE?

10 March 2024

In examining the future of the ABC amid the evolving media landscape and political pressures, it's crucial to consider recent developments and the broader context in which the broadcaster operates. The departure of Ita Buttrose as ABC's chair and the appointment of Kim Williams could mark a critical moment in the broadcaster's history, reflecting a necessary change in its approach to journalism and content creation.

The past five years under Buttrose's leadership have been disastrous, to say the least, with criticisms centred on perceived biases within its news coverage and political reporting, including accusations of the ABC acting as a mouthpiece for the Liberal Party—regardless of whether the Coalition is in government or not—signal deep-seated problems within its editorial practices. This perception is exacerbated by the recruitment of journalists from predominantly conservative media outlets, such as News Corporation, and a notable shift towards commercial news models, emphasising clickbait journalism over substantive reporting. Esteemed commentators and former ABC journalists, including Kerry O'Brien, have voiced concerns over the broadcaster's direction, highlighting a fixation on marketing and demographic targeting at the expense of foundational principles that are contained within the charter of the ABC.

In his recent critique, O'Brien shed light on a fundamental challenge facing the ABC: the balance between reaching younger audiences and maintaining the integrity of its content. The drift towards a commercial model, driven by a fear of losing traditional viewership, has sparked debates about the influence of marketing within the organisation and its impact on editorial decisions. The emphasis on appealing to younger demographics, while necessary for relevance in a digital age, risks diluting the ABC's public broadcasting mandate if not managed with a clear understanding of its core values. Younger audiences are not fools: why should the ABC dumb down its content in a misguided attempt to attract young adults and thirty-somethings who have a sophisticated understanding of media consumption and cultural tastes? Younger audiences are no different to any other demographic group—if the quality is not there, they are not going to engage.

The initial skepticism surrounding Kim Williams' appointment stems from his history within the Murdoch empire—Foxtel and News Corporation—raising questions about his commitment to public broadcasting. However, Williams' departure from Murdoch under contentious circumstances and his professed support for public broadcasting suggest potential for a positive shift in the ABC's leadership. His tenure will be closely watched, as the broadcaster needs strategic guidance to navigate the pressures of modern media consumption while staying true to its public service remit.

There have been many peculiar operational and editorial strategies implemented by the ABC in recent times. The broadcaster faces criticism for decisions perceived to undermine its quality and diversity, such as the axing of programs like *The Drum* and *Lateline*, and budget cuts to *Foreign Correspondent*, changing it from a hard-hitting documentary-style program focused on critical international affairs, to a lifestyle-influenced series based on human interest stories. These actions, coupled with a reliance on dated content and a controversial 24-hour news cycle which includes irrelevant content simply to fill up the time, reflect broader challenges in content strategy and resource allocation.

To reorient the ABC towards a future where it remains a vital, independent voice in Australian media, a comprehensive review of its editorial and operational frameworks is necessary. This includes re-evaluating the role of marketing, addressing biases in political reporting, and investing in diverse, high-quality content that appeals to as many people within the community as possible. The balance between traditional and digital media, along with the imperative to serve as a check on government power, highlights the need for a nuanced approach to public broadcasting in the modern era.

A BLUEPRINT FOR REDEMPTION: WHAT CAN THE ABC DO?

In an era characterised by the ever-shifting media landscape, the ABC finds itself dealing with substantial challenges. The organisation has compromised its impartiality, relies on antiquated content strategies, and lacks a clear direction in its digital transformation. Most critically, it has suffered a significant loss of credibility. For many years, the ABC was heralded as one of Australia's most trusted brands, consistently ranking in the top two positions.

Its mobile application boldly proclaims—if somewhat arrogantly—ABC News as "Australia's most trusted news" upon user engagement. However, this claim falls short of reality: in 2018, the ABC was ranked as Australia's fourth most trusted brand, as per findings by Roy Morgan Research. Recent studies have seen the ABC's trust plummet to the 18th position, a decline that coincides with Ita Buttrose's tenure. It is evident that under Buttrose's leadership, the ABC has experienced a notable decline, for which she needs to held accountable, as does the rest of the ABC board, as well as the managing director, David Anderson.

To reverse this trend, the ABC must embark on a comprehensive overhaul across various domains. This endeavour will demand a considerable investment of time, energy, and resources. Priority areas for immediate action include ensuring editorial independence, enhancing content diversity, implementing effective digital transformation strategies, fostering innovation and partnerships with independent content creators and producers, engaging with the community in meaningful ways, securing funding, and establishing robust leadership and governance structures.

At the core of any news organisation lies its unassailable commitment to editorial independence. However, critiques have surfaced, pointing towards a need for the ABC to recalibrate its editorial direction. The reinforcement of editorial guidelines, coupled with the strengthening of robust internal watchdog mechanisms such as the ABC ombudsman, could serve to realign the ABC with its previous high standards of unbiased reporting, and restoring public faith in its journalistic integrity. While the ABC did establish an internal ombudsman in 2022, this office seems to be too closely aligned to the ABC management—only five of 33 reports prepared by the ombudsman over this time have declared breaches of impartiality, and no breaches have been declared over the ABC's predominantly pro-Israel coverage over the conflict in Gaza.

The broadcaster has also faced criticism for a homogenisation of content, mirroring rather than differentiating itself from commercial networks, and quite often, it is difficult to discern the difference between ABC news and other commercial enterprises. This scenario highlights the necessity for a strategic change towards the investment in high-quality, original content that not only mirrors but celebrates Australia's multicultural identity, catering to a broad spectrum of audiences across the nation.

Digital disruption, presenting both formidable challenges and unprecedented opportunities, necessitates a strategic approach from the ABC. Expanding its digital footprint through enhanced streaming services, podcasts, and effective utilisation of social media platforms could significantly bolster its reach, especially among younger demographics. This digital expansion, however, must not detract from the ABC's core mission but should instead serve to reinforce its commitment to inform, educate, and entertain the Australian public.

Innovation and collaboration emerge as critical pathways forward in the redefinition of public broadcasting within Australia. The ABC is called upon to foster a culture of innovation, exploring new formats and storytelling methodologies. Collaboration with local creators and independent producers promises to yield content that not only engages but accurately reflects the diverse fabric of Australian society.

Audience engagement needs to be a central concern for the ABC to demonstrate its commitment to its public service mandate. By enhancing interactive platforms and deepening community engagement, the ABC can ensure alignment with the evolving needs and preferences of its audience, thereby solidifying its position as Australia's quintessential public broadcaster.

The broadcaster's financial stability and funding model represent ongoing challenges in an increasingly competitive media ecosystem. Advocacy for stable, sufficient public funding is critical, as is the exploration of alternative funding mechanisms to ensure financial autonomy and sustainability.

At the governance and leadership level, the ABC stands at a crossroads, and it requires leaders who are committed in their dedication to the values of public broadcasting. The articulation and implementation of a clear, forward-looking strategic vision, anchored in transparent reporting practices, are indispensable for navigating the broadcaster through the complexities of the contemporary media environment.

The national broadcaster has been failing in too many of these areas—an organisation that has been cowered by external conservative influences, lacked the desire to truly transform itself in the digital age, stalled on developing its cultural diversity—the ABC is still predominantly a white Anglospheric media outlet, not so far removed from its cultural makeup and output from the 1930s—and failed to protect its editorial independence. While it could be argued that the ABC's slow decline commenced in 1996 when the Howard government was elected and proceeded to attack and defund the ABC, there has certainly been a faster decline since the appointment of Buttrose as the chair in 2019, and it's unclear whether this decline will be, or can be, reversed.

AN UNCERTAIN FUTURE FOR THE ABC

The future of the ABC rests on addressing profound criticisms concerning its management and strategic direction over the past five years. Blueprints for change can always be recommended but there needs to be a political will and an organisation will within the ABC to make these changes, and it's evident that the current board and management is not equipped to deal with these changes that are necessary for the ABC to survive.

As the landscape of media continues to evolve, the necessity for the ABC to realign its mission with its foundational purpose—serving the public interest through independent news and investigative journalism—has never been more critical. The departure of Buttrose and the entrance of Williams as chair can open a new chapter, but it is a chapter that demands a rigorous examination of past missteps and a clear vision forward.

The ABC's mimicry of commercial networks, has been a disaster and has raised significant concerns about its identity and value proposition as a public broadcaster. The blending of its content with that of commercial networks, from breakfast shows to drama series, dilutes the unique role the ABC is meant to play in providing distinctive, high-quality programming unavailable elsewhere. This approach not only undermines its public mandate but also contributes to the homogenisation of Australian media, diminishing the diversity of voices and perspectives that are essential for a vibrant democracy.

The shift towards sensationalism and clickbait, driven by an apparent adoption of commercial models, compromises the ABC's commitment to rigorous and unbiased political coverage. The portrayal of political events, such as its coverage of the recent Dunkley by-election, through a lens favouring conservative perspectives, further alienates audiences seeking balanced and comprehensive reporting. This erosion of trust in the ABC's political journalism is exacerbated by programming decisions that prioritise entertainment and 'infotainment' over informative and critical discourse, as evidenced by the replacement of the political panel show *The Drum* with comedy entertainment programs like *Hard Quiz*. Journalism replaced with comedy: it's the sad story of the modern ABC, and it's an insult to its audiences.

The critique of the ABC's management extends to its strategic response to the digital transformation in media consumption. The proliferation of viewing and listening options has significantly altered audience behaviours, yet the ABC's adaptation to these changes has been lacklustre. A focus on lower-budget but more radical productions and a return to its core of true independence and investigative journalism could re-establish the ABC as a vital source of information and analysis for the Australian public.

The challenge ahead for Williams, and for the ABC as an institution, is formidable. The broadcaster must navigate a path that respects its heritage of public service while innovating to meet the demands of a fragmented media environment. This requires a departure from the pursuit of commercial mimicry towards a rejuvenation of the principles of public broadcasting—integrity, independence, and a commitment to serving the public good, above all else.

To achieve this transformation, a comprehensive overhaul of the ABC's editorial and managerial practices is imperative. This includes reassessing the influence of marketing within the organisation and facile 'engagement' of audiences, realigning content strategies to emphasise diversity and quality, and fostering an environment that prioritises investigative journalism. The chair's role in setting the cultural tone and strategic direction cannot be understated, and as such, Williams' leadership will be instrumental in steering the ABC back to its foundational principles.

The ABC stands at a crossroads and it's possibly at its lower ebb ever in its history, facing the dual challenges of restoring public trust and adapting to the demands of the digital era. The broadcaster's future success hinges on its ability to embrace its public service mandate, offering content that is not only distinctive and high-quality but also reflective of Australia's diverse society. This journey will require introspection, bold decision-making, and a steadfast commitment to the values that have long underpinned public broadcasting. Only through such a transformative approach can the ABC hope to reclaim its place as a valued and indispensable institution in Australian life.

***

THE GREAT AUSTRALIAN SILENCE IN GAZA

16 March 2024

In his address at the National Press Club last week, Yanis Varoufakis, the former Greek finance minister and renowned economist, took a firm stance on the ongoing crisis in Gaza, shining a spotlight on the Australian government's weak and often contradictory one-sided position. Varoufakis, whose expertise stretches beyond economics to encompass a broad understanding of global geopolitical dynamics, criticised Australia's implicit support for Israel's actions in Gaza, East Jerusalem, and the West Bank, actions he described as deliberate war crimes.

Varoufakis's poignant words, "children are not starving in Gaza today; they are being deliberately starved," underscore a grave accusation against Israel's policies, which is an intentional strategy to subjugate and eventually displace the Palestinian population. By drawing parallels with historical instances of apartheid and the ideological justifications used to erase native populations, such as the doctrine of *terra nullius* in Australia, Varoufakis not only condemned Israel's policies but also called out Australia's complicity in these actions, arguing that Australia's diplomatic defence of Israel's actions, uncritically supporting the right to self-defence—for Israel, but not for Palestinians—and its decision to defund the United Nations Relief and Works Agency, the only agency capable of alleviating the humanitarian crisis in Gaza, has tarnished its international reputation.

Varoufakis urged Australia to lead a campaign against apartheid in Israel–Palestine, reminiscent of its historical campaign against apartheid in South Africa in the 1980s, to restore equal civil liberties to both Israelis and Palestinians.

The Australian government's lacklustre response to the crisis in Gaza, suggests that it's primarily parroting U.S. policies without forging an independent foreign policy stance. The ongoing violence in Gaza, resulting in the deaths of over 32,000 Palestinian people in just five months, has been met with a cowardly silence from Australia, marked by a failure to unequivocally condemn the actions of the Israeli Defense Forces. This stance is a significant stain on the legacy of the Albanese government, raising questions about the moral and ethical lines that must be drawn in international relations and human rights advocacy.

The dialogue surrounding this issue highlights a broader critique of global inaction and the need for a concerted effort to address the root causes of the conflict in Gaza. The lack of a strong, principled stance from countries like Australia not only undermines their moral authority but also implicates them in the ongoing humanitarian disaster. As the international community watches, the call for Australia to revisit its foreign policy priorities and stand on the right side of history grows louder, urging an end to the violence and a move towards lasting peace and equality in the region.

THE UNACCEPTABLE REASONS FOR AUSTRALIAN COWARDICE

If people such as Varoufakis—and many others in the world community—can be so critical of the actions of Israel, why is it so difficult for political leaders to make the same strident calls? What are the barriers that make Australian leaders such as Prime Minister Anthony Albanese and Foreign Affairs Minister Senator Penny Wong so reluctant to call out the actions of Israel? What are the factors that have made them determine that supporting Palestinians—as well as being on the right side of history—will cause them far greater political and electoral damage, than calling out Israel for obvious war crimes, attempted genocide and ethnic cleansing?

At the heart of Australia's foreign policy are its strategic and diplomatic alliances, particularly with Western nations. The longstanding military and diplomatic co-operation between Australia and Israel, reinforced by mutual interests in the Middle

East, highlights a significant aspect of this relationship. The alliance with Israel aligns Australia with its primary ally, the United States, which exerts considerable influence over Australian foreign policy. This alignment reflects a broader geopolitical strategy, positioning Australia within a network of Western democracies facing shared security concerns.

Domestic politics also play a crucial role in shaping Australia's stance. The influence of the Jewish community, while numerically small, is notable in political and business circles. This community's support is seen as vital for political leaders of the Labor and Liberal parties, and there is a palpable fear among politicians of alienating these and other pro-Israel voters. This fear is compounded by the broader Australian public's perception of Israel some kind of like-minded democracy in a turbulent region, which many politicians are loath to challenge. Whether this notion of democracy is the case or not—Israel currently has an extremist far-right government that doesn't seem to be representative of the will of the electorate—this is the perception that exists within the Australian community.

The media's portrayal of the Israeli–Palestinian conflict significantly influences public opinion and, by extension, political stances. Media coverage often sympathetic to Israel's security dilemmas tends to shape a narrative that discourages overt support for Palestine and Australian leaders, wary of backlash or accusations of not supporting Israel, often find themselves navigating a media landscape that can be hostile to nuanced positions on the conflict.

The conflation of criticism of Israel with anti-Semitism is a significant factor in the Australian political discourse. Politicians are acutely aware of the fine line between legitimate criticism and being perceived as anti-Semitic—maniacally monitored and pushed by groups such as the Zionist Federation of Australia and the Australian Jewish Association—and it's this fear leads to more cautious public statements that often favour Israel or express neutrality, even when faced with significant evidence of humanitarian crises or disproportionate responses in conflicts like that in Gaza.

And, of course, there is the grand old sentiment of racism in Australia, which has historically had a fear of outsiders and people who are 'different to us', and this is an issue that cannot be underplayed.

Australia's cautious approach to the conflict in Gaza and the broader Israeli–Palestinian conflict reflects a complex interplay of strategic, domestic, ethical, religious, and racial considerations. The challenge for Australia lies in navigating these multifaceted issues while maintaining its strategic interests and upholding its values, necessitating a more assertive and principled stance in foreign policy. Whether or not Australia will rise to this challenge remains to be seen, however, it is evident that many politicians in federal politics—particularly within the Labor government—prioritise their political careers over the lives of the 32,000 individuals who have been lost in Gaza over the past five months.

A MORE INDEPENDENT COURSE

For most governments, attempted genocide, ethnic cleansing and apartheid would be reasons for political leaders to speak out, irrespective of where it's occurring in the world, but especially in a case where we can see exactly what is happening and have been constantly outraged by these events. Should Australia cultivate a more autonomous foreign policy direction, distinct from the overarching influence of the United States, so it can discuss more openly—and more accurately—the events that are taking place in Gaza?

The relationship between Australia and the U.S. is undoubtedly deep-rooted, characterised by extensive military, security, and intelligence collaborations. However, this intertwined relationship has sparked debates over the extent of Australia's foreign policy autonomy, particularly in its current position on Israel and the ongoing situation in Gaza.

The unwavering support of the United States for Israel, epitomised by President Joe Biden's unequivocal backing—a self-proclaimed Zionist—raises questions about the implications of such alliances for Australian domestic and foreign policy. While the solidarity with Israel may resonate with American political narratives, it simultaneously tests the waters of Australia's political leadership, challenging the

Prime Minister and Foreign Affairs Minister to navigate a complex geopolitical landscape.

Historically, figures such former prime ministers Bob Hawke and Paul Keating have demonstrated that Australian foreign policy can indeed be formulated with a degree of independence, mindful of the country's unique geographical and strategic interests. Their efforts to differentiate Australian foreign policy from that of its allies, while maintaining amicable relations, offer valuable lessons for the current administration. The proximity of nations like Indonesia, Papua New Guinea, India, and China highlights the strategic imperative for Australia to pursue a foreign policy that not only respects its alliances but also recognises the importance of its immediate neighbourhood.

By positioning itself as a significant middle power within the South-East Asia region—where it geographically belongs—rather than merely acting as a subordinate player to the United States, Australia could assume a more impactful role in international affairs. This shift would not only enhance Australia's standing but also provide itself with greater moral authority on issues in the Middle East, allowing it to address the death, destruction, and suffering of the Palestinian people more effectively, rather than continually overlooking these grave concerns.

The challenges facing the Foreign Minister are considerable as she endeavours to navigate the intricate landscape of international diplomacy and her goal is to strike a balance between maintaining Australia's long-standing alliances and advocating for a distinctive and principled stance in foreign policy. At present, it is a balance that is not being achieved. The ongoing debate over Australia's autonomy in foreign policy, especially highlighted by the Gaza conflict, prompts a wider discussion about the nation's role on the global stage.

ANTI-SEMITISM HAS LOST ITS MEANING

In the evolving narrative surrounding Australia's position on the Gaza conflict, criticism towards the Foreign Minister and the Labor government has intensified, underscoring a perceived failure to navigate the diplomatic tightrope with the finesse expected of a nation with Australia's international standing. The delayed decision to restore funding to the UNRWA for humanitarian aid in Gaza, as highlighted by former Foreign Affairs Minister Gareth Evans where he urged the government to "stop sitting on the fence", epitomises this critique. The eventual reinstatement of aid, while a positive step, has been overshadowed by the protracted hesitation that preceded it, casting a shadow over Australia's commitment to humanitarian principles.

There have also been incidents where Palestinians in Gaza, having been granted visitor visas to Australia, managed to escape from Gaza into Egypt and board flights to Australia, only to be told mid-flight that their visas had been cancelled, forcing them to return. Although over 2,000 visitor visas have been granted to Palestinians—and more than 2,400 to Israeli citizens—only 400 have actually arrived in Australia. Many have been left stranded due to these mid-flight visa cancellations, a situation influenced by pressure from Israeli lobby groups in Australia and political figures such as the Shadow Home Affairs Minister, Senator James Paterson.

Once again, a lacklustre justification was offered by Minister Clare O'Neil, stating that the government was investigating the manner in which some of these visa holders had exited Gaza "without explanation"—just a guess, but perhaps the daily bombings, genocide, and ethnic cleansing in Gaza could provide some context? This situation highlights the influence of the Israeli lobby and demonstrates the Australian government's readiness to perpetuate the persecution of Palestinians, extending the suffering initiated by the state of Israel. It's reminiscent of the ships of Jewish refugees turned back from the ports of the United States during Word War II, under the belief by the U.S. State Department that they could "threaten national security". Short memories.

The conversation around Australia's diplomatic language and actions—or the lack of action—regarding the situation in Gaza is marked by a palpable frustration. The government's rhetoric often resorts to what could be best described as "weasel words," a diplomatic contortion that fails to adequately address the gravity of the conflict or the disproportionate number of Palestinian casualties.

Amidst these critiques, voices within the Labor government, such as Tony Burke, Ed Husic and Senator Fatima Payman, have been acknowledged for their condemnation of the violence in Gaza—their outspokenness serves as a reminder that strong, principled stances on international human rights issues do not necessarily precipitate political fallout and these example highlights the possibility for the Australian government to adopt a more unequivocal stance in condemning the actions of the Israeli government and advocating for a ceasefire, without fear of reprisal from domestic political opponents or lobby groups. It shouldn't be necessary to point this out, but surely it's acceptable for political leaders to condemn genocide, ethnical cleansing, apartheid and the slaughter of over 32,000 Palestinians in Gaza and not be accused of anti-Semitism. *Surely*.

The discussion around response to the conflict also extends beyond diplomatic and humanitarian concerns, touching on broader issues of identity, morality, and the politics of criticism. The controversy surrounding writer-director Jonathan Glazer's Oscar speech, wherein he called out the genocide in Gaza—only for him to be accused of anti-Semitism by the Combat Antisemitism Movement and Holocaust Survivors groups—encapsulates the fraught terrain of public discourse on this issue, where even a small and legitimate criticism of the state of Israel and the actions of the Israel Defense Forces—whether it's a real or perceived criticism—brings on the torrents and waves of abuse and claims of anti-Semitism. What is the meaning of anti-Semitism if every course of debate has the label throw at it?

As Australia navigates its response to the crisis in Gaza, the calls for a more assertive and morally consistent foreign policy grow louder and the aspiration for an Australian foreign policy that aligns with the nation's values and international human rights standards, while managing diplomatic relationships, presents a challenge. Yet, it is a challenge that Australia must meet if it is to fulfill its potential as a force for good on the world stage, advocating for peace, justice, and the protection of human rights for all, irrespective of political pressures or alliances. The path forward requires courage, clarity, and a recommitment to the principles that should guide international relations in the twenty-first century. We're not seeing that at the moment.

***

THE RELIGIOUS DISCRIMINATION BILL IS A TEST OF AUSTRALIA'S SECULAR VALUES

23 March 2024

The proposed religious discrimination legislation in Australia has re-emerged in federal parliament, sparking a significant debate that stretches far beyond the confines of religious freedom and into the broader spectrum of discrimination, societal norms, and the balance between public funding and what are, essentially, private beliefs. At the heart of this issue is the question of whether religious institutions, particularly schools, should be granted the legal right to select staff and students based on religious beliefs—which are against the notions of Australia as a secular nation—and institutionalising a form of discrimination that has long been contentious.

This legislation ostensibly aims to safeguard religious freedoms, a move highlighted by promises made during the 2022 federal election campaign by now Prime Minister Anthony Albanese. These promises were in response to Scott Morrison's efforts to politicise religion and use it as a means to wedge the Labor Party during that campaign. The draft bill suggests giving religious schools the authority to employ and enrol individuals who align with their faith—raising concerns about the blurring lines between religious autonomy and an assumed right to discriminate, under the pretext of religious freedom.

Many of these institutions, especially schools, receive substantial funding from federal, state, and territory governments, highlighting a paradox where public funds may potentially support practices that contradict broader societal values of inclusivity and equality. Surely the argument can be made that if these schools benefit from public funding, they should adhere to the same principles of non-discrimination that govern other sectors of society. Why should religious institutions be exceptions to the rules that advocate for a more inclusive society?

This debate also brings to light the inherent classism within the education system, where private schools, through tuition fees, already enforce a form of economic discrimination. This existing disparity is compounded by practices that allow for the exclusion of students not meeting academic or behavioural standards, subtly reinforcing a selective system that privileges certain demographics. For these reasons, the proposed legislation is an extension of this exclusionary practice, aiming to codify the ability to discriminate on additional grounds such as sexuality or religious belief.

The hiring practices of these schools also need to be called into question, especially where there is a preference for candidates of the same faith over potentially more qualified individuals. This prioritisation of religious adherence over merit raises concerns about the priorities of educational institutions and their impact on the quality of education. Would students prefer their lessons to be taught by a superior science teacher who might be an atheist or from another religion, rather than someone who adheres to the faith but has limited knowledge of their subject matter?

If the goal of education across Australia is to provide the highest level of tuition possible, then the answer seems clear. Of course, there are many instances where an excellent teacher is also a strong adherent of a particular faith, but is it necessary to legally enshrine an option to undermine the processes of merit, based on someone's belief system? The proposal to enshrine such preferences in law is also puzzling, as it could make these discriminatory practices more susceptible to legal challenges and public scrutiny.

The proposed religious discrimination legislation has highlighted the ethical implications of funding discriminatory practices with public money, the societal values we seek to uphold, and the kind of education system we envision for future generations, and has reopened discussions—yet again—on how to balance religious rights with the principles of inclusivity and equality, discussions that we didn't really need to have.

AN INCLUSIVE SOCIETY CANNOT BE BASED ON EXCLUSIVITY

This debate is further magnified when we consider the implications on educational environments and the fundamental values that underpin our societal fabric. At the heart of this debate is the assertion that educational institutions, particularly those founded on religious principles, should not be limited to employing staff who exclusively share their religious identity. This standpoint challenges the notion that a teacher's faith directly impacts their capability to deliver education in subjects like mathematics or science, which are universally recognised as secular knowledge areas. The potential enrichment brought by cross-religious faculty appointments—such as a Catholic teacher in an Islamic school, or vice versa—speaks to a vision of educational environments as spaces of cultural and intellectual exchange, rather than fortresses of ideological homogeneity.

This perspective not only questions the underlying rationale for the proposed legislation but also the allocation of public funds to support schools that engage in discriminatory practices. The argument for moving towards a system without publicly-funded religious schools highlights a fundamental belief in education as a public good that should transcend religious divides and envisions an educational landscape where schools serve as microcosms of a diverse society, fostering mutual respect and understanding among students of different backgrounds.

The historical context surrounding the legislation's revival—originally pushed by former Prime Minister Scott Morrison and now revisited under Albanese's leadership—highlights the contentious nature of this issue within Australian politics. The internal divisions and public debate generated by the bill's initial introduction in early 2022 underscore the complex interplay between religious freedoms, educational policies, and societal values.

Australia is a secular state—where freedom *of* and freedom *from* religion coexists—and has a vision for a society where individuals are free to practice their faith without imposing it upon others. This vision aligns with the principle of inclusivity, advocating for an educational system and societal structure that respects and accommodates diverse beliefs without compromising on the fundamental values of equality and non-discrimination. Religious discrimination legislation that actively discriminates against different faiths—or of *no* faith—would undermine these values.

THIS IS ALL ABOUT POLITICS, AND NOT MUCH ELSE

The path towards the legislative enactment of these measures has been marked by political opportunism, deep ideological divides, and the inherent tension between preserving religious freedoms and upholding the principles of a secular state. The government's call for bipartisanship, as emphasised by Attorney-General Mark Dreyfus, highlights the need for a collaborative approach to address this highly contentious issue. This controversy has been primarily fueled by the leadership of the Liberal Party, which consistently aims to polarise the community. Instead of seeking unity, it focuses on ideological battles as part of its ongoing "culture wars"—a strategy that would have exhausted any other political party by now. However, the Liberal Party remains undeterred, continuing its divisive tactics now into the third decade of misdemeanours since the election of the Howard government in 1996.

Of course, Dreyfus has demanded bipartisanship—and why wouldn't he—surely such a piece of legislation, if it is going to be deemed by the political system that is something that is necessary (even if it's *not*), then a consensus view rather than the ideology of a single party would be expected, as well as legitimise the provisions of this legislation in the eyes of the broader Australian public.

However, the response from opposition leader Peter Dutton, characterised by demands for "further details" and a critical stance on the government's motivations—a tactic he used so destructively and decisively during the Voice to Parliament campaign—suggests a complex political situation where support for the bill is anything but assured.

Dutton opposes everything: this is his *modus operandi*. Dutton's approach mirrors tactics seen in other political debates—such as the Voice—revealing a strategy that is more about political positioning than genuine concerns over the legislation's content or implications.

The Liberal Party's opposition to the 1988 referendum on religious freedoms—serves as a reminder of the deep-seated political dynamics that influence the debate on religious discrimination. This backdrop highlights the perennial challenges of balancing religious freedoms with the principles of a secular democracy, where the state's neutrality in matters of religion is paramount.

Where does this lead us? The criticisms directed at previous versions of the bill under Morrison's leadership underscore the potential for religious discrimination legislation to be misappropriated in ways that could negatively impact marginalised communities, such as transgender individuals and the broader LGBTQI+ community, or to solidify discriminatory practices. The debate over legal safeguards for divisive, inflammatory, or derogatory remarks—such as those made by footballer Israel Folau in 2019, despite his contract mandating equal, fair, and dignified treatment of all individuals regardless of gender identity, sexual orientation, ethnicity, cultural or religious background, age, or disability—and the denial of services based on religious beliefs, highlight the intricate balance required between protecting religious expression and shielding individuals from harm.

Under Morrison's proposed religious discrimination bill, Folau could have made statements such as "homosexuals, atheists, hell awaits you... repent, turn away from your evil ways... God's plan for gay people is hell"—as he did in 2019—claim it as part of his religious beliefs, and face no repercussions. Hospitals owned by religious orders—such as St Vincent's Hospital in Sydney—could turn away patients from non-Catholic faiths, or LGBTQI+, or divorced people, if they wished to, based on "religious beliefs". Is this the direction we want for Australia, a modern secular state that prides itself on values of inclusivity and diversity?

It's crucial to separate the activities of the state from those of religious institutions, a fundamental aspect of maintaining a secular state. The blending of these boundaries, as witnessed under the leadership of Morrison, Tony Abbott, and John Howard, serves as a warning of the risks associated with allowing religious beliefs to excessively influence public policy and governance. The separation of church and state originated, in part, from church leaders' desires for protection from the state: in the 1600s, the Puritan minister Roger Williams advocated for a "high wall" between church and state to shield religious affairs from the "wilderness of governments".

However, this "high wall" also facilitated ongoing child sexual abuses by priests and staff within religious organisations, not only in Australia but worldwide. Initially intended to protect religious practices, this separation has, after countless instances of child sexual abuse and the legal hurdles that impeded the prosecution of clergy, resulted in churches now having the temerity to not only demand additional protections but also the legal right to discriminate against others under the guise of faith and religious beliefs.

It has become clear that the issue extends beyond the legal provisions of the religious discrimination bill itself: it encompasses broader questions about the nature of Australian society, the values it cherishes, and the kind of legal framework that best supports a diverse and inclusive nation. The challenge lies in crafting legislation that protects religious freedoms without compromising the rights of others or the secular character of the state—a task that demands careful consideration, broad consultation, and a commitment to upholding the principles of equality and justice for all Australians and ensuring that the rights of all citizens, regardless of their religious affiliation or lack thereof, are protected under the law.

**

SWEEPING CAMPAIGN AND DONATION REFORMS NEEDED FOR DEMOCRATIC RENEWAL

24 March 2024

In recent years, the discourse surrounding political campaign and donation reform in Australia has reached a tipping point and it's clear to most people that change is needed. Spearheaded by the crossbench, including the Australian Greens and independent politicians, there has been a renewed push for sweeping changes to how political campaigns are funded and how donations are regulated. This movement highlights a broader concern that the current system disproportionately benefits major parties—Labor, Liberals, and the Nationals—perpetuating a cycle that impedes genuine democratic reform. Despite the apparent need for overhaul, these parties have historically shown reluctance towards reform, primarily because the status quo serves their interests well. This inertia is particularly evident in the case of the Labor Party, which, despite its vocal support for reform while in opposition, has demonstrated a notable lack of action on this front upon assuming power.

The proposed reforms by the crossbench are comprehensive and aim to address several key issues that undermine the democratic process. Among these proposals is the introduction of truth in advertising laws and a significant reduction in the donations disclosure threshold from $16,300 to $1,000. These measures are complemented by proposals to ban donations from industries deemed socially harmful, mandate real-time disclosure of donations, and impose absolute limits on donation amounts, capped at $1.5 million. These initiatives collectively aim to mitigate the undue influence of wealthy donors and special interest groups on the political landscape, which have the potential to sway election outcomes in ways that do not reflect the will of the electorate.

The urgency for reform is further enhanced by the recent entry of individuals and entities such as Clive Palmer's United Australia Party, whose financial contributions have raised concerns about the integrity of the electoral process. The full public funding of campaigns is a viable solution to ensure a level playing field, particularly for smaller parties and independents, although in a recent Essential Poll, only 29 per cent of voters support either an increase, or full funded election campaigns from the public.

The support offered by Simon Holmes à Court's to the teal independent candidates in the lead up to the 2022 federal election, demonstrates a method of political financing that aligns with the values of transparency and accountability, contrasting sharply with the opaque and disproportionate spending by figures such as Clive Palmer, although simply replacing one conservative wealthy donor with another wealthy donor with progressive leanings doesn't solve the issue of individuals with the means and resources having the ability to sway electoral outcomes.

The debate over campaign and donation reform in Australia is not just a matter of regulatory adjustment but a question about the nature of democracy itself. The existing system, which allows for significant disparities in financial influence on politics, arguably distorts the democratic principle of equal representation. The reforms proposed by the crossbench aim to redress this imbalance, ensuring that the political arena is not unduly swayed by the wealthiest voices but reflects a broader, more equitable spectrum of the Australian populace. It is increasingly clear that the path to a more democratic and politically sustainable Australia lies not only in the enactment of these reforms but also in a cultural shift towards greater transparency, accountability, and inclusivity in political financing.

HOW MUCH MONEY IN POLITICS IS TOO MUCH?

The cost of democracy is high in Australia—the public cost of the 2022 federal election was $522 million, including public funding payments—but it's a price worth paying, especially in the context of the increasing influence of substantial financial contributions on Australian politics and significant concerns regarding the integrity of democratic processes. This phenomenon is not unique to Australia; however, the specific manifestations of financial influence in the Australian context reveal systemic vulnerabilities that undermine the principles of equitable representation and accountability.

The case of Palmer and other wealthy individuals spending exorbitant sums to sway political outcomes highlights a troubling trend where financial might can override the collective voice of the electorate. Palmer's expenditure, over $200 million across two election cycles, exemplifies how political influence can be bought, rather than earned through persuasive policy and principled leadership. Such actions not only distort the political landscape but also erode the foundational democratic principle that each citizen's voice should carry equal weight.

Setting higher limits on political donations inherently benefits conservative politics—consistently raised whenever the Liberal Party gains office, as was the case in 1996 and 2013—and always ignites debates about the fairness and impartiality of the current system.

The influence of wealth in politics has been linked to policy decisions that disproportionately benefit the affluent at the expense of broader societal interests, including resistance to effective taxation of the mining industry (in 2010 when the Rudd government sought to introduce a carbon emissions trading scheme and a super-profits mining tax), opposition to reforms on franking credits and negative gearing (during the 2019 federal election campaign) and policies that adversely affect marginalised communities, such as the cashless debit BasicsCard that was championed by mining magnate Andrew Forrest, even though he has no expertise in social policy. These policy outcomes illustrate the broader implications of allowing unchecked financial contributions to dominate political discourse and decision-making.

The phenomenon is not limited to direct electioneering efforts but extends to broader attempts to shape the political and ideological landscape. Movements such as the American Tea Party movement, financed in part by the Koch brothers, shows how strategic financial contributions have sought to install legislators amenable to a particular ideological agenda. This strategy aims not only to influence individual policies but to fundamentally alter the role and capabilities of government, reducing regulatory oversight and dismantling social safety nets in favour of a deregulated environment that privileges the interests of the wealthy.

The danger of such influence is the potential to erode democratic institutions and principles, fostering cynicism and disengagement among the electorate. When political success becomes closely tied to financial resources and well-heeled individuals, the essential democratic tenet of government being determined by the citizens of a nation, is imperilled. This situation raises profound questions about the nature of representation and governance in a democratic society and the extent to which the current trajectory can be altered to ensure a more equitable and participatory political process.

In light of these concerns, the push for campaign and donation reform in Australia is not only an administrative or regulatory issue but a fundamental and necessary challenge to the prevailing dynamics of power and influence. The goal of such reform is to restore public confidence in the democratic process, ensuring that political decisions are made in the public interest, rather than being dictated by the financial interests of a privileged few. The need for comprehensive reform that addresses the root causes of financial influence in politics is becoming increasingly urgent, and if these reforms are achieved, will pave the way for a more inclusive and democratic political landscape.

THE TRADITIONAL TWO-PARTY SYSTEM IS ERODING

The dynamic shifts within the Australian political landscape, particularly the decline in the combined primary vote for major political parties and the unprecedented rise of the crossbench—17 from a total of 151 lower house electorates—signify a burgeoning desire among the electorate for more diverse representation and a departure from traditional two-party dominance, which has dissatisfied the public for far too long.

This evolution reflects a broader trend of public disillusionment with established political entities and a craving for transparency, accountability, and genuine democratic renewal. The 2022 federal election, which recorded the lowest combined primary vote ever for the Labor Party and the Liberal and National coalition—68 per cent—alongside the largest crossbench in history, is a clear indicator of this shift. Such developments not only challenge the status quo but also highlight the critical need for comprehensive reform in campaign and donations rules to facilitate a more equitable and representative political process.

The relationship between the growing disenchantment with major parties and the ascendancy of independents and minor parties suggests that the public is increasingly wary of the influence wielded by substantial financial donors over political agendas and decision-making. The call for reforms, particularly those that aim to level the playing field, is not merely about altering the mechanics of political financing but about restoring faith in the democratic process. The potential introduction of these reforms in the context of a future minority government—which, based on the current trajectory is going to become the norm rather than the exception—highlights the inevitability of change and the urgency for current political leaders to proactively address these concerns.

Transparency in political funding is paramount, and the public's demand for it should transcend partisan lines: this would be desirable but we just know that in Australia, under the current two-party system which is no longer fit for purpose, this is never going to be achieved. Transparency is about ensuring that government is influenced by the will of the people rather than by the financial power of a select few.

The support from groups like Climate 200 for the teal independent candidates, also highlights the necessity of a framework that does not disproportionately favour those with access to significant financial resources, regardless of the political or ideological spectrum they occupy. While the contributions of donors such as Simon Holmes à Court and Graeme Wood to progressive causes should be acknowledged, influential donations usually flow into the coffers of conservative political interests, and the principle of limiting the influence of large donors remains paramount to preserving the integrity of the political system.

The debate over campaign and donation reforms is not just a matter of policy but a reflection of a deeper crisis of trust between the electorate and their representatives. The scrutiny of political donations is a manifestation of broader concerns about the motivations behind political decisions and the accountability of elected officials to their constituents rather than to their benefactors. This trust deficit, particularly pronounced among younger voters who exhibit diminishing support for traditional major parties, represents a critical challenge that must be addressed to ensure the long-term viability of Australia's democratic institutions.

The trajectory towards more diverse and representative governance in Australia, as evidenced by the shifting dynamics within the political landscape, necessitates a comprehensive overhaul of campaign and donations rules. Such reforms are not only essential for mitigating the undue influence of wealth in politics but also for enhancing democratic engagement and rebuilding public trust in the political process.

***

APRIL

THE DEATH OF AID WORKERS IN GAZA SPARKS GLOBAL OUTRAGE

6 April 2024

In the wake of the killing of Australian aid worker Zomi Frankcom and her colleagues by the Israel Defense Forces in Gaza, a storm of controversy and outrage has developed, not only for those directly involved but also the response—or lack of response—by the Australian government. The reports of this killing—which seems to be an execution based on the use of artificial intelligence and predictive technology—were marred by initial disinformation from Mossad attributing the deaths to Hamas, and the event has rapidly evolved into a focal point for broader discussions about Israel breaching international humanitarian law, war crimes, the ethics of warfare, and the complex web of geopolitical relationships that dictate international responses to such events.

    The Australian government's response, although more strident than most their commentary on Gaza over the past six months, has still been tepid and indecisive. Despite the gravitas of the situation, statements from Prime Minister Anthony Albanese and Foreign Minister Senator Penny Wong lacked the forcefulness for such a disaster, and played down the role of the Israel government. The killings in Gaza, which resulted in the deaths of seven aid workers from World Central Kitchen, should have been the clarion call for a stronger stance against the actions of Israel and the IDF, as well as lobbying for a ceasefire in Palestine and to end the war which has so far killed over 33,000 people in Gaza. Yet, the Australian leadership's reaction reflects a cautious approach, influenced by the intricate dynamics of international politics and Australia's strategic ties, especially with the United States, which maintains a complex and one-sided relationship with Israel.

While the world should have acted way before this specific event—the deaths of 33,000 Palestinians should have been the core reason for action—the deaths of the World Central Kitchen aid workers have ignited debates about the proportionality and justification of military actions performed by the IDF, the obligations under international humanitarian law, and the moral imperatives facing nations witnessing such conflicts. This incident constitutes a war crime—among many others committed by the IDF—and underlines the severity of the breach of laws designed to protect the most vulnerable, including those providing humanitarian aid in conflict zones.

The Australian government's lack of meaningful actions have not occurred in a vacuum. International reactions have varied, with some leaders, like U.S. President Joe Biden and U.K. Prime Minister Rishi Sunak, expressing more direct frustrations with Israel's actions—still with great limitations—and this divergence highlights the complexities of international diplomacy, where responses to conflicts are often tempered by strategic interests, historical relationships, and domestic political considerations.

The calls for tangible actions, such as recalling ambassadors and boycotting of Israeli products, are growing louder and reflects a growing impatience with this tepid diplomatic caution. Drawing parallels with the international isolation faced by the South African apartheid regime in the 1970s and 1980s, similar pressures could prompt a re-evaluation of policies and practices by Israel which are deemed in violation of international law and norms.

In this complex and evolving situation, it is clear that the Australian government faces a delicate balancing act. On one hand, there is a clear moral and legal imperative to condemn and seek accountability for actions that violate international humanitarian law. On the other, Australia must navigate its strategic relationships and the broader geopolitical landscape. But at what cost should this be, especially in the context of clear and obvious cases of apartheid, genocide and ethnic cleansing?

We should not only mourn the significant loss of lives in Gaza, but push the international community's commitment to uphold the principles of justice, accountability, and human dignity in the face of conflict and geopolitical complexities. Australia is part of this international community and domestic pressure must continue to be placed upon the Albanese government to also uphold these principles.

DOUBLE AND TRIPLE STANDARDS REMAIN IN VOGUE FOR POLITICAL LEADERS

Despite Prime Minister Albanese's historical advocacy for Palestinian rights and critical stance on Israeli policies—in 2002, his parliamentary comments openly and directly criticised the government of Israel for "creating a human rights and humanitarian crisis in Palestine", for provoking the Al-Aqsa Intifada, funding Hamas, and berated Israel for allowing "fundamentalists to build illegal settlements on Palestinian land"—his commentary in 2024, once he achieved the power where he could actually make a difference, has lacked vigour and the condemnatory force many people would have expected, based on his past positions. The cowardice from Albanese, now in a position to effect change, reveals that his strong statements and actions in 2002 were superficial and shallow words, and have shown him up as a politician who is weak and callow.

Of course, this shift in Albanese's tone highlights the complex pressures and responsibilities that come with leadership, especially on the international stage, where the balance between diplomatic relations and principled stances on human rights and international law must be carefully navigated. But how far can one's principles be bent and distorted, and credibility shredded in such a way? Albanese's past statements in Parliament, which emphasised the importance of adhering to international law and acknowledged the humanitarian crises faced by Palestinians, stand in contrast to his current commentary.

These criticisms should be extended beyond the Prime Minister and to other members of the Labor government, but this also highlights the divisions and the broader debate within Australian politics about the country's stance on the Israeli–Palestinian conflict. The frustration among rank-and-file Labor members highlights the tension between party unity and individual members' sympathies towards the Palestinian cause. This internal dynamic within the party mirrors the larger global debate on the conflict, where sympathies and political stances are often deeply personal and reflect a wide spectrum of views on justice, human rights, and national security.

The targeted IDF attack on World Central Kitchen has also been seen as a deliberate message to deter external aid to the Palestinian community in Gaza. This incident, referred to the British news presenter and commentator Richard Madeley as a "targeted execution", represents a significant escalation in the tactics employed in the conflict, raising serious questions about the rules of engagement and the protection of humanitarian workers in conflict zones. The Australian government's response to such incidents is not just about diplomatic relations with Israel but also about its commitment to upholding international humanitarian law and protecting civilians and aid workers in conflict zones. It's condemnation of Israel and the IDF should have been far stronger.

THERE IS SO MUCH MORE THE AUSTRALIAN GOVERNMENT CAN DO

There are many potential avenues through which Australia could exert pressure and signal its condemnation of the Israel government's actions, not only on the killing of one of its citizens performing humanitarian aid work, but of the 33,000 Palestinians in Gaza. Australia possesses a range of diplomatic and economic tools that could be deployed to express discontent and push for change, including recalling ambassadors, pausing military trade to Israel—52 Australian export licences were granted to Israel during 2023—and considering trade and cultural sanctions. These suggestions not only reflect potential policy actions but also highlight the expectations placed on Australian leaders to embody their historical stances on human rights and international law.

The local political ramifications of the government's stance, particularly for Prime Minister Anthony Albanese, suggest a broader discontent among constituents. The silent vigil outside Albanese's electoral office in Marrickville by the Palestine Action Group and his refusal to meet with them, illustrates a tension between political pragmatism and democratic responsiveness and a reflection of how the broader debate on Australia's foreign policy and can have implications for domestic politics. The electoral implications for Albanese in his historically safe seat of Grayndler, underscore the political cost of perceived inaction or inadequate response to international human rights concerns.

The potential for electoral backlash in Albanese's constituency, based on shifting public sentiment on the Israeli–Palestinian conflict, indicates a broader trend of increasing political accountability. While Albanese won the seat of Grayndler at the 2022 federal election by a margin of 67–33 per cent in two party preferred voting, previous election results—54–46 per cent at the 2010 federal election—have shown that with the right candidate and with the right campaign, the Australian Greens do have the potential to unseat Albanese at the next election. The unique dynamics of the Grayndler electorate—which shares state boundaries with the NSW state seat of Newtown, held by the NSW Greens—reveal a heightened sensitivity to issues of human rights and justice, and this presents a potential vulnerability for Albanese.

While there might be a political cost for the Prime Minister at a local level, Australia's response to the destruction of Gaza and the broader Israeli–Palestinian conflict reveals the complex interplay between international diplomacy, domestic politics, and the moral imperatives of human rights and justice. As Australia manages its role on the global stage, the actions it chooses to take—or not take—will not only impact its international relations but also reflect its values and priorities to its own citizens and the electorate. The call for a more assertive stance on the Israeli–Palestinian conflict is not only about foreign policy and geopolitics, but about the very identity and moral compass of the Australian nation.

***

SUPERMARKET SHAKE-UP: A NEED FOR STRONGER REGULATION

13 April 2024

The interim report of the Food and Grocery Code review sheds light on the significant power imbalances within Australia's supermarket sector, focusing particularly on the disparities between large supermarket chains such as Coles, Woolworths, and Aldi, and the smaller suppliers, farmers and producers they dominate. These large players currently operate under a voluntary code that lacks the enforcement teeth necessary to deter breaches. This gap in regulatory oversight has facilitated an environment where supermarket giants can, without fear of meaningful penalties, disregard the code, perpetuating practices that harm smaller producers and inflate consumer prices.

The financial figures are significant: Coles and Woolworths reported substantial profits in the 2023 financial year—$1.1 billion and $1.6 billion respectively—highlighting a market condition skewed heavily in favour of these large corporations at the expense of a competitive marketplace. Aldi's exact figures remain undisclosed—as a private company—but market analysts suggest that their profit margins are similarly high. This disparity not only highlights the disproportionate financial clout these corporations wield but also casts doubt on the effectiveness of current regulatory frameworks to foster fair competition and protect consumer interests.

Treasurer Jim Chalmers has advocated for transitioning from a voluntary to a mandatory code as soon as possible, equipped with stringent penalties and enhanced dispute resolution processes and such changes aim to rebalance the scales, ensuring that breaches of the code are met with substantial consequences. The author of the report, Dr. Craig Emerson, made the key point that current voluntary code is akin to having speed limits on the roads without penalties for violations—so why would anyone take any notice of the code—and it's a scenario that starkly illustrates the ineffectiveness of the existing system.

The need for reform is urgent—the lack of competition not only stifles market dynamics but also directly impacts consumers, who are currently face high prices amidst rising living costs. This critique extends to the broader economic model, where the natural trajectory of unchecked capitalism leads monopoly or duopoly conditions—which Australia has an abundance of in its corporate sector—diminishing the very competition that is essential for a healthy market economy.

In this context, the government faces substantial pressure to act decisively. The full report, due in late June, will likely lead to further discussions about competition policy in Australia and should become the catalyst for legislative changes in the near future. The effectiveness of these changes will ultimately be judged by their ability to bring about tangible improvements in market practices and consumer protections. This requires a careful, robust approach to regulatory overhaul that not only addresses the symptoms of the current market dysfunctions but also the structural inequities at their root.

A BALANCING ACT: AUSTRALIA'S COMPLEX INTERSECTION OF POLITICS, ECONOMY, AND SOCIAL PRIORITIES

This current debate in Australia transcends simple market mechanics, venturing deeply into the realm of political priorities and societal values. The government's approach to addressing these issues is not only a matter of regulatory intervention; it is also a reflection of what our society aims to prioritise: is it consumer affordability? Or fair prices for farmers and producers? Or is it the economic welfare of the workforce within the supermarket and retail sector? The massive profits that that been made by the supermarket giants have been built on the back of the low wages that many of their retail and support staff receive. Surely all these factors need to be taken into account when deciding what the results of new competition policy and legislation should be.

Within this complex picture, there are many priorities that are layered and intersect with each other. The most immediate concern for most politicians revolves around consumer prices—every voter is a consumer, and the sheer number of consumers makes this a significant political issue. However, ensuring lower prices for consumers without harming other stakeholders involves a delicate balance. Producers and suppliers, who are fewer in number but crucial to the economic ecosystem, need fair prices to sustain their operations and livelihoods. This is not just an economic issue but a matter of equitable market practices, ensuring that large supermarkets do not use their dominant position to unfairly squeeze suppliers' profit margins.

Further complicating this are the concerns regarding wages and working conditions within these supermarket chains. The substantial profits reported by the giants in the industry suggest that they have the capability to improve pay and conditions for their staff, many of whom earn minimal wages despite the significant role they play in the companies' successes. Yet, there is a persistent resistance to wage increases within the business community and conservative politics, often coupled by the argument that higher wages could lead to economic ruin—a refrain that is rarely substantiated by any meaningful economic data or evidence.

This resistance overlooks the potential economic benefits of wage increases. Higher wages leads to increased disposable income, which in turn stimulates demand for goods and services, benefiting the economy at large—including the supermarkets themselves. This cycle of wage increase and spending boost is often ignored by those who fear the immediate implications of increased labour costs.

There is also the political and public challenge for the Labor government of managing expectations. Even if the government implements all the recommended changes to enforce a stricter regulatory environment and potentially lower grocery prices, the actual impact on cost of living might not be immediately noticeable to the average consumer. Public perception of economic pressure and the "cost-of-living" crisis pushed forward by the media is now deeply ingrained and difficult to shift, and unless there is a visible, significant reduction in grocery prices, dissatisfaction with the government may persist.

This highlights the multifaceted nature of the issue at hand. The government's response needs to be equally comprehensive, targeting not just the symptoms—high prices at the checkout—but also the underlying causes: lack of competition, unfair pricing strategies, and inadequate wages. The success of any legislative or regulatory changes will be measured not just by the balance sheets of big supermarkets or the price tags in store aisles, but by the real improvements in the lives of all stakeholders involved, from the smallest supplier to the everyday consumer.

WILL THE CONCENTRATION OF THE MARKET BE FINALLY BROKEN?

It is becoming increasingly clear that the issues of concern within the supermarket sector are deeply entrenched within broader economic and political contexts, and other sectors within the economy. Australia's history of protecting certain sectors through legislation, effectively granting favourable conditions to big players, is not unique to supermarkets but is a recurring theme across many other industries, including telephony, the whitegoods and electronics retail market, and the mainstream media. This pattern has resulted in duopolies and low competition environments that invariably lead to inflated consumer prices, as large corporations leverage their market dominance.

The forthcoming reforms in merger approval and competition laws, slated for implementation in January 2026, signal the Labor government's recognition of the need for a more robust framework to ensure fair competition. However, the delay in these reforms taking effect indicates that significant relief in grocery prices—or any other prices in other sectors—may not be immediate. This delay is typical in political landscapes where substantial policy shifts require time for legislation, implementation, and to start showing effects.

Political responses to these issues also reflect broader ideological divides. Criticisms from the leader of the opposition, Peter Dutton, who dismissed the supermarket report as inconsequential and ineffective in controlling prices—claiming they were "Mickey Mouse"—underscore the challenges in achieving consensus on the approach to regulating key markets. His comments also highlight a common political tactic for the conservative politician: focusing on short-term headlines rather than long-term solutions. But this is who Dutton is—more interested in amplifying a perceived problem, than seeking a consensus; we shouldn't really expect anything better. Dutton was in government between 2013 to 2022, yet there was not one act from the Coalition to bring supermarket prices down, and to keep them down. The current system of corporate self-regulation was instigated by the Coalition, yet here they are arguing how terrible the system is, hoping that no-one in the electorate will remember that they are the ones with responsibility for the current calamity.

The necessity for regulation in the free market, particularly in sectors as vital as grocery retail, is evident. While proponents of a *laissez-faire* economy argue that the market self-regulates and will always arrive at a solution, the reality observed in protected sectors like supermarkets suggests otherwise. Without effective regulation, monopolistic and duopolistic tendencies develop, stifling competition and harming both consumers and smaller businesses.

The argument that substantial government intervention in markets equates to socialism—in February, the Prime Minister Anthony Albanese suggested that "we are not the Soviet Union" in response to a question about possibility of breaking down the supermarket duopoly—is a misrepresentation of the role of government in a capitalist society. That is true: we are not the Soviet Union, but neither do we exist in a land where free market capital and the law of the jungle prevails. Governments have a responsibility to ensure that markets operate fairly, that businesses adhere to ethical practices, and that consumers are protected from predatory practices. This responsibility justifies and necessitates a degree of regulation and oversight, particularly in sectors where the potential for abuse is substantial due to lack of competition.

Ultimately, the trajectory for supermarket competition in Australia and its regulation will be a balancing act between fostering an environment conducive to free market operations and implementing safeguards to protect consumers and ensure fair play. This balance is crucial not only for the economic health of the country but also for the welfare of its citizens. As the government navigates these complex issues, the outcomes will likely influence public opinion, potentially reshaping political landscapes and consumer expectations in the process. It remains to be seen how effective these changes will be and whether they can indeed usher in an era of more competitive pricing and fairer market practices in the supermarket sector.

***

FIXING AUSTRALIA'S HOUSING AFFORDABILITY CRISIS

14 April 2024

The issue of housing continues to be in the spotlight, driven by persistent concerns over affordability and access. Recently, two main factors have captured attention in Australia: the substantial portion of unoccupied housing stock and the contentious idea of using superannuation funds to purchase homes.

At any given time, approximately 10 per cent of all housing stock in Australia remains unoccupied, a figure that includes both temporarily vacant properties, such as those undergoing renovations or in the process of changing ownership, and those deliberately left empty, and about half of these vacant properties are not available for use due to reasons such as being land-banked, reserved as holiday homes, or kept vacant for speculative purposes such as Airbnb rentals. This strategic withholding of property not only skews market dynamics but exacerbates the housing shortage, impacting affordability and accessibility for many Australians.

In response to this, there has been a growing call for the implementation of a vacancy tax, aimed at providing incentives for property owners to release these homes into the market. Such a tax would ideally decrease the number of persistently vacant homes, increasing supply and help to stabilise or reduce housing prices. This approach is being seriously considered by state governments in New South Wales and South Australia and given the pressing nature of the housing crisis, these proposals merit not just consideration but swift enactment.

Critics of Airbnb and similar platforms argue that they have transformed from a means for homeowners to earn extra income by renting out spare rooms into a commercial enterprise that reduces the housing stock available for long-term residents. This shift has had a pronounced effect in areas such as the Gold Coast, where the scarcity of affordable housing close to employment hubs is impacting local economies, as potential employees cannot afford to live within a reasonable distance of their workplaces.

The tax incentives currently favouring property investors are also another area of concern. These benefits contribute to market distortions by encouraging investment in real estate primarily for speculative gains rather than for providing housing. This issue is deeply entrenched, with significant resistance to change likely due to the personal financial interests and ownership of investment properties by many members in Parliament.

As Australia attempts to deal with these challenges, the focus must also shift to alternative solutions that can provide immediate relief to those most affected. Subsidised rents or temporary housing solutions could serve as interim measures to assist those in dire need, such as individuals currently living in cars or temporary accommodations.

Addressing Australia's housing crisis requires a multifaceted approach that not only increases the supply of available homes but also ensures sustainable and equitable access to housing for all Australians. Whether through taxation reform, regulatory changes, or new and experimental financial mechanisms, the path forward must be guided by both immediate and long-term strategies to resolve this pervasive issue.

URBAN PLANNING AND GOVERNMENT INTERVENTION: THE COMPLEX TERRAIN OF AUSTRALIA'S HOUSING MARKET

The roles and interactions between government intervention and urban planning continues to significantly influence the Australian housing market. Historical initiatives such as the first homeowner grants, intended to assist Australians in purchasing their initial homes, have paradoxically contributed to inflating housing prices. While these grants were aimed at making homeownership more accessible, they inadvertently increased demand without a corresponding increase in supply, thus driving up prices and negating the grants' intended affordability benefits.

In addition, local council zoning laws across Australia have often been critiqued for being overly restrictive, particularly in how they delineate residential, commercial, and industrial spaces. Such restrictions have constrained the development of new housing, limiting supply in areas with high demand and exacerbating the housing shortage. This shortage has not only escalated prices but also limited living options, impacting the overall quality of urban life and sustainability of cities.

In response to these challenges, the New South Wales government has initiated the Transport Oriented Development program, an innovative approach which aims to increase the density of housing near public transport hubs—specifically, within a 400-metre radius of 31 train stations across the Sydney region. By rezoning these areas to allow for the construction of up to six-story apartment buildings, the plan seeks to capitalise on existing infrastructure while promoting a more sustainable urban lifestyle, reducing reliance on private vehicles and enhancing accessibility to jobs and services.

This strategy represents an extension of the urban consolidation efforts previously seen in New South Wales and reflects a broader shift towards denser, more efficient urban living arrangements. However, these changes have not been universally welcomed—local resistance and political contention are common, as debates over urban development often stir concerns about increased congestion, the strain on local services, and the preservation of community character.

Addressing these concerns, NSW Minister for Planning, Paul Scully, emphasised the government's commitment to tackling inherited housing challenges by delivering "well-located, well-designed, and well-built homes" that integrate seamlessly with the urban fabric. On the other side of politics, NSW Opposition Leader Mark Speakman highlighted the importance of engaging with local communities to tailor developments that meet their specific needs and infrastructure requirements, suggesting a more bottom-up approach to planning.

The tension between 'not in my backyard' and 'yes in my back yard' attitudes and the need for more inclusive, accessible housing solutions highlights a broader societal debate. This conflict often pits longer-term residents against newer, younger populations who may have different visions for their communities. Such dynamics necessitate difficult decisions from governments, which must balance immediate local concerns with the long-term strategic needs of urban areas across Australia.

The evolving nature of work, particularly the rise of remote work, also offers potential solutions for decongesting major cities like Sydney and Melbourne. Promoting remote work could alleviate the pressure on urban housing markets, encouraging population dispersal and making it feasible for more people to live in less densely populated areas. This shift could also help preserve historically significant architecture within cities by reducing the need for high-density developments in culturally sensitive areas.

It is imperative to consider sustainable living solutions that don't only respond to current demands but anticipate future needs. The goals must remain clear: to provide affordable, accessible, and suitable housing for all Australians, fostering communities that thrive both socially and economically.

SUPERANNUATION FOR HOME BUYING: A CONTROVERSIAL FIX THAT WON'T WORK

The ongoing debate over housing also includes the controversial proposal of allowing Australians to use their superannuation funds to purchase homes, and this approach is seen by some as a potential remedy to enable first-time home buyers to enter the market. However, detractors argue that this could lead to further inflation of housing prices by increasing demand without corresponding increases in supply and such a policy could also undermine the primary purpose of superannuation, which is to secure financial stability in retirement.

Recent polls, however, such as the most recent Essential Report, indicate a significant public backing, with 57 per cent of respondents supporting the idea of accessing superannuation for buying a first home. Despite its popularity, the policy has faced substantial criticism from economists and policymakers who caution that such measures would likely escalate property prices even further. This inflation is expected because withdrawing significant amounts of superannuation would increase demand without a corresponding increase in housing supply, thereby soaking up the available superannuation funds and potentially reducing individuals' financial security upon retirement.

This debate highlights a broader problem with short-term, politically driven decisions that have characterised Australian housing policy over the past 30 years. Such policies are often popular for their immediate benefits but have had detrimental long-term effects on the economic landscape and the housing market. For instance, similar interventions in the past—such as the first home buyers grant—have resulted in unintended but predictable consequences such as dramatic increases in home prices, which outstripped the initial financial support provided.

This pattern of policy-making highlights the need for a more educated and economically aware approach among Australia's political leaders. The current political environment, influenced by short electoral cycles and the selection of candidates more focused on personal or party gain rather than public service, exacerbates the issue. There is a call for substantial reform in political party dynamics and candidate selection, promoting leaders who prioritise long-term national interests over immediate electoral gains. While this is inherently a separate issue to housing, these factors are interlinked.

Any measure adding to demand—without increasing supply—will inevitably lead to higher prices and this is a fundamental concept that seems to be repeatedly overlooked in government interventions across various sectors, including housing. As observed with the first home buyers grant, initial assumptions about moderate price increases were vastly underestimated, demonstrating a profound misunderstanding of market dynamics.

Addressing these challenges requires a shift towards more sustainable economic policies that consider both immediate impacts and long-term outcomes. The suggestion that superannuation should be preserved exclusively for retirement is based on the principle of ensuring long-term financial security rather than being seen as an immediate solution to current problems like housing affordability.

This approach calls for a broader vision and more profound economic strategies that look beyond the next electoral cycle, focusing instead on creating robust systems that can support the country's economic health over decades.

Australia's housing crisis demands a multifaceted approach that includes reforming political processes, enhancing economic understanding among leaders, and implementing policies that genuinely address the root causes of the crisis. Only then can the nation hope to achieve a stable, affordable housing market that serves the needs of all Australians, ensuring that the dream of homeownership does not compromise the financial stability of future generations.

***

LEHRMANN CASE EXPOSES FLAWS IN AUSTRALIA'S DEFAMATION PRACTICES

20 April 2024

The Bruce Lehrmann defamation case provides a stark illustration of the complexities and challenges inherent in media coverage of legal affairs, particularly in the case of high-profile and sensitive issues such as sexual assault allegations. This case, which revolved around accusations made by Brittany Higgins that she was raped by Lehrmann in a parliamentary office in Canberra—an allegation Lehrmann denied but was never acquitted of in the 2022 criminal trial due to jury misconduct—culminated in a civil defamation suit filed by Lehrmann against Network 10 after their coverage of the allegations.

This lawsuit and its resolution highlight significant issues concerning the roles and responsibilities of the media in reporting on such cases. Justice Michael Lee's judgment against Lehrmann not only dismissed the defamation claims but also declared that, on the balance of probabilities, that Lehrmann raped Higgins. This finding highlights a critical divergence between criminal and civil law standards of proof—'beyond reasonable doubt' versus 'balance of probabilities', respectively, and it raises profound questions about the portrayal of truth in media and legal contexts, where the former often seeks a narrative clarity that the latter, bound by stringent evidentiary standards and procedural constraints, cannot always provide. But the fact remains: Bruce Lehrmann raped Brittany Higgins, and despite whatever Lehrmann and his supporters in the conservative media wish to believe, this is what Justice Lee asserted in a court of law.

The judgment also speaks volumes about the potential misuse of defamation law as a tool to manage reputations and manipulate public perception. Lehrmann's decision to pursue defamation charges, despite the complexities and risks involved, was a strategic misstep that ultimately led to a more damaging public rebuke. Media outlets, such as Network 10, operate under the constant threat of defamation suits, which can influence how they report on sensitive issues. The case exemplifies the balance the mainstream media must maintain between aggressive reporting and the legal risks of defamation.

The reactions from various media commentators, as highlighted in the initial statements, also reflect a broader skepticism about the motives behind such lawsuits and their implications for public discourse, which point to a growing public awareness and criticism of how defamation laws can be used to suppress legitimate journalistic investigation and reporting. This situation is particularly precarious in Australia, where defamation laws are notoriously plaintiff-friendly, often placing an undue burden on the media to prove the truth of their statements to avoid liability.

In light of these challenges, the Lehrmann case acts as a catalyst for a broader discussion on the need for media reform in Australia. The media's role in shaping public understanding and discourse is critical, and its capacity to do so responsibly and ethically must be supported by legal frameworks that do not unduly stifle journalistic freedom but also promote good behaviours from the mainstream media. Reforming defamation laws to better balance the right to reputation with the public interest in freedom of expression and press would also be a significant step forward. This would not only help protect media outlets from vexatious litigation but also ensure that they can continue to play their crucial role in a democratic society by informing the public and holding the powerful to account.

Such reforms could include the introduction of public interest defences, caps on damages, or stricter requirements for proving actual malice in cases involving public figures. These changes would help realign Australia's defamation laws with international human rights standards, fostering a more vibrant, fearless, and accountable media landscape.

A CALL FOR REFORM: SYSTEMIC FAILURES IN AUSTRALIA'S MAINSTREAM MEDIA

Mainstream media's role in influencing public perception and justice can sometimes cross ethical boundaries, as evidenced by actions such as Seven West Media's payment for sensational stories—in the case of Lehrmann, this also involved supply of drugs and sex workers. Such practices not only compromise journalistic integrity but also raise questions about the accountability mechanisms currently in place to govern media conduct. The involvement of prominent media entities in behaviour that perverts the course of justice points to a systemic failure, not just isolated incidents of journalistic lapse.

This brings us to a critical crossroad: the necessity for a Royal Commission into mainstream media, which has been necessary and requested by the public for some time, and the Lehrmann trial provides even more evidence for this. The Australian media industry, much like any other sector with significant public influence, must be subjected to rigorous scrutiny and reevaluation, and the call for a Royal Commission is about ensuring that media outlets operate within a framework that upholds journalistic ethics and public trust and such an inquiry would examine the extent of media malpractice and propose structural reforms to mitigate these issues.

There's also a pressing need to reassess the criteria and conditions under which media licenses are granted and maintained in Australia. The fact that major media players like Kerry Stokes and the Murdoch family retain their licenses despite recurring controversies suggests a gap in the regulatory framework governing media operations. Why have they not been stripped of their licenses, despite their repeated failures and constant interference in the legal system and influence within politics? This gap allows media owners and executives to hold disproportionate influence over public discourse, often at the expense of fairness and accuracy.

The media's dwindling viewership and engagement with traditional forms of news, as highlighted by declining newspaper sales and television ratings, reflects a broader shift in consumer trust and habits. This "death spiral" of traditional media consumption and the end of the advertising "rivers of gold" highlights the urgency for the industry to adapt and reform. The transition towards digital news and the concentration of news consumption around weekends signal changing consumer preferences that the industry must accommodate to stay relevant.

In addressing these challenges, comprehensive media reform in Australia should not only focus on punitive measures but also on fostering a more transparent, accountable, and ethical media landscape, which could also include: implementing clearer regulations and standards that define and enforce ethical journalism; establishing stronger oversight bodies capable of independent and effective action against media malpractice; encouraging media literacy among the public to enable more discerning consumption of news; and promoting diversity in media ownership to reduce the concentration of media power that can lead to bias and manipulation of information.

Such reforms are essential but is there a political will to implement them? Based on what we've seen from governments of all persuasions over the past 50 years or so, the answer is a resounding "no".

DEFAMATION LAW ALSO NEEDS TO BE SIGNIFICANTLY REFORMED

The paradoxical outcomes of recent high-profile defamation cases in Australia, where plaintiffs often emerge with reputations more tarnished than before, underscore the urgent need for reform in both media practices and defamation laws. The cases of Ben Roberts-Smith, Lehrmann, and the future case involving Senator Linda Reynolds exemplify the risky nature of defamation litigation, where efforts to salvage a public image instead lead to further public and legal scrutiny, often resulting in more significant reputational damage.

Defamation litigation, in its current state, seems to offer a punitive process rather than a path to vindication, although Lehrmann's defeat in his case did provide belated vindication for Brittany Higgins. This reflects a broader issue with the legal framework surrounding defamation in Australia—it is not only punitive but also often fails to accommodate the complexities of proving truth and intent in the digital age. The legal battles fought by figures like former Attorney-General Christian Porter and the actor Craig McLachlan highlight how defamation suits can extend the public and personal trauma of the victims involved in the case, with questionable benefits in terms of justice or reputational management.

These high-profile cases also reveal a concerning trend: individuals retreating from public life or even relocating as a consequence of the overwhelming negative publicity and social repercussions stemming from their legal battles, as was the case with Higgins, who has relocated to France, even though she was not the one who brought on this case. This phenomenon points to a deeper societal issue where the court of public opinion and the legal system intersect to create outcomes that can be disproportionate and destructive.

Reforms—if they are to achieve a better balance for all parties—must address several key areas, including revision of defamation standards, promotion of pre-litigation mediation, caps on damages payable, and greater support for witnesses, especially in cases that involve sexual assault and rape.

The necessity of these reforms becomes even more pressing considering the evolving role of media in society. As traditional media struggles with credibility and the rise of digital platforms transforms how information is consumed, the legal frameworks governing defamation must adapt. Without such reforms, the media and individuals may continue to engage in legal battles that serve no constructive purpose, potentially stifling free speech and journalistic integrity.

Ultimately, defamation reform in Australia should aim not only to protect individuals from undue harm but also to ensure that the media can fulfill its role with a democratic society without fear of oppressive litigation. By realigning defamation laws with contemporary values and technological realities, Australia can better protect both individual dignity and public discourse.

***

NAVIGATING THE COMPLEXITIES OF THE GAZA CONFLICT AND GLOBAL DIPLOMACY

21 April 2024

The escalation of the war in Gaza and its ripple effects extend far beyond the immediate conflict zone, touching on global politics and influencing national policies, including those of Australia. The recent increase in hostilities, marked by Iran's unprecedented direct missile and drone attacks on Israel, stems from a complex web of regional tensions and historical grievances. This act by Iran, a response to a provocative Israel Defense Forces attack on its embassy in Syria, signifies a dangerous broadening of the conflict's scope, which could lead to further instability in the Middle East.

This international conflict also has profound implications for Australian politics, especially concerning its foreign policy and domestic political discourse. Australia, with its significant Jewish and Muslim populations, finds itself in a delicate position, needing to balance its historical, if misguided, support for Israel with the growing calls for recognition of Palestinian statehood. The recent statements from Foreign Minister Senator Penny Wong highlight this shift, where she advocated a two-state solution as the only viable method to end the cycle of violence. It's inherently correct—the long-held view of a two-state solution can't be achieved if Palestine is not a state—and her comments have stirred controversy within Australia from the usual conservative players, reflecting a fractious debate on how the nation should navigate its diplomatic ties and moral positions on international justice and human rights.

The situation has also been a catalyst for wider discussions in Australia about the role of international law and the responsibilities of nations in upholding peace and security. The Australian government faces increasing pressure to align more closely with global consensus, which leans towards recognising Palestinian statehood. This is highlighted by the significant number of UN member states that support such a move—140 of the 193 members—though challenges remain, notably the potential for veto by permanent UN Security Council members, including the United States, which recently used its veto power to block Palestinian statehood.

Australian domestic politics also feels the strain as community groups and political factions express divergent views on the issue, mirroring the global division. The response from the conservative and self-interested Australian Jewish Association, which vehemently opposes recognising Palestinian statehood, contrasts sharply with the broader international and national movements towards a two-state solution. This dichotomy represents the deep ideological divides within Australia that mirror the global disagreements over the Israeli–Palestinian conflict.

The war in Gaza and the international responses to it, including from actors like Iran and Israel, significantly affect Australian political discourse and policy. As the conflict continues to evolve, Australia must navigate its diplomatic strategies carefully, balancing its domestic interests with its international obligations and moral stances on peace, justice, and human rights.

HOW THE ISRAELI–PALESTINIAN CONFLICT SHAPES AUSTRALIAN POLITICS

The domestic political landscape in Australia is intricately tied to its international relations, especially concerning the Israeli–Palestinian conflict. As the conflict escalates, comparisons are being drawn between Israeli Prime Minister Benjamin Netanyahu and former British Prime Minister Margaret Thatcher. Both leaders, facing political unpopularity, leveraged military actions to boost their domestic approval ratings. Netanyahu, like Thatcher with the Falklands conflict in 1982, is using the ongoing violence to solidify his position amid political instability.

This perception has sparked significant debate within Australia, impacting both public opinion and the stances of political leaders. Prime Minister Anthony Albanese and Senator Wong have faced considerable pressure, navigating the complex and often divisive reactions among the Australian populace—the Australian government, while officially supporting a two-state solution, appears to vacillate under the influence of powerful lobbies, such as the Australian Jewish Association. The situation is further complicated by Israel's actions, particularly under Netanyahu's leadership, are motivated by strategic interests in natural resources, such as gas reserves near Gaza, rather than purely security concerns.

Public response in Australia has varied widely, with community leaders and activists vocalising either staunch support for Israel or condemnation of its actions and calling for more robust support for Palestinian statehood. The Labor Party, historically more sympathetic to Palestine, has found itself at a crossroads, attempting to balance these complex international dynamics with domestic political consequences. The Australian government's approach has been characterised by caution, as it weighs the implications of fully endorsing Palestinian statehood against the backdrop of international relations and domestic electoral fallouts.

The controversy over Senator Penny Wong's shifting stance on Israel and Palestine highlights the broader political and ethical dilemmas facing Australia. Her nuanced position—to put it very generously—reflects an attempt to mediate between the humanitarian crises in Gaza and the powerful domestic and international interests that influence Australia's foreign policy. This balancing act is indicative of the broader challenges that Australia faces on the world stage, where it must navigate its values, strategic interests, and international obligations.

THE IMPACT ON AUSTRALIAN POLITICAL LEADERSHIP

The Israeli–Palestinian conflict continues to cast a shadow over Australian politics, influencing not just foreign policy decisions but also the dynamics within domestic political arenas. The leader of the opposition, Peter Dutton, recently took a controversial stance that starkly contrasts with the more measured approach of the government. Dutton's remarked that "whilst no one was killed during the protests... the events of the Sydney Opera House were akin to a Port Arthur moment in terms of their social and national significance ...Prime Minister Albanese has not driven risen to that moment, as John Howard did," a comment that was guaranteed to incite and cause yet another divisive debate within the community.

This discourse is not just about the events themselves but also about the role of leadership in times of national and international turmoil. Dutton's comments were intended to as a criticism of Prime Minister Albanese's handling of the issue of Gaza, suggesting a failure to rise to the occasion as past leaders have. However, this comparison has been met with backlash and ridicule from various quarters, including from within his own party, especially from the Liberal Party backbencher, Bridget Archer.

The government's Jason Clare commented that "if you want to run the country, you can't run your mouth. Last week, Peter Dutton took the sight of another country that killed an Australian citizen. This week, he is using the murder in cold blood of 35 Australians to try to make a political point. This bloke is all aggro and no judgment."

Dutton's behaviour resulted in a response that shows a broader discontent with what is seen as an opportunistic and divisive approach to politics and a style of irresponsible leadership that prioritises sensational rhetoric over substantive policy.

The fallout from Dutton's comments has also highlighted a schism within the Liberal Party, with figures such as Archer calling for a return to more principled politics, echoing a sentiment that many Australians find lacking in Dutton's approach. This internal party conflict mirrors the larger national debate over how Australia should engage with complex international issues like the Israeli–Palestinian conflict. The sharp critiques from within Dutton's own ranks—Archer wasn't the only Liberal Party to voice her dismay—suggest a party at odds with itself on the direction and tone of its leadership.

The broader Australian political landscape is witnessing a shift towards more grassroots movements, as indicated by the Climate

200 initiative's plans to support candidates in upcoming elections. This movement signifies a growing public demand for new political narratives that diverge from traditional party lines and address global issues like climate change and international conflict with a fresh perspective. Such movements pose a challenge to established figures like Dutton, who are perceived as out of touch with the evolving political consciousness of the Australian public.

The discourse surrounding the Israeli–Palestinian conflict not only shapes foreign policy but also deeply influences Australian domestic politics, challenging leaders to adapt to a rapidly changing political environment. As Australia deals with these complex global interactions, the political responses at home reflect a nation striving to reconcile its international engagements with domestic political accountability and integrity of leadership.

***

AUSTRALIA'S RISE IN THE GLOBAL ECONOMIC RANKINGS DOWNPLAYED BY THE MEDIA

27 April 2024

Australia's ascent in the global economic hierarchy is remarkable, with the country now ranked second among G20 nations for its economic performance, a stark contrast to its 14th place standing in 2021 during the final year of the Coalition's term. This is an impressive leap from the 107th position out of 116 economies in 2019, illustrating a dramatic turnaround in just a few years. Importantly, these rankings are sourced from the International Monetary Fund, an institution not swayed by partisan influences, countering any notion that the metrics might be biased by leftist think tanks or political agendas.

This upward trajectory has not always been mirrored in the media's portrayal of economic management concerning the achievements under Labor governments. Historical patterns indicate that since at least 1983—and likely earlier in the 1940s and definitively from 1972—Labor has managed the economy more effectively than the Coalition, especially in periods of long-term governance, such as the Hawke–Keating years between 1983–1996. This was evident when Australia deftly avoided the pitfalls of the 2008 financial crisis, a testament to the economic stewardship of figures like Wayne Swan, whose contributions are often overshadowed by those of Paul Keating, despite both receiving accolades as international finance ministers of the year—a recognition never bestowed upon their Liberal counterparts.

Despite these achievements, there is a pervasive reluctance within the mainstream media to acknowledge Labor's superior economic management. The narrative often favours the Coalition, despite its spotty record in economic stewardship, marked by ideologically driven policies more suited to times of economic boon rather than hardship. The Coalition's governance has seen Australia through cycles of economic mismanagement, most notably after the mining boom of the early 2000s, which left enduring budgetary challenges.

Current discussions around economic policy under the Labor government, led by Treasurer Jim Chalmers, reflects a certain level of optimism. His efforts to amend the structural damages wrought by nearly a decade of Abbott, Turnbull, and Morrison's leadership are commendable, yet the journey toward substantial reform is long and fraught with challenges. This cautious approach reflects a broader awareness that while macroeconomic indicators suggest robust health, public sentiment about economic conditions remains tepid.

As Australia navigates these complex economic waters, the shift from entrenched neoliberal policies to more progressive economic models is gradual but necessary. The transformation towards a New Keynesian framework is emblematic of this shift, indicating a deeper, more systemic reorientation of economic policy thinking that is essential for addressing contemporary economic challenges and ensuring long-term sustainable growth. This transition highlights a crucial moment in Australian economic history, one that requires a nuanced understanding of both the achievements and the ongoing challenges in governance and economic management.

A LONG-TERM VISION IS REQUIRED TO SHAPE AUSTRALIA'S ECONOMIC FUTURE

This perspective on economic management, voiced by Chalmers during his recent visit to the United States, emphasises the necessity of investing strategically for long-term gains. Chalmers articulates a vision where investments are not just immediate but staggered over time, reflecting a deep understanding of how economies evolve. The planned reforms in the upcoming Australian budgets are described as "big" and "substantial" by Chalmers, yet tempered to unfold across a medium to longer term period. This approach is designed to manage inflation while simultaneously fostering growth, highlighting a strategic patience that aims to match investment impacts with economic cycles.

The areas Chalmers highlights—energy transformation, housing, and human capital—are central concerns, and they represent sectors where Australia has significant potential to leverage its natural and human resources to forge a more dynamic and competitive economy. The emphasis on energy transformation, in particular, speaks to an urgent global need and presents Australia an opportunity to lead in a sector that is increasingly defining economic models worldwide. Such transformation is not only industrial but is fundamentally about reshaping the economic landscape to be more sustainable and resilient.

The need for agility in economic policy highlights a historical lesson: economies that fail to adapt to changing circumstances risk stagnation or decline. Looking at the history of economic performance in Australia, economic successes were often attributed to a single booming sector rather than a diversified approach—agriculture in the 1950s and mining in the early 2000s—and this illustrates the dangers of over-reliance on specific industries. The contemporary Australian economic strategy aims to rectify these past oversights by promoting agility and diversification, ensuring that the economy is robust enough to withstand future challenges.

The call for reforms to be community-focused is also a critical reminder that economic policies must serve the broader population, not just the economic metrics. This principle is fundamental to democratic governance and ensures that economic progress translates into real improvements in people's lives. What is the point of an economy that ranks second in the OECD if people can't afford to purchase a home at a reasonable cost, or afford to adequately feed their families? This is the criticism often leveled at neoliberal policies, which often prioritises economic efficiency at the cost of social equity.

The narrative around economic management in Australia often revolves around the dichotomy between the Labor and Liberal parties. On most economic indicators, Labor governments manages the economy better during challenging times—in the early 1970s during the oil crisis; during the recession left behind by the Fraser government in 1983; the global financial crisis in 2008; and now, the dire economic circumstances left behind by nine years of the Abbott–Turnbull–Morrison governments; while the Liberal Party promotes economic conditions that benefit the wealthy and squanders good economic circumstances—and these factors points to a deeper ideological divide over economic policy and its social implications. This ideological battle shapes public perceptions and is influenced by conservative media narratives, often obscuring the underlying economic realities.

This discussion of economic reforms and strategic investments comes at a critical time. As Australia prepares for future budgets under the Labor government—at least one more budget before the next federal election—the focus remains on how these policies will not only enhance economic statistics but also how they will impact the everyday lives of Australians, fostering a more equitable and sustainable future. This ongoing economic recalibration seeks not only to address immediate needs but to lay down the foundational structures that will support future generations. This broad, inclusive approach to economic management, despite often lacking sufficient recognition in the mainstream media, is crucial for building a consensus on the way forward, ensuring that the economy serves all segments of the community.

ECONOMIC SUCCESS AND POLITICAL POPULARITY: THE PARADOX OF LEADERSHIP

The critical dissonance between government performance, public perception, and media representation reveals a complex landscape in Australian politics, particularly with the economy. Despite the Labor government's strong economic track record as articulated by Treasurer Chalmers and evidenced by significant improvements in the IMF rankings, public approval for Prime Minister Anthony Albanese remains lukewarm.

During the United States Presidential Campaign in 1992, Bill Clinton asserted "it's the economy, stupid," suggesting that successful economic management is the number one priority for a political leader and, if this is managed successfully, political success is guaranteed. However, this is not always the case, and it appears that in the case of Albanese—and the broader Labor government—his electorate standing has been influenced by factors beyond economic performance. His support for the Voice of Parliament in 2023, for instance—or his lack of support for the Palestinian cause in Gaza—has been a flashpoint in public opinion, possibly exacerbating his negative approval ratings amidst underlying societal currents. Such complexities highlight that economic achievements alone may not suffice to garner broad public support in a diverse and at times divided electorate.

The negative portrayal of Labor's economic management by mainstream media also further complicates the public's understanding and appreciation of the government. Despite Labor's substantial economic successes, financial publications and broader media outlets often downplay these achievements, influenced by longstanding biases or commercial interests that favour conservative narratives, especially the narratives presented by News Corporation. This skepticism from the media is striking. Critical voices from the *Australian Financial Review* and News Corporation undermine significant achievements, such as delivering a budget surplus—a long-held gold standard of fiscal responsibility. Yet, when a Labor government achieves this, it is mocked for not using the appropriate fiscal lever at the necessary time.

This media bias not only shapes public perception but also plays into the political dynamics, where divisive figures such as Peter Dutton can achieve a positive approval rating—for the first time ever as leader of the opposition—despite his objectively less competent track record and propensity for social division at every opportunity. This phenomenon highlights the role of media in crafting political landscapes, often irrespective of underlying economic realities.

The upcoming budget in May represents a critical point for the Labor government to reinforce its economic credentials and shift public and media narratives. However, the government's approach suggests a resolve to prioritise long-term economic strategies over immediate political gains. The decision to ignore the often partisan media critique and focus on sustainable economic policies may ultimately serve the broader interests of the Australian community, and emphasises the need for governance that transcends short-term popularity and remains steadfast in its commitment to national prosperity.

The challenge for the Labor government lies not only in managing the economy but also in navigating the complex pieces of media influence, public perception, and political opposition. The ability to maintain a focus on equitable and sustainable economic policies, despite these pressures, will be crucial for their long-term success and for the advancement of Australia's national interests. Economic success must be coupled with strategic communication and engagement to truly resonate with and serve the community and the electorate.

***

MAY

MEN, WE HAVE A PROBLEM: AUSTRALIA'S ESCALATING DOMESTIC VIOLENCE CRISIS

4 May 2024

Domestic violence perpetrated by men against women and children remains an urgent and ongoing issue in Australia. Despite being widely recognised as a critical concern, efforts to address it have been frustratingly sluggish and often mired in political complexity and grandstanding. The impetus for reform, however, has never been clearer or more urgently needed.

In Australia, the magnitude of domestic violence is alarming. Reports and rallies, such as the recent "No More" gatherings in Canberra and other cities, underscore the pervasive nature of this crisis. The last major report, released in October 2022, culminated in a national plan to end violence against women and children. Yet, the subsequent actions have fallen short of the sweeping reforms needed. The federal government has now pledged significant funds, including $925 million aimed at helping victims escape abusive environments, and proposed legal changes to combat deep fake and violent pornography. These measures, while beneficial, are insufficient without a broader societal and cultural shift towards addressing the root causes of gender-based violence.

The political landscape surrounding domestic violence reforms is fraught with challenges and initiatives often become entangled in partisan debates, as seen in the discussions about Prime Minister Anthony Albanese's attendance at the "No More" rally in Canberra. Political figures can, unfortunately, overshadow the core issues, with their presence at such events sparking controversy over intentions rather than focusing on the victims' needs. This recent politicisation diluted the momentum for change and distracted from the essential goal of protecting vulnerable individuals.

Cultural norms and societal behaviours play a substantial role in perpetuating domestic violence and the prevailing attitudes towards masculinity and violence need profound transformation. Current measures still place undue burden on women to protect themselves rather than addressing male aggression directly and it is this skewed responsibility which highlights the broader societal reluctance to confront uncomfortable truths about gender and power dynamics.

The political response to domestic violence is often reactive rather than preventive. While funding for victim support services is crucial, it does not address the systemic issues that give rise to violence in the first place. Issues such as alcohol abuse and gambling are frequently overlooked in discussions about domestic violence. These factors, coupled with financial stress and societal pressures, create environments where violence can thrive and addressing these contributing elements is essential for long-term change.

The integration of domestic violence policies across various sectors where government is involved is also vital. For instance, adequate housing policies and social support payments play a crucial role in providing safe alternatives for those seeking to escape abusive situations. Incremental policy changes and funding increases are steps in the right direction, but they must be part of a larger, more cohesive strategy that includes education, legal reform, and economic support.

According to the CEO of Domestic Violence NSW, Delia Donovan, tackling domestic violence in Australia requires many approaches that go beyond temporary fixes and addresses the underlying social, cultural, and economic factors. Political challenges must be navigated with a focus on bipartisanship and the common goal of eradicating violence. It is imperative for policymakers, community leaders, and all stakeholders to commit to sustained and meaningful action that ensures safety and justice for all affected individuals, and this commitment must be matched with accountability, comprehensive reforms, and a shift in societal attitudes to create a safe and equitable environment for women and children.

SHOULD HE STAY OR SHOULD HE GO? A REFLECTION ON LEADERSHIP AND COMMUNITY ENGAGEMENT

Political events such as rallies can serve as significant platforms for leaders to address pressing issues. However, they can also become pitfalls for political figures, as illustrated by Prime Minister's appearance the "No More" rally. This event highlighted not only the ongoing struggles against domestic violence in Australia but also the complexities and missteps in political leadership regarding sensitive societal issues.

At the rally, Albanese aimed to demonstrate the government's commitment to addressing domestic violence, noting the substantial financial resources allocated to this cause, and spoke of government actions, such as funding for domestic violence workers and the implementation of domestic leave days. Yet, his speech, which spanned almost ten minutes, was criticised for being overly focused on financial commitments rather than offering substantive policy advancements or empathetic engagement with the audience's concerns.

The rally turned contentious when the issue of whether Albanese should speak was put to the audience, revealing a lack of coordination and prior understanding between the organisers and the Prime Minister's office. This situation was exacerbated when Albanese, in response to claims that he had not engaged with the event organisers—also asserting "well, I am the Prime Minister"—and such a defensive posture in a context that called for sensitivity and solidarity with victims of domestic violence exemplified a disconnect between political leadership and the needs of the community. And it was this action—whether it was intentional or not—the lead the media narrative throughout the days ahead, rather than the *actual* issue of domestic violence.

The aftermath of Albanese's participation at the rally serves as a case study in the political challenges inherent in addressing important social issues such as domestic violence. The response to his speech and the dynamics at the event reflect a broader issue where political actions are often scrutinised through a partisan lens, regardless of the intentions behind them. Supporters of the Prime Minister may view his actions as appropriate within the constraints he faced, while critics may see his responses as inadequate or misjudged, highlighting the polarised nature of political discourse.

The "No More" rally highlighted a significant challenge in political leadership: the need for politicians to transcend party lines and genuinely engage with community issues in a manner that respects and amplifies the voices of those directly affected. In scenarios like these, political figures must navigate the delicate balance between speaking out on critical issues and stepping back to listen and learn from those living the realities of such crises.

This misstep by the Prime Minister—thoroughly and gleefully magnified by the mainstream media—reveals the intricate balance of political engagement with sensitive social issues. It exemplifies the potential for political disasters when leaders fail to align their rhetoric with the expectations and emotional contexts of their audiences. For meaningful progress in combating domestic violence, political leaders must not only advocate for policy changes and allocate funding but also demonstrate genuine solidarity and sensitivity towards the victims and advocates at the forefront of this struggle.

A CALL FOR IMMEDIATE ACTION AND SYSTEMIC CHANGE

Despite various government efforts over the years, the statistics on domestic violence remain deeply concerning. The recent increase in domestic violence homicides by 30 per cent over the past year and the overall rise in incidents since the onset of COVID-19 demand a reassessment of the efficacy and direction of current interventions.

The recurrence of domestic violence across all socio-economic brackets illustrates its pervasive nature, and it is not confined to any single demographic but is a widespread issue affecting many communities. The statistics are staggering: one in six women experience physical or sexual violence from a current or former partner, and economic abuse affects a similar number of women. These figures underline the severity of the crisis, which according to KPMG costs the Australian economy an estimated $26 billion annually.

Political inertia is also a significant barrier to progress, where governments tend to react rather than proactively address issues, often only mobilised by sustained public pressure and advocacy. This reactive stance has led to piecemeal solutions that fail to address the root causes of domestic violence or create sustainable change, and it is not only a matter of insufficient funding but also of misdirected efforts that do not tackle the structural issues enabling domestic violence.

A prime example of this was a recent summit hosted by the NSW Premier Chris Minns on women's violence, which was primarily composed of male and religious leaders, and this exemplifies the missteps in addressing gender-based violence. The lack of representation of women, who are predominantly the victims of this violence, in such forums is a critical oversight that distorts the framing and solutions proposed for these issues.

Prominent voices in the field, such as academic and criminologist Vincent Hurley, have expressed frustration with the political handling of domestic violence, where they argue that extensive discussions and commissions, while necessary for oversight, often delay direct action that could provide immediate relief to victims. Hurley's call for denying bail to individuals with a history of violence is an example of specific, actionable measures that can be implemented to protect victims more effectively.

The broader societal implications of domestic violence extend beyond immediate physical and emotional damage to long-term societal costs, including healthcare, lost productivity, and intergenerational trauma. Addressing these issues requires a holistic approach that encompasses not only law enforcement and judicial reforms but also educational and cultural changes to alter attitudes toward gender and violence.

The reduction of domestic violence in Australia is usually hindered by political, cultural, and systemic challenges, and the path forward must include a robust re-evaluation of funding allocations, legal frameworks, and community engagement strategies. It demands a shift from reactive policies to proactive, comprehensive reforms that address the underlying causes of domestic violence. This shift requires a commitment to genuine and sustained action, transcending political cycles and aiming for long-term cultural change. For real progress, it is crucial that all levels of government, supported by the community and advocacy groups, prioritise the safety and dignity of women and children, and aim to eradicate domestic violence entirely. Such an endeavour not only fulfills a moral obligation and a duty of care to all citizens but is essential for the health and wellbeing of society as a whole.

**

UN VOTE ON PALESTINE EXPOSES AUSTRALIA'S INCONSISTENT FOREIGN POLICY

11 May 2024

There was another vote at the United Nations on the weekend, aiming to provide Palestine with additional observer status rights. Unlike the vote in April, which the United States blocked through the UN Security Council, this time the draft resolution had undergone changes to address the previous objections. The revised vote was passed by the United Nations by a substantial majority of 143 votes to 9, despite the vehement protests from the Israeli Ambassador. Although this change was small, it signified progress in the pathway for Palestine being fully recognised as a state. This vote did not concern full UN membership for Palestine, which typically involves a cyclical pattern of vetoes from permanent members of the United Nations—the United States vetoed the vote in April and is expected to do so again if a resolution for full Palestinian membership arises, and in the unlikely event that it did either support the vote or abstain, the permanent members usually conspire so that one of the other members—either Britain or France—can find some fault with the resolution, perpetuating the diplomatic stalemate.

Australia's stance on this matter continues to highlight the inconsistency in its foreign policy regarding the Israeli–Palestinian conflict. The rhetoric of a two-state solution, frequently reiterated by Australian officials, rings hollow without recognising both Israel and Palestine as sovereign states. Australia's abstention from the vote in April—to provide Palestine with full UN membership—reflects a lack of courage and commitment to meaningful progress in the region and while it did support this vote, it did it's best to downplay the significance of this support, leaving people wondering why they supported it in the first place. Foreign Minister Penny Wong had been engaged in discussions with ministers from Germany, the United Arab Emirates, and New Zealand, yet substantial political will is still lacking. In an election year for the United States and Britain—and possibly Australia—these countries are unlikely to shift their positions, further complicating efforts for change.

Comparisons have been also been made between the situation in Palestine and the historical context of East Timor in 1999. Indonesia's long-standing control over East Timor, driven by strategic interests in the region's resources, seemed intractable until international pressure and political will culminated in an end to the Indonesian occupation and East Timor's independence in 2002. While each international situation is unique, there are lessons to be learned from East Timor that could be applied to Palestine and the broader Middle East. However, this requires a significant shift in political will from the international community, which is currently absent concerning Gaza and Palestine.

Australia's involvement in East Timor was also marred by controversial actions, including the disproportionate appropriation of gas resources and allegations of spying on the East Timorese government. These actions highlights the importance of supporting smaller nations rather than exploiting them, a lesson that seems not fully absorbed when it comes to Gaza. The ongoing reluctance to join the global consensus in protecting Palestinian rights and sovereignty reflects a persistent failure in Australian foreign policy. This failure is particularly stark given the context of Palestinian resistance against what they view as foreign interlopers taking their land, especially when consideration of Australia engaged in exactly the same action in 1788 which its own Indigenous population. It is crucial for Australia, and the international community, to engage in self-reflection and adopt a more just and proactive stance on Palestine.

DEBATE OVER PALESTINIAN STATEHOOD HIGHLIGHTS HYPOCRISY AND INACTION IN AUSTRALIAN FOREIGN POLICY

The ongoing debate over what constitutes a Palestinian state has also dominated international discussions recently. Central to this debate is whether the borders should be based on the pre-1967 lines or include Gaza and the current West Bank, which has been increasingly encroached upon by illegal Jewish settlements over the past 57 years. The pre-1967 borders are unequivocally unacceptable to the current Israeli leadership. Yet, it's crucial to acknowledge that, as a state founded on Zionism, Israel is unlikely to ever accept the establishment of any kind Palestinian state, irrespective of how small it is. Consequently, any vote on the state of Palestine is improbable to succeed in the near term, especially during an election year in the United States. Australia, with an election looming possibly by the end of this year or by May 2025, is likely to maintain its pro-Israel stance under Prime Minister Anthony Albanese's government.

Albanese's recent actions starkly contradict his positions when he was in opposition. This perspective was evident in his conversation with former Liberal Party treasurer Josh Frydenberg—who appears to be revelling in role of director of pro-Israel propaganda documentaries for Sky News—when Frydenberg asked Albanese if the phrase "from the river to the sea" extremely violent and said it had no place on Australian streets, Albanese readily agreed. And to further show which side he now supports, in a recent 3AW interview when asked to comment on the pro-Palestine university protests and encampments, Albanese said "I reckon if you asked those people chanting it [from the river to the sea], heaps of them wouldn't have a clue, wouldn't be able to find the [river] Jordan on a map". Not much solidarity with the people who Albanese would have been protesting with on campus, in his previous life in student politics. But, as Lord Acton once said "power tends to corrupt and absolute power corrupts absolutely".

This stance raises questions about the perceived violence of words versus actions. While the phrase is deemed offensive and violent towards Israelis, the massacre and bombing of over 35,000 Palestinians, predominantly women and children, is not similarly condemned by these leaders. This selective outrage reflects a profound hypocrisy. Frydenberg, Albanese and many other leaders seem to overlook the equally inflammatory and violent rhetoric from Israeli leaders. Not long ago, Israeli Prime Minister Benjamin Netanyahu asserted that Israel must control the entire area "from the river to the sea"—so, it seems, words are deemed violent and unacceptable if uttered by Palestinians, but appear to be ignored when the same words come from an Israeli leader.

The double standard extends further. Albanese recently reprimanded Education Minister Jason Clare for his balanced stance on protests and slogans, where Clare emphasised that while protests are a fundamental part of democracy, there is no place for hate, prejudice, discrimination, intimidation, anti-Semitism, or Islamophobia, and pointed out the ambiguous interpretation of slogans like "from the river to the sea," which have been used by both Palestinian advocates and Israeli political parties. Clare's call for a two-state solution, where two peoples could live side by side in peace without fear, terrorism, checkpoints, or occupation, was a plea for reason and balance. Yet, Clare's very moderate comments and statements on Israel were shut down by Albanese, and criticised as being highly inflammatory and anti-Semitic by the Israel and Zionist lobby groups, and News Corporation.

This hypocrisy is stark. The selective condemnation of rhetoric depending on its source highlights a broader issue in international politics regarding Palestine. The same words are branded as violent when spoken by Palestinians but are brushed off when articulated by Israeli officials. This double standard not only undermines the legitimacy of calls for peace and justice but also perpetuates the cycle of violence and occupation in the region. Albanese's shift in stance from opposition to leadership further exemplifies the political expediency that often trumps genuine efforts towards a fair resolution of the Israeli–Palestinian conflict.

Australia's lack of action and the inconsistency in its foreign policy reflect a broader unwillingness to confront the complex realities of the Israeli–Palestinian conflict. This reluctance to take a firm and principled stand, whether driven by electoral considerations or international alliances, ultimately contributes to the ongoing suffering and instability in the region. It is imperative for leaders to transcend partisan politics and adopt a genuinely balanced approach that advocates for the rights and sovereignty of all peoples involved.

ALBANESE'S SHIFTING STANCE ON PALESTINE UNDERMINES HIS CREDIBILITY

Albanese's stance on Palestine presents a troubling inconsistency that has become increasingly evident over his tenure. While Albanese has shown strong leadership on various issues, his approach to the Israeli–Palestinian conflict starkly contrasts with his earlier, more principled positions. True leadership entails adhering to values consistently, and deviating from these values can erode a leader's credibility over time. This divergence is particularly glaring given Albanese's history of pro-Palestinian advocacy and other issues, such as his previous support for increasing social welfare payments. His current positions not only diminishes his moral authority but also raises questions about his commitment to justice and human rights.

Albanese's shift on Palestine, alongside his reluctance to support raising Jobseeker payments, marks a significant departure from his past advocacy and this change reflects a broader trend in politics where electoral calculations often outweigh moral imperatives, and it's a pragmatic but ethically dubious approach, especially given the ongoing humanitarian crisis in Gaza. As reports of massacres and uncovered mass graves continue to emerge, Albanese's support for Israel becomes increasingly indefensible. Certainly, the electorate may not prioritise Middle Eastern policy in their voting decisions on election day, and this is a calculation that both Albanese and U.S. President Joe Biden are relying on. However, dismissing the ethical and moral dimensions of the Gaza conflict undermines the very principles that should guide leadership.

When leaders abandon long-held beliefs, they need compelling reasons for doing so. In the case of Albanese, such reasons have not been convincingly presented. He was pro-Palestine when he was was opposition but now that he's a leader of government, he's pro-Israel and dismissive of any calls for action on alleviating the situation for the people of Gaza. This lack of transparency and deviation from core values is troubling. The government must rediscover its soul, purpose, and reason for being. Albanese's leadership on this issue—or lack thereof—demands a re-evaluation of priorities, guided by the principles of justice, equality, and human rights.

The ongoing developments at the United Nations regarding Palestine highlight the need for strong, principled international leadership. Australia's failure to take a decisive stand on this issue reflects broader systemic problems in how foreign policy is conducted. The hypocrisy in supporting Israel despite the clear humanitarian crisis in Gaza cannot be justified by electoral pragmatism alone. Leaders must be held accountable for their actions and the values they espouse.

True leadership requires unwavering commitment to one's values, especially in the face of complex international issues. Albanese's shifting stance on Palestine not only undermines his credibility but also reflects a deeper problem within political leadership today. The international community, including Australia, must take a more active and principled role in resolving the Israeli–Palestinian conflict, guided by a genuine commitment to human rights and justice for all.

***

A FEDERAL 2024 BUDGET TO ADDRESS FISCAL PRIORITIES AND POLITICAL CHALLENGES

18 May 2024

The release of the federal 2024 Budget has created the usual firestorm of media criticism and debate, highlighting the complexities of governments managing financial planning and the public reception, especially when it comes to Labor governments. Key players in the media landscape, such as News Corporation and Nine/Fairfax, have been particularly scathing in their evaluations of this Budget, often focusing on the negatives. This contrasts with the perspectives of leading economists such as Chris Richardson, who views the Budget as a beacon of fiscal positivity, promising substantial tax cuts and increased government spending designed to bolster the economy swiftly and reduce inflation significantly.

Amidst this backdrop, the portrayal of Treasurer Jim Chalmers in the media as either a jester or a confused and foolish politician on the cover of the *Daily Telegraph* highlights a continuing trend of antagonism towards Labor governments, a biased right-wing lens through which such budgets are often scrutinised. This depiction forms part of a broader media strategy that perennially cast Labor Budgets and financial initiatives in a dubious light, irrespective of their actual efficacy or intent.

Leading banking economists and market responses, indicated by the rise in the ASX 200, suggest a more favourable reception, recognising the potential of the Budget to stabilise and stimulate economic growth within the Australian economy. This narrative is often lost in mainstream media coverage, which tends to emphasise minor negative aspects, overshadowing broader economic benefits and such coverage raises questions about the influence of media biases on public perception and the potential consequences for political accountability and governance.

Historical comparisons highlight an inconsistency in economic management reputations between different governments, which promote Liberal governments as prudent and spectacular, whereas Labor governments are depicted as reckless, hopeless and incompetent. However, transformative economic reforms under Labor leaders such as Bob Hawke and Paul Keating during the 1980s, and effective crisis management during the global financial crisis under Kevin Rudd and Wayne Swan in 2008 provide evidence of competent Labor stewardship, challenging the stereotype of Labor's fiscal irresponsibility.

Yet, the Budget's reception is mired in a cacophony of mainstream media skepticism which tends to amplify dissenting voices like that of conservative economist Warwick McKibbin, while underplaying supportive economic assessments. This selective amplification contributes to a polarised view that may not fully reflect the broader economic consensus or the substantive content of the Budget measures.

Is the 2024 federal Budget good for the economy? Or *not* good for the economy? It's probably best not to look at assessments arising from the mainstream media, amid their predictions of the falling sky and an economic Armageddon just around the corner, because their habit is to always criticise the performances of Labor governments. It's the golden rule of Australian economic journalism.

DISSECTING THE DISCREPANCIES IN GOVERNMENT SPENDING AND SOCIAL COMMITMENTS

In the analysis of the Budget, a discrepancy emerges between the government's projected economic path and the realities of its financial allocations. With a hefty budget of around $730 billion, the allocation decisions reflect both the government's priorities and the political constraints it faces. Despite significant public and political pressure, the government has resisted raising the JobSeeker payment to 90 per cent of the pension level—or an increase from $381 to $500 per week—a change advocated by various social service groups and even segments within the business community. This resistance is damning, given the Labor Party's historical advocacy for more robust social safety nets, leading to criticism that the party is not living up to its principles or the expectations it set while in opposition, where it constantly demanded the Coalition make a substantial increase to unemployment benefits.

There is a historical comparison between Anthony Albanese's reluctance to increase JobSeeker and former Prime Minister John Howard's reluctance to apologise to the Stolen Generations, and this illustrates a deeper political fear—a fear of facing backlash from conservative media outlets, which usually attack increased welfare spending as supporting 'dole bludgers', or providing a disincentive to work. Increasing JobSeeker rates would be politically advantageous at this stage but Albanese, like Howard on the apology, refuses to budge on this issue. This highlights the political will that is often shackled by perceived media narratives and the fear of electoral repercussions, which in turn stifles progressive reforms.

The Budget speech by Treasurer Jim Chalmers emphasised a vision of resilience and prosperity, aiming to address immediate pressures while fostering long-term growth. However, this vision is somewhat contradicted by continued large-scale subsidies to the fossil fuel industries, totalling around $11 billion annually, and this allocation persists despite widespread acknowledgment of its environmental and fiscal inefficiency. It's a legacy issue that no government has dared to fully tackle due to the political influence of powerful industry groups, as evidenced by past campaigns against resource taxation reforms, especially the campaign against the mining tax in 2010, which ushered in and fast-tracked the removal of then Prime Minister, Kevin Rudd.

In contrast, the allocation of $21 billion to the 'Future Made in Australia' scheme, which supports renewable energy and rare mineral exploration, represents a strategic shift towards sectors where Australia has competitive advantages. While this initiative is commendable and necessary for transitioning to a sustainable economy, it is juxtaposed against underfunding in other critical social areas such as housing and the creative industries. For example, only $6.5 billion is earmarked for social housing and homelessness—sectors in desperate need of investment.

The Budget also fails to address other significant revenue opportunities or tax reforms, such as revising negative gearing and franking credits, which continue to benefit wealthier segments of society disproportionately. These omissions highlight a cautious approach to fiscal management by the Labor government, influenced by fear of political backlash rather than economic prudence or social equity.

There is also a broader concern with the Labor government's apparent loss of nerve upon assuming office, a pattern observed since the end of the Hawke–Keating era in 1996, and this timidity in governance contrasts sharply with the bold visions articulated in opposition—the historical reminder of Rudd's retreat in the face of mining industry pushback exemplifies this issue. The current government's reluctance to confront similar challenges suggests a continuation of a defensive and risk-averse strategy that prioritises political survival over transformative policy-making. There should be better ways to manage government and implement a progressive agenda but it appears this hope is being pushed into a faraway place somewhere on the distant horizon.

THE OPPOSITION'S BUDGET RESPONSE

The response of the opposition to the Budget has been as contentious as the Budget itself, reflecting the deeply polarised nature of contemporary Australian politics. Leader of the Opposition, Peter Dutton, criticised the budget heavily—even before it was released—attributing any perceived successes to the policies of the previous Coalition government, discrediting the Labor government's strategies and blaming them for ongoing economic challenges such as inflation and high energy costs.

In this fantasy land of the Coalition, the positive effects in the current state of the economy are somehow the result of their economic management between 2013–22—even though they almost destroyed the economy—yet, any negative effects are only caused by the management of the Labor government since they assumed office in 2022, as if the economy discerns the actions of the government of the day, sifts through the good and the bad of the economy, and allocates it according to party lines.

Dutton's remarks highlight the typical adversarial dynamic in politics, where achievements are minimised and failures are magnified across party lines. His characterisation of the Budget as "inflationary" and detrimental to families and small businesses highlights a significant divide in economic philosophy between the government and opposition. His metaphor of the Budget as a "band-aid on a bullet wound" vividly conveys his reactionary perspective that everything is a problem—even if it's not—but it is a critique which aligns with traditional conservative concerns about neoliberal economic policies, particularly regarding spending and its impact on inflation and interest rates.

This lack of coherence in the opposition's critique—along with the performances of Shadow Treasurer, Angus Taylor, who usually claims that a solution to every economic problem is just a matter of "getting back to basics"—weakens their position, and when everything just becomes a sound grab for the media, it just reduces their effectiveness in holding the government accountable. The opposition's narrative, focused more on condemning the government rather than proposing viable alternatives, also diminishes their credibility with the electorate, especially if the electorate perceives it as political posturing rather than substantive economic critique.

As this Budget is likely to be the last before the next federal election, it does carry significant weight for the government. It is designed to consolidate support and address criticisms of economic management—a strategic move in light of the impending election. The distribution of benefits, such as the $300 electricity rebate which has been universally applied rather than means-tested, could be seen as an attempt to appeal broadly to voters, though it has attracted criticism from various quarters for being either too generous or not targeted enough.

The legacy of the previous Coalition government is also relevant when compared with the current Budget, with a lack of substantial achievements or positive reforms from past Coalition Budgets, who appeared to squander their opportunities in government to navigate the economy through difficult times and spread the benefits to as many people as possible throughout the community. This historical context frames the 2024 Budget as not just an economic document but as a corrective measure, aimed at rectifying past mismanagements. While the Budget has been criticised for not being transformative enough, it should also be seen as part of a larger, more gradual process of repair and renewal.

The 2024 Budget is more than a financial statement; it is a political instrument shaped by and shaping the country's economic and political landscape. It reflects the government's priorities and strategies for navigating a challenging economic environment, while also revealing the tensions and conflicts inherent in the political process. The opposition's response, marked by traditional criticism and lacking in coherent alternatives, highlights the adversarial nature of politics, which often complicates rather than clarifies the economic choices facing the nation. The electorate's challenge is to navigate these complex narratives and discern which criticisms are valid and which are part of the typical political theatre surrounding national budgets.

***

JUSTICE DENIED: DEEP FLAWS IN WHISTLEBLOWER PROTECTION AND ACCOUNTABILITY

19 May 2024

The conviction and subsequent imprisonment of David McBride starkly illustrate the perilous path whistleblowers often tread when exposing governmental or military misconduct. McBride, who revealed alleged war crimes by the Australian Special Forces in Afghanistan, now faces a prison sentence of over five years, with a non-parole period of 27 months. This punishment has sparked considerable controversy and debate about the treatment of whistleblowers within the Australian legal system and the broader implications for governmental transparency and accountability.

McBride's disclosure led to a significant investigation by ABC's *Four Corners*, which subsequently led to the Brereton investigation and report. This investigation found credible evidence of war crimes committed by the Australian Special Forces, suggesting that such actions were not isolated incidents but part of a troubling pattern of behaviour. The report's findings highlighted the necessity of McBride's actions, revealing systemic issues that required public scrutiny and institutional accountability.

Despite the gravity of the crimes exposed, the individuals implicated in these offenses remain uncharged and free, highlighting a disconcerting disconnect between the severity of the crimes committed and the legal repercussions for those responsible. In contrast, McBride, who brought these issues to light, has been subjected to legal reprisals and jail time that is disproportionately harsh. This disparity raises fundamental questions about the priorities and values of the justice system and whether it serves to shield the powerful while punishing those who seek to expose wrongdoing.

Andrew Wilkie, the independent member for Denison, criticised the government's punitive approach to whistleblowers, suggesting that it aims to silence dissent and discourage others from coming forward and the systemic suppression of whistleblowers is not only a failure of the government to protect those who expose wrongdoing but also a broader failure to uphold principles of justice and transparency.

The legal ordeal faced by McBride and the government's response to his actions reflect a troubling stance on whistleblowing and it signals to current and potential whistleblowers that the personal cost of exposing wrongdoing may be exceedingly high. It is a situation that not only undermines efforts to maintain governmental accountability but also discourages civic engagement and the pursuit of ethical governance.

The treatment of McBride should prompt a reevaluation of the mechanisms in place for protecting whistleblowers and ensuring that they can come forward without fear of severe repercussions. It also highlights the need for robust legal protections that not only prevent retaliation against whistleblowers but also ensure that they are supported and vindicated when their disclosures reveal genuine misconduct.

GAPS IN LABOR'S COMMITMENT TO TRANSPARENCY AND PROTECTION

The plight of McBride also raises significant questions about the sincerity and efficacy of government promises, particularly those made by the Labor government regarding whistleblower protections and transparency. Upon assuming office, the Prime Minister, Anthony Albanese, provided a robust commitment to transforming the landscape of public interest disclosure in Australia and his assertions in 2020 suggested a change from the culture of secrecy which become a hallmark of the Morrison government, to one of openness, championing not only the protection of journalists but also the expansive safeguarding of whistleblowers, who play an instrumental role in the accountability framework of democratic governance.

However, despite these pronounced commitments to enhance transparency and protect those who expose wrongdoing, progress under the Labor government remains markedly absent. The lack of movement on these promises is not just a bureaucratic delay; it is a profound failure that undercuts the very principles of justice and accountability that form the bedrock of democratic societies. This inaction is particularly glaring in light of high-profile cases like McBride's, which continue to spotlight the vulnerabilities and risks faced by whistleblowers under current legal frameworks.

The introduction of the National Anti-Corruption Commission by the Labor government in 2023 was a step in the right direction, signaling a willingness to tackle corruption. However, this measure alone is insufficient if it is not accompanied by comprehensive reforms in other areas critical to transparency and accountability. The stagnation in advancing freedom of information reforms and strengthening whistleblower protections as initially promised illustrates a troubling inconsistency between the government's rhetoric and its actions and this discrepancy prioritises political expediency over the foundational democratic values of transparency and accountability.

This lack of progress in reforming whistleblower protection laws directly impacts individuals like McBride, who find themselves penalised rather than protected for their acts of conscience. The current state of affairs not only discourages potential whistleblowers from coming forward but also jeopardises the integrity of the institutions they aim to hold accountable, and serves as a potent deterrent that may silence other potential whistleblowers, allowing misconduct and corruption to flourish unchecked.

While national security concerns are legitimate, they should not preclude the operation of a fair and just legal system where the rights of individuals to a fair trial and the public's right to information are preserved. Courts have mechanisms to handle sensitive information without compromising public safety or national security, suggesting that these concerns are often overstated to suppress whistleblower activities and discourage disclosures that could embarrass or implicate government agencies.

The government's failure to act decisively on its prior commitments not only undermines public trust but also raises critical ethical questions about the nature of justice and governance in Australia. If those who expose wrongdoing are punished more severely than those who commit the crimes, it sends a chilling message about the values and priorities of the government.

THE ONGOING STRUGGLE FOR WHISTLEBLOWER PROTECTIONS AND OPEN GOVERNANCE

There is a broader systemic issue that plagues democratic governments worldwide: the inherent tension between the public's right to know and the state's desire for secrecy. This tension is not peculiar to any one government or political party—it is a ubiquitous challenge that transcends political lines, impacting various administrations regardless of their professed allegiance to transparency prior to assuming power.

In Australia, the bipartisan inclination towards secrecy has manifested starkly in recent years. Historical instances such as former Prime Minister Scott Morrison's undisclosed appointment to multiple ministerial roles in 2020 and 2021, and attempts by the Governor-General David Hurley and Morrison to orchestrate a secretly funded leadership initiative, illustrate how deeply embedded the culture of secrecy is within the political fabric of the nation. These examples highlight not just a reluctance to share power or information with the public but also a more concerning propensity to actively conceal actions and decisions that have significant public implications.

The challenge of shifting from this entrenched secrecy to a more transparent governance model appears to be formidable. Labor's failure to follow through on its promises to improve whistleblower protections and reform freedom of information laws suggests a disheartening disconnect between campaign rhetoric and governmental action. This pattern of inaction highlights a broader political reality: real change often requires a combination of pressure from a strong, informed electorate and the strategic influence of a diverse and robust legislative assembly, involving a significant crossbench presence or a minority government situation where no single party has absolute control.

This dynamic is further complicated by the plight of other whistleblowers such as Richard Boyle, whose experiences highlight the dire consequences of current legislative inadequacies. Boyle's potential 46-year prison sentence for exposing questionable practices within the Australian Taxation Office demonstrates the severe risks faced by those who dare to challenge institutional misconduct. The severe retaliatory measures they face not only threaten their personal freedom and wellbeing but also affect broader societal efforts to ensure accountability and ethical governance.

The electoral implications of these whistleblower cases are profound and multifaceted, and they have the potential to influence voter perceptions and behaviours significantly, particularly in constituencies where issues of transparency and government accountability resonate deeply. As seen in recent elections, voters are increasingly willing to reject traditional party loyalties in favour of candidates who credibly commit to reforming governance practices and adhering to those commitments once in office.

For the Labor Party—or any party in power—the ongoing neglect of whistleblower protections and freedom of information reforms poses not just a moral dilemma but a potential political hazard. The electorate's growing awareness and concern over these issues could result in significant electoral shifts, particularly if alternative independent candidates or parties can convincingly promise and subsequently deliver genuine reforms.

Ultimately, addressing the systemic issues highlighted by the McBride case requires not only legislative change but also a cultural shift within government institutions—a shift towards valuing transparency over secrecy and integrity over expediency. This may involve difficult decisions, including pardoning whistleblowers such as McBride or reforming punitive laws that disproportionately penalise those who expose wrongdoing.

The resolution of McBride's case on appeal—and a quick release from incarceration—and the broader reform of policies affecting whistleblowers will be a true test of the government's commitment to the principles of transparency and accountability. As the public's tolerance for secrecy wanes and demand for governmental integrity grows, political leaders must decide whether to perpetuate a culture of concealment or to embrace a new model of openness and ethical governance.

The Labor government must reconcile its actions with its articulated vision of a transparent, accountable governance structure where whistleblowers are seen not as liabilities, but as essential guardians of the public interest.

***

ISRAEL INCREASINGLY ISOLATED OVER GENOCIDE IN GAZA

25 May 2024

The International Criminal Court has issued arrest warrants for Israeli Prime Minister Benjamin Netanyahu, his defense minister, and the leadership of Hamas, on the grounds of war crimes and crimes against humanity. This move, while contentious, is a significant step in the ongoing conflict between Israel and Palestine. For decades, the Israeli–Palestinian conflict has been marked by violence predominantly perpetrated by the state of Israel, extreme political machinations, and international diplomatic interventions, with both sides committing actions that have drawn widespread condemnation. In this case, however, the ICC's decision is based on extensive documentation of alleged war crimes, particularly since the escalation of violence since October last year.

Israel has faced accusations of committing war crimes and genocide against Palestinians over many years, a claim that has gained traction especially since the intensification of hostilities. On the other hand, Hamas's actions, particularly those on 7 October 2023, have also been classified as crimes against humanity. The international response to these developments has been polarised—support for Israel, while still significant, appears to be waning, with many advocating for adherence to international law and due process as stipulated by the ICC.

Domestically, reactions have also been divided along political lines. Prime Minister Anthony Albanese has refrained from commenting on the legal proceedings, maintaining a stance of non-interference with the judicial process. Conversely, the Leader of the Opposition, Peter

Dutton, has vehemently criticised the ICC's actions, describing them as "an abomination" and threatening to withdraw Australia from the ICC's jurisdiction if the Liberal Party were to come into power after the next election, a reaction which is consistent with his historical stance of ignoring legal processes that conflict with his political agenda.

Internationally, the situation is equally complex. Albanese has the dubious distinction of being the first Australian political leader referred to the ICC for his support of Israel in their actions in Gaza, a position that contrasts sharply with the ideals he once held about ending the Israeli occupation of Palestine. Meanwhile, the Netanyahu government is increasingly seen as morally compromised, especially as the death toll among innocent Palestinians rises—over 36,000—and protests within Israel grow louder. The shift in global sentiment is further evidenced by countries such as Norway, Spain, Malta and Ireland recognising Palestine as a state, indicating a significant change in the international community's stance.

The potential repercussions of the ICC's actions are profound. There is a possibility that the court itself could face challenges to its authority, particularly from powerful nations such as the United States, which usually seeks to undermine its legitimacy when its decisions are not favourable to the political and military agenda of the U.S. As more Western countries without direct ties to the conflict begin to voice their support for Palestine, it becomes evident that a significant shift is underway. Whether this will lead to a peaceful and just resolution remains to be seen, but the changing dynamics suggest that the status quo is no longer tenable.

AUSTRALIA'S RESPONSE REFLECTS A PREDICTABLE STANCE

Closer to home, the responses in Australia have been predictable and politically unsophisticated. The Australian government has largely disengaged diplomatically from the Israeli war on Gaza and seems content not to position itself as a leader with any gravitas or independence in this conflict. Dutton has criticised Albanese for what he perceives as equivocation regarding the ICC's announcement, while most politicians have lined up to condemn the ICC. Prominent Liberal figures such as Senators Simon Birmingham,

James Paterson and Jane Hume have all taken pot shots at both the Labor government and the ICC decision, while government MPs have all been in unison that there is no "moral equivalence" between Hamas and Israel, voicing their strong support for the state of Israel, reflecting a broader trend of political appeasement towards the Israel lobby in Australia.

It is undeniable that Hamas and the Israeli government are not equivalent entities; they have distinct motivations and methods. However, both have committed war crimes and crimes against humanity. Hamas's actions on 7 October last year and Israel's sustained violence—36,000 deaths in Gaza, the continual operation of an apartheid state since 1948 and oppression of Palestinians in both Gaza and the West Bank—are egregious and have been widely documented. Statements from Israeli Defense Force leaders, the Israeli government, and Prime Minister Benjamin Netanyahu himself have confirmed these actions.

Palestinian human rights lawyer Diana Butu, commenting on the ICC announcement, has emphasised that while it is a significant step, it has taken "far too long to reach this point". The occupation of Palestine has persisted for almost 80 years, and starting the timeline on 7 October 2023 rather than when Palestine signed on to the ICC in 2015 reflects a lack of context and depth to this case. Nonetheless, she sees this as an essential first step towards holding Israeli leaders accountable for their actions. Butu hopes that this will lead to more substantial actions, including indictments, to bring an end to what she describes as Israel's genocide.

The prolonged suffering in Gaza must end, regardless of who has committed the crimes. In the case of the alleged war crimes, punishment and sanctions are necessary for those responsible but the priority at this stage must be to halt the extensive human suffering. The global community is growing increasingly intolerant of the ongoing violence, and Netanyahu must face accountability for his actions. His continued aggressive policies are efforts to avoid internal prosecution in Israel for historical corruption, but this cannot justify the immense loss of life in Gaza. The world demands an end to the violence and a move towards justice and peace.

IRELAND LEADS EUROPEAN RECOGNITION OF PALESTINE

> "On January 21, 1919, Ireland sought international recognition of its right to be an independent state, emphasising its distinct national identity, historical struggle, and quest for self-determination and justice. Today, Ireland uses the same language to support the recognition of Palestine as a state, grounded in the belief that freedom and justice are fundamental principles of international law and that permanent peace can only be secured through the free will of a free people."
>
> Prime Minister of Ireland, Simon Harris, announcing that Ireland will recognise the state of Palestine.

In his statement, Simon Harris highlighted the powerful political and symbolic value of recognition, asserting that Palestine holds the full rights of a state, including self-determination, self-governance, territorial integrity, and security. This recognition also places obligations on Palestine under international law and supports those in Palestine advocating for a future of peace and democracy.

The Irish government announced its intention to recognise Palestine as a state, a move to be followed by Spain, Slovenia, Norway, and Malta, with speculation that France and Belgium might soon join. This shift in recognition from influential European nations signals a major impetus for change—historically, Palestine's recognition was often limited to smaller, less influential countries, but now, significant European states are taking a stand, reflecting a growing global consensus against Israel's immoral and illegal actions in Gaza and the West Bank.

This movement is not confined to diplomatic recognition alone—the International Criminal Court has issued arrest warrants for Israeli leaders on war crime charges; the International Court of Justice has brought a case of genocide against Israel; a recent United Nations vote increased the rights of the state of Palestine, albeit slightly; FIFA is considering banning Israel from the Football World Cup. Protests and awareness of the plight of Palestine around the world is increasing, with a global outcry demanding an end to the occupation of Palestine.

Israel is becoming increasingly isolated due to its actions in Gaza and the West Bank—the United States remains a steadfast ally, as does Britain, and the upcoming general election in the U.K. is likely to delay any significant change in their stance. However, the international community's patience with Israel's ideological, political, and military overreach is wearing thin, and it can no longer look away.

Despite this international momentum, Australia's response to these developments has been weak and embarrassing. By closely aligning itself with the United States' unwavering support for Israel, Australia has chosen a path of least political resistance domestically, despite knowing about the human rights abuses, war crimes, and genocide. The Liberal Party's overwhelming support for Israel and Zionism contrasts sharply with the more cautious stance of the Labor government. However, the government's response to the events in Gaza and Israel has been disappointing, reflecting a lack of courage and clarity compared to the governments of Ireland, Spain, Norway, Slovenia, and Malta, which have taken decisive and principled stands.

The Australian government should look to these European nations for direction. Despite some commentary from parliamentarians such as Senator Fatima Payman, Tony Burke, Ed Husic and several others, the overall support for Palestine has been insufficient. Many federal cabinet members, including the Prime Minister, had previously supported the rights of Palestinians, and while foreign affairs are complex and subject to change, being on the right side of history is a goal worth striving for.

As support for Palestine gains momentum in Western Europe, it signifies a significant shift in global politics. Australia should aim to facilitate this change rather than cling to the status quo, and the recognition of Palestine and the end of the genocide in Gaza are crucial steps toward a more just and peaceful world. The international community's increasing intolerance of Israel's actions should serve as a wake-up call for Australian political leaders to show greater courage and align themselves with the global movement for justice and peace.

***

JULIAN ASSANGE: THE GOVERNMENT'S INADEQUATE AND WEAK DIPLOMACY

26 May 2024

Julian Assange's ongoing incarceration in Belmarsh prison and the inadequate efforts by the Australian government to secure his release highlight a deeply troubling and concerning issue. Stella Assange's recent impassioned plea that the case has taken "an enormous toll on Julian, and now is a right moment for the Biden administration to drop the case", highlights the gravity of the situation, calling for an immediate end to what she describes as a shameful attack on journalism, the press, and the public. For over five years, Assange has been under immense pressure, confined within the high-security walls of Belmarsh prison, while his case continues to languish in legal limbo, with no indication for when it will ever be resolved. The call for the Biden administration to abandon the case resonates with a sense of urgency and justice, as the prolonged ordeal is taking a significant toll on Assange's mental and physical wellbeing.

The recent decision by the London High Court granting Assange the right to appeal his extradition to the United States represents a minor yet crucial legal victory, and this right to appeal hinges on challenging the assurances provided by the United States regarding the protection of freedom of speech, the avoidance of prejudice due to nationality, and the removal of the death penalty as an outcome of any legal proceedings. These assurances are fraught with complexities, particularly given the contentious nature of the death penalty in the U.S. legal system, which permits its federal application under certain circumstances, including for non-citizens. The intricacies of federal law and the broader implications of Assange's case raise significant concerns about the fairness and impartiality of the legal proceedings he faces.

The Australian government's role in this protracted saga remains ambiguous and disheartening. A look at the recent treatment of David McBride—whose trial the Attorney-General Mark Dreyfus could have halted but chose not to—casts doubt on the Australian government's commitment to protecting its citizens from international or domestic legal overreach, and the limited and seemingly ineffective efforts to secure Assange's release suggests a lack of political will or diplomatic prowess. The small legal step of being able to appeal extradition, while better than no recourse at all, pales in comparison to the broader need for the United States to entirely drop the charges against Assange. This outcome would represent a significant step toward justice and the protection of journalistic freedom.

The U.S. Supreme Court's interpretation of the Constitution, particularly concerning freedom of speech, further complicates Assange's predicament. The principle of freedom of speech is foundational to the American legal system, intended to safeguard the right to criticise the government without fear of undue repercussions. Assange's actions, primarily facilitating the publication of documents in the public interest that were critical of the U.S. government actions in Iraq, fall within the purview of this fundamental right. The charges against him, and the resulting extradition battle, reflect a troubling level of insecurity within the U.S. system and the prolonged pursuit of Assange contradicts the ethos of a liberal republic, which should ideally uphold and protect freedom of speech rather than stifling it.

The narrative surrounding Assange has shifted over the years, with initial criticisms of his personal conduct giving way to a broader recognition of his role as a symbol of the fight for free speech. The vilification he faced early on has been overshadowed by the more significant implications of his prosecution. In many ways, Assange has become a martyr for a cause that strikes at the heart of democratic principles and the United States' continued efforts to extradite and prosecute him only serve to reinforce this perception, undermining the very values the country purports to defend. The

Australian government's failure to assertively intervene exacerbates this injustice, leaving Assange's fate precariously balanced on the edge of an international political and legal quagmire.

HAS THE AUSTRALIAN GOVERNMENT DONE ENOUGH TO RELEASE ASSANGE?

The incarceration of Assange in Belmarsh prison, despite the lack of concrete charges against him, casts a long shadow over the Australian government's purported efforts to secure his release. Official statements from both Coalition and Labor governments over the years assert that they have done all they can, yet the reality of Assange's continued detention suggests otherwise. Assange has been held in London for over five years, largely due to his involvement with WikiLeaks and the release of a 2010 video depicting a U.S. airstrike on civilians in Baghdad. Chelsea Manning, the American whistleblower who initially leaked the footage, was imprisoned for seven years before receiving a pardon from President Barack Obama in 2017. The discrepancy in treatment, where the provider of the original U.S. secrets has been free for seven years, while the publisher of the secrets remains in jail and untried, raises questions about the actual crimes attributed to Assange, which remain allegations at this stage, rather than proven charges.

The legal and political landscape surrounding Assange's case is rife with inconsistencies and missed opportunities. Under U.S. federal prosecution principles, and with directives from the President, the U.S. Attorney-General Merrick Garland has the power to drop the charges. Stella Assange's appeal highlights this potential path to resolution, yet no such action has been taken. This inertia points to a glaring lack of pressure from the Australian government, which ostensibly should have significant leverage over its ally. The ANZUS Treaty, the Quad relationship, Pine Gap, and the controversial AUKUS agreement all signify strong ties between Australia and the United States. Yet, despite these strategic and diplomatic connections, Australia's government appears reluctant to engage in the necessary tough negotiations with the U.S. to secure Assange's release.

This reluctance is further magnified by the Australian government's treatment of other whistleblowers, notably David McBride, whose case was marked by double speak and a lack of decisive action from Australian authorities, mirroring the broader pattern of a lack of support for whistleblowers. While Australia has successfully negotiated the release of its citizens from Chinese jails, for example, it seems impotent in the face of securing Assange's freedom from Belmarsh prison and the potential legal peril he faces in the U.S. This disparity is particularly stark given that the countries involved—Britain and the United States—are among Australia's closest allies.

The hope that the U.S. court system might eventually see reason and deliver justice to Assange is tempered by a prevailing skepticism about its current reliability and impartiality. The broader implications of this case extend beyond Assange himself, striking at the core principles of freedom of speech and the protection of journalistic endeavours and it serves as a sobering reminder of the fragile state of these freedoms in an era increasingly dominated by security concerns and governmental overreach.

The Australian government's failure to secure the release of Julian Assange from Belmarsh prison is a troubling testament to its inadequate diplomatic efforts and the broader systemic issues at play. Assange's prolonged detention, couples with what appears to be concocted charges of espionage, reflects poorly on the efficacy and commitment of Australian authorities to protect their citizens and uphold the principles of justice and free speech. The need for decisive action and genuine political will is more pressing than ever, not just for Assange's sake, but for the integrity of democratic values worldwide.

***

JUNE

THE MEDIA'S BROKEN MIRROR EXPOSES AUSTRALIA'S RACIAL DIVIDES

1 June 2024

In a recent address at the Sydney Writers Festival, senior ABC journalist Laura Tingle made a comment that Australia is a "racist country," setting off a chain of reactions that exposed deep divisions within the nation's media and political landscapes. Tingle's comments, made during a discussion on immigration, suggested that the political discourse led by certain leaders such as leader of the opposition Peter Dutton was not only divisive but actively harmful, giving "license to be abused" to those who "look different." Her assertion highlights a persistent challenge in Australian society—how it deals with issues of race and the legacy of its policies.

The backlash against Tingle—and the ABC—was swift and severe, particularly from conservative corners and News Corporation. Figures such as Sophie Ellsworth from Sky News quickly positioned Tingle's remarks as evidence of a supposed broader problem within the ABC—impartiality—and damage to its credibility, and then went on to frame the situation as a "nightmare" for ABC chair Kim Williams, amid further calls to defund the ABC and privatise it for commercial interests.

Tingle's comments rekindled discussions on Australia's historical and contemporary issues with racism, and it's very clear that Australia does have a significantly racist and unjust history—the White Australia Policy, Indigenous exclusion under the doctrine of *terra nullius*, and more contemporary examples of social exclusion and systemic institutionalised bias are prime examples of this. Once again, this situation highlights an Australia at odds with itself—caught between its purported ideals of egalitarianism and the stark realities of its historical and ongoing racial tensions.

This discourse is not only about whether Australia is or isn't racist—it's about recognising the multifaceted nature of racism. It's not just the overt discrimination, but also the subtle, systemic kinds that shape public policy and everyday interactions. Tingle's assertion, and the polarised responses to it, reveal a society still dealing with its past, its present, and its future: trying to reconcile a contentious history with aspirations for a more inclusive nation. This, however, is further complicated by political imperatives that often prioritise immediate, palpable gains over deep, structural reforms.

In this heated debate, the role of the media becomes crucially significant. As gatekeepers of information and framers of discourse, journalists and their platforms shape public perception and understanding. The reaction to Tingle's comments highlights that balance they must maintain between delivering hard truths and keeping the maniacal conservative media at bay, whose behaviour in being able to find and magnify material they don't like—even if it at a relatively obscure public event—and then go on to call for punishment and retribution, is akin to a Soviet-era spy agency.

The fallout from Tingle's comments—purely concocted by News Corporation—is a microcosm of a larger national debate on race, identity, and the role of the media in shaping political discourse. It encapsulates the tensions between freedom of expression and the responsibilities of public broadcasters, between historical acknowledgment and contemporary reality, and between the diverse elements of an increasingly pluralistic society.

THE ABC'S STRUGGLE WITH IDEOLOGICAL PRESSURES

The tension between the ABC and News Corporation highlights a broader ideological battleground within Australian media and politics. The ABC, historically perceived as a bastion of independent journalism—although it could be argued that with the continuous interference from the Liberal Party during their time in government, it has been less than independent in recent years—now finds itself increasingly scrutinised and attacked by News Corporation, a media conglomerate often aligned with conservative interests, including those of the Liberal Party. This scrutiny manifests not just in critiques of content but in calls for drastic actions such as defunding or sacking journalists who deviate from certain conservative social and political lines approved by News Corporation, as seen in the case of Laura Tingle.

This scenario typifies how News Corporation leverages its media influence to shape public discourse and, by extension, political agendas. It portrays a media landscape where News Corporation rarely reports news in a factual manner but actively participates in the political process, aggressively setting the terms of debate and determining what is permissible discourse.

The reaction from the ABC's management to the controversy surrounding Tingle is telling. Rather than robustly defending the principles of free speech and the diversity of opinions that a national broadcaster should embody, the response from the ABC's director of news, Justin Stevens, was tepid and bordering on apologetic. This capitulation points to a deeper issue within the ABC: a growing concern about offending conservative powers and, therefore, reporting in a manner that avoids offending these conservative powers. Such conservatism not only contradicts the ABC's charter, which mandates it to provide informative, educational, and entertaining content that reflects Australia's cultural diversity, but it also hinders the broadcaster's ability to engage in and foster meaningful national debates.

In the context of such controversies, it becomes evident that there is an uneven playing field in terms of what is considered acceptable commentary. While right-leaning perspectives, even controversial ones, often receive a platform on ABC programs such as *Insiders* or *Q&A*, progressive views like Tingle's are met with fierce opposition and demands for censorship. This dichotomy undermines the ABC's mandate to reflect a plurality of views and suggests a troubling drift towards a more conservative, restrictive media environment, influenced heavily by external pressures from powerful media players like News Corporation.

The stark contrast in how different ideological perspectives are treated points to a larger cultural and political division within Australia. If the ABC yields to pressures to conform to a narrower view of acceptable discourse, it risks losing its integrity as a public broadcaster committed to impartiality and diversity, an integrity which has perhaps already been lost. Such an outcome would not only diminish the ABC's role in Australian society but also impoverish the public discourse necessary for a vibrant democracy.

Ultimately, the treatment of Tingle and the broader implications for ABC illustrates the significant problems that exist for Australian media and journalism. The challenge lies in balancing a commitment to impartial reporting and a diverse range of opinions against the backdrop of intense media scrutiny and political polarisation. How the ABC navigates this will be crucial for its future role in shaping an informed, engaged, and inclusive Australian public.

ABC'S LACK OF DEFENCE OF ITS OWN JOURNALISTS THREATENS PRESS FREEDOM

The recurring issue of the ABC not adequately defending its journalists against external attacks, particularly from entities such as News Corporation, raises profound questions about the broadcaster's role and responsibilities in Australia's media landscape. The cases of Stan Grant, Yassmin Abdel-Magied, Emma Alberici, Nick Ross and now Laura Tingle illustrate a worrying pattern where ABC journalists facing criticism or controversy from conservative quarters—often sparked by their candid assessments of sensitive topics—are left to fend for themselves. This perceived lack of support not only affects the individual journalists but also sends a chilling message to others within the organisation about the limits of editorial freedom and the potential consequences of inciting the ire of powerful external critics.

This situation is further exacerbated by the nature of the criticisms often levied at ABC journalists by conservative media outlets. The attacks are not just professional critiques but are frequently *ad hominem*, sometimes straying into the personal, and the departure of Stan Grant and the overseas relocation of Yassmin Abdel-Magied after sustained campaigns against them are cases in point. Both were prominent figures who contributed significantly to public discourse in Australia, yet faced overwhelming pressure largely as a result of their visibility and the uncomfortable truths they were willing to articulate.

Laura Tingle stands out in this narrative not just for her role as a senior journalist and a member of the ABC board but also for her forthrightness in discussing Australian politics and societal issues. Her statement of calling Australia a "racist country"—reflect a willingness to confront Australia's historical and contemporary challenges head-on. Yet, the pattern of ABC responses, or lack thereof, to the subsequent fallout suggests a continuity of the broadcaster's feckless approach, prioritising organisational safety and conservative interests, over journalistic integrity.

The fundamental issue here extends beyond individual controversies to encompass the broader role of the ABC as a national broadcaster funded by the public. When the ABC fails to protect its journalists from orchestrated external attacks, it risks undermining its own credibility and authority as an independent voice in Australian media. This perceived vulnerability is especially concerning in an era where public trust in media is both more crucial and more fragile than ever.

While the focus has been on the weak and tepid response from ABC management, including the director of news and the managing director, criticism must also be directed towards the Minister for Communications, Michelle Rowland, and Prime Minister Anthony Albanese, for their lack of support. As a public broadcaster, the ultimate responsibility rests with government, in this case, Rowland and Albanese. However, they have allowed the continuous attacks from News Corporation to fester without offering any support for the ABC. Why are they so willing to allow the reputation of ABC to be trashed so comprehensively?

The manner in which these controversies are handled also reflects broader societal divisions over what constitutes acceptable discourse. The term "woke," as used pejoratively by critics of the ABC and its journalists, exemplifies how certain perspectives are dismissed as overly progressive or politically correct, marginalising voices that challenge the status quo. This delegitimisation of dissenting voices undercuts the very purpose of a public broadcaster in a democratic society, which is to foster a well-rounded public dialogue that includes all perspectives, even those that may be uncomfortable or unpopular.

For the ABC to fulfill its mandate and maintain its integrity as a public broadcaster, it must not only provide a platform for diverse voices but also vigorously defend those voices when they are challenged. This involves a more robust and principled stance in support of its journalists, who should feel assured that their employer backs them when they are targeted for fulfilling their role. Strengthening this support is essential not only for the personal wellbeing of its journalists but also for safeguarding the broader democratic values of freedom of expression and informed public debate in Australia.

***

A SECOND TERM FOR LABOR? A BALANCE BETWEEN GOVERNING AND POLITICS

2 June 2024

The Labor government's strategy for securing a second term in office is slowly unfolding amidst a complicated political and economic landscape. As the current parliamentary term continues, Prime Minister Anthony Albanese's announcement to the Labor Caucus about "crafting" their next-term offer has sparked discussions on timing and priorities, suggesting a pre-emptive move towards election readiness. While no election is imminent—more than likely to be held after the Queensland election in October this year and further complicated by seat redistributions yet to be announced by the Australian Electoral Commission—the announcement suggests that Labor is preparing its electoral strategy and policy outlines for its second term, if it manages to get there.

Economic management remains a critical aspect of the government's agenda, with recent inflation figures rising to 3.6 per cent, slightly above the target band of 2–3 per cent. This economic indicator not only reflects the immediate financial health of the nation but also influences public perception of the government's competency. Inflation, coupled with ongoing issues such as housing affordability, domestic violence, and energy pricing, forms a significant part of the government's current challenges that will undoubtedly spill over into the next term.

These persistent societal and economic challenges highlight the balance that the government must maintain between managing immediate political issues and establishing a long-term vision and the government's effectiveness in addressing these issues will play a crucial role in its re-election campaign. However, the focus on early campaign strategising—although the current term could potentially extend to September 2025, it is highly unlikely—also highlights the inherent difficulties of three-year electoral terms. Such terms often see substantial policy implementation constrained by the need for continuous electoral campaigning and in contemporary politics, as soon as one election concludes, governments begin their campaigns to win the next, creating a never-ending cycle.

The political dynamics within Australia also suggests a landscape where Labor must navigate not just opposition from traditional parties such as the Liberal Party but also manage the rising influence of smaller parties and independents. The spectre of a minority government after the next election looms, with potential scenarios involving negotiations with disparate groups, from Green-leaning independents to hard-right figures such as Bob Katter and One Nation, complicating future legislative processes. This environment requires Labor to not only solidify its base but also strategically appeal to a broader electorate to prevent erosion of its majority. As this term progresses, the clarity of Labor's agenda and its execution will be critical in shaping the electoral outcomes and defining the government's legacy.

LABOR'S GOVERNANCE CHALLENGES AMIDST DISCONTENT IN THE RANKS

The Labor government's approach to governance and implementation of policy has led to significant disquiet within its own ranks, particularly among the rank-and-file members who expected a more distinct departure from previous conservative administrations between 2013–22, and the government's handling of various crises and cautious approach to policy initiatives has frustrated some supporters who were hoping for more transformative policies.

The government's response to immigration issues, including deportation policies and managing net overseas migration, has become a contentious point, with leader of the opposition Peter Dutton and the Liberal Party intensifying their focus on these issues as a political strategy. This situation, among many others, exemplifies the ongoing challenges faced by Labor in balancing pragmatic governance, vociferous negativity from the opposition, and the ideological expectations of its base.

To alleviate some discontent within Labor ranks, supporters have suggested that the government has spent most of its first term laying the groundwork for a prolonged period in government and they argue that it is in its second term that a more progressive and "Labor-like" agenda will be implemented. However, there is no historical evidence to suggest that a second Albanese term will be more adventurous than the first. For instance, was the Whitlam government's second term more adventurous than its first term from 1972–74? Was the Hawke government's second term from 1984–87 more "Labor-like" than its first? Assessing the second term of the Labor government from 2010–13 is difficult, as it was under a different Prime Minister, Julia Gillard.

Will a second term for Albanese result in a shift in stance on Middle East politics, particularly regarding the genocide in Gaza? To date, Albanese has staunchly supported Israel, often ignoring or criticising pro-Palestine advocates in Australia. His response to every massacre in Gaza typically involves a media release carefully crafted not to offend the interests of local Israeli lobby groups. How might this approach change in the future? Typically, a government's second term is less ideologically ambitious than its first and in any case, Albanese has yet to indicate a clear trajectory that deviates markedly from its first-term agenda, leading to skepticism about whether any dramatic changes can be expected if re-elected.

Critics from within the party also argue that the government has strayed from core Labor values, particularly in areas such as taxation, foreign affairs, and housing. The government's support for the Stage 3 tax cuts—albeit a modified version—and the AUKUS security pact, for instance, has positioned it closer to centrist or even right-leaning policies, alienating traditional supporters on the left. This perception is compounded by a lack of aggressive action on housing, a cornerstone issue for Labor, traditionally tackled with robust policies by predecessors such as Curtin, Chifley, Hawke, and Keating. Certainly, the Labor government has moved on some of these issues but have they done enough?

The disappointment extends to broader economic and cultural policies, where the government is seen as continuing neoliberal practices that blur the ideological lines between Labor and the Liberal Party which, in turn, shifts national political debates towards "culture war" issues, sidelining the more substantive reforms that are required within Australia. Influential figures within the party such as Jim Chalmers and Katy Gallagher need to assert more influence and steer the government back towards a governance style that aligns more closely with traditional Labor principles.

As the government navigates these internal and external pressures, the challenge remains on how to reconcile the pragmatic demands of governance with the ideological aspirations of its members, and setting a course that will influence its electoral prospects in the upcoming term.

THE QUEENSLAND ELECTION IS A CRUCIAL TEST FOR LABOR'S DIRECTION

As the Labor government contemplates its "offerings" for a second term, one influence appears to be the impending Queensland state election on 26 October this year, and the outcome of this election could potentially serve as a barometer for federal Labor's policy directions, particularly in terms of public support for certain types of government interventions and welfare enhancements.

The strategy of Queensland Premier Steven Miles, including policy announcements such as the "50-cent fares" for public transport across the state—although branded as an election gimmick—highlights a broader shift developing within state Labor at least, where they are moving away from a user-pays approach, to more universal service delivery models in public services like transport, health, and education. And why wouldn't they? These are the types of policies that the electorate expects to see from Labor governments so it makes sense for the Miles government in Queensland to continue to announce these types of policies. Such measures, which result in community-wide benefits, may inform federal Labor's policy adjustments or introductions, particularly if they resonate well with voters in Queensland.

However, the broader context of fiscal management and budget concerns still remains a primary focus for the federal government. Despite a performance that many economists suggest has been successful, the general lack of acknowledgment from the media and public could signify a challenging environment for promoting and implementing bolder, distinctly Labor policies. The Labor Party's apparent hesitance to fully embrace its traditional policy initiatives—often seen as too bold or risky in the current political climate—is also causing frustrations within its ranks.

While the federal government considers aspects like health and education, the Queensland election could serve as a litmus test for the viability of these policies at the federal level. For instance, reductions in healthcare costs, childcare, early education, schooling and student debts could follow the model of Queensland's transport fare reduction, aiming to reduce the cost of living and increase disposable income for ordinary Australians. The era of cost-based recovery accounting for governments should have ended some time ago—the massive government support provided during the first two years of the COVID pandemic demonstrates that alternative economic models involving government intervention are achievable—and the Labor government has the potential to extend much further along this path.

Could the government consider reducing the GST from 10 per cent to 7.5 per cent to alleviate cost pressures, even if it is only as a temporary measure? Such a move, while likely to be controversial and challenging to implement given its broad economic implications, would signal a strong commitment to easing financial strains on Australians—a key concern that resonates across the electorate.

Federal Labor will be watching Queensland politics closely over the next five months and is likely to gauge the public reaction to state-level policies that could end up influencing its own platform. The electoral outcome in Queensland will not only impact their tactical decisions but could also offer a blueprint for Labor's policy offerings on a national scale, aiming for broader appeal while staying true to core Labor values of universal service provision and social welfare.

**

FRYDENBERG'S FAILED COMEBACK REVEALS BIG PROBLEMS IN THE LIBERAL PARTY

8 June 2024

The re-emergence of the former Treasurer Josh Frydenberg as a potential Liberal Party candidate in Australian federal politics has resulted in a broad spectrum of reactions, from fervent enthusiasm to outright rejection and dismay, reflecting deep divisions within both the media landscape and the electorate. The narrative of Frydenberg's political comeback centres not just around the man himself, but around the broader dynamics of media influence and leadership vacuums within the Liberal Party.

Frydenberg's decision to step away from politics completely following his 2022 defeat to independent candidate Monique Ryan was initially viewed as a definitive closure to his parliamentary career, when he stated a desire to focus on "spending more time with family" and work within the private business sector—which, of course, many politicians cite when exiting the stressful arena of politics. However, the media, particularly outlets such Sky News, never let this narrative settle, instead, there has been a persistent media-led campaign over the past six months, suggesting not just a return but a necessary resurgence for Frydenberg to fill perceived leadership gaps within his party and, by extension, the nation.

The nation needs Frydenberg? *Really?* The campaign led by News Corporation was so exaggerated that it seemed as if a new Robert Menzies had been discovered; as though the sun itself was following the learned guru toward a rapidly approaching horizon, while the seas parted and the heavens opened, providing a pathway for the balding messiah to lead the Liberal Party back to the promised land of electoral nirvana.

Yet, Frydenberg is nothing like Menzies. Robert Menzies was not only a major figure in the creation of the Liberal Party in 1944 but also a leading figure in Australian history and centre-right conservative politics. While there is contention about Menzies's effectiveness as Prime Minister, with some belief that his political skills lay more in creating and magnifying divisive problems for the Labor Party during the 1950s and 1960s rather than focusing on national development in the post-war era, he is still regarded as one of Australia's leading political figures, especially in terms of longevity.

These media portrayals often gloss over substantial differences in political stature and context between Menzies and Frydenberg, sometimes bordering on a revisionist enthusiasm that overlooks the nuanced realities of contemporary political challenges. While Menzies was a towering figure within Australian politics, Frydenberg registers as a smaller footnote in history, ranking among the poorer performing Treasurers. His preference for political gamesmanship over national unity is also evident, as shown by his frequent partisan and negative commentary against the Victorian government during the early stages of the COVID-19 pandemic.

The push for Frydenberg's return also highlights the broader strategic machinations within conservative media circles. Outlets like Sky News have not only been vocal but almost prescriptive in their commentary, often promoting a dissatisfaction with the current Labor government and a nostalgic longing for the type of governance Frydenberg represents which, of course, is more of the same type of neoliberalist ideology that News Corporation supports and benefits from. This has been particularly evident in interviews and discussions where Frydenberg's potential candidacy is discussed less in terms of 'if' and more as a matter of 'when', despite his repeated dismissals of such speculation.

The interactions between Frydenberg and the media, particularly with figures like Sharri Markson of Sky News, reveal a tension between personal agency and media-driven narratives. These dynamics raise important questions about the role of media in shaping political careers and, conversely, the extent to which politicians can and do manipulate media narratives to their advantage. It also paints a broader picture of the current state of the Liberal Party—riddled with leadership uncertainties and strategic anxieties—it looks towards familiar faces to reinvigorate its ranks amidst evolving political landscapes and voter demographics. However, if Frydenberg is supposedly the messiah for the Liberal Party, why was he so comprehensively defeated by Ryan at the 2022 federal election? Is Australia *really* needs the leadership of Frydenberg, why did he not offer himself for preselection for the seat of Kooyong when candidates were called for nomination several months ago?

The situation also encapsulates a fundamental tension within modern democratic systems: the oscillation between leadership as a reflection of public will versus leadership as a construct of media influence and internal party machinations. Frydenberg's saga, whether he returns to the political fray at some point in the future or remains on the sidelines, serves as a contemporary case study in the complex interplay of media dynamics, personal decision-making, and political strategy within the fraught arena of Australian politics.

AN UNFULFILLED POLITICAL RETURN AND ITS IMPLICATIONS

Analysing the implications of Frydenberg's potential but ultimately failed return to Australian federal politics requires an understanding of his tenure and the broader political context. Frydenberg's political career, particularly his time as Treasurer, draws mixed reviews that influence perceptions of his suitability for leadership. His political skills in the *game* of politics, while significant—he was in politics for 12 years and achieved the second-most important position in politics—often attracted scrutiny and criticism, and an concerted partisan ability to get people offside, as exemplified by his contentious interactions when he was energy minister within the Turnbull government between 2015–2017.

The exchange between Frydenberg and former South Australian Premier Jay Weatherill in 2017 highlighted one of the most infamous moments in Frydenberg's career. Frydenberg initially claimed credit for a renewable energy program initiated by the South Australian government. Yet, several months later, during an extreme weather event that caused severe blackouts in the state, he blamed the same renewable program for the energy failures and criticised the South Australian government for its alleged irresponsibility. This incident was emblematic of Frydenberg's tenure—marked by political strife and contentious policy implementation, which arguably clouded his effectiveness and leadership potential, as well as constantly moving blame—or creating blame—onto Labor governments in South Australia, Western Australia, Queensland and Victoria. It's a type of political leadership that Australia definitely does not need.

Frydenberg's tenure as Treasurer of Australia also faced criticism for an inadequate preparation for economic downturns, especially around the time of the COVID pandemic. Despite the government's assurances that the economy was set to be "back in black," indicating a return to surplus, the reality was quite different. In early 2020, Australia was on the brink of a recession, and had already experienced a per-capita recession during 2019, before the recession was confirmed in September 2020. Although it was difficult to foresee the full economic effects of COVID, this assessment was supported by many leading economists at the time, suggesting that the economic strategies in place were not sufficient to avert the downturns.

In addition, Frydenberg's desire for a political comeback, often hinted at but never fully embraced, reflects a common pattern among politicians who find the allure of public office hard to resist. However, the lack of enthusiasm for his return from significant portions of the electorate, coupled with mixed assessments of his previous tenure, poses substantial barriers. These barriers are not just personal but are emblematic of the broader challenges facing the Liberal Party, struggling to redefine its leadership and direction in a rapidly changing political landscape.

The discussion around Frydenberg's return to politics—and subsequent failure—is not just about him but reflects broader issues of leadership, effectiveness, and public accountability in Australian politics. The Liberal Party's leadership void and the electorate's reaction to Frydenberg's political behaviours highlights a critical period of introspection and potential transformation within the party.

As the party struggles to deal with these challenges, the lessons from Frydenberg's career and the public's response to his failed comeback might inform its strategies and choices ahead, defining not just its future leaders but its path forward in an evolving political arena.

LIBERAL PARTY FACES MANY INTERNAL CHALLENGES

The broader issues within the Liberal Party extend beyond the potential return of Frydenberg and reveals systemic challenges and ideological shifts that the party faces. The dynamics within the Victoria branch, marked by political infighting and the influence of conservative religious groups—Mormons and Pentecostals—exemplify the internal complexities that threaten the party's unity. This backdrop raises substantial questions about the party's direction and its ability to address the concerns of a diverse electorate.

The selection of Amelia Hamer in the seat of Kooyong represents a strategic response by the Liberal Party to adapt to the evolving political landscape, particularly in response to the defeat of Frydenberg by independent candidate Monique Ryan at the federal election in 2022. Hamer—a younger and moderate candidate—signifies a shift towards moderation, reflecting a broader strategy to recalibrate the party's appeal. The emphasis on selecting a moderate candidate, akin to the successful teal independents, suggests at least an acknowledgment of the electorate's shifting priorities and the necessity for the Liberal Party to evolve beyond hard-line conservatism.

However, the challenges of reinventing the party are steep. The presence of deep-seated factions and the influence of external ideological forces complicate efforts to present a unified front. The task is not only about finding suitable candidates but also about fundamentally reassessing the party's values and strategies to resonate with contemporary Australian society.

In this context, the fixation on figures such as Frydenberg and the constant speculation about their political futures can distract from more pressing organisational reforms. While individuals like Frydenberg can play significant roles, the focus on individual comebacks should not overshadow the need for systemic and ideological renewal within the party. The situation in Victoria, with its particular political complexities, serves as a microcosm of the national challenges facing the Liberal Party and the engagement with local issues and responsiveness to the electorate's changing demands are crucial for the party's revival.

The Liberal Party of Australia faces a critical challenge in regaining its relevance and appeal among the broader electorate. To do this effectively, the party needs to engage authentically with both internal and external challenges. This includes selecting candidates who resonate with a wider range of voters, as well as redefining its ideological boundaries to better reflect the values and expectations of contemporary Australians.

While current polling, such as the Newspoll, shows the party holding a competitive position with 50 percent in the two-party preferred vote, this surface-level metric doesn't fully capture the underlying issues within the party and, besides, an election is not on the immediate horizon and the electorate is not yet fully engaged with the issues that will determine the next election. Since 1996, the Liberal Party has also focused on creating division on issues such as climate change and culture wars, and this focus might have overshadowed more pressing concerns for many Australians, potentially alienating voters who are more interested in pragmatic solutions to immediate economic, social, and environmental challenges.

Given the increasingly competitive and diverse political landscape, the Liberal Party's ability to adapt and address the deeper structural issues it faces, while refocusing on the real, everyday concerns of Australians, will likely determine its future success.

However, the question remains whether the party is currently equipped to undertake such significant changes. The evidence, as it stands, suggests challenges in this area. The party's emphasis on divisive issues over the past few decades and its struggle to resonate broadly with modern Australian values will hinder its ability to transform effectively, and it remains to be seen whether can align its philosophies and practices with the needs and expectations of contemporary Australia.

***

NACC IGNORES ROBODEBT CORRUPTION: IS ACCOUNTABILITY AT RISK?

15 June 2024

In a highly contentious decision, the National Anti-Corruption Commission has decided that it will not pursue corruption investigations into six public officials implicated in the scandalous Robodebt scheme between 2016 and 2020. This decision marks the NACC's first significant public announcement since its inception, and it has been met with widespread criticism and disappointment. The NACC's rationale for this decision hinges on its desire to avoid duplicating the efforts of the Australian Public Service Commission and the findings of the Robodebt Royal Commission, however, this reasoning has not quelled public outcry nor addressed the expectations of rigorous accountability that were central to the establishment of the NACC.

The Robodebt scheme, implemented by the former Coalition government, has been one of Australia's most damaging social policy failures in recent memory, if not ever. Its design, which involved the automated tallying of welfare debts that erroneously and aggressively targeted vulnerable Australians, has had disastrous consequences. Lives and livelihoods were disastrously impacted, leading to immense financial and emotional stress among affected individuals. The subsequent Robodebt Royal Commission was scathing in its critique, not only of the scheme's operational failures but also of the government's oversight, describing the initiative as not just flawed but "terrible and awful and evil," designed to exploit the most vulnerable layers of society.

Against this backdrop, the "sealed" section of the Robodebt Royal Commission's report named 16 individuals suspected of corrupt practices linked to the scheme's administration, and six of these were directly referred to the NACC by Catherine Holmes, the head of the Royal Commission, marking a critical test of the NACC's resolve and effectiveness—or so we were told at the time. The public and political expectation was that the NACC would act as a robust mechanism of accountability, particularly given the grave nature of the allegations and the societal impact of the scheme. However, the decision to not pursue investigations into these referrals has cast serious doubts on the NACC's commitment to its fundamental purpose of investigating corruption.

The NACC's reluctance to initiate its own investigation highlights a potentially troubling approach to accountability. While it is rational for a new entity to consider resource optimisation and efficiency, the gravity and public sensitivity of the Robodebt scandal necessitate a more assertive stance. The optics of this decision are particularly damaging; it appears to contradict the very essence of why the anti-corruption body was established.

The argument that existing inquiries by other bodies might cover the same ground does not adequately address the unique investigative powers and mandates that the NACC holds, and an independent investigation by the NACC could potentially uncover new evidence or provide a more focused exploration of corruption-specific dynamics that broader inquiries might not sufficiently address. The decision raises an important question about the effectiveness of multiple oversight bodies operating in parallel; it suggests a potential reluctance to engage in investigations that are politically sensitive or that involve high-level officials.

As the political ramifications of this decision unfold, there is a broader implication for the Labor government, which campaigned on the promise of effective governance and robust anti-corruption measures. The handling of this issue could significantly impact public trust and voter confidence in the government's willingness to enforce accountability, especially in high-stakes, high-impact cases such as Robodebt. If the NACC's decision stands as a precedent for future actions, it could also undermine the body's credibility and effectiveness, turning a potentially powerful tool for transparency into a symbol of bureaucratic hesitancy and inefficiency.

THE FALLOUT FROM NACC'S DECISION

The decision strikes a chord of deep frustration and betrayal among the Australian public, and is particularly poignant given the immense human cost associated with Robodebt—highlighted by the reported 2,000 deaths linked to the stress and financial hardship imposed by the scheme. The label of the "most disastrous public policy ever implemented in Australia," as described by numerous observers including the former Prime Minister Malcolm Turnbull, highlights the gravity of the scheme's impact and the purported role of the NACC in addressing such profound governmental failures.

The unfolding controversy around the NACC's refusal to investigate is compounded by the expectations set by the Robodebt Royal Commission—the deferral of its final report by Holmes, explicitly to align with the NACC's operational commencement on 1 July 2023, was a clear indicator of the Royal Commission's trust in the NACC's capacity to pursue justice and accountability rigorously. The subsequent decision by the NACC to sidestep this responsibility not only confounds the public but also raises serious questions about the commission's autonomy and its willingness to confront powerful political figures and entities.

This issue is not only administrative but deeply political. The NACC was a cornerstone of the Labor Party's platform in the lead-up to the 2022 federal election, which likely influenced their election success—the party's commitment to establishing a robust anti-corruption framework was seen as a direct response to the previous government's failures, of which Robodebt is perhaps the most glaring. As a result, the inaction on such a high-profile case undermines the credibility of the government's commitment to reform and accountability and suggests a disconcerting continuation of past apathy towards systemic issues within the government's own machinery.

This situation also has broader implications for the political landscape in Australia. The electorate's trust in governmental institutions and mechanisms designed to ensure accountability is crucial for the healthy functioning of democracy. When these institutions fail to act on clear mandates, particularly in cases involving extensive public harm and governmental malfeasance, it erodes public trust and dampens civic engagement. For many Australians, the NACC's inaction on Robodebt might confirm their cynicism about the effectiveness of governmental reforms and anti-corruption efforts, which could have lasting impacts on public confidence and future voter turnout.

In the context of political fallout, it's essential to consider the broader spectrum of promised reforms that have not been effectively implemented by the Labor government. The lack of progress on key issues such as AUKUS, and the continued incarceration of high-profile whistleblowers such Julian Assange, David McBride and Dan Duggan—locally and abroad—compounds the sentiment of disillusionment and this pattern of unmet expectations raises fundamental questions about whether the issue at hand is one of inexperience or points to deeper issues of a lack of political will.

The government needs to demonstrate not only a capacity to govern effectively but also a willingness to stand by its principles of transparency and accountability. Failing to do so could jeopardise its mandate and its future at the next federal election, due before May 2025.

A DOWNWARD SPIRAL OF PUBLIC TRUST IN OUR INSTITUTIONS

In 2023, Prime Minister Anthony Albanese and Government Services Minister Bill Shorten expressed strong condemnation of the Robodebt scheme, emphasising its unlawful nature and the severe impact it had on vulnerable Australians. Their words painted a picture of a new government ready to take decisive action against not only the failings of its predecessors but also the structural injustices that allowed such a scheme to flourish. Yet, the recent silence from these leaders following the NACC's announcement contrasts sharply with their earlier vigorous critiques, suggesting a retreat from their commitments to accountability and justice for vulnerable Australians.

This silence is particularly jarring given the context of the Robodebt scheme's consequences—financial ruin, severe emotional distress, and tragically, the numerous deaths that can be attributed to the scheme. It was a system that, as the Royal Commission pointed out, operated not just outside of legal boundaries but in a manner that was manifestly unjust. Taking these factors into account, the expectation was not only for an acknowledgment of these failures but for a robust response that could prevent such a catastrophe from recurring.

Critics now argue that the NACC's refusal to act, coupled with the government's lacklustre response to this decision, signifies a broader reluctance to engage with the systemic issues revealed by the Robodebt saga. The comparison with the New South Wales Independent Commission Against Corruption is telling: ICAC's history of vigorous investigations, which have led to high-profile resignations and reforms, starkly contrasts with the NACC's tentative beginnings, and this comparison raises uncomfortable questions about the effectiveness and independence of national anti-corruption efforts in Australia. Indeed, ICAC's first major case in 1992 resulted in the resignation of the NSW Premier Nick Greiner: in 2024, the NACC can't even proceed with a case where the corruption has clearly been identified.

The failure to investigate, as voiced by victims of the Robodebt scheme and echoed in public forums, paints the NACC as an institution lacking the courage to confront powerful interests or to address corruption in high places. This perception undermines the very purpose of the Commission and could have long-lasting implications for its legitimacy and the public's trust in governmental institutions more broadly.

The broader implications of this are significant. If the public perceives that even the bodies explicitly designed to combat corruption are toothless or unwilling to tackle substantial issues, the damage to the civic fabric could be extensive, and it may lead to increased public cynicism about the political process, lower voter engagement, and a weakening of the democratic accountability that is vital for a healthy political system.

A NEED FOR DRASTIC REFORM IN ANTI-CORRUPTION MEASURES

The hesitant approach to tackling issues such as the Robodebt scheme—as well as the subsequent decision to not investigate corruption within Tourism Australia over incidents related to the misuse of travel expenses—suggests that there may either be legislative difficulties or competency issues at NACC—headed by Paul Brereton—and this is a stark departure from the more assertive and proactive stance of other anti-corruption bodies around Australia, which have set a high bar by actively pursuing corruption within governments that established the respective commissions, demonstrating a commitment to integrity over political loyalty. This vigorous approach historically has highlighted a crucial ethos: anti-corruption agencies must operate with an unwavering dedication to transparency and accountability, irrespective of the political sensitivities involved.

The decision by the NACC to not investigate the Robodebt or Tourism Australia scandals, as well as the weak reasons provided for not pursuing the investigations, not only undermines its credibility but also sets a concerning precedent for future governance. This was the NACC's first round of major public announcements and conveys a message that political and bureaucratic machinations can potentially shield individuals from scrutiny and accountability, regardless of the scale of wrongdoing. This perception is damaging to the public's trust in government and its institutions, suggesting that there are limits to accountability when facing politically sensitive or high-profile cases.

The implications of this decision extend beyond immediate political repercussions; and suggests a systemic reluctance to enforce accountability. This is especially troubling in light of historical patterns seen in New South Wales and South Australia, where government interference has occasionally sought to undermine anti-corruption efforts through strategies like funding cuts when investigations got too close to core political interests. The example of former NSW Premier Gladys Berejiklian, whose administration interfered with

ICAC funding during ongoing investigations, illustrates the perils of such interference and highlights the need for anti-corruption bodies to operate without fiscal or political constraints.

It is obvious that the NACC's approach needs a fundamental recalibration. To restore public confidence and ensure robust accountability, the operations of the NACC should be transparent, especially once investigations reach a point where the public has a right to understand the processes and outcomes involved. Transparency not only safeguards the investigated but also ensures that the public can see justice being served, reinforcing trust in the system's ability to handle even the most politically sensitive cases. For those found guilty, public accountability is essential—it demonstrates that no one is above the law, reinforcing the principles of justice and equity foundational to democratic governance.

In the immediate aftermath, the Inspector of the National Anti-Corruption Commission, Gail Furness SC, has received nearly 900 individual public complaints about the decision by the NACC to not to commence a corruption investigation into the Robodebt Scheme, and will now perform her own inquiries into the decision. This is to be welcomed but the issue remains that it should never have got this point and the NACC has failed in its first major test.

The NACC's tepid response to the Robodebt scandal should serve as a wake-up call for all stakeholders involved and it presents an opportunity to recalibrate its commitments to an uncompromising and transparent fight against corruption. If the NACC is to be an effective instrument of justice, capable of maintaining public trust and holding power to account, it requires a significant overhaul—a reset that repositions it as a truly independent and fearless custodian of integrity in Australian public life.

***

DUTTON'S CONSERVATIVE STANCE AND CLIMATE WARS WILL ISOLATE AUSTRALIA

16 June 2024

The re-emergence of climate politics in Australia, spearheaded by leader of the Liberal Party Peter Dutton, highlights a significant ideological and strategic dissonance within the party's ranks, particularly following their significant losses in the 2022 federal election. These losses, primarily to the teal independents who campaigned heavily on progressive climate policies, might have suggested a moment for reflection and realignment towards more environmentally friendly policies. Instead, the party, under Dutton's leadership, along with the support role of the National Party leader, David Littleproud, seems poised to double down on a more conservative, pro-nuclear, anti-climate action stance.

Dutton's rhetoric, coupled with Littleproud's comment that the Coalition will place a cap on funding for renewable energy projects, should they win the next federal election, is a retreat from proactive climate action. His outright dismissal of Labor's climate targets for 2030 as "unachievable", and his unchallenged critique that pursuing such goals would lead to skyrocketing power prices, paints a grim picture of the Liberal Party's climate strategy. This stance is not just a rejection of Labor's policies but also signals a withdrawal from the Paris Agreement, an international commitment to combat climate change and reduce rising global temperatures. Such a move would not only isolate Australia on the global stage but also contradict the desires of the electorate that ousted numerous Liberal candidates in many metropolitan areas in favour of those advocating for stronger climate action.

In contrast, Prime Minister Anthony Albanese's response highlights the broader implications of Dutton's approach, framing it as an abandonment of Australia's international obligations and a threat to future investment in clean technologies. Albanese's remarks suggest that walking away from the Paris Agreement equates to standing with nations that are either embroiled in conflict or are international outliers—Yemen, Libya and Iran—further illustrating the potential diplomatic and economic isolation that could result from such a policy shift.

The strategy of reigniting the so-called "climate wars" does not only reflect a policy preference but seems to be a calculated, if misguided, political gamble by Dutton, a gamble that presupposes that the backing of powerful media proprietors—Kerry Stokes and Rupert Murdoch—could sway public opinion enough to counteract the clear environmental concerns expressed by voters during the last election. However, the electoral defeat of key figures such as former Liberal Treasurer Josh Frydenberg, despite favourable media coverage, challenges the effectiveness of this strategy, and the 2022 election results, certainly in the seat of Kooyong, suggest that voters are increasingly discerning over issues relating to climate change, prioritising substantive policy positions over partisan narratives.

The inclusion of nuclear power in the policy mix introduces another layer of complexity and public resistance. While nuclear power offers a low-emission alternative to fossil fuels, the issues of prohibitive costs, waste management and the 'not-in-my-backyard' sentiment significantly complicate its deployment as a feasible or popular solution in Australia. Dutton's advocacy for nuclear power, however, is more of a diversion rather than a viable policy shift, highlighting a potential misreading of public sentiment and the practical challenges of energy policy.

This situation presents a paradox where the Liberal Party, in an attempt to differentiate itself from its opponents, is moving further away from the very constituents it needs to regain. The persistence of this strategy could either be a testament to a deep-seated ideological commitment to traditional energy sources or simply a misjudgment of the electorate's priorities. Either way, it signals a turbulent time ahead for the Liberal Party, as it navigates through the combination of media influence, voter sentiment, and the urgent global need for effective climate action.

THE LIBERAL PARTY CONTINUES TO ALIENATE KEY ELECTORATES

Dutton's decision to also withhold specific climate targets until he wins the next election reflects a broader trend in his political engagement—promising results without providing substantive plans or details. This tactic not only risks alienating voters who demand clear and immediate action on climate change but also undermines the transparency expected in democratic processes.

The resistance to committing to detailed climate plans before an election is particularly problematic in the context of the seats the Liberal Party lost to teal independents and the Australian Greens. These seats, such as Kooyong, Goldstein, North Sydney—a seat which is also subject to a redistribution by the Australian Electoral Commission—Warringah, Macarthur, Wentworth, Ryan and Brisbane, are characterised by a voter base that has shown a strong preference for proactive environmental policies. The independents who won these seats did so by presenting detailed, ambitious climate policies, directly countering the less defined and more conservative environmental approaches of the traditional parties. Dutton's vague promises and his reluctance to engage with climate science and a lack of detailed policy planning do not resonate with these electorates.

Dutton's strategy appears to focus heavily on consolidating his highly reactionary base, primarily engaging through platforms such as News Corporation, Sky News and 2GB, which cater to a more conservative audience. This tactic might solidify his support in certain demographics but does little to address the broader national concerns about climate change and environmental sustainability. It also potentially isolates him from a segment of the electorate that is crucial for any significant electoral victory—those in the middle ground who may be swayed by substantive policy offerings rather than partisan alignment.

The leadership style that Dutton exemplifies—marked by a lack of flexibility and tactical acumen—raises questions about his capacity to navigate the complex and shifting political landscape of Australia. The emphasis on nuclear energy, a contentious issue within Australia, without providing details or engaging with the community concerns about cost, waste management and safety, further illustrates this disconnect. His dismissive attitude towards demands for more detailed environmental and energy policies not only alienates potential voters in crucial seats but also provides fertile ground for opposition parties to critique and campaign against his leadership.

The comparison drawn between Dutton's secretive approach to policy details and his criticisms of the Labor Party's detailed Voice to Parliament referendum in 2023 exemplifies a perceived hypocrisy in his political stance, undermining his credibility and the trust voters might place in him. Such discrepancies between what is critiqued and what is practiced could lead to voter apathy or backlash, particularly in areas sensitive to political and policy integrity.

Ultimately, Dutton's current strategy may secure certain rural and outer urban seats where conservative values are more prevalent, but it neglects the inner urban and suburban seats that form a crucial part of the electoral landscape. The risk here is that by focusing too narrowly on a conservative base that is already secured, Dutton and the Liberal Party may fail to address the broader national issues that are critical to winning elections, such as effective climate action and transparent governance. This approach not only threatens their chances in upcoming elections but also suggests a broader issue within the party: a lack of viable leadership alternatives who can realign the party's strategies with the evolving priorities of the Australian electorate.

ELECTORAL RISKS IN THE LEAD UP TO THE NEXT FEDERAL ELECTION

As the next federal election approaches—due before May 2025 with a small chance of being held in November this year—the stakes for Dutton and the Liberal Party become increasingly clear, especially in light of government projections suggesting that Australia is on track to achieve a 42 per cent reduction in emissions by 2030, one percentage point under the target. This progress, made despite the Coalition's historical resistance to climate policies, indicates a broader global shift towards sustainability that Australia risks being left behind from if it does not participate. The international market for electric vehicles and renewable energy sources—especially China and, increasingly, the United States—presents massive economic opportunities that Australia could capitalise on, yet the strategy proposed by Dutton shies away from these prospects.

This outright and hostile rejection to set clear climate targets reflects a broader strategic vulnerability for the Liberal Party. Dutton's decision to defer revealing any climate targets until potentially winning the next election opens him and his party to criticisms of opacity and lack of commitment to critical national and global issues. This tactic, reminiscent of his stance during the Voice to Parliament campaign where he advocated a conservative approach to change, could be politically weaponised against him. The phrase "If you don't know, vote no," used effectively against the Voice to Parliament proposal, might just as effectively be turned against Dutton himself, as voters may prefer transparency and decisiveness in policy-making, particularly on issues as critical as climate change.

Polls showing the Coalition neck and neck with the Labor government or even trailing slightly—the recent Resolve poll even shows Dutton ahead of Albanese as preferred Prime Minister for the first time—indicate a volatile political environment where public opinion could shift rapidly, especially as environmental and economic issues take centre stage. The electorate's engagement levels may not currently be high, but as the election nears and campaigns intensify, Dutton's continued emphasis on divisive or opaque policies could further alienate moderate and swing voters, as well as those in key seats concerned about environmental issues.

Dutton's public persona as a tough but negative character—"a muscular brand of politics", in the words of a certain ABC political commentator—might not resonate well outside his conservative base. Even if described by some media outlets as a strong and decisive leader, this image does not seem to hold much traction beyond those predisposed to support him. In contrast, a perceived lack of genuine leadership and innovation in policy could dampen enthusiasm among broader segments of the electorate, who are looking for proactive and positive leadership, especially in areas like climate policy where Australia has both much to gain and much to lose.

The Liberal Party, under Dutton's leadership, faces complex challenges. To regain lost seats and secure new ones, they must navigate a course that increasingly values substantive action on climate change and clear, forward-thinking policies. The upcoming election presents not just a test of political strategy but of the party's ability to align itself with the evolving values and priorities of the Australian electorate. The outcome will likely hinge on whether the Liberal Party can convincingly address these critical issues or if they will continue down a path that may lead to further political isolation and electoral challenges.

***

THE WRECKING BALL OF AUSTRALIA POLITICS: NUCLEAR NOT IN THE PUBLIC INTEREST

22 June 2024

The decision by the Liberal and National parties to unveil their nuclear power station program highlights the paucity of public debate and complexities of energy policy in Australia. At the heart of this move is a blend of rank opportunism and cynicism, aiming to reshape the political narrative surrounding climate action in Australia and diminish the use of renewable energy.

The announcement to construct seven nuclear power stations comes at a time when Australia is entrenched in the ongoing "climate wars", which the Coalition wages whenever it faces political difficulties, irrespective of whether it's in government, or in opposition. The decision to propose nuclear energy—specifically at sites of retiring coal plants around Australia—is presented by conservatives and vested interests as a bold vision towards sustainable energy solutions. However, the political motivations behind it are driven by a desire to control the political narrative, rather than a genuine commitment to transformative energy policy, and primarily to destroy the pursuit of renewables.

From a political standpoint, the selection of the proposed nuclear sites is telling. Placing them predominantly in safe Liberal and National seats strategically minimises political risk and backlash in those regions. Obviously, this choice is aiming to avoid the "not in my backyard" syndrome which often accompanies such developments but it's a high degree of cynicism that utilises these proposals more as electoral and propaganda tools than feasible energy solutions. The lack of serious consideration for the implications of these nuclear sites is further highlighted by the absence of a detailed cost analysis—or *any* cost analysis—which remains undisclosed, raising questions about the transparency and viability of the Coalition's proposal.

Economically, the move towards nuclear energy is fraught with challenges. The initial setup and ongoing maintenance costs of nuclear power are substantially higher compared to renewable energy alternatives. Despite claims to the contrary by leader of the opposition, Peter Dutton, the reality of nuclear economics stands in stark contrast. Countries around the world, including notable examples such as Germany and the United Kingdom, are increasingly investing in renewable energies, achieving significant portions of their energy supply from these sources. These examples contradict Dutton's assertions and highlight a global shift towards more sustainable and cost-effective energy solutions: nuclear energy contributes around 10 per cent of the world's energy supplies—a number that is decreasing—while renewables currently contribute around 30 per cent, a number that is rising dramatically.

In the public area, the proposal has sparked a wide range of reactions, from skepticism to outright opposition. Critics argue that the plan is not only economically unsound but also poorly timed, considering the global urgency to reduce carbon emissions and the available alternatives that promise quicker and cheaper results. The public's trust in government-led large-scale infrastructure projects is waning, given past failures such as the National Broadband Network and the continuous infrastructure issues surrounding the Snowy Mountains 2.0 scheme. This history makes the nuclear proposal a hard sell to the Australian electorate, which may view it as another potentially unfulfilled promise.

COALITION'S HIGH-RISK STRATEGY LACKS CLARITY AND FEASIBILITY

The unveiling of the nuclear energy program is a gamble, reflecting a high-risk political strategy with minimal transparency and significant gaps in detail. Why would anyone in the electorate support such a proposal based on a politically motivated four-page media release and announcement, without costings? This lack of clarity, coupled with an absence of firm commitments on the specifics of the nuclear reactors, highlights not only a disregard for informed policy-making but also a broader strategic aim that prioritises political positioning over practical energy solutions.

The proposed nuclear reactors, with unspecified types and sizes, represent a critical void in the plan and this ambiguity extends to the lack of a clear timeline and budget, raising serious questions about the feasibility of the project. The Coalition has not provided substantial information on the technology they plan to employ, whether it be yet-to-be-invented small modular reactors or more traditional nuclear designs, some of which remain purely theoretical and untested at scale. This vagueness suggests a detachment from the technical realities of nuclear power development, which requires precise planning and rigorous safety protocols, especially in a country such as Australia which is geographically prone to natural disasters like floods, bushfires and earthquakes, which pose additional risks to nuclear facilities.

It can also be seen that the underpinnings of the Coalition's proposal has dual intent: to extend the life of the coal industry under the guise of transitioning to nuclear power, and to leverage this transition as a political tool against the Labor government and support the vested interests of the Coalition. This tactic is primarily an attempt to delay substantive action on climate change, and maintaining the status quo under the pretext of innovative progress.

Aside from these issues, there are pronounced constitutional hurdles and the rights of the states, notably the required approval from state Premiers, who have been unequivocally resistant to endorsing the proposed sites for nuclear development. This uniform opposition from state leaders not only complicates the logistical execution of the plan but also indicates a broader misalignment between federal ambitions and state-level energy policies.

The political landscape within the Liberal Party itself also reflects a broader ideological shift, with the marginalisation of moderates and the ascendancy of figures such as Dutton, who now embody the party's strategy. This shift towards a more conservative, reactionary stance on energy policy will alienate some electoral segments, further complicating the party's position with the electorate. The promise of nuclear energy, in this context, is less about a tangible shift towards sustainable energy and more about political posturing, presenting a facade of action to a public that is increasingly aware of and concerned about climate issues.

THE COALITION'S NUCLEAR RUSE CONTRASTS WITH THE GLOBAL SHIFT TOWARDS RENEWABLES

The Coalition's nuclear energy ambitions against the global trend of decommissioning and moving away from nuclear power starkly illuminates the anachronistic nature of their proposal. Internationally, the trajectory is clear: nations are gradually reducing their reliance on nuclear energy—most, but not all—in favour of renewable sources. This global shift is not just a matter of energy policy but a reflection of broader economic, environmental, and social priorities that increasingly favour sustainability and public safety over the complex challenges associated with nuclear power.

Japan's experience with Fukushima Daiichi in 2011 serves as a sobering reminder of the potential dangers associated with nuclear energy. The disaster remains an unresolved environmental catastrophe, influencing Japan's decision to significantly scale back its nuclear operations and this incident highlights the inherent risks of nuclear power, which even with advancements in technology, cannot be entirely mitigated. Fukushima was a turning point for Japan, and it highlighted the critical oversight issues and the devastating consequences of underestimating the risks involved with nuclear energy management.

Similarly, Germany's decision to decommission all its nuclear power plants and shift towards renewable energy is indicative of a broader, deliberate move towards sustainability. Germany, an industrial leader in Europe, if not the world, has successfully demonstrated that economic vitality does not solely depend on nuclear power. Instead, it has embraced a future-oriented approach by investing in renewable energies, decommissioning its final nuclear power station in 2023 and aiming for a completely renewable energy grid by 2035. This transition is not only about reducing carbon emissions but also about enhancing energy security and public safety, distancing the country from the problematic legacies of nuclear power.

In contrast, the Coalition's proposal is out of step with these international trends. While nuclear energy does provide certain benefits, such as stable base-load generation and relatively low emissions compared to fossil fuels, the economic and social costs associated with it are considerable. The lack of a clear, detailed plan, the potential for high infrastructure and decommissioning costs, and the substantial risks of environmental disasters make the proposition less appealing, especially when compared to the rapidly falling costs and increasing efficiency of renewable energy technologies.

The ideological inclination of the Coalition towards privatisation of energy assets further complicates the scenario. The Australian public has witnessed the detrimental effects of privatising essential services, where profit motives often supersede public interest, leading to reduced investments in maintenance and safety. The example of Fukushima, where privatisation played a role in the mishandling of the plant's safety protocols, is a cautionary tale that resonates deeply within Australia. While the Coalition has stated that these nuclear power stations will be government owned, there's no question that they would sell these assets as soon as it would be possible to do so, further adding to the risk of these assets, if held in private hands, as was the case in Fukushima Daiichi.

This approach is reminiscent of past policies where actions by Liberal governments have been more about garnering votes and catering to corporate interests than addressing public concerns or environmental responsibilities—as evidenced by the Coalition's history with infrastructure projects, which often prioritise political and vested interests over public interests.

PARTISAN POLITICS AND VESTED INTERESTS UNDERMINE SUSTAINABLE ENERGY GOALS

The leader of the National Party, David Littleproud's statement on capping government spending on renewable projects such as offshore wind farms highlights a direct effort to manipulate energy policy in a way that discourages renewables in favour of nuclear solutions. The criticism that offshore wind farms are an "eyesore"—some 20 kilometres off the coast—is an example of how ridiculous aesthetic judgments are used to undermine environmentally beneficial projects, despite their placement far from shore and their minimal visual impact. This stance not only serves to halt progress towards more sustainable energy solutions but also appeals to their "cooker" base that holds misconceptions about the supposed health impacts of wind farms—misconceptions that have been consistently debunked by scientific research.

The ties between key political figures and the uranium mining industry reveal a concerning overlap between personal financial interests and public policy making. Figures such as Gina Rinehart and entities associated with Rupert Murdoch have been noted proponents of uranium mining, an industry that stands to gain significantly from a shift towards nuclear energy. The involvement of these figures in pushing for nuclear energy, coupled with Dutton's interactions with these influencers at costly events funded by taxpayers—in 2023, Dutton charged taxpayers $23,000 to fly to an event hosted by News Corporation and sponsored by Rinehart's Hancock Prospecting—suggests a deep entanglement of politics with corporate profit motives, often at the expense of more equitable and sustainable energy policies.

The Coalition has been historically inept in managing national infrastructure projects, such as the NBN and the Snowy Mountains 2.0 scheme, and not even having the wherewithal to construct car parks as part of the infrastructure rorts back in 2019. It's obvious that the Coalition is not the party of infrastructure unless it can find a beneficial use for one of its benefactors or other vested interest. This inefficacy not only casts doubt on their ability to undertake a project as complex and demanding as nuclear energy infrastructure but also raises concerns about their overall capability to manage public resources responsibly.

In this light, the push for nuclear energy is a strategic move to support specific economic interests within the party's support base, rather than a genuinely considered strategy aimed at transitioning Australia to a more sustainable energy future. It highlights a pattern of governance where policy decisions are often skewed by partisan and personal interests, which could ultimately undermine public trust and the efficacy of governmental action in addressing critical national issues such as energy security and climate change.

NUCLEAR POLICY MISSTEP WILL GIVE RISE TO CLIMATE 200 AND INDEPENDENT MOVEMENTS IN AUSTRALIAN POLITICS

While the Coalition might consider that its nuclear energy announcement will give it an unlikely political fillip—despite its lack of detail and disregard for the broader public interest—it inadvertently serves as a catalyst for mobilising climate action groups and other independent political movements in Australia. This strategic misstep by the Coalition provides a significant opportunity for Climate 200 and the Australian Greens, who are poised to capitalise on the growing disenchantment with traditional party policies, particularly regarding environmental and energy issues.

Climate 200, founded by Simon Holmes à Court, has already demonstrated its ability to influence Australian politics by successfully supporting independent 'teal' candidates in previous federal elections, especially in 2022. With the announcement of targeting additional seats in the upcoming election, the group is strategically positioned to further erode the traditional stronghold of major parties. The nuclear proposal, a backward step in the context of global energy trends, enhances the appeal of independents and smaller parties who advocate for more progressive and sustainable energy policies.

The shift away from major parties has been a notable trend in Australian politics since the mid-1980s, with primary vote shares consistently declining, recording 69 per cent in the 2022 federal election. The Coalition's nuclear energy policy proposal could accelerate this trend, as it aligns poorly with the growing public sentiment favouring renewable energy and more transparent, accountable governance. The nine federal seats targeted by Climate 200, especially those with smaller margins in the 2 to 4 per cent band, become particularly vulnerable in this context, providing fertile ground for independents and small party candidates who can offer credible alternatives to disillusioned voters.

The Australian Greens also stand to benefit, particularly in urban areas such Melbourne and Sydney, where environmental concerns are pronounced and the party already has a substantial supporter base. The Coalition's gamble on nuclear energy could be perceived as out of touch with the progressive environmental policies more popular among urban voters, potentially boosting support for the Greens.

The Coalition's commitment to nuclear energy and vested interests rather than public good, will also strengthen the resolve and appeal of independent candidates, who often campaign on platforms of integrity, transparency, and community-focused initiatives—direct counters to what many see as opaque and interest-driven policies from the larger parties.

While the Coalition views its nuclear energy policy as a means to gain power and attract voters looking for firm energy solutions, the move will paradoxically undermine their position. By alienating environmentally conscious voters and those frustrated with traditional political dynamics, the policy may drive these constituents towards independents and smaller parties like the Greens, who promise a more sustainable and community-oriented approach to governance. The true impact of this strategy will become clearer in the upcoming federal election—due before May 2025—but it does hold the potential to reshape the Australian political arena in favour of those advocating for real change.

***

THE STRUGGLE FOR PRESS FREEDOM AND WHISTLEBLOWER ADVOCACY CONTINUES

29 June 2024

Julian Assange is finally free, marking the end of a long saga that began in 2010 when WikiLeaks released footage of the United States military killing civilians and journalists in Baghdad—an incident regarded by many as a war crime, which saw no charges laid against anyone involved, except for the people who reported the war crimes: Assange and Chelsea Manning. Throughout Assange's imprisonment, successive Australian governments displayed varying degrees of indifference to his plight, with some politicians vocally supported his release while in opposition, only to retreat from these positions once in power.

Of particularly note was the stance of former Prime Minister Julia Gillard who claimed in 2010 that Assange was "guilty of illegality"—even though no charges had been laid that stage, and also going on to say that she didn't have a "great deal of respect" for Assange releasing the scores of material depicting possible war crimes committed by U.S. forces in Iraq and Afghanistan, and believed there was "no moral purpose" behind his actions.

This was indicative of the attitudes of many political leaders and mainstream journalists at the time—and continued for most of the time Assange was in jail—and he was left to languish, facing the possibility of execution in the United States, until a significant shift occurred once Anthony Albanese became Prime Minister. While in opposition, Albanese had campaigned on a platform that included justice for Assange, a promise he continued upon assuming office.

The quiet and slow diplomacy was initially met with skepticism and criticism for its sluggishness, but ultimately proved effective, leading to Assange's release. Jennifer Robinson, Assange's legal counsel, highlighted the extensive global support for Assange that played a central role in this outcome, as well as Albanese's leadership and diplomacy, which she credited as instrumental in securing Assange's freedom.

This event has reignited discussions about the nature of WikiLeaks' other disclosures, particularly those that influenced the 2016 U.S. presidential election. Critics argue about the appropriateness of the material released against Hillary Clinton during that campaign, but the core issue remains the public's right to know about the actions of their governments—we can't pick and choose or have preferences over the type of material that is released, and whether it was 2010 Baghdad attacks or the 2016 U.S. election, governments and the players within the political system need to be held to account. Assange's release does not negate the divisive views on his actions; rather, it highlights the complexities of freedom of speech and the press.

When considering the broader implications of Assange's incarceration, it is crucial to weigh up the effect it may have had on journalism, and the charges and prolonged legal battles faced by Assange highlighted the risks journalists endure when exposing governmental misconduct. While opinions on Assange's methods and motivations vary widely, the principle that underpins his ordeal is the essential right to hold power to account—a principle that vital to a functioning democracy.

DEEP FLAWS IN THE U.S. ESPIONAGE ACT: A CALL FOR REFORM AND TRANSPARENCY

The charges against Assange have raised debates about the U.S. *Espionage Act* and its implications on freedom of the press and the right to information. Originally enacted in 1917 amid fears of communist influence following the Russian Revolution, the *Espionage Act* was intended to protect national security by preventing the sharing of state secrets with foreign governments. However, its application has often extended far beyond these initial intentions, targeting not just spies but also those perceived as ideological threats to the U.S. government.

In Assange's case, his acceptance and dissemination of classified documents through WikiLeaks was seen as a violation of this act, despite the public interest argument supporting the need for such information to be disclosed. Assange's U.S. lawyer, Barry Pollack, highlighted this conundrum: acknowledging the technical breach of the law, while also arguing for First Amendment protections for Assange's actions. This duality highlights the conflict between national security interests and the principles of transparency and freedom of information that are foundational to democratic societies.

The legal battle surrounding Assange also reflects broader concerns about how laws such as the *Espionage Act* can be used to stifle journalistic practices that are critical of governmental actions. The historical use of the Act against ideological opponents, rather than genuine threats to national security, raises questions about the balance of power and the safeguarding of civil liberties. For instance, the case of Julius and Ethel Rosenberg during the McCarthy era, who were executed under the auspices of the *Espionage Act*, still sparks debates in the United States about legal overreach and miscarriages of justice.

In Australia, similar legislation was enacted with the amendment of the *Crimes Act* in 1926, aimed at suppressing communist activities. This paralleled the U.S. approach, demonstrating a common legislative reaction against perceived ideological threats. The subsequent legal battles and political actions by conservative governments, such as the 1951 referendum in Australia to ban the Communist Party, further illustrate the contentious nature of such laws and their impact on political discourse and individual rights.

Assange's ordeal, culminating in a plea deal and an implied acknowledgment by the chief judge Ramona Manglona that the application of the *Espionage Act* may have been misguided in this case, reveals the complexities involved in applying outdated laws to contemporary issues of governance and information dissemination. This case not only highlights the need for legislative reform to better align with current realities and ethical standards but also serves as a reminder of the ongoing struggle between governmental authority and the pursuit of truth.

A STRANGE COALITION FOR FREEDOM AND TRANSPARENCY

The case of Assange has created an odd coalition across the political spectrum, both in the United States and Australia, demonstrating an uncommon consensus on issues of freedom of speech and the limits of governmental authority. In the U.S., the alignment of figures as ideologically diverse as Alexandria Ocasio-Cortez and Marjorie Taylor Greene on Assange's case highlights a rare bipartisan agreement. Similarly, in Australia, the support for Assange crossed various political boundaries, involving members from the Australian Greens, independents, the Labor Party, and the National Party, including Barnaby Joyce and George Christensen. While there were some MPs from within the Liberal Party's also supported the release of Assange, the party did oppose a motion advocating for Assange's return to Australia in May 2024, once again showing them to be on the "wrong side of history".

This unusual political alignment reveals a significant shift in how issues related to freedom of the press and whistleblowing are perceived across the political landscape. Traditionally viewed through a partisan lens, the Assange saga has prompted a re-evaluation of these issues as fundamentally about democratic rights rather than simple political positions.

Prime Minister Albanese's role in this scenario has been central to the release of Assange. His involvement has not only been about supporting Assange but also about advocating for the principles of justice and transparency that the case represents. The international dimension of this support, facilitated by diplomatic figures such as the U.K. High Commissioner Steven Smith and U.S. Ambassador Kevin Rudd, illustrates the complexity and global impact of Assange's situation. The Australian government's proactive stance under Albanese, offering not just verbal support but also tangible diplomatic assistance, sets a precedent for how such cases might be handled in the future.

The broad and diverse backing for Assange's release and the criticism of the extended legal proceedings against him highlight a growing public and political acknowledgment of the need for reform in how whistleblowers and journalists are treated. This case has become a focal point for discussions on the balance between national security and the public's right to know, challenging governments and individuals to reconsider their positions on these pivotal issues.

A MEDIA DIVIDE AND CALLS FOR STRONGER WHISTLEBLOWER PROTECTIONS

The release of Assange is a significant victory for media freedom and a moment of relief for his supporters and advocates of free speech. However, the journey to this outcome was fraught with challenges—over 14 years—and marked by a notable absence of support from many within the mainstream media. Initially, many journalists, including some from ABC—who are now ensconced on the ABC *News Breakfast* program, effectively managing an early retirement and superannuation package—distanced themselves from Assange, questioning his status as a journalist and expressing indifference or even approval of his potential extradition to the U.S. This stance from parts of the media industry—and there was a clear schism between establishment media and independent media—not only highlighted the divide within journalism about what constitutes legitimate journalistic activity but also highlighted the precarious position of whistleblowers who expose uncomfortable truths.

While Assange's release is a triumph, it should also highlight the plight of other whistleblowers who continue to face severe consequences for their actions of information the public about government malfeasance. The cases of David McBride and Richard Boyle are particularly alarming. McBride, a former military lawyer, was imprisoned for disclosing information about alleged war crimes by Australian forces in Afghanistan. Boyle, a former Australian Taxation Office employee, faces legal challenges—and a potential 46 years in prison—for revealing aggressive debt collection practices that allegedly led to unfair treatment of taxpayers. Both whistleblowers acted in the public interest, yet found themselves prosecuted rather than protected. Their ongoing prosecutions raise critical questions about the inconsistency of support for whistleblowers and the application of laws meant to shield them.

The Australian government's approach to whistleblowers such as McBride and Boyle suggests a selective interpretation of what constitutes the public interest. The fact that the Attorney-General, Mark Dreyfus, has not intervened in these cases, despite having the authority to do so, indicates a concerning disregard for the principle of transparency. This inconsistency in handling whistleblowers not only undermines trust in the government's commitment to justice but also discourages future whistleblowers from coming forward, for fear of reprisals.

It's important for governments establish robust mechanisms to protect and support whistleblowers, as these individuals play a critical role in a healthy democracy by holding institutions accountable and exposing wrongdoing, and establishing a Public Informant Office could be a step in the right direction. Such a system should ensure that genuine whistleblowers are shielded from retaliation, while also incorporating safeguards against malicious allegations. This dual approach would maintain the integrity of the system while encouraging responsible whistleblowing.

Ultimately, the broader implications of Assange's case and the ongoing challenges faced by other whistleblowers such as McBride and Boyle offers an opportunity for the governments to re-evaluate how democratic societies treat those who expose the truth. It's a value that's instilled from childhood—to speak out against wrongdoing—and this must be upheld by our institutions, ensuring that those who do so are celebrated rather than condemned. The hope remains that the resolution of Assange's case will bring in a new era of enhanced protections for whistleblowers, reflecting a true commitment to transparency and accountability in governance.

***

JULY

THE SLIGHT ON THE HILL: A SCHISM WITHIN LABOR'S MEMBERSHIP

6 July 2024

The drama surrounding Senator Fatima Payman and her departure from the Labor Party is more than a personal or political narrative: it's a reflection on the internal dynamics and ideological battles within the party itself. This situation has unfolded in a way that has brought significant attention not only to Senator Payman but also to the foundational principles and the operational tactics of the ALP, and the issues to the heart of party alignment, Caucus solidarity, and the broader implications for political representation of minority groups in Australia and contentious international issues such as the recognition of Palestine.

Senator Payman's actions and the subsequent reactions from the ALP parliamentary leadership highlight a contradiction between the party's proclaimed values contained within the Labor Platform and its actions, once it gets into office. Labor, historically a champion of the working class, social justice, and minority rights, has now sidelined a young, articulate Senator from an Islamic background because she took a stand that aligns with her constituents' and her personal beliefs on Palestine, rather than strictly adhering to party lines. It also raises critical questions about the role of individual conscience versus party unity in parliamentary democracies.

Her choice to cross the floor and support an Australian Greens' motion calling for the Australian government to recognise the state of Palestine was not a policy divergence—Labor's Platform clearly calls for the recognition of Palestine *as a priority*—but a symbolic act loaded with implications for her role in parliament and for the Labor Party.

The official reason given for her suspension—a breach of Caucus rules—thinly veils the real reasons—adopting a position that is offensive to the lobbyists and supporters of Israel in Australia— and the mainstream media narrative condescendingly suggested naivety and susceptibility to manipulation by political rivals, painting a picture of a Senator who is out of her depth. However, such interpretations fail to recognise Payman's agency and commitment to what she sees as a just cause, reflecting a broader pattern of political parties undermining or patronising their own members who come from minority backgrounds.

This incident also highlights the historical patterns of dissent within the Labor Party. The ALP has, throughout its history, experienced several splits based on deep ideological differences, from conscription and economic policy, to the role of communism in party ideology in the 1950s, with each split reflecting a tension between the evolving demands of the party's base and the strategic directions chosen by its parliamentary leadership. The treatment of Senator Payman hints at a possible brewing of another such moment of reckoning within the Labor Party, as issues of global significance intersect with internal party politics and the representation of diverse Australian communities.

Senator Payman's resignation and shift to an independent is not just a loss of a party member but a critical commentary on the ALP's current trajectory. It also signals a shift in how minority representatives might view their roles and align themselves within Australian politics, especially when they feel that the party no longer serves as a platform for their advocacy or aligns with their principles. This could have significant electoral implications for the ALP, especially in engaging with a demographic that is increasingly aware and sensitive to issues of global justice and representation.

RECOGNITION OF PALESTINE AND THE DIVERGENCE FROM THE LABOR PLATFORM

The ALP's Platform clearly supports the recognition of both Israel and Palestine within recognised borders, and highlights the urgency of addressing this issue as a priority for the government. Yet, despite this clear stance in the party Platform, there has been a lack of progress on the recognition of Palestine since Labor came into office in May 2022. This gap between the Platform and practice raises critical questions about the ALP's governance and its responsiveness to the values and expectations of its members and supporters.

Senator Payman's situation highlights the broader struggle within the party between adhering to Caucus discipline and staying true to the party's foundational principles and promises. While Caucus solidarity is crucial for political strategy and unity, it also poses a dilemma when it suppresses significant voices within the party, particularly on issues that resonate deeply with the party's base. The Senator's decision to cross the floor reflects a courageous commitment to her principles on Palestine and the interests of her constituents, challenging the party's leadership to align its actions with its declared policies.

This conflict within the ALP is reflective of a broader historical pattern where the party has often found itself at crossroads, torn between progressive aspirations and pragmatic governance. The divergences on issues such as the recognition of Palestine spotlight the ongoing tensions between the party's rank-and-file members—who often hold more idealistic views on international justice and human rights—and the parliamentary party, which prioritises broader political and diplomatic considerations.

The comparison with Ireland's recent recognition of Palestinian statehood highlights a contrasting situation where a similar act can be implemented in other countries with little controversy. Of course, Ireland's history and political landscape allowed for a more straightforward acknowledgment of Palestine, a stark contrast with Australia's fraught political machinations on the same issue. However, if Ireland can recognise the state of Palestine—with almost unanimous political support—why is it so difficult for Australia to follow? What is the Labor government so afraid of?

The threat of a split within the ALP over this issue is not just theoretical; it could have tangible consequences for the party's cohesion and its future electoral prospects. History shows that political parties can endure only so much internal strife before they either transform or fracture. The unfolding situation around Senator Payman and the recognition of Palestine may serve as a critical point for the Labor Party, testing its ability to reconcile the demands of governance with the principles it purports to uphold.

THE TENSIONS BETWEEN CAUCUS SOLIDARITY AND MODERN POLITICAL DYNAMICS

It's clear that the treatment of Senator Fatima Payman and her subsequent resignation, brings to light significant structural and ideological rigidities within Caucus that are increasingly at odds with the dynamic political and social landscape of today and it's a schism that highlights a broader issue: the tension between Caucus solidarity and the party's ability to adapt and respond to contemporary issues and the will of its rank-and-file membership.

This situation reflects not just a single issue of policy disagreement but a systemic rigidity that stifles individual voices and progressive stances within the party. Senator Penny Wong referred to her own experience of refraining from criticising the Caucus decision not to support marriage equality when a private member's bill was presented in Parliament in 2012 as the correct method of dealing with personal issues that may conflict with decisions made by the Caucus.

But where is the merit in Wong's actions at the time? Over 65 percent of the community—and 80 percent of Labor members—supported marriage equality in 2012. Wong's initial silence and later support for marriage equality, which only came to fruition under a different government in 2017, serve as a potent example of how Caucus solidarity can delay or even derail significant social reforms. How did Caucus solidarity serve the public interest in 2012, or the gay and lesbian community that Wong is a part of? It didn't: Labor had an opportunity to highlight its credentials on progressive issues—and a policy position on marriage equality that was firmly entrenched in the Labor Platform—but when the time came to actually introduce marriage equality, it couldn't find the courage to support it and left it to a future Prime Minister, Malcolm Turnbull, to implement it many years later.

In this context, the insistence on Caucus unity appears not as a strength but as a liability for the Labor Party, especially when it conflicts with the party's publicly professed values and the expectations of its members. This rigidity is sclerotic in a rapidly changing world and this approach alienates not only party members but also the wider electorate, who may view the party's inability to adapt as a failure of leadership and vision.

The influential factions within the party, such as the leadership of certain unions and conservative elements, exert disproportionate influence on Caucus decisions and this reveals a deeper issue—this influence often does not reflect the broader membership's progressive aspirations, leading to decisions that may align with internal power structures but not with the party's stated goals or the progressive ethos it claims to represent.

The paradox within the ALP, where the leadership appears to be at odds with the grassroots and progressive segments of the party, is not unique to this issue or to the Labor Party—the Liberal Party has had many MPs in recent years crossing the floor of parliament against the wishes of the Liberal party room—but it is symptomatic of a larger pattern. This disconnect raises fundamental questions about the nature of representation and accountability in modern political parties, and ongoing and significant internal conflicts, as the gap between the leadership's actions and the membership's expectations widens.

A CRISIS OF CONSCIENCE

This situation has not only stirred discontent within Labor's rank and file—the Leichhardt branch of the Labor Party in Albanese's own seat of Grayndler passed a motion of support for Senator Payman, adding that they share her "strong support for Palestine and respect the courage and integrity she has demonstrated on this issue"—but has also amplified the issue in ways that may have been avoidable, revealing deeper strategic and ideological flaws within the party's leadership.

Prime Minister Anthony Albanese's response to Senator Payman's actions seems to signal an attempt to manage party discipline and external perceptions simultaneously. By addressing the concerns of the Israel lobby while managing internal Caucus dissent, the Prime

Minister escalated a policy disagreement into a significant political crisis. This approach contrasts sharply with historical precedents within the party, where figures such as Tom Uren, Jim Cairns, and Kim Beazley senior crossed the floor on matters of principle in 1968, and went on to serve as respected senior figures within the party. Their actions were eventually seen not as breaches of discipline but as expressions of deeply held convictions, enriching the party's democratic and moral fibre.

The current party leadership's handling of the issue has inadvertently spotlighted the inconsistency between the ALP's stated foreign policy objectives—particularly its commitment to recognising Palestine—and its actions. This inconsistency is further compounded by the ongoing approval of military export permits to Israel and significant contracts with Israeli military tech firms—a $917 million contract was agreed to with Elbit Systems, a company which has supplied technology to the military junta in Myanmar and installed systems on military hardware which have been used to kill Palestinians—which starkly contradict the humanitarian values that many within the Labor Party advocate.

The decision to suspend Senator Payman could have been managed in a way that highlights the party's commitment to robust debate and democratic values, perhaps even strengthening its image as a genuinely progressive force. Instead, the leadership's actions have not only alienated a segment of its base—and the migrant community, especially those of Islamic backgrounds—but have also risked portraying the party as intolerant of dissent and resistant to the very ideals it purports to uphold. The issue of Palestine serves as a litmus test not just for the party's foreign policy but for its internal coherence and fidelity to its own principles.

It also presents the ALP with both a challenge and an opportunity—the challenge lies in reconciling the demands of party unity with the imperative to remain true to its democratic and progressive values. The opportunity is to reframe the narrative around this incident from one of discord to one of diversity of thought and commitment to principle, revitalising the party's appeal to a broader, more ideologically driven electorate.

While these opportunities are a long-term proposition—by which time, it may be too late—the ALP might consider embracing this episode as a catalyst for broader reforms within the party, particularly in terms of how it handles internal dissent and aligns its policies with its Platform. Failure to do so could not only diminish its credibility but also pave the way for a schism that could have long-term implications for its political future. The current situation could mark a significant turning point for the ALP, calling into question its capacity to adapt to the evolving political landscape and the expectations of its constituents. As the party navigates this crisis, the lessons it learns and the changes it implements could very well determine its trajectory in the coming years.

PUBLIC OPINION AND INTERNAL CHALLENGES SIGNAL CRITICAL TURNING POINT FOR ALBANESE

The resignation of Senator Payman is an issue that arrives at an unfavourable time for the Prime Minister, where opinion polls are suggesting a continuing dip in his approval ratings. Despite maintaining a lead as the preferred Prime Minister over Peter Dutton, Albanese's net approval rating has dropped to its lowest point in the Essential Point—a net negative of 9 points—indicating public disquiet with his leadership. This decline is particularly telling because it suggests that the electorate is responsive not only to large-scale policy decisions but also to the manner in which the party handles internal dissent and adheres to its stated principles.

Opinion polls, while not definitive predictors outside of election periods, do offer a snapshot of public sentiment that can inform party strategy. They highlight a vulnerability for the ALP, stemming from perceived inconsistencies between its Platform and its actions, especially on issues like the recognition of Palestine. This situation illustrates the broader challenge facing the party: aligning its internal governance and its external policy commitments with the expectations of its members and the electorate.

The specifics of Senator Payman's case reflect a wider issue within the ALP regarding its approach to international policy and minority rights, which has broader implications for voter perception and electoral outcomes. The controversy surrounding the suspension may seem minor in isolation, but it contributes cumulatively to shaping public perceptions of the ALP's integrity and responsiveness. This is particularly relevant in constituencies with significant Middle Eastern populations in western Sydney and outer Melbourne, where the issue of Palestine resonates on a deep, personal level, transcending from simple political debates to touch on significant aspects of human rights and international justice.

This also serves as a cautionary tale for the ALP leadership, highlights the importance of foresight and sensitivity in handling internal disputes that have external political ramifications. But in this case, the Labor Party has decided that stalling on the recognition of Palestine as a state—and avoiding conflicts with Israel lobby groups in Australia—is more important than losing a valuable seat in the Senate. The loss of Senator Payman's vote in the Senate—a crucial factor in future legislative processes—exemplifies the tangible consequences of internal party disagreements.

Albanese is an experienced politician, with 28 years in Parliament, and a lifetime in politics. An experienced politician should have been able to manage the process of recognising the state of Palestine, keeping the Israel lobby group at bay, and keeping a Senator whose vote is crucial to implementing the legislative agenda of the government. That Albanese has not been able to achieve any of these suggests that he's not as clever at politics as was previously understood, or that the 28 years in Parliament has made him impervious to the issues that really matter to the community and, ultimately, the membership of the Labor Party.

The party's ability—or inability—to reconcile its parliamentary actions with its Platform, manage internal dissent constructively, and uphold its commitments to both its members and the broader values it espouses will likely play a decisive role in shaping its future political fortunes. Its leadership would do well to consider not just the immediate impacts of their decisions but also the long-term implications for party cohesion, public trust, and electoral viability.

***

NAVIGATING ISLAMOPHOBIA IN AUSTRALIAN MEDIA AND POLITICS

13 July 2024

The narrative surrounding multiculturalism and media representation in Australia presents a complex and often contradictory narrative. The recent remarks by the Leader of the Opposition, Peter Dutton, exemplify a troubling pattern where political rhetoric not only reflects but exacerbates societal biases. Dutton's comments, which linked the prospect of a minority government with the inclusion of Muslim candidates from Western Sydney, implicitly cast these potential representatives as threats to political stability, in his words, "a disaster". Such statements are not isolated incidents but are part of a broader narrative that often surfaces in Australian political discourse.

The recent resignation of Senator Fatima Payman from the Labor Party to sit as an independent further fueled the media's engagement with themes of race and religion. Payman, a refugee from Afghanistan—*and visibly Muslim*—has been at the centre of what can be described as a media spectacle, with her actions and statements scrutinised and interpreted through a lens of racial and religious stereotypes. The coverage by various media outlets, from Seven West Media, the ABC and through to News Corporation, has varied in tone, but a common undercurrent of skepticism and fearmongering about Islam and its adherents persists.

Commentary provided by figures such as Andrew Bolt—who breached the *Racial Discrimination Act* for publishing racist material in 2009—claiming that with Payman's shift, "Australian politics just got more dangerous", illustrates how media figures can influence public perception by perpetuating narratives of fear and *otherness*. Bolt's derogatory remarks about Muslim victimhood and his targeting of Payman's background as a refugee highlights a broader media trend that often borders on—and surpasses—Islamophobia. Such narratives not only distort public discourse but also reinforce societal divisions by emphasising differences rather than commonalities.

This media portrayal does not exist in a vacuum. It interacts with and shapes the political landscape, where the fear of the 'other' can be a powerful tool in mobilising electoral support. The political utility of Islamophobia, as seen through the actions and words of some Australian politicians, raises questions about the role of media in either challenging or perpetuating these divisive strategies. While there are exceptions, such as the efforts of broadcasters like SBS to present a more nuanced and diverse perspective, the dominant media narrative tends to favour a portrayal of Australian society that prioritises Anglo-centric views and marginalises minority voices.

The presence in the media of figures such as Waleed Aly, Stan Grant, and Fauziah Ibrahim does offer alternative viewpoints, yet they often face a paradox. While their perspectives are crucial in fostering a more inclusive dialogue, their acceptance and success are contingent upon aligning with a predominantly conservative mainstream narrative. In Grant's case, when he strayed away from this narrative and offered his perspectives as an Indigenous Australian, he was severely criticised and ushered out of the media industry.

This dynamic illustrates the challenges faced by minority voices in gaining traction within a media landscape that is predominantly Anglo, male, and oriented towards centre-right political narratives.

Media representations and political rhetoric in Australia reveals a landscape fraught with challenges for minority communities, particularly for Muslims and especially since the events of 9/11 in the United States in 2001. The narrative not only reflects existing societal biases but also has the potential to shape political and social outcomes. Understanding and addressing these dynamics is crucial for moving towards a truly inclusive and representative Australian society.

THE STRUGGLE FOR SECULARISM AND DIVERSITY IN AUSTRALIAN PARLIAMENT

As Australia manages the ideals of multiculturalism and secularism, the practices within its political institutions reveal a continuing struggle to reconcile tradition with a diverse and changing demographic landscape. The recitation of the Lord's Prayer to commence Parliament—reintroduced by the Howard government in 1996—symbolises this tension. This ritual, ostensibly benign and reflective of moral aspirations, inadvertently highlights the incongruence between Australia's secular commitments and its ceremonial practices, marginalising non-Christian parliamentarians and, by extension, the diverse populace they represent.

The use of the Lord's Prayer as a parliamentary opener is more than just a formality; it is a symbolic act that highlights the perceived primacy of Christian values at the core of governmental proceedings, alienating members of other faiths and those with no religious affiliation. It also highlights how deeply embedded and normalised Christian norms are within the structures of Australian governance, despite the nation's secular policy and diverse religious landscape.

The representation in Parliament, although becoming more diverse, still lags behind the actual demographic makeup of Australia. The 2022 federal election brought in more representatives from various backgrounds, yet the political and cultural infrastructure has been slow to adapt. This sluggishness in embracing true diversity is further compounded by the media and political narratives that often view non-Christian participation, particularly Islamic, with suspicion and as a potential threat rather than a reflection of societal diversity.

The historical context of Australia's foundation as a secular nation, highlighted by the *Australia Act* of 1986, provides a constitutional backing for broader religious freedom and representation. The legacy of figures such as Alfred Deakin at the time of Federation in 1901 and his engagement with spiritualism and theosophy highlight the varied spiritual undercurrents that have shaped Australian public life, which are often overshadowed by the dominant Christian narrative.

The discussion around whether to remove the practice of reciting the Lord's Prayer in Parliament is not only about a procedural detail; it is emblematic of a larger debate about what values Australia wants to project and whose interests and beliefs it aims to reflect. The persistence of such a debate reveals the challenges that lie in fully actualising a secular and inclusive governance structure that respects and represents its citizens' diverse religious and cultural backgrounds.

This situation calls for a thoughtful re-evaluation of traditions that no longer serve the intended purpose of inclusivity and unity in a modern, multicultural society. Such re-evaluation is not an indictment of Christianity or any religion but a recognition of the need for Australia's political practices to mirror its democratic, pluralistic, and secular ideals. This ongoing tension between tradition and modernity in Australian politics highlights the need for a more conscious and deliberate approach to inclusivity, one that not only recognises diversity in parliamentary representation but also respects it in practice.

THE WANING INFLUENCE OF THE MAINSTREAM MEDIA ON AUSTRALIAN POLITICS

The downward spiral of media influence in Australia, particularly in the context of political outcomes, reflects a complex interaction between traditional media power and the shifting dynamics of public engagement and technological change. This transformation is evident in the declining ratings and influence of legacy media outlets, which have traditionally played a central role in shaping political debate and public opinion in Australia.

The decreasing relevance of mainstream media is highlighted by significant shifts within the industry itself, such as staff redundancies at major corporations like News Corporation, which is the largest employer of journalists and media staff in Australia. These changes are symptomatic of a broader transformation where the diversification of media platforms and the advent of digital media have fragmented the audience, offering alternatives that cater to a wider array of interests and viewpoints.

This fragmentation is mirrored in the political sphere, where the rhetoric of politicians such Dutton, who frequently frames Islam as a threat, or commentators like Bolt, who perpetuates negative stereotypes about Muslims, no longer uniformly sway the electorate. Instead, there appears to be a growing scepticism towards the media's portrayal of these issues, suggesting a deeper, more critical consumption of media content by the public. This shift implies that while mainstream media still has the power to reinforce existing prejudices, its ability to convert or significantly alter political views is waning.

The recent political events such as the election of the Albanese government in 2022 and the results of the Voice to Parliament referendum illustrate this nuanced role of the media. In both instances, despite strong media campaigns for opposing outcomes, the public voted differently, indicating that while media narratives can influence public opinion, they do not dictate it. This scenario suggests a more discerning electorate that engages with media content that aligns with their pre-existing beliefs rather than being passively shaped by it.

In addition, the general distaste for Dutton's public offerings, despite media efforts to bolster his image as a decisive leader, further demonstrates the limits of media influence in modern Australian politics. The public's disappointment with the Albanese government, on the other hand, reflects not just media criticism but also broader societal expectations and the complex realities of governance.

This evolving media landscape highlights a significant shift from a passive reception of media content to an active, critical engagement by the public. The growing schism between the politicians and media on one side and the electorate on the other indicates a changing dynamic where traditional media must adapt to remain relevant—if, indeed, it is not too late. This suggests that while the media still plays a critical role in political debate, its influence is modulated by a more informed and critical electorate capable of independent analysis and decision-making.

CAN POLITICAL BEHAVIOUR ADAPT TO THE CHANGING MEDIA LANDSCAPE

In the evolving dynamics between Australian politics and media, the relationship, although altered by digital transformations and shifting public perceptions, remains fundamentally interconnected. Politicians, irrespective of their ideological leanings, continue to rely on mainstream media to disseminate their messages, despite the decline in the media's sway over public opinion. This persistent dependency highlights a deep-seated inclination towards traditional platforms of communication, which, though waning in effectiveness, still hold symbolic and practical value for political figures.

The media's influence, while diluted, is far from extinguished and maintains a psychological hold over politicians, who often measure their own relevance and the impact of their policies through the lens of media coverage. This is reflected in the attention they pay to headlines and news stories, where visibility in mainstream outlets is still equated with political potency. Consequently, even as the power of these outlets wanes in the digital era, their endorsement or criticism remains a coveted prize in political circles.

This enduring relationship reveals a conservative approach to political communication, where innovation is often sacrificed for familiarity. The reluctance to fully embrace newer, more direct methods of engagement such as social media or alternative news platforms highlights a hesitancy to break away from established norms. This is not only a matter of habit but a calculated decision rooted in the perceived risks of alienating traditional media power bases, most notably players such as Kerry Stokes and Rupert Murdoch. Politicians, aware of the media's capacity to shape narratives, are cautious of incurring their ire, which can amplify opposition and stir public sentiment.

However, this dynamic is not without its critics and potential for reform. The suggestion of a governmental inquiry into media ownership and the regulation of media licenses points to a growing recognition of the need for greater media diversity and accountability. Such measures, though fraught with political risk due to potential backlash from powerful media conglomerates, could significantly alter the landscape of political communication. By diminishing the concentrated power of a few media entities, the government could encourage a more pluralistic media environment that better represents Australia's diverse population and offers a wider array of viewpoints.

Taking these issues into account, the challenge is one of courage and political will. The transformation of the media–political nexus would require not only regulatory changes but also a cultural shift within politics itself, where short-term gains through conventional media channels are weighed against the long-term benefits of a more engaged and representative public discourse. The inertia of the status quo is a formidable barrier, with governments often opting for the path of least resistance, which sustains existing power structures and communication strategies.

While the influence of mainstream media on political outcomes may be diminishing, its role within the political process remains significant and the future of this relationship hinges on the ability of politicians to adapt to new realities of media consumption and public engagement. Forging a new path will involve rethinking not just the tools of communication but also the underlying assumptions about power and influence in the digital age. As Australia continues to go through the challenges of racism and Islamophobia, the evolution of this media–political landscape will be crucial in shaping more inclusive and effective governance.

***

RELIGION IN POLITICS: SHOULD WE BE WARY OR ACCEPT ITS INFLUENCE?

14 July 2024

The emergence of the Muslim Vote group in Australia signifies a new dynamic in the political landscape. Unlike a traditional political party, this group focuses on educating and mobilising voters on specific issues, particularly those related to events and international injustice in Palestine. By supporting independent candidates in Labor-held seats in Western Sydney and Melbourne, the Muslim Vote mirrors the strategy of Climate 200, which successfully supported independents in Liberal-held seats during the 2019 and 2022 federal elections. However, the Muslim Vote has sparked significant backlash from the mainstream media and establishment politics, with sensationalist claims about the impending imposition of Sharia law and dire warnings about Australia's future.

The criticism of the Muslim Vote highlights a deep-seated inconsistency in Australian politics, where religious influence is selectively tolerated. For instance, former prime ministers Kevin Rudd and Scott Morrison openly expressed their faiths while they were in office, as does the current Prime Minister Anthony Albanese, albeit to a much lesser extent. The Speaker of the House of Representatives, Milton Dick, is scheduled as a guest speaker at the ROAR Leaders Summit in September, organised by the evangelist Breakthrough Church to explore the Seven Mountains Mandate to conquer the key spheres of influence in society and "what God is doing in various spheres of influence" and the "importance of kingdom leadership".

The Christian Democrats have also maintained a political presence in New South Wales Parliament over many decades and although they are a very small political player, they do regularly feature in federal campaigns. This selective acceptance is evident in the continued recitation of the Lord's Prayer in parliament and this raises questions about why Islamic influence is viewed with suspicion while other and sometimes more extreme and reactionary religious influences are accepted.

The argument could—and should—be made that religion must be entirely absent from politics, reflecting the doctrine of separation of the church from state, a key feature of democratic systems for almost 400 years. However, since religious influence is already entrenched in Australian politics, is it fair to discriminate against Islamic participation while tolerating other faiths? The electorate, as the ultimate decision-maker, should determine the acceptability of religious influence through democratic processes. The current trend in Australia shows a decline in religious adherence, with fewer people attending church or other religious gatherings than ever before. Nonetheless, can the presence of religious individuals and their participation in politics be respected, provided it aligns with democratic principles?

The political landscape in Australia has seen the detrimental effects of religious factions within political parties, particularly the influence of Pentecostalism. The Victorian Liberal Party, for example, has faced significant challenges due to the dominance of Pentecostal factions, rendering it unelectable in many respects. In contrast, the NSW Liberal Party appears to be cautiously navigating this issue, learning from the Victorian experience to avoid similar pitfalls. The upcoming state election in Queensland will further test the influence of religious factions within the Liberal–National Party.

The case of Katherine Deves, a prominent Pentecostal figure who ran as a candidate for the Liberal Party in the 2022 federal election on religious–transgender issues and failed to reclaim the seat of Warringah from Zali Steggall, highlights the limited appeal of overtly religious candidates. Steggall, a relatively secular candidate, managed to resonate with her community more effectively, suggesting that voters prioritise local representation over religious affiliation—religion seems to be acceptable, as long as it remains a *private matter*. This trend is likely to influence the broader acceptance of groups like the Muslim Vote, as long as they focus on informing and empowering their communities on key issues such as Palestine *as a political issue*, rather than imposing religious doctrines.

A POTENTIAL GAME-CHANGER IN THE UPCOMING FEDERAL ELECTION

The influence of the Muslim Vote group on the next Australian federal election, especially in Labor-held seats in Western Sydney, is an issue of considerable interest. Drawing parallels to the British Muslim Vote group, which successfully supported four independent candidates against Labour contenders and reduced majorities in many other constituencies, the potential impact in Australia is significant. Although the British Parliament's 650 seats render four victories relatively minor, the Australian Labor Party must take notice, especially given their narrow five-seat majority in a 151-seat parliament and the possible nominal loss of one seat due to electoral redistributions.

The Muslim Vote group's focus on Justice for Palestine is prominently displayed on their website and resonates with the concerns of many Muslim and non-Muslim Australians concerned about the ongoing genocide in Gaza. Key seats in Western Sydney, such as Watson and Blaxland, held by Tony Burke and Jason Clare respectively, have substantial Islamic populations—approximately 25 per cent in Watson and 31 per cent in Blaxland. While an Islamic background does not guarantee support for an independent candidate from the same background, even half of these populations voting independently could shift these seats into marginal territory, although the ultimate effect will depend on the quality of the independent candidates and the broader electoral context.

Critics might argue that the influence of Muslim Vote in only a few seats is negligible. However, in a tightly contested election where every seat counts, this could be critical. Comparing the Muslim Vote to the Teal movement from 2019 onwards, or even further back to the rise of One Nation in 1997, provides a framework for understanding its potential impact. One Nation, though vastly different ideologically, similarly represented a group of disaffected voters finding a political voice and disrupting the status quo. The Prime Minister at the time, John Howard, used strategic "dog-whistling" and manipulative management of One Nation voters to bring them back to the Liberal Party, and these tactics highlight how mainstream parties can mitigate the effects of such movements, if they have the will and the skill to do this.

For the Labor Party, understanding and addressing the grievances of Muslim Australians and others in the electorate who are deeply concerned and distressed about the government's indifference to the events in Gaza, is crucial. This includes differentiating between legitimate concerns and misconceptions, many of which are perpetuated by sensationalist media coverage. The portrayal of the Muslim Vote as a gateway to Sharia law reflects a lack of understanding and a tendency to invoke fear rather than engage with the real issues. The vast majority of Muslims do not support such extreme interpretations, highlighting the diversity of thought within Islam—a complexity often overlooked by the media.

Addressing the concerns of the Muslim Vote group does not imply yielding to extremist demands but rather recognising and integrating the legitimate aspirations of a significant community within Australia's multicultural society. This approach could prevent the marginalisation of Muslim Australians and strengthen the democratic fabric of the nation. The upcoming federal election will test the extent to which the Labor Party can adapt to this new political reality and whether they can successfully engage with and integrate the voices represented by the Muslim Vote.

THE GOVERNMENT'S MISGUIDED STRATEGY OF FAVOURING CONSERVATIVE JEWISH GROUPS

The current political behaviour of the Labor government regarding the Palestine issue is perplexing, especially given the historical context of political leaders navigating conflicting issues with skill—Howard's adept and cynical management of One Nation is a case in point, demonstrating how a leader can keep various sides of an issue satisfied (to some extent) and minimise political risks to the government of the day.

However, the Labor government's approach to the Palestine issue seems to lack this nuanced strategy. They have already lost a Senator over this issue and risk losing additional seats in Western Sydney due to their alignment with Israel over Palestine. This approach not only jeopardises their standing in specific constituencies but also fails to offer any clear electoral advantage elsewhere in the country. Why would a government continue down a path that has lost a member of Caucus, produced great hostility with its membership and supporters, and could ultimately result in losing either its parliamentary majority, or losing government entirely at the next federal election?

The influence of the right-wing Israel lobby within Australian politics is evident in these actions and the decision by Prime Minister Anthony Albanese to appoint a special envoy to combat antisemitism, Jillian Segal, further illustrates this point. While addressing antisemitism is undoubtedly important, the choice of Segal, who is known for her pro-Israel and Zionist stance, and support of the Israel Defense Forces' actions in Gaza, raises serious concerns, and the appointment favours conservative Jewish lobby groups while sidelining progressive Jewish voices.

This appointment has been criticised by members of the Jewish community who feel it misrepresents the diversity of Jewish perspectives on Israel and Palestine. Sarah Schwartz, CEO of the Jewish Council of Australia, did emphasise that antisemitism is a serious and rising issue, but suggested the government's choice of envoy who lacks a background in fighting anti-racism and, instead, has a history of lobbying for Israel, could be used politically to stifle voices supporting Palestinian rights and does not enhance the safety of Jewish people in Australia.

The Labor government's siding with the conservative side of the Jewish community, particularly in the context of appointing a pro-Israel envoy, illustrates their alignment with certain influential lobby groups. This strategy, however, overlooks the broader spectrum of Jewish opinions and fails to address the legitimate concerns of those who support Palestinian human rights. By not engaging with these progressive voices, the government risks alienating a significant portion of the electorate that values a more balanced and human-rights-focused approach to the Israel–Palestine conflict.

SYMBOLIC GESTURES FALL SHORT IN ADDRESSING BROADER ISSUES OF DISCRIMINATION

Prime Minister Albanese announced that he would also appoint a special envoy to combat Islamophobia, but this announcement seems to have come as an afterthought rather than a serious commitment. Islamophobia has long been a significant issue for the Islamic community in Australia and if the government was genuinely committed to combating discrimination, why not announce the special envoy for Islamophobia simultaneously with the one for antisemitism? The staggered approach suggests a reactive rather than a proactive stance, casting doubt on the sincerity of these initiatives.

The necessity and efficacy of these special envoys are debatable. Australia already has an Anti-Discrimination Commissioner and a Human Rights Commission that have been effectively addressing issues of discrimination for years. Appointing additional special envoys seems redundant and politically motivated, serving more as a token gesture than a genuine solution. Antisemitism is unacceptable, as is any form of discrimination. However, creating specific envoy positions without a comprehensive strategy appears to be more about appeasement than about real change.

The broader issue at stake is how to combat *all* forms of discrimination and ensure that every Australian citizen lives safely and peacefully, without harassment based on their background or beliefs. The focus should not be on protecting certain segments of society while neglecting others but on fostering an inclusive environment for all. The government's current strategy, marked by knee-jerk reactions and a lack of comprehensive planning, falls short of this ideal.

A more thoughtful approach would involve a genuine commitment to addressing *all* forms of discrimination equally and transparently. This means listening to and incorporating the voices of all affected communities, not just the most politically influential ones. It means leveraging existing frameworks such as the Human Rights Commission more effectively rather than creating redundant positions. Ultimately, it requires a shift from reactive to proactive governance, where the safety and wellbeing of all citizens are paramount.

The Labor government's current handling of the Palestine issue and its approach to addressing discrimination reflect a problematic strategy driven more by political appeasement than by genuine commitment to justice and equality. A more inclusive and proactive strategy is essential to ensure that all Australians, regardless of their background, can live free from discrimination and harassment.

***

THE SURREAL STATE OF AMERICAN POLITICS

20 July 2024

The recent attempted assassination of U.S. Presidential candidate Donald Trump during a public rally is a reminder of the unpredictable and often surreal nature of contemporary American politics. In a country where bizarre and shocking events are becoming almost routine, this incident still managed to stand out due to its sheer audacity and the subsequent controversies it has sparked—the shooter, positioned on a rooftop in clear view of the rally attendees, initiated a sequence of events that felt more like a scene from a Hollywood thriller than real life, and the Secret Service's inept response and the overall security lapse have drawn intense scrutiny and debate.

After the assassin was killed by Secret Services, the scene escalated dramatically, with Trump appearing as a defiant, bloodstained figure, pumping his fist before being hurried off stage. This image alone has fueled a wave of speculation and conspiracy theories, with many questioning the authenticity of the event and it is this scepticism that highlights the deeply polarised and distrustful state of American politics.

Trump's reaction to the incident, notably his decision to make a public show of defiance immediately afterward, aligns with his known penchant for dramatic and often reckless behaviour. Comparing this incident to the 1981 assassination attempt on President Ronald Reagan highlights the differences in security responses—Reagan was swiftly shielded and removed from danger without theatrics, whereas Trump's response was more visibly chaotic and less controlled.

The broader implications of this event are significant. It highlights the deteriorating trust in political narratives and the increasing tendency of the public to question official accounts. However, it is Trump's history of public deceit since his 2015 campaign that complicates the public's ability to discern truth from fabrication and this erosion of trust in the political system is symptomatic of a deeper malaise affecting American democracy.

Adding to this complexity is President Joe Biden's unexpected decision to withdraw from the 2024 election campaign, and this development introduces a new layer of uncertainty and speculation into an already volatile political climate. While he will remain President until January 2025, Biden's withdrawal is a pragmatic response to his poor political campaign performance and the growing turmoil and polarisation, and a strategic move within a broader, more convoluted game of political chess being played out by the Democrats.

Within the context of these extraordinary events, the challenges of restoring trust and ensuring effective governance in the United States become ever more daunting, and these factors set the stage for a deeply contentious and unpredictable political future, not just for America, but the international community as well.

THE POLITICAL SPECTACLE AND THE RAMIFICATIONS

In the days following the attempt, Trump made a dramatic and extravagant appearance at the Republican convention, sporting a conspicuous bandage on his ear, serving as a poignant reminder of the attempt on his life, ensuring the event remained fresh in the minds of the public and reinforcing his narrative of victimhood.

Trump's fist-pumping moment, captured with blood on his face against the backdrop of the American flag, was a masterclass in political theatre. The Secret Service's pause on the stage seemed to allow photographers to frame the perfect shot leading to many people believing the incident was choreographed but whatever the case, the image evoked a powerful response from Trump, in his attempt to solidify his media persona as a defiant patriot who narrowly escaped death.

In politics, such moments are invaluable and it's obvious that a political party—especially a U.S. Republican party—will exploit the circumstances for political gain. The comparisons to the Reichstag fire of 1933, where the Nazis exploited the event to consolidate power by blaming their opponents, are not far-fetched. MAGA Republicans quickly pointed fingers at Biden and the Democrats for responsibility for this attack, despite the shooter being a registered Republican. The truth of the attack's origins and the intentions behind it became secondary to the narrative that Trump was a survivor of an assassination attempt and this narrative alone was potent enough to galvanise his base supporters and frame the election campaign narrative.

For Trump's base, this incident reinforced their loyalty, portraying him as a martyr under siege. Conversely, the Democratic base, already fragmented and uncertain, was thrown into further disarray, until the moment that Biden withdrew his nomination. The incident didn't seem to sway undecided voters or shift the polls significantly, although it may be too early to see how the voting patterns will be affected by this event. Unlike more mainstream candidates, Trump's support base is deeply entrenched, driven by a mix of admiration and revulsion that leaves little room for neutrality.

The announcement of JD Vance as Trump's vice-presidential pick the day after the assassination attempt was a strange move, one fraught with risk, considering that he is an even more polarising and ideologically-driven candidate than Trump, despised by both Republicans and Democrats. This choice might parallel Sarah Palin's selection by John McCain in 2008—a move that initially energised the base but ultimately alienated broader support. This choice could also deter swing voters and those disenchanted with Trump's antics, potentially weakening his position despite the initial rallying effect of the assassination attempt.

The shooting, initially dominating the news cycle, quickly receded as the focus shifted to Trump's vice-presidential announcement and Trump's strategy appears to be a high-risk gamble that hinges on maintaining the fervour of his core supporters while trying to navigate the broader electorate's complex landscape.

This incident encapsulates the surreal and often bewildering state of American politics. The attempted assassination, instead of becoming a sobering moment of reflection and unity, has been weaponised in the relentless pursuit of political gain. As the dust settles from this dramatic week of an attempted assassination on Trump and Biden's resignation from the campaign, it remains unclear how this will influence the broader dynamics of the 2024 election. The narrative of Trump's survival and his subsequent choices reflect a political environment where spectacle often overshadows substance, and the line between reality and performance becomes increasingly blurred.

GLOBAL REACTIONS AND DEMOCRATIC CHALLENGES

The Prime Minister Anthony Albanese expressed solidarity with the American people, condemning the violence and emphasising shared democratic values and his response highlights the global resonance of such events and the intricate web of political and cultural ties that bind nations like Australia and the United States.

Albanese's statement highlighted the fundamental principles of democracy: the right to express views, debate disagreements, and resolve differences peacefully. His remarks, while supportive and diplomatic, also reflected a sense of disbelief and concern about the state of American politics. The pervasive gun violence, epitomised by the Capitol Hill riots in 2021 and frequent mass shootings, paints a picture of a nation dealing with deep-seated issues. Despite these challenges, American leaders, including Biden, have repeatedly stated that such violence does not define the nation, claiming that "this is not who we are". However, the persistence of these issues suggests otherwise: this is exactly what America is.

Trump's rhetoric has consistently been a catalyst for division and violence. His refusal to accept the 2020 election results and his incitement of the Capitol Hill riots are prime examples of his incendiary approach. His public statements often flirt with calls for retribution, violence and chaos, which resonate with a significant portion of the electorate that seems to thrive on the unpredictability and drama he brings to the political arena. This chaotic atmosphere characterised much of his first term in office, leading to discussions about invoking the 25th Amendment due to his perceived unfitness for the presidency.

The tumultuous nature of Trump's presidency, marked by corruption, incompetence, and daily drama, raises serious questions about his suitability for office. Despite these concerns, his base remains steadfast, yearning for more of the same chaos and instability. The charges against him and the possibility of further legal consequences—remembering that Trump is already a convicted felon for illegally influencing the outcome of the 2016 election—also highlight the gravity of his actions. Yet, his support remains robust, particularly in the context of polling data that, despite being hard to believe, shows him as a serious contender in the 2024 election.

The international perspective, as seen through the reactions from Australian leaders and public discourse, reveals a mixture of bemusement and concern. Australia's political landscape, while different in many respects, still shares the values of democratic governance and peaceful resolution of conflicts, although Trump's behaviour after the 2020 election and the subsequent Capitol Hill riots suggests that this is not always the case.

THE LOOMING THREAT OF A TRUMP VICTORY AND GLOBAL IMPLICATIONS

Many commentators—and betting markets—are now suggesting that a Trump victory in the 2024 presidential election seems almost inevitable, unless the Democrats can rally behind a strong replacement for Biden, who is likely to be Kamala Harris, the current Vice-President. With the election just four months away, the political landscape is still volatile, and anything could happen, and history is littered with examples where candidates were predicted to win an election, yet unexpectedly failed at the final hurdle: Michael Dukakis in 1988, George H. Bush in 1992, Al Gore in 2000, Hilary Clinton in 2016. It's a cliché but polls are meaningless in deciding elections: it's the tally of the vote on the election day that matters the most.

However, it feels as though American politics is being swept along by the chaotic force that is Donald Trump, and his brand of politics is far more disruptive and damaging that anything seen before in contemporary American politics and is supported by a cadre of dangerous ideologues.

The emergence of figures associated with Project 2025 and the conservative Heritage Foundation signals a more organised yet ominous approach than Trump's previous term as President between 2017–2021. If elected, Trump would likely be more prepared to implement his agenda, but in ways that could further destabilise American democracy through a lethal mixture of fascism and evangelism.

Prime Minister Albanese has emphasised the shared values between the U.S. and Australia, but the alignment needs to stop short of endorsing the extreme elements backing Trump. These ideologues represent a dangerous shift that Australia, and the world, must be wary of. The potential for a second Trump presidency brings significant concerns, particularly in the context of global power dynamics. With China's continuing rise, another term for Trump might accelerate America's decline as the pre-eminent global power. While the U.S. is expected to survive even a Trump presidency, the damage to its institutions and international standing could be profound and Australia would be wise to reassess its relationship with the U.S. if Trump returns to power, given the likely negative repercussions.

Generally, there is a deep and abiding reverence among the American people for institutions such as the Supreme Court and the office of the presidency. This respect is something that Trump has repeatedly undermined, and it could be his undoing with moderate voters. The Project 2025 manifesto, seen by many as a thinly veiled fascist agenda, threatens the foundational values of American democracy and Trump's disregard for institutional norms may alienate the political centre, potentially thwarting his bid for re-election.

The initial shock of the assassination attempt on Trump has faded into the background, and has been overshadowed by subsequent events and controversies. The focus has now shifted to Kamala Harris as the Democratic frontrunner, with Trump and the Republicans launching crude and unhinged attacks against her, again, a reaction that highlights the bizarre and volatile state of American politics, especially from the reactionary parts of the Republican party.

In this strange and unpredictable time, the 2024 election promises to be a watershed moment. The direction America takes will have profound implications not only for its own future but for global stability and democratic values worldwide. The challenges posed by Trump's potential return to power, coupled with the internal difficulties within the Democratic Party, set the stage for a fiercely contested and important election. The outcome will determine whether the U.S. can navigate through this tumultuous period and emerge with its democratic institutions intact.

***

ICJ RULING CONDEMNS ISRAEL'S OCCUPATION OF PALESTINIAN TERRITORIES

27 July 2024

The International Court of Justice has unequivocally ruled that Israel's occupation of Palestinian territories is illegal under international law and the court's findings highlight numerous breaches of international statutes by Israel, mandating an immediate cessation of the occupation and full reparations for the extensive damage inflicted since 1967. This landmark ruling represents the most definitive legal condemnation of Israel's actions by an international judicial body to date.

Despite the historical tendency of major powers to dismiss unfavourable rulings from international institutions, the ICJ's decision has intensified calls for tangible actions, particularly from the Australian government. In response, Foreign Minister Senator Penny Wong issued a statement urging Israel to halt the expansion of settlements and to curb settler violence in the West Bank and the Albanese government, which keeps saying it is "committed to a two-state solution" without doing anything to move towards that position, is now evaluating potential measures, including financial sanctions and travel bans on specific Israeli settlers and groups implicated in violence.

Senator Wong emphasised that sanctions are "a significant measure", usually reserved as a last resort in foreign policy, with individuals targeted by these sanctions have been involved in severe acts of violence against Palestinians in the West Bank, including beatings, sexual assaults, and torture, resulting in serious injuries and fatalities. While Senator Wong insists that these sanctions reflect careful consideration, the measures have been criticised as insufficient, reflecting a continued reluctance to alienate influential pro-Israel lobbies within Australia.

The actions of the Israel Defense Forces are undeniably acts of genocide, particularly given the deliberate targeting of non-combatants, children, and the destruction of essential infrastructure such as schools and hospitals, and this factor adds a grave dimension to this issue—despite what the government of Israel continues to claim, this is not a conventional military conflict but a systematic campaign against a civilian population, demanding a swift and robust international response which, so far, has been lacking.

Senator Wong's call to stop settlement expansion in the West Bank without an equal demand to withdraw, also suggests a tacit acceptance of the current status quo, which many argue is insufficient and advocates insist on a reversion to the pre-1967 borders, a stance supported by a substantial segment of the international community. Some commentators argue that a return to the 1948 borders is critical, though this is viewed as politically impractical by most experts—at this stage. The two-state solution, while contentious among Palestinians, remains the most widely endorsed framework for resolving the conflict.

The Australian government's position, while rhetorically firm, continues to navigate the delicate balance of international diplomacy and domestic political pressures. The ICJ's ruling, however, injects renewed urgency into the debate, compelling nations such as Australia to reconcile their foreign policy with the imperatives of international justice and human rights, and ignore the demands and influence of domestic conservative Israel lobby groups. This path forward is fraught with challenges, but the strong calls for justice and accountability cannot be ignored forever.

AUSTRALIA CAN ASSERT INFLUENCE AND SUPPORT PALESTINE THROUGH STRONGER DIPLOMATIC ACTION

While the Australian government would not be expected to take extreme measures such as physically or militarily intervening in the conflict, there remains a broad spectrum of actions it could undertake to support Palestine, including imposing sanctions on the Israeli government, severing trade relationships with Israel, recalling the Israeli ambassador, and recognising the state of Palestine—which the Labor Party promised when they returned to government—and extending travel bans to more Israeli citizens involved in the occupation and violence. Such actions would signal a significant shift in Australia's foreign policy, demonstrating a commitment to holding Israel accountable for its violations of international law.

Critics may argue that these measures will not immediately halt the ongoing violence in Gaza, and they would be correct. However, the weight of the ICJ's ruling provides a legal and moral foundation for these actions. By aligning its policies with international law, Australia can exert increased pressure on Israel to change its behaviour in the occupied territories, including a withdrawal from the West Bank and Golan Heights, as well as ceasing and removing the military slaughter in Gaza. The initial sanctions targeting seven Israeli settlers and a youth group are a minimalist first step, but they must be expanded to create meaningful impact.

Drawing parallels with the anti-apartheid movement in South Africa, history has shown that sustained economic and diplomatic pressure can lead to significant political change. It took years of concerted international efforts to dismantle apartheid, and a similar approach is necessary to address the Israeli occupation. While immediate political solution for those suffering in Gaza is unlikely, a robust and persistent stance by the international community, including Australia, can contribute to longer-term solutions. However, Palestine cannot wait as long as South Africa did to end apartheid, which essentially took over 30 years: immediate action is required by the international community to end the genocide in Gaza and bring lasting peace to the Middle East.

The role of Australia's foreign minister is undeniably complex, particularly in the delicate arena of Middle Eastern politics. Directly confronting allies, such as the United States, is not a straightforward option, given Australia's limited influence in the region and its broader strategic interests and this geopolitical reality necessitates a nuanced approach, balancing diplomatic relations while advocating for justice and human rights.

Despite these constraints, Australia can still assert its independence and express strong, principled views. Diplomatic channels can be used effectively to convey Australia's stance without jeopardising essential alliances. Senator Wong—or any foreign minister—must navigate this fine line, articulating Australia's positions firmly but tactfully. The challenge lies in reconciling Australia's strategic interests with its commitment to upholding international law and supporting human rights.

Recognition of the state of Palestine would be a powerful statement, aligning Australia with the growing number of countries acknowledging Palestinian statehood. Such recognition would not only bolster Palestine's international standing but also highlight Australia's commitment to a just and lasting peace in the region. Similarly, recalling the Israeli ambassador and severing trade ties would send a clear message of disapproval of Israel's actions, reinforcing the international community's calls for accountability.

Extending travel bans to more Israeli citizens involved in the occupation and violence would further isolate those responsible and increase pressure on Israel to change its policies. While these measures alone will not resolve the conflict, they represent critical steps towards a comprehensive international response. However, these actions also involve political courage and the Australian government has shown little empathy for the plight of the Palestinian people so far. Certainly, the diplomatic path is fraught with challenges, but the pursuit of justice and peace demands bold and decisive action.

CHINESE-BROKERED UNITY DEAL MARKS A MAJOR DEVELOPMENT IN MIDDLE EASTERN DIPLOMACY

A significant event has also taken place that has largely gone unreported in the Australian media: a unity deal brokered by the Chinese government involving Hamas, Fatah, and 12 other Palestinian political groups. This development is particularly noteworthy as Fatah and Hamas have been political adversaries for decades and the accord, which fosters political accommodation among these 14 groups, marks a potential turning point for Palestinian governance and unity.

The efficacy of this accord remains uncertain as it has not yet been tested. However, it represents a crucial step towards the full recognition of the state of Palestine. One common criticism has been that Palestine lacks a unified government capable of effectively governing, yet, it is crucial to consider the severe constraints faced by any Palestinian administration: governing an area likened to an open-air concentration camp, under blockade by land and sea, subjected to apartheid-like conditions by Israel, deprived of free movement, and continuously bombarded and attacked by Israeli Defense Forces and settlers in the West Bank. The conditions are such that running an effective government is an extraordinary challenge.

This unity deal is significant for several reasons, not least because it signals China's entrance into Middle Eastern diplomacy in a substantial way. By brokering this deal, China is stepping into a role traditionally occupied by Western powers, which have historically exacerbated problems in the region and this move can be seen as China asserting that it can resolve conflicts in the Middle East more effectively than the West. While the deal will not end the conflict immediately, it is a critical development that could pave the way for more significant changes.

Historically, the disunity among Palestinian resistance groups has been a major obstacle and this lack of cohesion among these groups has meant that the Palestinian people had little choice but to follow fragmented leaderships. The unity brokered by China could be a game changer, and bringing together factions that have historically despised each other means there is now a potential for concerted and effective action.

China's intervention also signifies its growing role on the world stage. By facilitating this unity deal, China is demonstrating its capability and willingness to engage in high-stakes international diplomacy, a domain where it has previously been reticent. This development is likely to provoke a strong reaction from Western media outlets, especially those aligned with the interests of the News

Corporation empire, as it highlights a diplomatic achievement that the West has failed to secure.

The United States, in particular, has been largely dormant in Middle Eastern diplomacy over the past couple of decades and its current approach is a relic of Cold War politics, inadequate for addressing the contemporary complexities of the region. China's proactive stance in brokering the Palestinian unity deal exposes the limitations of the American and broader Western diplomatic strategies, potentially heralding a new era of Chinese influence in the Middle East. The impact of this deal remains to be seen, but it undoubtedly represents a critical shift in the dynamics of the Israeli-Palestinian conflict and the broader geopolitical landscape.

LABOR PARTY FACES INTERNAL TENSIONS AND ELECTORAL RISK OVER PALESTINE

Amidst these international developments, the recent NSW Labor Conference held at Sydney Town Hall highlights the growing internal tensions within the Australian Labor Party regarding the recognition of Palestinian statehood. The conference—again—voted to urge the Australian government to promptly recognise Palestine as a sovereign and independent state, echoing a similar motion approved at the previous year's national conference. This repeated call, which also reflects the contents of the Labor Plarform agreed to in 2021, raises a critical question: what is the Labor government waiting for?

A clear schism is developing between the parliamentary members and the Labor rank-and-file membership, where the latter are striving to adhere to core Labor values of justice, human dignity, and solidarity, while the former appears indifferent and cautious, potentially gambling on the belief that this issue will not critically affect their safe seats in Western Sydney at the next election. However, this assumption may prove to be a significant miscalculation.

The frustration and impatience within key Labor-held electorates are palpable. Western Sydney, with its substantial and vocal pro-Palestinian community, is particularly aggrieved by the federal government's inaction. This discontent was visibly manifested when a large crowd of pro-Palestinian protesters gathered outside the Town Hall during the conference, some of whom heckled delegates as they exited. The activists voiced their frustrations over the government's failure to recognise Palestine and demanded more robust diplomatic actions against Israel, which has been responsible for the deaths of over 40,000 Palestinians in Gaza over the past 10 months and, according to *Lancet* magazine, possibly up to 186,000 deaths.

This growing dissatisfaction poses a potential electoral risk for the Labor government and the party's traditional support base in Western Sydney, which has historically delivered safe seats, may not be as secure as assumed. If the government continues to delay decisive action on Palestinian statehood, it risks alienating a significant portion of its voter base, who are deeply committed to justice for Palestine. This issue could become a focal point in the next federal election, with voters seeking to hold their representatives accountable for their stance on this critical international issue.

The broader implications of inaction extend beyond electoral politics. By failing to respond decisively to the calls for recognising Palestinian statehood, the Labor government undermines its own professed values and principles, and it also risks diminishing Australia's credibility on the international stage as a nation committed to upholding human rights and international law.

Of course, the current hesitation to take stronger action will be influenced by various factors, including geopolitical considerations and domestic political calculations. However, the growing discontent within the party and among the electorate suggests that the Labor government cannot afford to remain passive. Recognising Palestine as a sovereign state would not only align with international legal standards, as emphasised by the decision by the ICJ, but it would also resonate deeply with the values and expectations of many Labor supporters, as well as many members of the general community.

The Labor government's lack of action in addressing the concerns of Palestinians and recognising Palestinian statehood may have significant repercussions in the next election and the discontent within the party and among key electorates in Western Sydney cannot be ignored. The government must reconcile its policies with the core values of justice and human dignity that it professes to uphold, or it risks facing a strong electoral backlash. Recognising Palestinian statehood and taking decisive diplomatic actions will not only fulfill a moral and legal imperative but also secure the trust and support of its voter base, ensuring a stronger and more unified party moving forward.

***

UNPACKING THE AUSTRALIAN MEDIA'S PREOCCUPATION WITH A U.S. ELECTION

28 July 2024

In recent weeks, the Australian media landscape has been saturated with exhaustive coverage of the U.S. presidential campaign, despite the election still being four months away and Australians not having a vote in its outcome. This intense focus has sparked a debate on the appropriateness and impact of such extensive foreign political coverage, especially when positioned against significant domestic issues that arguably warrant more attention.

The recent events in U.S. politics have indeed been dramatic and newsworthy: a shocking assassination attempt on former President Donald Trump, and an unexpected withdrawal by President Joe Biden from his re-election campaign, presumably paving the way for Vice President Kamala Harris to assume the Democratic nomination. These developments have understandably dominated global headlines due to their implications on international relations and global stability.

However, the extent of the coverage by Australian outlets raises questions. For example, the ABC prominently featured U.S. politics across its platforms, with such stories consistently topping its most viewed articles. Similarly, major publications like *The Guardian* and the *Sydney Morning Herald* have followed suit, leading with U.S. political news over local Australian stories.

To keep pushing the issue of U.S. politics in different ways after the more substantial stories began to ebb, *The Guardian* went to the effort and expense of surveying 1,137 Australians last week, asking who they would vote for in the U.S. election if they could, even though Harris is not yet the endorsed Democratic candidate, even though the election is still four months away, and even though Australians cannot vote in U.S. elections. It's hard to see how a vanity exercise of this kind serves the public interest for an Australian audience. Is it essential to know that 29 percent of those surveyed would vote for Trump and the Republicans, or that 37 percent would vote for Harris and the Democrats?

This phenomenon isn't merely a matter of media preference but reflects a deeper global interconnectivity where American political shifts significantly influence economies and policies worldwide. Nevertheless, the saturation of U.S. politics in Australian media has had unintended consequences, primarily the overshadowing of pressing local issues. At a time when Australian politics also faces unprecedented developments, the predominance of U.S. news stories seems disproportionate.

Critics argue that this focus diverts attention from critical Australian issues that need addressing, from environmental policies and economic reforms to social justice initiatives. The rapid cycle of news coming out of the United States, including the rapid consolidation of Democratic support around Harris, mirrors a media fascination with American politics that often eclipses local content, leaving citizens less informed about their own governmental affairs. This has implications for public understanding and engagement with complex issues, both domestic and foreign.

The debate over the volume and tone of U.S. political coverage in Australia raises a central question about the role of media in shaping not just what people think, but what they think about in the first place.

SPECTACLE VS. SUBSTANCE: THE IMPACT OF PERSONALITY-DRIVEN COVERAGE ON POLITICS

The portrayal of political leaders in the media often reflects not just the society's interest in their personalities and policies but also the media's own business-driven need to attract viewers and readers. This dynamic is exemplified in the case of Donald Trump, whose media coverage often resembles more of a spectacle than a serious political discourse. This phenomenon is not unique to Trump; a range of global political figures including Boris Johnson in Britain, Jair Bolsonaro in Brazil, Viktor Orbán in Hungary, and locally, Scott Morrison, Tony Abbott, Pauline Hanson, Clive Palmer, *et al*, have similarly been highlighted and promoted, often for their more outlandish or controversial traits rather than substantive policy discussions.

This pattern of coverage reflects a broader trend where media focus on personalities who can generate immediate and intense public interest. Trump, with his unpredictable statements and flamboyant style, draws comparisons to a stand-up comic or a reality TV star more than a traditional politician. Similarly, figures like Johnson and Bolsonaro engage the public through a mix of humour, shock, and direct communication, often bypassing conventional political discourse and engaging directly with the populace in ways that traditional media find hard to ignore.

However, this focus on the sensational aspects of these leaders has significant implications for political reporting and public perception. The continuous emphasis on "idiot politician syndrome" shifts the focus from policy and governance to personality and scandal. This can detract from a more nuanced understanding of the political landscape and reduces complex political realities to simple narratives that are easier to consume but less informative.

The dominance of such figures in media coverage also skews public perceptions, making it seem as though flamboyance or controversy are more widespread in politics than they actually are. This can also lead to a cycle where the most sensational figures receive the most coverage, which in turn enhances their visibility and influence in a feedback loop that can distort electoral outcomes. For example, the coverage of Harris in the Australian media often highlights a comparative analysis of her negatives rather than her policies or leadership qualities. Such framing can influence public perception by focusing on personal flaws or controversies rather than substantive differences in policy or vision for the country.

The consequences of this style of media coverage are profound. It risks diminishing the public's ability to engage critically with political information and to make informed decisions at the polls. Instead of a well-informed electorate, the focus on political drama and personality flaws can lead to voter apathy or cynicism, which undermines democratic processes.

The Australian media's recent heavy focus on American politics, particularly its most sensational aspects, can crowd out coverage of critical domestic issues. This can leave Australian citizens less informed about their own government's actions and policies, which directly affect their lives more than foreign political developments.

While the media's obsession with figures like Trump and other controversial leaders can be explained by the immediate engagement they generate, it presents a challenge to the depth and quality of political journalism. As media outlets worldwide continue to navigate the shifting landscapes of digital news consumption and global politics, the balance between coverage that attracts viewers and that which informs and empowers them remains a critical concern.

THE MEDIA'S OBSESSION WITH THE FREAK SHOW

The pervasive focus of the Australian media on U.S. politics, particularly the sensational aspects embodied by figures such as Trump, highlights a broader trend within the industry: the prioritisation of ratings and a battle over diminishing advertising revenues, rather than substantive reporting. This phenomenon raises significant concerns about the media's role in serving the public interest, particularly when it comes to informing citizens about crucial political developments.

It's apparent that the media's fascination with the freak show of U.S. politics is not about the public interest but about capitalising on the spectacle to draw viewers. This strategy is evident in the coverage of Kamala Harris, whose emergence as the likely Democratic nominee has shifted the narrative around the U.S. presidential race. Despite her serious demeanour and policy-focused campaign, much of the media coverage remains superficial, focusing more on her as a personality rather than on her policies or vision for America.

This approach reflects a media landscape—locally and internationally—that is increasingly driven by the need to secure eyeballs and generate clicks, and it is this environment that often rewards sensationalism over depth and controversy over clarity. While the media industry has always relied on sensationalism to engage viewers, readers, and listeners, in the past, this strategy was used to attract audiences to more substantial content that informed the public. However, in the modern era, sensationalism is used primarily to attract audiences to even more sensationalism and, as a result, the news, information and current affairs the public truly needs to know about are often relegated to insubstantial narratives, if reported at all.

The implications of such a media strategy are profound, especially in terms of how it shapes public perception and understanding of politics. Instead of fostering a well-informed electorate, this leads to an amused, bemused and misinformed public, where sensational stories overshadow critical issues and complex policy discussions.

The intense focus on U.S. politics by Australian media, despite the lack of direct electoral influence by Australian citizens, suggests a mismatch between the content provided and the actual informational needs of the audience. While the outcomes of U.S. elections certainly have global ramifications, the disproportionate coverage comes at the expense of more relevant domestic issues that directly impact Australians.

Harris's rise in the U.S. opinion polls and the narrative shift from Trump as an inevitable winner to a potential loser illustrate how quickly media narratives can change, yet these changes often remain on the surface. The deeper, more substantive aspects of her candidacy and what it signifies for U.S. politics—and eventually, Australian and global politics—are frequently glossed over in favour of more digestible, albeit less informative, storylines.

As the media continues to struggle with the challenges of a changing technological and viewer consumption landscape, the need for a more responsible approach becomes clear. Such an approach would prioritise the public interest and strive to provide coverage that not only informs but also enriches public debate. This would entail a significant shift from the current practices, focusing more on in-depth analysis and less on the spectacle, fostering a more engaged and informed electorate. As the global media landscape evolves, the call for such a transformation becomes increasingly urgent, compelling media organisations to reassess their roles and responsibilities in a democratic society.

***

AUGUST

IS THE NATIONAL ANTI-CORRUPTION COMMISSION LIVING UP TO EXPECTATIONS?

3 August 2024

The establishment of the National Anti-Corruption Commission in 2023 was heralded as a crucial step towards enhancing transparency and accountability within governmental operations in Australia, and this development came in response to long-standing public concerns about corruption and misconduct among high-ranking officials. However, the NACC's operational effectiveness has been increasingly questioned, particularly in light of its selective investigative processes and apparent reluctance to pursue high-profile figures and cases.

The Robodebt scheme, implemented by the former Liberal–National Government, was the controversial welfare debt recovery program that was eventually ruled unlawful. The scheme not only caused significant distress and financial hardship for many affected individuals but also raised serious questions about the ethical conduct of those at the highest levels of government. The decision by the NACC last month to refrain from further investigation into this matter, coupled with the Australian Federal Police's decision not to pursue allegations of perjury against Scott Morrison at the Robodebt Royal Commission, raises critical concerns about the commission's priorities and its commitment to uncovering truth and ensuring justice.

In its first year of operation, the NACC has seemingly devoted more effort to delineating what *not* to investigate rather than proactively uncovering instances of corruption, as shown by the large number of referrals it has decided to overlook—over 83 per cent of all referrals. While it could be assumed that within a total of 3154 referrals, some would be from vexatious claims and frivolous litigants, but having such a high percentage that has not passed the first point of inquiry suggests that either the legislation for the NACC is not strong enough, or it's an institution that cannot effectively carry out its work.

This approach not only undermines the very purpose of its creation but also erodes public trust in the institution. The appointment of Paul Brereton as the Commissioner, a figure with a military background, further complicates these perceptions. His military expertise, while extensive, might not translate effectively into leading a complex, civil anti-corruption agency focused on nuanced legal and ethical issues.

There is a pressing need for restructuring the commission to ensure it is led by individuals with legal and judicial expertise—people who are independent and relentless in the pursuit of uncovering corruption, without the spectre of political bias or insufficient capability. This shift would not only align the commission more closely with its foundational goals but also restore public confidence in its ability to act as a genuine watchdog for government integrity.

As it stands, the National Anti-Corruption Commission's initial performance has been underwhelming, marked by missed opportunities and a lack of aggressive pursuit of justice. For the NACC to fulfill its potential as a critical instrument of accountability, significant reforms are essential. These reforms should focus on enhancing investigative performance, ensuring leadership that is both capable and suited to the task, and aligning the commission's operations with the clear, unequivocal pursuit of uncovering and addressing corruption wherever it may lie.

THE FIRST YEAR: A REVIEW OF NACC'S EFFECTIVENESS AND TRANSPARENCY

The NACC at this stage also appears to be a Kafkaesque "bureaucratic black hole," where referrals are made without substantial follow-through. A further test for the NACC will be a recent referral from the Australian Greens concerning a $2.25 billion contract with a British subsidiary company—ASC Shipbuilding—which has escalated to $15 billion. Such defence contracts, often shrouded in 'commercial-in-confidence' secrecy, represent just the type of high-level corruption the NACC should be poised to investigate due to the enormous sums and significant implications involved.

However, the pattern that emerges from past misdemeanours is disconcerting. Retrospective scandals from previous administrations, such as the questionable $30 million land sale from Liberal Party donors at Western Sydney Airport for land valued at $3 million, and various dubious water licensing deals and relationships with entities in the Cayman Islands, appear to have been sidestepped.

The referral numbers might be staggering in their volume but are minuscule in their prosecutorial outcome, with only five cases making it to court, resulting in only two convictions. Certainly, such cases can be complex and require a substantial amount of legal resources to arrive at an outcome, but such a mediocre result does not instill confidence in the NACC's ability to fulfill its mandate.

The lack of transparency is another critical issue. The NACC's operations are opaque, with little information available about why certain cases are dismissed and others are pursued. This opacity not only fuels public cynicism but also diminishes the perceived integrity of the commission. The question arises: why have nearly two and a half thousand referrals been dismissed without any explanation? This practice contributes to a perception that the NACC may be serving more as a political shield than a robust anti-corruption agency.

While the work of Paul Brereton in his previous role in exposing war crimes committed by Australian soldiers in Afghanistan was effective—although no charges have been laid against anyone—his approach has not yet reassured the public or political observers that he is the figure to steer the NACC toward a path of aggressive and impartial corruption investigation. There needs to be a different style of leadership—similar to the leadership provided by inaugural commissioner of the NSW Independent Commission Against Corruption, Ian Temby—who can rejuvenate the NACC into the formidable anti-corruption entity it was intended to be—one led by someone with legal acumen and a relentless commitment to justice, rather than a figure perceived as compliant within the political framework.

FEDERAL V. STATE: HOW WOULD NACC DEAL WITH GLADYS BEREJIKLIAN?

The recent inability of former NSW Premier Gladys Berejiklian to overturn findings of serious corrupt conduct highlights a disparity in the effectiveness of anti-corruption mechanisms across Australia. Berejiklian's case, adjudicated by the NSW Independent Commission Against Corruption, shows the rigorous standards some state-level bodies maintain in addressing corruption. However, its quality and effectiveness casts a shadow over the national body's capability, or lack thereof, to handle similar cases with the same level of tenacity and transparency.

The NSW ICAC, recognised as one of the toughest and most comprehensive anti-corruption bodies globally, has shown a resolve that the National Anti-Corruption Commission appears to lack. This distinction is particularly alarming given there has been some speculation that had Berejiklian been under the purview of the NACC, her political career would not have suffered the same consequences, the serious corruption she engaged with would never have been uncovered, and she'd still be the Premier of New South Wales.

This leniency feeds into a broader narrative of a systemic tolerance for corruption among Australia's powerful elites. Berejiklian's subsequent appointment as a senior executive at Optus, despite the serious allegations against her, exemplifies how high-ranking individuals often continue to thrive, escaping significant repercussions. This situation reveals a disturbing pattern: while lower-level officials may face the consequences of corrupt actions, those with substantial influence and resources frequently evade similar accountability.

The perception that the NACC acts as a "toothless tiger," primarily targeting relatively minor infractions while neglecting substantial corruption among politicians and senior bureaucrats, undermines its purpose and effectiveness. If the NACC continues to demonstrate a selective approach to investigations, it risks becoming irrelevant or, worse, viewed as a protective mechanism for political and bureaucratic elites rather than a bulwark against corruption.

Ultimately, the effectiveness of anti-corruption measures hinges not just on the ability to prosecute but on the broader impact those actions have on public trust and institutional integrity. Without visible and meaningful consequences for those found guilty of corruption, these bodies will fail to deter misconduct, leading to a cynical view of justice that can erode the very fabric of democratic governance.

For Australia—or any other nation—the goal should be not only to punish corruption but to foster an environment where integrity and accountability are the hallmarks of public service. This requires robust, effective, and fearless anti-corruption agencies that are empowered to act decisively against malfeasance at all levels of government, ensuring that these bodies are not only capable of fighting corruption but are also seen as effective and equitable in their pursuit of justice.

***

AUSTRALIA'S ELEVATED TERROR ALERT: NATIONAL SECURITY OR POLITICS AS USUAL?

10 August 2024

> "Terrorism has changed the world, and Australia is not immune, but the way of life that we value so highly must go on. Our security agencies have been upgraded and are ready to detect, prevent and respond to terrorism. We can work together to protect our way of life—be alert, but not alarmed."
> Howard government television advertisement, 2001.

The federal government's decision to raise Australia's national terrorism threat level from "possible" to "probable"—based on a recommendation from ASIO—is a decision that goes beyond the immediate concerns of national security and into the field of public perception, political strategy, and the broader socio-political landscape.

Prime Minister Anthony Albanese's statement sought to project an image of decisiveness and transparency but it also raises questions about the underlying political motivations. Albanese was quick to clarify that "probable" does not imply an imminent threat, yet the very act of elevating the threat level inevitably stirs public anxiety.

The rationale behind this heightened alert level, according to the head of ASIO, Mike Burgess, is based on the assessment that more Australians are embracing a 'broader range of extreme ideologies'. This diversification of extremist thought, coupled with the increasing willingness of individuals to resort to violence, presents a complex challenge for national security agencies. Yet, the ambiguity surrounding what "probable" actually means raises concerns about the effectiveness and the intent of such warnings.

Of course, it's not possible to overlook the timing of this decision in the context of recent global and domestic events—the ongoing war inflicted by Israel in Palestine has seen escalations in violence that resonate far beyond the Middle East. The recent rise in far-right extremism and racially motivated violence, particularly in Western nations like England, adds another layer of complexity to the threat of terrorism and these events, coupled with the increasing polarisation of political debate, has created a fertile ground for radicalisation. The government's decision to raise the terror alert might be seen as a response to these external and internal pressures, and a way to signal to the public that they are aware of the growing risks but the broader implications of this move cannot be ignored.

Historically, public announcements about terrorism in Australia—especially from conservative governments—have often been mired in political agendas and the pursuit of increased funding from security agencies. The Australian Federal Police and ASIO, like many security organisations globally, operate in a competitive funding environment where the perceived threat level directly influences budget allocations and raising the terror alert could be viewed as a strategic move to secure additional resources.

POLITICAL MANIPULATION OF TERROR ALERTS

The strategic use of terror alerts by governments, particularly when facing political challenges, has long been a tool used by incumbents seeking to shift public focus, from Billy Hughes, through to Robert Menzies, John Howard and Tony Abbott. When the Coalition was in office, they frequently used terror-related announcements as a means of deflection when faced with political scandals or declining public support, and a sudden terror alert or the arrest of an individual—preferably of "Middle Eastern appearance"—on terror-related charges often served to distract the electorate.

While it's clear that the role of the Australian Federal Police and ASIO is not just as a prop for the government of the day to be used to raise fears within the community—the raids on several houses in Surry Hills in 2017 foiled a plot to blow up an Etihad plane and resulted in 40-year jail terms for Khaled Khayat and Mahmoud Khayat—other acts have not been so clear, such as the raiding of Labor Party offices and union bosses, or the homes of people from Islamic communities in Western Sydney and Melbourne, where the charges against individuals arrested under the banner of terrorism were quietly dropped, leaving the public with little information about the validity of the initial accusations.

Labor, now in power, appears to have recognised the effectiveness of this political tactic and this elevation in the terror threat level should be seen through this lens. While the government insists that this decision is based on intelligence and the evolving security environment, the lack of clarity surrounding what "probable" truly means leaves room for skepticism.

The shift from "possible" to "probable" also raises the question: At what point does a threat move from one category to the next? And what are Australians meant to do with this information? The vague nature of the alert offers little in the way of guidance for the public. Unlike in the past, where citizens might have been encouraged to report suspicious activity, today's environment is more complex.

The difficulty in infiltrating nationalist and cultural groups, which often operate in secrecy, also compounds the problem, and ASIO and other security agencies face significant challenges in tracking the activities of far-right extremists, neo-Nazis, and other violent groups. While it is possible that these agencies are more effective than the public realises—national security and spy agencies are hardly going to telegraph their every movement—the classified nature of their operations leaves taxpayers in the dark. Without transparency, it is hard to gauge the effectiveness of these agencies, and the public is left to place their trust in the government's public assurances.

This lack of transparency also plays into the hands of those in power. By keeping the details of security operations classified, the government can selectively release information that suits its narrative. Arrests are announced, but the outcomes are rarely publicised, leaving the impression that the threat is ever-present. This approach not only keeps the public on edge but also distracts from other pressing issues, such as the cost of living and the state of the economy.

The Coalition was particularly adept at this, often creating distractions through race issues, culture wars, or terror alerts to keep the electorate occupied with something other than the real problems. While Labor tends to avoid race baiting and cultural wars, the temptation to use terror alerts as a distraction remains strong.

For the average Australian struggling with rent, loans, and daily expenses, the shift from "possible" to "probable" offers little comfort and it is difficult to see how such an announcement, with its vague implications, addresses the real concerns of the populace. The government's use of this tactic may be an attempt to garner political support or for security agencies to secure additional funding but it does little to alleviate the burdens faced by ordinary citizens.

BALANCING NATIONAL SECURITY AND POLITICAL STRATEGY

Although Albanese's announcement was more subdued compared to the bombastic displays of previous Coalition leaders like Scott Morrison, Malcolm Turnbull, and Tony Abbott, it still carries significant weight—the absence of a sea of Australian flags that were the hallmark of Abbott's security announcements, and the measured tone that reflects Albanese's more restrained style, does not diminish the strategic underpinnings of such a move. It is, however, evident that this is also a calculated attempt to bolster the Labor government's credibility on national security, an area traditionally dominated by the Coalition.

Historically, the Coalition has positioned itself as the stronger manager of national security, a perception reinforced by their frequent, high-profile terror-related announcements and this narrative has been deeply embedded in the Australian political psyche. The frequent use of terror alerts, ASIO raids, and media conferences brimming with patriotic symbolism has kept the electorate's focus on security, often to the detriment—or at least the distraction—of other issues. Labor, during its time in opposition did limit its criticism of this approach, wary of being perceived as unpatriotic and "un-Australian", but also recognised the political dividends it brought the Coalition. Now in power, it seems Labor may be adopting a similar strategy, albeit with a different tone.

The use of fear as a political tool is not new, but it is particularly effective when it comes to national security. Fear is a powerful motivator, one that can rally public support and distract from other pressing issues. Under a Labor government, the overt fear-mongering may be less pronounced, but the underlying strategy remains. By elevating the terror threat level and making announcements about potential dangers, the government taps into the electorate's deep-seated anxieties, subtly reinforcing its authority on security matters.

However, this approach is not without its nuances. While the Coalition has mastered the art of leveraging national security for political gain—and still does so, even from the opposition benches—Labor's more restrained approach might be an attempt to differentiate itself, to show that it can handle these issues without resorting to the same level of hyperbole. Will it work? In a political landscape where anything is *possible*, and now, with the elevated threat level, anything is *probable*, the line between genuine security concerns and political opportunism becomes increasingly blurred.

Trust in governments on national security is always going to be a double-edged sword. On one hand, the public's fear of terrorism and the desire for security can lead to broad support for increased funding and expanded powers for ASIO. On the other hand, the lack of concrete information and the tendency for these threats to fade from the public eye when no attacks occur can breed skepticism. If no attack happens, the narrative shifts to one of "prevention success," yet the public is left wondering whether the threat was ever real or simply a tool for political gamesmanship and agency funding.

The public, understandably, does not want a terror attack, and any move to prevent such a tragedy is seen as necessary. However, when these alerts are used as political tools, their effectiveness in truly protecting the nation is called into question. As long as the motivations behind these alerts remain murky, and as long as they serve dual purposes of national security and political gain, there will always be a tension between genuine safety concerns and the politics of fear.

***

THE ETHICAL DILEMMA OF USING GAMBLING TO SUPPORT THE WORLD'S WORST MEDIA

17 August 2024

The debate surrounding the potential banning of gambling advertising and the link with the survival of free-to-air mainstream media is a situation laced with historical vested interests, and the recent remarks by senior government minister Bill Shorten have ignited a broader discussion about the role of government in supporting an industry in decline due to technological disruption, changing consumer habits and its own ineptitude.

Shorten's comments highlight a dilemma faced by many governments worldwide: the balancing act between regulating harmful industries such as gambling, alcohol and tobacco, and ensuring the viability of traditional media outlets. He candidly acknowledged the severe impact that digital platforms such as Facebook have had on traditional media, especially free-to-air channels, which have seen their advertising revenues plummet as advertisers flock to more targeted and data-rich online platforms. This shift has left traditional media in a precarious position, increasingly reliant on any available sources of revenue, including those from gambling advertising.

This reliance is not only about maintaining profitability: it's about survival. Shorten's perspective is that while the ideal situation might be to eliminate gambling advertising due to its societal harms, the reality is that such a move could cripple the already struggling free-to-air media sector. This sector, despite its flaws, is seen by some, including Shorten, as vital for maintaining a diverse media landscape and ensuring access to information, particularly in areas underserved by broadband internet or where people rely on television for news and local content.

Shorten—reflecting the government's cautious stance on most issues—has framed gambling advertising as a 'necessary evil' to prevent a greater loss, which would be the collapse of an entire media sector. His view, however, raises significant ethical questions, as it pits the welfare of a traditional industry against the broader societal impacts of gambling, such as addiction and financial hardship, which are exacerbated by pervasive advertising.

Historically, Australian media has been cushioned by various government policies aimed at shielding it from market and technological pressures. From the legislative protections in the 1980s and early 1990s, to the media bargaining code of 2021, these measures have often been justified as efforts to maintain a healthy, diverse media environment. Critics, however, argue that these protections have served to maintain outdated business models and stifle innovation, and is a form of protectionism that has kept the media industry risk-averse, conservative, and overly reliant on sensationalism and outrage—a far cry from the dynamic and diverse media landscape that modern Australia might expect or require.

The evolution of media consumption patterns, with the rise of streaming services and on-demand content, has fundamentally altered how people interact with media. The traditional model of scheduled programming is increasingly irrelevant in a world where viewers are accustomed to watching what they want when they want. This shift raises the question of whether propping up traditional media through gambling revenue is just delaying the inevitable need for these companies to innovate or fundamentally restructure.

This debate about media dependency on gambling advertising is also a reflection of broader societal issues—a paradox in relying on an industry that harms public wellbeing to fund a sector that is meant to serve the public interest, but is only serving its own vested interests. Is the short-term survival of traditional media worth the long-term costs of increased gambling harm? Or is it time to rethink not just the regulations around advertising, but the very nature of the media industry itself in Australia? Is mainstream media an industry worth saving?

GOVERNMENT PROTECTION OF OUTDATED MEDIA MODELS

The historical approach to media regulation and government support in Australia contrasts with broader economic trends, particularly the steady withdrawal of subsidies from other industries. Sectors such as textiles and footwear in the 1970s, and car manufacturing in the 2010s, saw their governmental lifelines cut as part of a broader neoliberalist agenda. Yet, the media industry, particularly free-to-air television, has been consistently shielded from similar fates through various legislative protections and sometimes direct financial interventions, such as the controversial $30 million payment made by the Turnbull government to Murdoch-owned Foxtel in 2017, ostensibly to promote women's sport, although there is no evidence to support this funding was ever used in this way, and there's no indication about how this money was spent.

Such protection has led to a media landscape that is not only outdated but also uncompetitive. The slow response to digital trends and the failure to develop new business models have left traditional media in Australia lagging behind their international counterparts, where outlets such as the *New York Times* and *The Guardian* have made significant strides in adapting to and capitalising on the digital age.

This, of course, extends to the type of journalism that dominates Australian free-to-air television, which has poor reporting standards and a reluctance to challenge powerful figures and interests. It's no secret that figures such as Rupert Murdoch and Kerry Stokes wield considerable influence over the Australian media and political landscape, yet government actions often pander more to these media moguls than to the principles of a diverse and dynamic media environment.

The Australian media landscape, as it stands, is not just a relic of past economic policies but also a current example of the government's failure to adapt to new realities. While there are exceptions such as SBS, which has managed to maintain high standards despite a wide range of political and funding challenges enforced by the government, most of the mainstream media industry is a wasteland of conservative interests in dire need of reform and modernisation.

GOVERNMENT'S ROLE IN TRANSFORMING MEDIA ETHICS

The government's support of a media industry which has persistent issues around workplace culture, particularly misogyny and racism, as highlighted in a recent exposé on the ABC's *Four Corners*, also highlights a deeper problem within this relationship. While *Four Corners* focussed on the unhealthy and disastrous work culture within Seven West Media, where allegations of protecting problematic figures and fostering discriminatory practices persist, there are systemic problems in all mainstream media outlets, including the ABC, and the continuing support and provision of legislative and financial support from governments cannot rectify this.

Taking this into account, the role of government should move from ensuring the survival of these entities to actively fostering their evolution into more ethical and responsible organisations. The government's financial lifeline through legislative changes, while crucial for those industries in the short term, offers an unprecedented opportunity to mandate substantial reforms. If government is going to provide this legislative and financial support, why not develop a legislative response that not only preserves jobs and services but also improves the ethical standards, quality and inclusiveness of these media outlets?

The suggestion by the Australian Greens to implement a 'tech tax' on major digital platforms such as Meta, Google, Twitter and TikTok, and redirect these funds to support legacy media, is a step in the right direction but it should come with caveats. This approach should not only be about handing over funds to media companies but about tying this financial support to clear, enforceable standards of corporate behaviour and journalistic integrity. This could involve setting higher benchmarks for diversity in hiring practices, enforcing strict anti-harassment policies, and requiring a shift away from sensationalist and divisive content towards more fact-based and inclusive reporting. The mainstream media has shown, historically, that it can't trusted on any of these areas of diversity, quality, integrity and good corporate behaviour, so why should the public—and governments—tolerate this situation?

This debate about the role of gambling advertising in media financing further complicates the government's position. While the financial benefits of such advertising are clear, especially in propping up a struggling industry, the ethical implications are profoundly troubling. Gambling advertising, much like tobacco and alcohol advertising in the past, plays a significant role in normalising behaviours that can have destructive personal and social consequences. The argument that these advertisements are a necessary evil to support media operations, as Shorten has suggested, reflects a troubling willingness to compromise public health and welfare for corporate profits.

The government's approach should focus not on sustaining outdated business models through ethically questionable means but on promoting a transition towards more sustainable and socially responsible media practices. Banning gambling advertising outright, as has been recommended by the cross-party Standing Committee on Social Policy and Legal Affairs, would align with this approach. Historical precedents with tobacco and alcohol suggest that such industries can adapt to advertising restrictions without facing extinction. More importantly, it would signal a commitment to prioritising public welfare over corporate profits, slowing down an industry that thrives on exploitation and reducing the social harms associated with gambling.

By leveraging legislative power to enforce reforms and curbing harmful advertising practices, the government can help foster a media industry that not only survives the digital transition but also emerges as a more inclusive, responsible, and ethical pillar of Australian society. This is not just an opportunity but a profound responsibility—to reshape the media landscape into one that truly serves the public interest. Isn't this what Labor governments are meant to achieve?

***

AUKUS IS JEOPARDISING AUSTRALIA'S INDEPENDENCE AND ECONOMIC STABILITY

18 August 2024

The revised AUKUS agreement presents a serious imbalance in the legal rights and commitments among its signatories—Australia on one side, and the United Kingdom and the United States on the other—and exposes Australia to significant geopolitical and financial risks without any recourse to redress or withdraw from this agreement. The deal, now extended until 2075, highlights a substantial shift from the initial expiry at some ethereal point in the 2040s, embedding Australia deeper into a complex trilateral naval pact which was supposedly aimed at enhancing undersea and strategic capabilities through the sharing of nuclear submarine technologies.

Central to the concerns over the amended deal is the clause that allows the U.K. and the U.S. unilateral rights to terminate the agreement with 12-months' notice, if they perceive the deal as counterproductive to their own submarine projects or broader national interests. But what about Australia's interests? There isn't a reciprocal right for Australia, which doesn't have the ability to exit the agreement under similar circumstances, nor to seek compensation should the pact be dissolved. This discrepancy not only places Australia in a vulnerable strategic position but also at a financial disadvantage, given the extensive investments already committed to the project over the past three years.

Australia's obligations under the agreement include hefty financial contributions and indemnifying the U.S. and U.K. against liabilities, including those arising from nuclear risks, without limits or conditions. Such terms raise questions about the degree of influence and security Australia gains in return, and this is a transaction heavily skewed in favour of its partners. The payments made so far—totaling $13 billion to the U.S. and U.K. ($4.7 billion each), and to settle the cancellation of a prior contract with the French Naval Group ($3.4 billion)—also highlights the economic burden shouldered by Australia without tangible assets or guarantees of delivery.

The geopolitical implications of this lopsided agreement extend beyond immediate financial strains as it positions Australia as a junior partner in a strategic pact that could influence its foreign and defence policies for decades, while offering almost no leverage over these terms. The long duration of the deal—51 years—a period which is likely to see shifts in international politics and the global technological military landscape, further complicates Australia's predicament. Since the original deal was created in 2021, Australia has had two different prime ministers, Britain is now onto its third prime minister, and the U.S. will have a new president in early 2025. Will China be a different type of international player in another decade or two? Will the U.S. be more hostile towards Australian interests by 2050?

The world is in a constant state of flux. This lack of a termination clause for Australia reveals a significant oversight or misjudgment in diplomatic negotiations, and underestimates the strategic shifts that could occur over the lifespan of the agreement. The deal not only represents a significant policy challenge for Australia but also a crucial test of its ability to navigate complex and shifting alliances in an increasingly changing world.

ASSESSING AUSTRALIA'S FUTURE IN AN EVOLVING MILITARY WORLD

The employment opportunities in Australia generated by AUKUS—as yet, unseen and unknown—are often highlighted as a significant benefit, ostensibly supporting high-tech industries and sustains high-wage jobs and, for sure, the prospect of long-term employment in constructing and maintaining a fleet of submarines is an appealing economic stimulus. This employment might indeed serve as a temporary economic buffer, providing jobs in advanced manufacturing sectors and resulting in further technological development.

However, the critical question remains: what value do these jobs create if the output—nuclear submarines—becomes obsolete or redundant in the evolving landscape of military technology over the next twenty to thirty years? This is not a distant hypothetical. The trajectory of military technology is veering sharply towards unmanned systems, drone and cluster technologies, which promise more flexible, cost-effective and advanced capabilities than traditional manned submarines. These systems are not only less detectable but can be operated at a fraction of the cost and risk, rendering large, manned submarine fleets obsolete in future strategic developments.

This exchange in the Senate Estimates Committee on Defence between the Australian Greens Senator David Shoebridge and Vice Admiral Jonathan Mead, highlights the precariousness of Australia's position:

> Shoebridge: Does the agreement provide that, if the United States does not provide us with an AUKUS submarine, we get our money back?
>
> Mead: The U.S. will provide us with an AUKUS submarine.
>
> S: Did you not understand that my question wasn't about some future hypothetical? I'm asking about what's in the agreement. Is the reason you won't answer what's in the agreement that it embarrassingly fails to have that?
>
> M: You're talking about a future hypothetical.
>
> S: I'm talking about what's in the agreement now.
>
> M: The U.S. will provide two submarines and one on procurement.
>
> S: I suppose it may be embarrassing that you've entered into an agreement that sees Australian taxpayers shelling out $4.7 billion which we don't get back if we don't get a nuclear sub. That might be embarrassing, but that's not a reason not to answer it. Does the agreement have a clawback provision?
>
> M: I reiterate my statement. The U.S. is committed to transferring two U.S. submarines.
>
> S: The only way of reading that answer is 'no', and it's embarrassing and it's a gamble.

The initial promise of two Virginia-class submarines from the U.S. by 2025 has already been halved—*to one!*—and even this reduced commitment seems tenuous. Senator Shoebridge's line of questioning reveals a crucial absence of protective measures in the deal, such as a clawback provision in the event that the promised submarines are not delivered—which, at this stage, seems very likely.

The inherent risk in tying Australia's economic and military strategies to an aging technology in an evolving field is obvious. While the immediate economic benefits of job creation are tangible, what are these jobs for? It's almost like a complex work-for-the-dole scheme and could divert resources away from more pressing national security concerns and the development of technologies that could genuinely enhance Australia's defence and strategic capabilities in a future dominated by automated and cyber warfare technologies.

THE PUBLIC HAS A RIGHT TO KNOW ABOUT THE DETAILS OF AUKUS

The AUKUS agreement, as currently structured, highlights a broader pattern of unchecked defence spending and unclear decision-making that marginalises taxpayer oversight and democratic accountability in Australia. It's a similar situation on national security and the Australian Federal Police: whatever these agencies ask of the government, these agencies always receive.

This agreement's design essentially reduces Australia to a dependent status, compromising its ability to act independently on the global stage. Such a dynamic not only diminishes Australia's leverage in the AUKUS partnership but also within the broader international community, where strategic autonomy is crucial for negotiating geopolitical challenges and opportunities.

The massive financial outlay committed by Australia—at least $368 billion with little to no safeguard mechanisms—exposes the country to significant economic risk without guarantees of strategic gain, as well as locking in current and future generations into paying for a strategy that may well be outdated within a decade or two.

The notion of tying Australia's defence strategy to the procurement of a small number of submarines to patrol its extensive coastline is optimistic—a *Yes Minister* level of 'optimism'—and exemplifies a strategic misalignment with contemporary defence needs and realities. The evolving nature of military threats and technologies calls for a defence strategy that is adaptive and forward-thinking rather than one anchored in the military thinking of yesteryear.

Australia's strategic partnerships should reflect a balance of power, mutual benefits, and flexibility to adapt to changing global circumstances—an ideal treaty would not only secure Australia's defence interests but also preserve its financial integrity and strategic autonomy, and involve a broader set of regional allies and contain provisions that allow for adaptation to technological and geopolitical shifts, unlike the rigid and asymmetric commitments now enshrined in AUKUS.

The AUKUS deal is a classic example of policy shaped more by the egos and immediate political interests of its architects—Scott Morrison, Joe Biden and Boris Johnson—than by a judicious assessment of Australia's long-term national interests. It would be better to renegotiate the terms of this agreement—or cancel it entirely—to better align with the country's real defence needs and strategic aspirations, one that serves Australia's national interest and maintains its true independence.

***

CONSERVATIVE RACE-BAITING POLITICS IN THE SPOTLIGHT YET AGAIN

24 August 2024

The accusations of racism levelled against the Leader of the Opposition, Peter Dutton, and by extension the Liberal Party, highlight a complex and contentious aspect of contemporary political debate. Central to this controversy is the accusation made by the independent member for Warringah, Zali Steggall, who accused Dutton of racism on Sky News—in Parliament, where speech is protected, such accusations are safe from legal reprisal; outside Parliament, however, the stakes are much higher.

Instead of reflecting on his behaviour—unlikely, given his entire political career has been based on attacking people who are not stock-standard white bread material—Dutton's response to Steggall's accusations was to consider legal action. His history as Immigration Minister provides substantial material evidence to support claims of racist behaviour: his comments on "African gang violence" in 2018 and the need for migrants to integrate into Australian society, singled out and negatively stereotyped black African communities. This is contrasted by his supportive comments and completely different tone towards white South African farmers, whom he described as hardworking and well-integrated into Australian society, and he would "always look at ways" for the then Coalition government to fast-track visa applications, an act which would have been against Australia's non-discriminatory migration policy.

This split in Dutton's statements raises critical questions about racial bias in his policymaking and public rhetoric. The selective compassion evident in his differential treatment of migrants—perceiving white South Africans as desirable while casting aspersions on the character and behaviour of black African migrants—feeds into the narrative of racial bias.

There are other examples: Dutton's actions towards the Murugappan family—denying medical care to their Australian-born children—and his policies on asylum seekers, further compromise his public image. His approach to immigration detention; his walkout protest during the Stolen Generation speech in 2008, and his stance on the Voice of Parliament in 2023, all suggest a pattern that aligns with a broader, racially insensitive and racist agenda.

Legalities aside, the essence of racism in politics often boils down to both the impact and the intent behind words and actions. Dutton's policies and statements suggests a worldview that implicitly, and *explicitly*, differentiates between races in ways that disadvantages non-white Australians.

Actions speak louder than words in assessing Dutton's behaviour. If racism, as commonly understood, involves prejudice, discrimination, or antagonism directed against other people because of their race or ethnic origin, then the evidence presented in public life suggests there is a significant cause for such claims to be made against him.

THE ETHICS OF BANNING PEOPLE FLEEING A WAR ZONE

A recent focal point for Dutton was his stance on visa applications for Palestinian refugees from Gaza, where he declared a complete prohibition on entries from Gaza, which then raised ethical and policy-oriented questions about the treatment of individuals fleeing conflict zones: this is the purpose of Australia's humanitarian visa program but Dutton was only too happy to play the race card and seek favour from the right-wing Israel lobby at the same time. It's also a moot point: Israel controls who can leave the occupied Palestinian territories through Israeli-issued exit permits and, since May, no one has been allowed out of Gaza anyway.

This policy stance taken by Dutton, however, does not operate in isolation but rather reflects a broader narrative within the Liberal Party, characterised by an overt appeal to xenophobic sentiments.

The manner in which this policy was communicated suggests an aggressive, public doubling down on divisive racial rhetoric, an approach which serves to not only polarise the community but also to court a specific segment of the electorate known for its highly conservative views on immigration and race.

The strategic implications of such a stance are complicated. On one hand, it solidifies the Liberal Party's appeal among voters who prioritise stringent immigration controls or who harbour suspicious views about Middle Eastern conflicts and the impact they might have in Australia. On the other hand, it alienates broader sections of the electorate, including moderate conservatives and centrists, who view such policies as unnecessarily harsh or morally questionable.

The scrutiny of Dutton's policies and actions, especially those that are racially charged or unjustly discriminatory, highlights the role that civic institutions can play in questioning and holding leaders accountable. However, the discussion needs to move beyond the semantics of political correctness and engage with deeper, more systemic issues of racism and intolerance within political leadership—in Dutton's case, he seemed to be more offended by the label of "racist" than by his actual racist commentary, and this points to a troubling disconnect between perception and reality in public discourse.

In this context, the role of media scrutiny becomes even more critical, where they should not only be reporting on these issues but also interpreting and contextualising them for the public, areas where they have so far been lacking. This is an essential issue, not just for informing the electorate but also for guarding the integrity of democratic institutions against the corrosive effects of the division that are usually created by conservative politicians.

DUTTONISTAN: QUEENSLAND'S DISTINCT POLITICAL LANDSCAPE

The distinct political culture in Queensland—shaped by historical figures such as Joh Bjelke-Petersen in the 1970s and 1980s and the long-standing influence of the National Party—has created a stronghold for the now merged Liberal–National Party at the federal level, despite mixed success in Queensland state elections.

This entrenched conservatism in Queensland is often characterised by a unique blend of social and economic policies, and Dutton, as a product of this Queensland political environment, embodies these conservative ideals, which have consistently secured his electoral success in the seat of Dickson since 2001, when he was first elected to Parliament.

The approach taken by Dutton and the Queensland L–NP—which relies on stoking fears about immigration and leveraging racially charged rhetoric—has proven electorally successful in Queensland but faces significant challenges elsewhere. This style of politics, while resonating within certain demographics in Queensland, does not translate well across the broader Australian electorate, which tends to be more diverse and, particularly those with urban centres such as Sydney and Melbourne, more progressive and moderate views usually prevail—often but not always.

The disparity in electoral success between state and federal levels in Queensland complicates the L–NP's strategy. While the party has maintained significant control federally—consistently holding between 20 and 25 of the 30 federal seats over the past 30 years—their state-level performance has been less impressive, where they have only been in office for five years since 1989, highlighting a disconnect between the regional conservative base and the broader state electorate's preferences.

This dichotomy also poses a strategic dilemma for the L–NP: should they continue with a proven but potentially limiting conservative approach, or should they adapt to a changing political environment that may favour more moderate or centrist policies? In any case, a shift to a more centrist position would not be a task for Dutton: moderation is not one of his political tools, and if such an unlikely shift were to occur, it would be viewed with great skepticism by the electorate.

While the L–NP faces organisational and credibility challenges across Australia—despite a landslide victory for the Country Liberal Party in the Northern Territory election on the weekend—internal divisions between moderates and conservatives are exacerbating the party's difficulties. These challenges are not isolated to the L–NP but reflect a broader trend in Australian politics where traditional party structures and strategies are being slowly dissolving, and new political movements and independents are gaining traction, as evidenced in the 2022 federal election and a slow decline in the two-party primary vote since 1984.

The political future for Dutton and the L–NP hinges on their ability to navigate these dynamics and balancing the conservative base's demands with the broader electorate's evolving preferences. This balancing act is crucial not only for electoral success—as it is for all political parties—but also for maintaining relevance in an increasingly diverse and fluid political landscape.

UNMASKING THE RACISM OF AUSTRALIAN PARLIAMENT

> Senator Mehreen Faruqi: This week, this place has broken me with its racism, with its attacks on Muslims, on Palestinian refugees, on disabled people and on women. Those who are not piling on hate and racism are standing on the sidelines or gaslighting, or worse, trying to shut us up, because that's what you want: You want us to be silenced because you don't like us holding a mirror to you. You don't like the truth you see in the mirror because you can't handle that truth. The roots of the racism in this country and the problems in this country sit right here in this Parliament.

Of course, in a week that was dominated by a debate over whether Dutton's actions and behaviours are racist *or not*, the forgotten world of everyone else on the margins continued to clean up and deal with the effects of collateral damage.

The sentiments expressed by Senator Faruqi highlights a critical and disheartening aspect of contemporary political debate in Australia—the pervasive and systemic nature of racism within the highest echelons of political power, and the emotional and professional toll it places on individuals who are often its targets.

The roots of racism in Australia are certainly entrenched in the structures of power and governance, exemplified by the ongoing debates and policies that emerge from Parliament, which reveal a significant divide in understanding and addressing racial issues within the governing bodies. The role of parliamentarians is not only to reflect the views—and prejudices—of their constituents but to challenge and reshape them towards a more inclusive and equitable society: Parliament should strive to be more than a mirror reflecting societal attitudes—it needs to be an institution for reform and progress. It is not enough for members of Parliament to passively reject racism; they must actively confront and dismantle the structures and practices that allow it to thrive.

When leaders like Dutton engage in racially charged rhetoric or support divisive policies, it not only impacts the immediate political landscape but also confirms and supports existing societal norms and behaviours, perpetuating cycles of racism and exclusion. This is the part that needs to change and it's depressing that this constantly needs to be pointed out to conservative politicians. There needs to be a systemic overhaul of how issues of race are addressed within legislative processes and this requires a commitment to transparency, accountability, and inclusivity in policy formulation.

It's critical for the health of the Australian democracy and the integrity of its institutions that these challenges are met with courage and a relentless pursuit of equality. Parliament, as both a symbol and a mechanism of governance, has a central role in leading this change, ensuring that the principles of justice and equity are not just upheld but cherished.

***

THE STRUGGLE TO DEFINE THE GOVERNMENT'S VISION AND DIRECTION

30 August 2024

The current political landscape presents a curious contradiction, with Prime Minister Anthony Albanese facing a slow and steady decline in popularity despite the relatively poor performance of the leader of the opposition, Peter Dutton. According to recent Essential Poll, Albanese's approval ratings have reached their lowest levels since taking office, with 50 per cent of respondents expressing dissatisfaction with his performance, reminiscent of the declining support for former Prime Minister Scott Morrison in the lead-up to the 2022 federal election. While it is not uncommon for a sitting Prime Minister to experience fluctuations in public support, the critical question is why Albanese's approval ratings have dropped so sharply and what this means for the future of this government.

One issue within the current polling data is the relatively small percentage of undecided voters—10 per cent—suggesting that the electorate has largely made up its mind about Albanese's leadership and this sentiment presents a challenge for the Prime Minister, as shifting public opinion once it's entrenched is notoriously difficult. The reasons for Albanese's unpopularity are varied and complex, reflecting a confluence of economic, social, and political factors that have coalesced into a broader dissatisfaction with his government.

Economic concerns, as they usually are, are at the forefront of the electorate's discontent—the rising cost of living, coupled with housing affordability issues, has placed pressure on many people in the electorate, and the perception that the government has not done enough to address these issues has undoubtedly contributed to Albanese's declining support. While the economy has shown signs of improvement, the benefits of this recovery have not yet been felt by many households, leading to a disconnect between the government's optimistic economic outlook and the lived experiences of the electorate.

Beyond economic issues, there are also significant concerns about the government's stance on various international and domestic matters. The AUKUS agreement, for example, is a contentious issue, with some voters feeling that the government's commitment to this alliance compromises Australia's sovereignty and security. Similarly, the government's indifference on the genocide in Gaza committed by Israel has alienated a segment of the electorate that expected a more assertive stance on international human rights.

Domestically, the government's strained relationship with the CFMEU has raised questions about the party's commitment to its unions and its working-class base. The tension between the government and the unions is emblematic of a broader challenge facing Albanese: the inability to craft a cohesive narrative that resonates with a diverse electorate. This failure to effectively communicate the government's vision and accomplishments has left many voters, especially from younger demographics, feeling disconnected from the party that they feel should be offering more.

However, it is important to note that unpopularity does not necessarily consign a Prime Minister to electoral defeat—history offers several examples of leaders who have managed to turn around their fortunes and secure re-election despite low approval ratings. Paul Keating in 1993 and John Howard in 2001 and 2004 both faced significant challenges yet managed to win the subsequent elections, if not win over the electorate. The key to their success was the ability to build a compelling narrative—Keating's focussed on the GST and the economy, while Howard focussed on national security and "trust"—that ultimately resonated with voters.

For Albanese, the challenge is to find a way to rebuild his political capital before the next election and this will require a delicate balance of addressing immediate concerns, while also articulating a clear and cohesive vision for the future. Complicating matters for Albanese is the presence of Peter Dutton: while Dutton is also unpopular, his political resilience should not be underestimated, irrespective of how bereft of talent he might be. The unexpected rise of figures like Tony Abbott and Scott Morrison to the Prime Ministership serves as a reminder that even seemingly unlikely candidates can succeed under the right circumstances. If the electorate's dissatisfaction with Albanese continues to grow, it could create an opening for Dutton to position himself as a viable alternative, despite his own significant shortcomings.

Ultimately, the Albanese government must navigate complex and rapidly evolving political circumstances. The government's ability to connect with voters on a broader range of issues will be critical to its success, especially in the context of the upcoming federal election, which is due before May 2025.

UNMET EXPECTATIONS AND MISSED OPPORTUNITIES

The Albanese government's current struggles can be further understood through the lens of unmet expectations and the shifting political mindset of the electorate. The 2022 federal election was a decisive moment, with voters sending a clear message that they were tired of the politics-as-usual approach and desired a government that would bring about meaningful change. The Labor Party was seen as the vehicle for this transformation, promising a departure from the policies and behaviours of the previous Coalition government and, in particular, former prime minister Scott Morrison.

One of the core issues lies in the perception that the Labor government is not delivering the transformative policies that were anticipated by its supporters. The COVID-19 pandemic fundamentally altered the public's expectations of what governments can and should do, where during the pandemic, the Coalition government implemented significant economic support measures, such as JobKeeper, that are anathema for conservative governments typically averse to such interventionist policies. Money that the government usually claims is never available for the public good, was magically found: governments can always spend money, it's just a question of political will. This created a belief that a Labor government, traditionally more inclined towards social welfare and public investment, would not only maintain but expand upon these initiatives.

Instead, what many voters have observed is a government that, while different from its predecessor in certain respects, seems to be drifting without a clear and bold vision. The perception that Labor has been pulled to the right on various issues, partly due to pressure from the Liberal–National opposition, has further eroded the sense of a distinct and progressive agenda.

Is the Labor government squandering its time in office? With nearly every government in Australia currently controlled by the Labor Party—aside from Tasmania and more recently, the Northern Territory—there was an opportunity for a coordinated and cohesive effort to push forward a progressive agenda. However, the federal government's slow and steady approach has been perceived as a lack of urgency, particularly in a political environment where bold action was necessary to address pressing issues.

While it's always easy to make comparisons to the Whitlam government between 1972–75, Gough Whitlam's tenure, though brief and tumultuous, is remembered for its ambitious reforms and the lasting legacy it left on Australian society. The Albanese government, in contrast, seems to be at risk of fading away, as the initial momentum of its electoral victory fades into a more cautious and conservative mode of governance. While there are certainly achievements that Labor supporters can point to, these accomplishments are often overshadowed by the perception that the government is not fully seizing the moment.

There is also the question of whether the Albanese government is being unduly influenced by various lobby groups, which is steering it away from its core values and objectives and these pressures from religious, industrial, social, and cultural groups, as well as the need to appease certain sectors, can dilute the government's ability to act decisively in the national interest. This balancing act, while an inevitable part of governing, has led the Labor government to compromise on issues where it should be more assertive in pursuing what is best for the country as a whole. In this case, if too many compromises are made, what is the real purpose of a Labor government if it is intent to occupy the treasury benches without following its own agenda, and genuflecting to the wishes of others, who are quite often hostile to its interests?

THE MISSING NARRATIVE: A STRUGGLE TO CONNECT POLICIES WITH A COHESIVE VISION

The Albanese government's struggles are not only rooted in policy decisions but also in the absence of a compelling and cohesive narrative that connects these decisions to a broader vision for the country. In the field of politics, *the narrative* helps the electorate make sense of the various policies and changes that are implemented. Unfortunately, the current Labor government has often failed to provide this connecting narrative, leaving many voters confused and disconnected from the government's agenda.

Storytelling in politics is crucial because it provides context and justification for policies, especially when those policies may not immediately seem beneficial or necessary to the public. The lack of such storytelling in the Albanese government's approach has been glaringly evident in several key areas; for example, the Housing Australia Future Fund was introduced earlier this year as a significant initiative to address housing affordability, yet the rationale behind structuring it like a hedge fund was never adequately explained. This left room for the narrative to be dominated by others, particularly the Australian Greens, who criticised the fund as insufficient and poorly conceived (which it was). The debate was left to fester, and the government's position appeared weak and reactive.

Similarly, on the issue of JobSeeker payments, the government's failure to provide a clear explanation for why it did not substantially raise these payments, despite campaigning on this issue in opposition and receiving a great level of support from the business community to do this, further eroded trust. This decision, which could have been framed within the context of broader economic challenges or fiscal constraints inherited from the previous government, was instead met with stonewalling and the government's refusal to at least engage in a meaningful dialogue about this choice left many supporters feeling betrayed.

The handling of the Stage 3 tax cuts is another prime example of the government's narrative shortcomings. Labor had the opportunity to address this controversial policy head-on from the moment it took office. Instead, it allowed the issue to linger for 18 months, during which time the public discourse was dominated by criticism and speculation. By the time the tax cuts came into effect in July 2024, the narrative had already been shaped by negative headlines and internal party divisions, and the government's eventual actions were barely noticed.

The government tried to make a virtue of 'keeping a promise' on Stage 3 tax cuts, despite the immense inequity of the policy. Instead of just taking the right course of action in the first place, as well as upholding the principles of the Labor Party, Albanese allowed the negative headlines to linger for another 18 months and broke the electoral promise anyway. This was excruciatingly bad politics, and the worst of both worlds: a promise that the electorate wanted the government to break, which *was* ultimately broken and gave the government 18 months of negative headlines in the media.

The broader issue at play here is that without a strong narrative, the government's achievements are easily overshadowed by perceptions of failures pushed by its enemies. Labor has enacted policies that have had positive impacts and helped ease inflationary pressures, which is now far lower than at the time they inherited government in May 2022. However, the lack of a connecting narrative has allowed these successes to be dismissed or minimised in public discourse. The narrative vacuum has been filled by critics who frame these policies as inadequate or misguided, reinforcing the perception that the government is not doing enough.

This failure to articulate a strong, cohesive narrative is not just a communications problem; it reflects a deeper issue of leadership and vision. The electorate is unforgiving when it feels that a government is not delivering on its promises or lacks direction. Voters are not particularly concerned with the difficulties of governing; they want to see results and understand how those results fit into a larger plan. The absence of a compelling story that ties together the government's various policies and actions has left voters feeling that the Labor Party is lacking the boldness and clarity that is expected from progressive governments.

THE STRUGGLE TO BALANCE PRINCIPLES AND POLITICAL STRATEGY

These difficulties are also compounded by the apparent attempts to appease conservative forces within and outside the political landscape, allowing these operatives to unduly influence the government's agenda. This approach, which seems driven by a desire for bipartisanship and a misguided sense of political civility, has resulted in a dynamic where Dutton—despite his overtly divisive and often uncivil tactics—has been allowed to control much of the narrative around key issues. In attempting to achieve a level of cooperation with Dutton, Albanese has compromised on the very principles that should define his government, weakening its position and alienating significant portions of its base. When the Coalition is in office, they rarely take notice of Labor or progressive policies and are often dismissive and hostile towards the interests of working people. If that's the case, when Labor is in office, why is it always so keen to accommodate the interests of conservatives when that action is never reciprocated?

This disparity has led to a situation where Dutton sets the terms of the debate—with the assistance of a dutifully obliging mainstream media—while the Labor government struggles to assert its own narrative. Treasurer Jim Chalmers' forceful critique of Dutton exemplifies the kind of rhetoric that should have been a consistent part of the government's strategy.

> **Chalmers:** "Dutton is a divisive figure, and I believe he is too divisive to be the prime minister of a great country like ours—divisiveness is his defining and disqualifying characteristic. When most people look around the world and see the divisiveness in politics overseas, they want to reject it, and he seems to want to embrace it. His focus is on dividing people, and that's because that's all he knows, and it's all that he does."

Yet, this kind of firm stance has been the exception rather than the rule, with the government often appearing hesitant to confront Dutton and the opposition directly.

The lack of courage displayed by the Albanese government is not just a matter of political strategy; it reflects a broader failure to stand firm on issues that are crucial to its supporters. This reluctance to take bold positions has been evident in various areas, from foreign policy to social issues. On the issue of Palestine, for example, the government's fear of offending the conservative Israel lobby has led to a cautious and, in many eyes, morally compromised stance. This has not only alienated pro-Palestine advocates but has also fed into the perception that the government is more concerned with appeasing powerful interest groups than standing up for justice.

Similarly, the government's decision to initially exclude questions on LGBTQI+ issues from the 2026 census, only to reverse course after a significant backlash, highlights its tendency to fold under pressure from conservative elements. The initial decision seemed to be driven by a desire to avoid conflict with the Australian Christian Lobby and other socially conservative groups, even though this meant breaking a promise made to the LGBTQI+ community and an issue that is specifically contained with the Labor Platform. This kind of backtracking not only damages the government's credibility but also creates unnecessary division, undermining its own stated goal of avoiding such conflicts.

This trend of sidelining and unnecessarily antagonising important constituencies is dangerous for the Labor Party, especially as it prepares for the next election. The party's left flank, which includes many of the voters who helped secure its 2022 victory, is increasingly disillusioned with a government that seems to be drifting away from the progressive principles it championed from opposition. While it is true that governing often requires difficult decisions and compromises, the Albanese government appears to be losing sight of the need to maintain the support of those who brought it to power in the first place.

This is particularly problematic given the rising threat from the Australian Greens, who are increasingly positioning themselves as a progressive alternative to Labor. The Greens, with their distinct political and policy agenda, are already looking to outflank Labor on the left, capitalising on the dissatisfaction among voters who feel that Labor has failed to deliver on its promises.

The danger for the Albanese government is that it may squander the political capital it came into office with, leaving it vulnerable to a the Liberal–National parties on the right, and a growing challenge from the left. While some Labor supporters argue that the government needs more time to undo the destructive damage of nine years of Coalition rule between 2013–2022, there is a growing sense that the current trajectory is leading to disappointment rather than the bold reforms many hoped for.

The next election will be a critical test of whether the government can reclaim its narrative, reconnect with its base, and deliver on the promise of change that brought it to power. If it fails to do so, the Albanese government risks being remembered not for its achievements but for its missed opportunities and its failure to stand up for the very principles that it once championed.

***

RECLAIMING THE PUBLIC INTEREST AND CHALLENGING THE POWER OF THE SUPER RICH

31 August 2024

The influence of the super wealthy in Australian politics is a persistent and troubling issue that has deep roots in the nation's history, yet continues to evolve with the changing dynamics of global capitalism. The recent presentation by Gina Rinehart at the Bush Summit, an event funded by her own Hancock Corporation and presented by News Corporation is a reminder of this undue influence—Rinehart's speech, predictably self-serving, highlights the problems of this link between immense private wealth and public policy in Australia.

Rinehart, like many of her wealthy peers, advocate for a contradictory set of demands: she insists on more government spending while simultaneously calling for lower taxes, particularly in ways that benefit her own interests and those of the mining industry. This is reflective of the broader trend among Australia's wealthiest, who demand that the state serve their interests while vilifying any form of regulation that might curb their profit margins.

The call for the reduction of "red tape" and regulation, without any clear articulation of where these supposed bureaucratic obstacles lie, is a classic strategy employed by those who seek to operate with minimal oversight. This tactic, paired with an advocacy for downsizing the government, reflects a broader ideological assault on the role of the state in regulating industry and protecting public interests. The narrative that all government is inherently obstructive is a powerful one that plays out in the community, particularly when amplified by figures who hold significant economic power. However, this perspective is deeply flawed and fails to recognise the essential role that government plays in maintaining the balance between private profit and public good.

Rinehart's alignment with figures such as Donald Trump, and her financial support for his political endeavours—as well as her membership of Trump's high society female supporters, *the Trumpettes!*—highlights the global reach of this issue. Her rhetoric mirrors the populist, right-wing discourse that has gained traction in various parts of the world, advocating for aggressive resource exploitation (*"drill, baby, drill"*) without regard for the environmental or social consequences. This approach is not only short-sighted but dangerous, prioritising immediate profits over the long-term sustainability of the planet and the wellbeing of future generations.

Rinehart's proposals, such as compulsory military service—only for *"biological"* men and women"—and an Israeli-style Iron Dome system for Northern Australia, reveal a worldview that is outdated, psychotic and detached from the realities of contemporary Australian society. These ideas, reminiscent of her father Lang Hancock's controversial views—who announced in 1984 that he wanted to poison the waterholes of Indigenous people and "breed them out", as well as making business deals with the Romanian dictator, Nicolae Ceaușescu—highlight the grotesque political philosophy of some of Australia's wealthiest individuals, a philosophy that is rooted in a deep-seated belief in the primacy of wealth and power over social equity and justice.

Rinehart's tax practices further diminish the legitimacy of her public pronouncements—while the taxes paid by Hancock Corporation are according to the law and sail close to the wind, governments should be forcing a wealth tax or higher mineral royalty rates, not pandering to their interests. The media, out of fear or vested interest, especially in the case of Rupert Murdoch and Kerry Stokes who own significant resources interests, often fails to hold these individuals accountable, allowing them to shape the narrative in ways that serve their narrow interests.

This is where the distinction between wealth and class becomes critical: The super wealthy in Australia often lack the social consciousness and responsibility that should accompany their financial power. Their philanthropic efforts through charity, sportswashing and greenwashing, while touted as evidence of their benevolence, pale in comparison to the potential social benefits that would arise if they were taxed appropriately and those funds were distributed through public channels. This perpetuates a flawed system where the rich not only control the means of production but also the means of social reproduction, further entrenching their power.

The example of Norway provides an excellent example of Australia should proceed in the management of these issues. Norway's sovereign wealth fund, derived from its North Sea oil and gas reserves, is managed in the *public interest*, ensuring that the benefits of the country's natural resources are distributed more equitably. In Australia, even though the Constitution stipulates that natural resources belong to the Commonwealth, governments of all persuasions have implemented policies that effectively hand these resources over to private corporations, allowing them to reap enormous profits with minimal return to the public.

THE HYPOCRISY OF WEALTH: HOW AUSTRALIA'S ELITE MANIPULATE POLITICS FOR PERSONAL GAIN

The entanglement of Australia's super wealthy with the nation's politics is not just a matter of undue influence but also a reflection of a broader ideological project that seeks to reshape society in their image. They hold a set of beliefs that are both politically naive and economically unsound, yet these ideas continue to gain traction, largely due to the enormous financial resources these individuals possess.

The irony in their positions is glaring, where they regularly denounce the role of government, advocating for reduced taxes or the outright elimination of taxes, all in the name of fostering a freer, more entrepreneurial society. However, this rhetoric is little more than a smokescreen for their true intentions: securing favourable government support and subsidies that directly benefit their businesses. Hancock Corporation's joint ventures into the rare mineral sector, for instance, are bolstered by government funding that is not only unnecessary but also serves to further entrench the economic dominance of those who are already at the top.

This selective engagement with government—where support is welcomed when it benefits the wealthy but decried when it aids the less fortunate—reveals a clear double standard. Individuals like Gerry Harvey, who lobbied successfully for changes to the impost of GST on international purchases to protect his business interests, while also suggesting that giving money to the homeless was to "help a whole heap of no-hopers survive for no good reason", exemplify this hypocrisy. The case of Andrew Forrest and the BasicsCard, which was tied to the Indue card company with connections to former Liberal Party MPs, further illustrates this point. Here, we see the super wealthy leveraging their political influence to shape policy in ways that benefit them personally, often under the guise of promoting the public good.

This stance reveals a disturbing lack of empathy and a deep-seated belief in their own superiority—an assumption that their wealth somehow makes them more deserving of government support than those who struggle to make ends meet. The belief in the inherent superiority of the wealthy is a dangerous fallacy, one that has been propagated by figures like Ayn Rand and other proponents of neoliberal ideology. This narrative suggests that business success is a marker of intelligence and capability, on par with or even surpassing the achievements of scientists, academics, and other professionals. However, this notion is demonstrably false. The wealth of these individuals is more often a product of privilege and inherited opportunity than of exceptional intelligence or hard work—they are not particularly innovative or bright; they are simply beneficiaries of a system that rewards the accumulation of capital above all else and a case of being in the right place at the right time.

Australia faces a choice: to continue down the path of increasing inequality and oligarchic rule, or to take bold steps to reclaim the political system from the grip of the super wealthy. This means not only challenging the undue influence of individuals like Rinehart, Harvey, and Forrest but also rethinking the very structure of the economy that allows such extreme concentrations of wealth to exist in the first place.

GOVERNMENT NEEDS TO ACT IN THE PUBLIC INTEREST

The central part of this issue is that the influence of the super wealthy over Australian politics is not just a matter of skewed priorities—it's a direct assault on the public interest. When governments, including Labor governments, cater to the whims of billionaires and corporate elites, it is the taxpayer who ultimately bears the cost. The case of the mining industry is perhaps the most blatant example, but it is far from the only one. Across various sectors, from health to superannuation, the influence of the wealthy and their corporate interests has led to a situation where public funds are increasingly funneled into private hands, exacerbating inequality and undermining the public good.

The health sector is a prime example of this trend. Projections indicate that in just a decade, *more* government funds will be allocated to private health subsidies than to Medicare. This shift is not accidental; it is the result of sustained lobbying by major health corporations and their army of lobbyists. These entities have managed to convince malleable governments that subsidising private health is in the national interest, when in reality, it serves to deepen the divide between those who can afford top-tier private care and those who rely on an increasingly underfunded public system.

Similarly, the superannuation sector is set to absorb more government subsidies than the government makes in pensions payments within the next 15 years. This too is a consequence of government policy being shaped by the interests of the wealthy, who benefit disproportionately from superannuation tax concessions. These concessions, often justified as necessary incentives for retirement savings, largely benefit those who are already well-off, while ordinary workers see little of the supposed benefits.

The aged care sector further illustrates this dynamic, where government support is channeled into private enterprises rather than public services, ensuring that the profits flow to shareholders rather than improving care for the elderly. This is a perverse outcome of neoliberal policies that prioritise privatisation and deregulation, often at the expense of those who most need support.

There is also a massive gap between the wealth class and the income class in Australia. The wealth class—those who derive their income from shares, property, and capital ownership—enjoys a system that is heavily skewed in their favour. They benefit from lower tax rates and numerous concessions, while the income class—ordinary working people—shoulders a much heavier tax burden through PAYG income taxes. This disparity is not just unfair; it is unsustainable. It reflects a broader neoliberal agenda that has dominated Australian politics for decades, where the state increasingly subsidises private institutions and the wealthy, often at a greater cost than if the government had simply provided these services directly.

This is not just an economic issue but a moral one. The government's role should be to protect and uplift its citizens, not to cater to the demands of the wealthy few and Labor governments, in particular, should be at the forefront of resisting this trend. The party's traditional base is not the corporate elite but the working people of Australia—those who rely on a fair and just government to safeguard their rights and interests. For too long, Labor has been caught in a bind, trying to appease both its base and the wealthy interests that exert so much influence over Australian politics.

It is time to reassert the public interest over corporate interests. This means raising taxes on the wealthy to ensure they pay their fair share—something they have been evading for far too long. It means rejecting the constant demands for subsidies and concessions that only serve to enrich the already rich. It means saying no to the undue influence that billionaires and corporate elites have over public policy.

Instead, the government should focus on those who truly need support. It should lift up those who have been left behind by decades of neoliberal policies that prioritise profits over people. This should be the core of the Labor narrative: a commitment to equity, fairness, and the public good. The party should champion policies that close the gap between the wealth class and the income class, that strengthen public services like Medicare, education and aged care, that ensure the benefits of economic growth are shared by all, not just the privileged few.

A Labor government should be the voice of the less powerful, those who have been systematically marginalised. This is not just a matter of political strategy but of moral responsibility. There needs to be a fundamental shift in the way we think about wealth, power, and the role of government in creating a fair and just society. The rewards—an Australia that is fairer, more equitable, and more just—are worth fighting for.

***

SEPTEMBER

WILL SUPER-PROFITS AND WEALTH TAXES UNLOCK A FAIRER FUTURE?

7 September 2024

The growing calls for the introduction of a super-profits tax and wealth tax in Australia reflect a wider discontent with the existing taxation system, which disproportionately favour large corporations and the wealthy. These proposals are becoming a focal point in the broader conversation about economic equity, as more Australians begin to question whether the burden of taxation is being shared fairly. The fundamental issue at stake here is whether those who benefit most from the economic system are contributing enough back into it, especially when so many individuals and smaller businesses continue to shoulder a disproportionately high tax burden.

The idea of a super-profits tax is not new to Australia: in 2010, the Labor government introduced a similar concept, although it was quickly diluted and applied only to the mining sector and this limited application resulted in a policy that failed to address the broader structural imbalances in the taxation system. The current debate surrounding a wealth tax has gained further momentum in recent years, even receiving cautious endorsement from unexpected quarters such as the CEO of the Commonwealth Bank, Matt Comyn, where he pointed out that Australia's reliance on income tax is outdated and inefficient, calling for a shift toward taxing wealth more substantially.

The Australian Greens have been the most vocal advocates for both a wealth tax and a super-profits tax, but their proposals have been met with skepticism from the major parties. The Labor government, wary of being perceived as too aligned with the Greens, has dismissed these ideas as "attention-seeking" measures, while the Coalition, traditionally pro-business, has offered little appetite for reforms that would impose greater taxes on the wealthiest individuals and corporations. This political deadlock reveals a deeper problem within Australia's tax policy debate—one that prioritises short-term political gamesmanship over long-term structural reform.

Australia's tax system is one of the most complex in the world, and this complexity benefits those who can afford to navigate it. A super-profits tax, if implemented properly, could begin to address many economic issues by targeting extreme concentrations of corporate wealth. The concept is straightforward: once a company reaches a certain and significant threshold of profit, its tax rate also increases significantly. Such a policy would ensure that companies benefiting from Australia's economic landscape are contributing their fair share to the public good, without placing undue strain on smaller businesses or individuals. Similarly, a wealth tax could serve to level the playing field by taxing the accumulated assets of the richest Australians, rather than relying solely on income taxes, which often miss the vast sums of wealth that sit untaxed in investments and property.

Yet, the resistance to such reforms is deeply ingrained, especially within the neoliberal framework that has dominated Australian economic policy for decades. The narrative, often propagated by powerful media moguls and corporate interests, is that taxation is an undue burden on wealth creators—but this is not only about redistributing wealth; it is about ensuring that the public infrastructure, services, and institutions that allow businesses to thrive are adequately funded.

COMPLEXITY IS A BARRIER TO REFORM AND AN ADVANTAGE FOR THE WEALTHY

The complexity of Australia's taxation system is one of the most significant barriers to meaningful reform, particularly when it comes to implementing taxes that could address wealth inequality. The existing structure, with its sprawling 14,000 pages of tax law, is symptomatic of a system that is both cumbersome and opaque, allowing those with access to the best legal and financial advice to exploit loopholes and minimise their tax obligations. This complexity doesn't serve the broader public interest but instead benefits a small, wealthy class that can afford to navigate its intricacies.

For large corporations and wealthy individuals, the complexity of the tax system becomes a tool for tax avoidance and this ability to structure earnings in such a way that they are either taxed at a lower rate or not at all is a privilege that most Australians don't have, making the system inherently unequal.

This imbalance has led many economists, surprisingly, to support the introduction of a wealth tax and, to a lesser extent, a super-profits tax, as tools to level the playing field. However, these ideas face substantial barriers, not just in terms of political will but in aligning the various interests that influence the taxation debate. Corporations, legal professionals, lobbyists, and politicians all have a stake in maintaining the status quo, or at least ensuring that any reforms do not significantly disrupt the current balance of power and wealth. Governments, too, tend to act based on political instincts, opting for policies that are more likely to secure their re-election rather than those that might introduce meaningful but difficult reforms.

One of the major proposals to overcome this political inertia is to take taxation out of the hands of politicians altogether, much like the Reserve Bank operates independently to set monetary policy. The idea is that an independent body could be tasked with redesigning the tax system in a way that promotes equity and simplicity, without the short-term political calculations that often undermine reform efforts.

However, this approach is not without its own risks. The Reserve Bank of Australia, once a model of independence, has recently come under fire for decisions that seem to align suspiciously with the political cycle, and this has led to concerns that so-called "independent" institutions are not always free from political influence. Any independent taxation body would need to ensure that it remains genuinely impartial, representing the interests of all Australians rather than the wealthy elite or corporate sector.

The other consideration is that taxation is not just an *economic* issue; it's inherently *political*, and decisions about who gets taxed and how much they pay are tied to broader questions about the kind of society Australians want to live in. Should the wealthy contribute more to the public good, or should they be allowed to retain the bulk of their earnings? Should corporations be required to pay higher taxes on extraordinary profits, or should they be allowed to reinvest those earnings in ways that they argue benefit the economy?

A truly independent body might be able to overcome these political hurdles, but it would have to be carefully constructed. It would need representation not just from economists and business leaders but from a broad cross-section of society, including those who understand the impact of taxation on low-income earners and vulnerable populations. Without this balance, any reforms are likely to be seen as either overly technocratic or, worse, as a continuation of policies that favour the wealthy.

The Labor Party's experience in the 2019 federal election is also a cautionary tale of how politically charged tax reforms can be. After proposing to reform capital gains tax, negative gearing, and franking credits, Labor suffered a surprising defeat, largely attributed to a scare campaign that framed these proposals as an attack on retirees and middle-class Australians. This loss has made the current Labor government risk-averse when it comes to tax reform, despite growing public support for changes that would make the system more equitable.

What is clear is that the current situation is unsustainable. Australia's taxation system is not only inefficient and complex, but it also fails to address the growing wealth inequality that is eroding social cohesion. Without significant reform, the country risks entrenching a two-tiered system, where the wealthy can continue to avoid their tax obligations while ordinary Australians bear an increasing share of the burden.

A PATH TOWARD FAIRNESS AND ECONOMIC RESTRUCTURING

The challenge of implementing a super-profits tax or a wealth tax in Australia is undoubtedly complex *politically*, but governments should not shy away from pursuing these reforms, particularly given the significant potential benefits for the broader population. Despite the knee-jerk reaction from conservative parties, who label such proposals as part of a "socialist" or "communist" agenda, these taxes are fundamentally about fairness and equity, not about antiquated ideological battles. They aim to ensure that those who can afford to contribute more are doing so, especially during times of economic difficulties experienced by many people in the community. In the current landscape of growing national debt and underfunded public services, governments have a compelling narrative to justify the introduction of these taxes: the need to raise funds for essential services that will benefit all Australians. So why don't they push these narratives that would allow them to implement these reforms?

The role of government should be to improve the quality of life for as many people as possible. Taxes on wealth and super-profits provide a clear path toward this goal, unlocking much-needed revenue for infrastructure, education, health care, and other critical areas. By framing these reforms as necessary steps to restore balance to the system, governments should be able to win public support for these measures.

Accusations of populism are often leveled at such proposals, with conservative critics suggesting that they appeal to voters' base instincts without delivering real solutions. But if right-wing populism, driven by promises of tax cuts and deregulation, can dominate the political landscape, why can't a form of left-wing populism do the same? It's not populism for the sake of it—it's about acknowledging the reality that Australia's wealth is concentrated in the hands of a few, and that the tax system should reflect this.

Contrary to the argument that higher taxes on the wealthy would disincentivise entrepreneurship or wealth creation, the levels being discussed would affect only a tiny fraction of the population. Would Gina Rinehart's ability for further wealth creation be damaged if her wealth decreased from $28 billion in 2020, down to $14 billion, after the application of a super-profits tax? She certainly has enough excess profits to sponsor Australia's Olympic swimming team and other sportswashing activities.

Those impacted by a wealth tax or super-profits tax would largely be people who have already accumulated significant fortunes or companies generating extraordinary profits. These taxes would not stifle economic growth or innovation but would ensure that a fair share of the wealth generated within the country is returned to society in the form of public services and social welfare programs. And by redistributing some of the nation's wealth, the government would also be better able to support those who are struggling, especially in areas where private-sector solutions have failed.

In sectors such as private childcare, early education and aged care, the inadequacies of privatisation have become increasingly apparent. The profits being made in these industries are not being sufficiently reinvested in the services themselves but are instead funneled upwards to boards, executives and shareholders. This leaves workers—educators, aged care workers, and others—underpaid and overworked, while families struggle to afford basic care. In such cases, it is clear that the private sector has failed to deliver the outcomes that it promised. Instead of reducing costs and improving quality, privatisation has driven profits into the hands of a few while leaving the services themselves underfunded and inefficient. This is a prime example of how an unchecked focus on privatisation and a brazen pursuit of profit can harm society as a whole.

Ultimately, the introduction of a super-profits tax or wealth tax is not just about raising revenue; it is about reshaping the economy to better serve the needs of the entire population. It would signal a shift away from the failed policies of neoliberalism that have dominated Australian politics for the past 40 years, toward a system that values fairness, equity, and social responsibility. While implementing these changes will be politically difficult, the potential rewards—both in terms of electoral success and societal benefits—make the challenge worth pursuing.

***

LABOR'S FIGHT FOR PROGRESSIVE REFORM IN THE FACE OF COALITION SABOTAGE

14 September 2024

The Labor government has long expressed a desire to introduce significant reforms, particularly in areas of economic governance, such as restructuring the Reserve Bank of Australia to include a specialist interest rate setting board. Despite the importance and urgency of these reforms, the Liberal–National Coalition has made it clear that they will not participate in negotiations, leaving the Labor government in a bind. While bipartisanship is often seen as a desirable way to pass lasting and broadly accepted reforms, the question arises: why does Labor continue to pursue cooperation with a party that, in opposition, consistently obstructs rather than collaborates?

Since the 2022 federal election—and even before, between 2007–2013—the Coalition has operated with a strategy of relentless and maniacal opposition. When in government between 2013 and 2022, they pursued their agenda with little concern for reaching agreements that appeal to the Labor Party. Now, in opposition, they have returned to a familiar role of blocking reforms rather than engaging in constructive debate. Their refusal to participate in the Reserve Bank reforms reflects a deeper political reality—bipartisanship has become an empty ideal, at least where the Coalition is concerned.

Treasurer Jim Chalmers has made no secret of his reluctance to negotiate with the Australian Greens, a party that, while smaller, has shown a greater willingness to engage with Labor on reformist policies. Yet, despite the Coalition's entrenched resistance, Chalmers has made it clear that he would still rather avoid dealing with the

Greens, if possible. This raises an important question about the current state of Australian politics: why does Labor, a party ostensibly committed to progressive reform, still push for cooperation with a conservative Coalition that seems incapable of offering it?

Part of the answer lies with the political optics that govern economic policy in Australia: by engaging with the Greens, the Labor government risks being seen by certain sectors, particularly in the world of finance and the media, as aligning with "economic extremists". The Coalition has long played into this narrative, framing the Greens as a radical, unreliable partner on issues such as fiscal policy, resources, climate change, and economic reform. In reality, however, this strategy of demonising the Greens is less about substance and more about maintaining a neoliberal economic orthodoxy that the Coalition clings to, despite its growing irrelevance in a changing world. And if the Greens are considered to be too extreme, then what exactly are the National Party?

Politics is not just about ideology; it is about power. While it is true that Labor's leadership, including Chalmers, may prefer to avoid dealing with the Greens, the reality is that in the current parliament, they have no other choice. The Coalition's refusal to engage leaves Labor with few alternatives but to seek alliances with the Greens and like-minded crossbenchers such as David Pocock who hold considerable sway in today's fractured political landscape. In contrast to the Coalition's nihilism, these crossbenchers can negotiate and participate in constructive dialogue, even if they don't always agree with the government.

Peter Dutton's leadership of the Liberal Party has only exacerbated the Coalition's drift toward political destruction. Far from being a party of responsible governance, Dutton's Liberals have become the true anarchists of Australian politics. His approach is one of obstruction and sabotage, not of dialogue or cooperation. Labor may not like dealing with the Australian Greens, but the Greens, for all their differences, are not political wreckers. They may push for policies Labor finds too radical or impractical, but their politics is rooted in a desire for constructive progressive change, unlike the

Coalition, whose sole mission in opposition is the undermining of any government agenda.

This destructive tendency in the Liberal Party is not new, but it has been amplified in recent years, whether they are in government or opposition. The nine years of Coalition rule, even under ostensibly a moderate leader such as Malcolm Turnbull, demonstrated the lengths to which the party's right-wing factions would go to sabotage their own leaders, let alone the opposition. Dutton, as leader, is the pinnacle of this tendency: his leadership style is characterised by a willingness to throw bombs at any reform effort, a refusal to engage in meaningful debate, and a desire to cater to the most reactionary elements of his party's base.

In this context, it is difficult to understand why Labor continues to hold out hope for bipartisanship with a party that is, in effect, no longer interested in the art of compromise. If Labor is serious about implementing its reform agenda, it needs to recognise that the political landscape has shifted and the Coalition, in its current form, is not a partner for responsible governance. Also, Labor's continued attempts to negotiate with the Coalition only serve to legitimise their obstructionism. By continually offering the hand of bipartisanship to a party that has made it clear they are not interested, Labor risks wasting valuable political capital.

THE NEED FOR A PROGRESSIVE COALITION AMIDST COALITION OBSTRUCTION

No issue is too small for the Coalition to oppose, and their current issue of choice is the process for appointing members to the Reserve Bank Board, where they argue the proposed reforms could lead to "board stacking," and appointments skewed to favour certain ideological positions or political allies. This argument is disingenuous and lacks credibility when looking at recent political history. The Coalition, when in government, has consistently engaged in the very behaviour they now railing against. From stacking the boards of the Reserve Bank to the Fair Work Commission and various public institutions such as the ABC, Australia Post and the Human Rights Commission, their track record on this issue is undeniable: The Coalition stacks; *that's what they do.*

The hypocrisy of the Coalition's position is clear. Their sudden concern about the integrity of the appointment process is more a tactic of obstruction than a genuine critique. In fact, it is a continuation of their broader strategy to prevent any meaningful reform that does not align with their neoliberal ideology. What Dutton's Liberal Party truly fears is the possibility of structural changes that reduce their ability to influence key economic institutions in the future.

Also, the Liberal Party has shown time and again that it is more interested in blowing up parliamentary processes than contributing constructively and intent on dismantling any reforms that would modernise Australia's economic and political structures. Yet, despite the Coalition's clear lack of good faith, Labor's hesitation to negotiate with the Australian Greens is puzzling when taking their increasing electoral significance into account.

With around 12 per of the primary vote at the 2022 federal election, the Greens are not an insignificant political force. The Liberal Party, by comparison, receives roughly 24 per cent of the vote. Certainly, while this is almost double the Greens' support, it's not a vast difference in relative terms—especially when considering the National Party's 7 per cent and far-right fringe dweller One Nation's 5 per cent of the primary vote. These figures show that the Greens are closer to mainstream political support than their far-right counterparts, who receive far more political respect and media attention.

Despite these realities, anti-Green sentiment remains pervasive in the political and media landscapes. The media often perpetuates the narrative that the Greens are "extreme" and "unreasonable", which serves to marginalise them in political debates. The Shadow Treasurer Angus Taylor is a prime example of this bias, where he suggested the Greens are "economic radicals" who want to "take over" the Reserve Bank and the broader banking system, a narrative designed to stoke fear and suspicion. This framing creates the false impression that negotiating with the Greens is inherently dangerous or irresponsible, despite their substantial electoral base and the growing popularity of many of their policies.

This media narrative, in turn, creates a political environment where Labor feels compelled to avoid engaging with the Greens, where such negotiations would be framed as a capitulation to extremism. Yet this framing ignores the reality of the Coalition's intransigence. Who are the *real* extremists here? Labor's preference to negotiate with the Coalition over the Greens may be based on a desire to appear moderate and responsible, but it is increasingly a political liability. The Coalition is not a partner for reform—it is a political force determined to block Labor's agenda at every turn.

The current situation leaves Labor with two clear options: continue the futile pursuit of bipartisanship with the Coalition, or shift focus to building an alliance with the Greens and other crossbenchers. While the Coalition's obstructionism is predictable, Labor's hesitation to embrace the Greens as potential allies risks leaving them with no clear path forward on critical reforms such as those proposed for the Reserve Bank.

The hesitation to deal with the Greens is not just a tactical mistake—it is a failure to recognise the evolving political reality. In a parliament where the crossbench holds significant influence, Labor needs to adapt to the new dynamics of power. This requires abandoning the notion that the Coalition can be a reliable partner in governance and embracing the potential of a progressive coalition that includes the Greens and like-minded independents. The risks of this approach are outweighed by the potential rewards: the ability to pass meaningful reforms, reshape Australian politics, and isolate the Coalition as a party of obstruction and irrelevance.

As it stands, Labor's unwillingness to engage the Greens is a symptom of a broader political malaise: a lack of boldness and an over-reliance on outdated strategies that no longer serve the party or the country. If Labor wants to be seen as a party of progress and reform, they must be willing to embrace those who share their commitment to change—even if it means dealing with parties and politicians that challenge their comfort zone.

BIPARTISANSHIP IS DEAD: WHY LABOR MUST EMBRACE ITS MANDATE AND GOVERN ASSERTIVELY

It's apparent that Labor government's pursuit of bipartisanship has increasingly become a liability rather than an asset and the reality is that this effort has consistently yielded few tangible results. The National Anti-Corruption Commission was introduced with an aim of broad bipartisan support, yet the Coalition offered little cooperation, except for changes that it found favourable and allowed them to escape scrutiny for their own corrupt behaviours during their time in office between 2013 and 2022. When it came to the Voice to Parliament referendum, despite Labor's overtures to the Coalition, it was met with outright hostility and sabotage: the desire for bipartisanship is undermining Labor's ability to govern effectively. What did these attempts at bipartisanship achieve? Absolutely *nothing*: the NACC has been a failure and the Voice to Parliament was comprehensively defeated.

Politics is, at its core, about wielding power to implement policy. When a party wins an election, it is given a mandate to pursue its agenda, not to pander to the party that lost. The Labor government seems to have forgotten this fundamental principle: instead of focusing on implementing their policies through effective negotiation with those who are willing to engage constructively (that is, *anyone but the Coalition*), they are trapped in a futile cycle of seeking approval from a party that has no intention of granting it.

John Howard's approach to governing is instructive here. As Prime Minister, he was known for his hard-nosed negotiation style, working with minor parties like the Australian Democrats and the independent Brian Harradine to pass key pieces of legislation. Howard understood that you don't get your agenda handed to you in politics—*you have to fight for it*, inch by inch, concession by concession. He didn't bend over backwards to appease the opposition but instead, focused on building alliances where he could, pushing his policies through sheer political will and shrewd negotiation. While this Labor government is diametrically opposite to the Howard government—or, at least, *it should be*—it could learn from Howard's tactics and strategies.

Essentially, these Reserve Bank reforms are a minor issue that few people would care about, but the way the government is handling the process reveals a larger problem. Instead of using its electoral mandate to move forward assertively, Labor appears hesitant and unwilling to challenge the Coalition head-on. After spending so long in opposition, Labor seems unsure of how to wield power effectively now that they are in government. This timidity, this refusal to fully embrace their right to govern, is hindering their ability to dismantle the destructive legacies of the previous government.

The NACC, for example, was hailed as a breakthrough in accountability. Yet, the NACC has so far failed in all its major tests of holding the previous Coalition to account. It might currently be investigating six serving and former ministers—unknown at this stage—but it has not yet demonstrated the kind of robust, fearless action needed to hold those truly responsible for past abuses to account. This failure is emblematic of a government that is not fighting hard enough to remove the toxic remnants of the last decade of Coalition rule. From Robodebt to AUKUS, there is a long list of Coalition policies and legacies that Labor should be systematically dismantling—not negotiating around.

The Labor government has a clear example in its own history of what it looks like to fight effectively while in power. Anthony Albanese himself once proudly declared, "I fight Tories. *That's what I do*". Yet, since becoming Prime Minister, we've seen little evidence of this fight. Great Labor leaders of the past—Paul Keating, Bob Hawke, Gough Whitlam—never stopped fighting, even when they did succumb to certain neoliberalism ideals of the time. Even Kevin Rudd and Julia Gillard, who governed in the most fractious of circumstances, kept swinging at the Tories until the very end. Labor has a long tradition of fighting for its policies and vision for the country, yet this current government seems reluctant to fully embrace that role.

This reluctance to fight is not just bad politics: *it's bad policy*. Without a willingness to engage in the tough political battles necessary to push through reforms, Labor risks squandering its time in government. There is no room for compromise when the opposition party's strategy is to obstruct and destroy. Instead of treating the Coalition as potential partners, Labor should recognise them for what they are: political adversaries and nihilists intent on preventing the government from achieving its goals.

The consequences of this hesitancy are already starting to show. Labor's support in opinion polls is waning, and a minority government after the next election—or worse, a return to power for the Coalition—is becoming a real possibility. While some might dismiss this notion this as alarmism, recent Australian political history is full of surprises. Few thought Tony Abbott would become Prime Minister, until he *did* become Prime Minister, yet his rise—and the damage his government inflicted on the country—still reverberates almost a decade later. The same mistake cannot be made with Dutton, a leader who, like Abbott, thrives on wrecking and opposition.

Labor must toughen up, embrace its mandate, and govern with the assertiveness that its electoral victory entitles it to. This means no longer kowtowing to the Coalition in a futile attempt at bipartisanship. Instead, it means building coalitions with those who are willing to negotiate in good faith, not the retrograde forces of the Liberal Party under Dutton.

Labor's responsibility is to fight for its policies, its vision, and its supporters. Only by doing so can they avoid the possibility of a minority government or, worse, the nightmare scenario of a Dutton-led Coalition returning to power. In the end, governing is not about appeasing your opponents—it's about fighting for what you believe in, even when the path forward is difficult. The Labor government has the tools, the mandate, and the moral authority to implement the changes Australia desperately needs: it just needs the will to fight for them.

***

THE SANITISATION OF WAR AND THE HUMAN COST OF THE LAND FORCES EXPO

15 September 2024

The recent Land Forces exposition held in Melbourne is yet another troubling mix of commerce, militarisation, and violence, and its existence provokes deep ethical questions that should concern many Australians. As an international military conference, the expo is not only a display of technological innovation but a marketplace where global arms manufacturers peddle tools of destruction to government representatives who, in turn, defend the rights of these manufacturers to display their killing field machines. It's an event that offers no public transparency, operating in a sphere of selective admission—not open to the general public—where those with power, broker deals in the shadow of secrecy.

The protests that erupted in opposition to Land Forces were a direct response to the moral and human costs that arise from such an event, where around 2,000 people, backed by nearly 50 activist organisations, unified under the "Disrupt Land Forces" banner to challenge the ethics of such a gathering. Their concerns are valid and pointed, focusing not only on the immediate harms of militarised violence but also on the broader, systemic impact that the global arms trade has on civilian populations. These weapons, flaunted for their precision and lethal value, often find their first real-world applications in conflicts involving civilians—Gaza, Yemen, Sudan, Ukraine, and many other active conflicts around the world. Such locations have become testing grounds for weaponry that, after proving its efficiency in destruction, is marketed to governments eager to bolster their military capabilities.

The moral contradiction at the heart of the global arms trade is difficult to ignore. On one hand, there is the recognition by many sociologists and peace advocates that conflict is a perennial part of the human condition, and as such, the goal should be to minimise violence and end conflict swiftly when it does arise. On the other hand, the arms trade flourishes in direct opposition to this ideal, driven by a pursuit of profit that thrives on the continuation, and often the escalation, of war. The United States, which holds a 40 per cent share of the global arms market, is the epitome of this paradox: while there is widespread acknowledgment that the world should be moving toward peace, the economic interests tied to the production and sale of weapons continue to fuel global instability.

For the protestors, it is especially galling that such an expo takes place in Australia, a country that, while geographically distant from many of the world's major conflicts, plays an increasing role in the global arms trade. The question arises: who is this expo really for? The Australian military knows what it needs and already has access to the global arms market through existing channels—in an age where information and trade can be conducted over the internet, the rationale for a physical gathering of this kind is tenuous.

The ethical implications become even more pronounced when we consider the nature of the protests themselves. The clashes between demonstrators and police, which have involved the use of tear gas, pepper spray, foam bullets and, in response, acid being thrown at law enforcement, highlight the extent to which these concerns have polarised communities. While such violence is regrettable, it also highlights the desperation felt by those who oppose the militarisation of society. The use of weapons designed to subdue protestors, whether tear gas or rubber bullets, is a reminder of the very industry that the expo represents—an industry that profits from control, domination, and, ultimately, the suppression of dissent.

Land Forces may seem like a niche event, but its broader implications can't be ignored. It is a symbol of a global arms trade that prioritises profit over human life, exacerbates conflicts rather than resolves them, and tests its deadly wares on the world's most vulnerable populations. As such, it is no surprise that the expo is met with such fierce resistance, nor is it surprising that these protests sometimes escalate into violence. In a world where weapons of war are treated as commodities, the lines between defence and aggression, between peacekeeping and warmongering, are increasingly blurred. It is a dynamic that will continue to provoke protest, and justifiably so, as long as the global arms trade remains as profitable, perverse and pervasive as it is today.

AUSTRALIA'S ROLE IN THE GLOBAL ARMS TRADE

The sanitisation of warfare through slick, polished events is a disturbing trend that disconnects the public from the brutal realities of modern conflict. Inside the expo's pristine conference rooms and exhibition halls, weapons of war are displayed not as instruments of death, but as technological marvels—gleaming, advanced, and indispensable, and there is a dissonance between the sterile, commercialised environment of the trade show and the devastation these weapons cause. These tools of destruction are showcased as feats of human ingenuity, but they are designed to kill, often indiscriminately, and their most common victims are civilians—women, children, and the elderly—whose lives and communities are irrevocably shattered.

This sanitisation is not unique to Land Forces—similar events take place globally, making the militarisation of society appear normal. Certainly, warfare today no longer looks like the historic battles of Gallipoli or World War II, where soldiers fought face-to-face on defined battlefields: it has evolved into a state where unmanned drones, autonomous weapons systems, and long-range missiles can obliterate targets thousands of miles away with the push of a button, often hitting civilian populations and critical infrastructure.

A common refrain, echoed by proponents of the military industry, is that it's not *weapons* that kill people, but the *humans* who deploy them, an argument which mirrors the rhetoric of the destructive U.S. gun lobby, where firearms are presented as neutral tools, with the responsibility for violence placed solely on the individuals wielding them. However, this reasoning is simplistic and fails to account for the immense social, political, and economic structures that make warfare profitable and perpetual. Arms manufacturers are not passive actors in global conflict; they actively lobby governments, exploit geopolitical tensions, and provide the tools that fuel wars. It is naïve to suggest that these actors simply exist to respond to a dangerous world when *they*, in fact, are deeply involved in creating and sustaining that danger.

Australia, though often perceived as playing a minor role in global conflicts, is more deeply entrenched in the arms trade than it publicly acknowledges. The country has aligned itself with major global powers through agreements like AUKUS and controversial military installations like Pine Gap, which plays a crucial role in U.S. military operations. The presence of Israeli defence companies at Land Forces is a reminder of how closely Australia's arms trade is linked to global human rights abuses. These companies tout their weapons as "battle-tested" but fail to mention that this "experience" comes from decades of military operations in Palestine, where civilians have borne the brunt of Israeli military aggression, especially over the past year in Gaza. For Australia to buy into this narrative without questioning the ethical implications of supporting such industries—and actually using special Victoria riot police forces to enforce this narrative—is deeply troubling.

This move toward a more prominent role in the global arms market can be traced back to former Defence Minister Christopher Pyne, who in 2017 expressed his desire for Australia to become a top-ten international arms producer. This ambition signals a shift in Australia's identity—moving from a nation that has historically focused on regional peacekeeping and defence to one that seeks profit in the global arms race. Australians would likely be shocked if they fully understood the extent of their country's involvement in the arms trade, the nations receiving these weapons, and the atrocities that are committed by using these arms. Much of this information flies under the radar, hidden from public scrutiny, leaving citizens in the dark about how deeply their country is enmeshed in an industry that profits from global instability.

While it is true that a defence force is necessary for most countries, and that military personnel often play critical roles in disaster relief and humanitarian efforts, this does not justify the normalisation of the arms trade or the glamorisation of military technology. The defence of a nation should not be conflated with the uncritical acceptance of an industry that profits from war. The display of military hardware at events like the Land Forces Expo serves no real defence purpose but rather feeds into a culture of militarisation that seeks to make war palatable, even desirable, under the guise of security and technological advancement.

What Australia truly needs is a more mature and thoughtful approach to defence—one that prioritises diplomacy, peace-building, and conflict resolution over the pursuit of profit through the arms trade. As the world evolves and new security challenges emerge, it is important that Australia rethinks its approach to military engagement. War in the 21st century does not resemble the conflicts of the past, and our understanding of what it means to defend a nation must adapt accordingly. Rather than showcasing military might and buying into the arms race, Australia should be leading efforts to promote peace and stability, using its influence to reduce global conflict rather than exacerbate it.

Failing to reassess these priorities risks leaving Australia trapped in a cycle of militarisation, where economic interests in the arms trade take precedence over the moral imperative to pursue peace. Without significant changes in how the country views defence and warfare, Australia may find itself increasingly entangled in the very conflicts it claims it wants to avoid.

***

THE LABOR–GREENS INFIGHTING OVER HOUSING LEAVES AUSTRALIANS IN LIMBO

21 September 2024

The debate between the Australian Labor government and the Greens over housing policy has descended into an unedifying spectacle and bitter political standoff. What should be a critical conversation about addressing the housing crisis, a fundamental issue for millions of Australians, has instead become a platform for political theatre, childish name-calling, and a clash of egos that reflects a deepening divide on how best to address housing affordability. And, as usual, the public is being left behind.

The current standoff is based around two bills proposed by the government: "Help to Buy" scheme is designed to assist 40,000 potential homebuyers through a government equity contribution, enabling them to purchase homes with as little as a 2 per cent deposit; and the "Build to Rent" program which seeks to incentivise private developers to create rental housing, with 10 per cent of those units offered at below-market rates. For Labor, these policies represent pragmatic, incremental solutions to a crisis that has left millions struggling to afford rent or buy homes.

However, the Greens, led by their housing spokesperson, Max Chandler-Mather, argue that these measures fall woefully short, and the Help to Buy scheme does little more than inflate house prices by injecting more demand into an already overheated market without addressing the structural issues behind the housing shortages. Chandler-Mather has also criticised the Build to Rent proposal, claiming that offering just 10 per cent of rentals at discounted rates is insufficient and is calling for a much more radical approach: a public housing initiative where the government itself acts as a developer, building homes to rent and ensuring long-term affordability, with rent increases capped at 2 per cent annually.

The gulf between these two positions is wide, but the rhetoric accompanying the debate has made negotiation almost impossible. Prime Minister Albanese's dismissal of Chandler-Mather's criticisms as immature and spiteful only entrenches the Greens' position further. Meanwhile, the finance minister Katy Gallagher's accusation that the Greens are working hand-in-hand with Peter Dutton and the Liberal Party to block legislation feeds the narrative that the Greens are playing politics rather than seeking substantive change.

The irony here is that the Greens' demands are more closely aligned with traditional Labor values than the current government's proposals. Public housing, rent controls, and government intervention in the housing market are policies one could expect from a Labor Party rooted in social democratic ideals. Yet, this Labor government is quick to dismiss the Greens' position as unrealistic, claiming that their proposals would harm renters and buyers by reducing housing supply and making homeownership less affordable.

But the real question remains: is this political impasse necessary? There are many Australians living with housing insecurity, and the longer this battle between the two progressive parties drags on, the longer those Australians will wait for solutions. The argument that the Greens are just playing politics to raise their profile misses the larger point—that the Labor government, too, is engaging in political games. If these policies are as crucial as Labor claims—and they truly are—why not make some concessions or agree to further negotiations on future housing measures?

The housing crisis is not an issue that can be solved by rigid adherence to one policy framework or another, and both sides would be better served by exploring ways to bridge their differences. The Greens are within their rights to push for more ambitious policies; after all, they represent a growing base of Australians who are frustrated by years of housing inaction from the mainstream political parties.

However, for their part, they need to find a way to present their demands that doesn't come across as petty obstructionism. In reality, the two parties should be natural allies, especially when facing a Liberal Party that remains largely opposed to interventionist housing policies, and the challenge lies in navigating these negotiations without losing sight of the larger goal: fixing Australia's broken housing market.

A BATTLE OF BETWEEN PRAGMATISM AND IDEALISM IN LEFT-OF-CENTRE POLITICS

This standoff also highlights the broader dynamics of left-of-centre politics, where ideological alignment is often complicated by tactical and strategic considerations. It's clear that the policies at the heart of this dispute are *not* fundamentally at odds with either party's core principles. In fact, the Labor Party's platform traditionally emphasises social justice, public welfare, and a proactive role for government in addressing market failures like housing shortages. Similarly, the Greens' push for more affordable housing is well within the realm of progressive policy-making, and it speaks to the same voter concerns that Labor claims to represent.

So why the entrenched hostility?

In part, this dispute exposes the internal machinations of political parties, where pragmatism often collides with ideological purity, and where perceived slights from years or even decades ago can have a disproportionate influence on current negotiations. The Greens' insistence on more ambitious housing policies represents not just an idealistic push for better outcomes, but also a challenge to Labor's credibility as the party of working Australians. Meanwhile, Labor's refusal to entertain some of these demands reflects a deeper anxiety: that conceding to the Greens would make them appear weak or too closely aligned with a smaller, more left-wing party that often challenges their authority on progressive issues.

In a purely policy-driven world, it would seem reasonable for the two parties to meet somewhere in the middle, *if possible*. If the Greens are pushing for 100 per cent affordable rentals and Labor is offering 10 per cent, why not negotiate a half-way compromise that allows both sides to claim a victory for housing reform?

This reluctance to find common ground also signals a broader trend in modern politics, where the question of "*but-where-will-the-money-come-from*" for policy initiatives has become both a tool for deterring bold reforms and a source of contention. During the COVID-19 pandemic, governments around the world, including in Australia, managed to mobilise unprecedented financial resources to deal with the crisis. This demonstrated that when the political will is there, money can be found—even when governments keep telling the electorate that it supposedly doesn't exist. If a government could spend billions on pandemic relief—a fiscally conservative Coalition government, no less—it can surely afford more ambitious housing policies.

Yet, this debate about funding also reveals something deeper: a reluctance within Labor to fully embrace key elements of its own platform. Housing, in particular, is an area where market-driven solutions have historically failed to deliver equitable outcomes, and where government intervention—whether it be through public housing, rent control, or subsidies—does play a crucial role in leveling the playing field. The Greens' proposals, far from being antithetical to Labor's platform, could be seen as an extension of the party's historic commitment to social justice. So why isn't Labor more open to negotiation?

The tensions between Labor and the Greens are not just about housing; they are part of a larger struggle over the future direction of progressive politics in Australia. As the Greens grow in influence, particularly among younger voters and in urban areas, they present a challenge to Labor's traditional dominance of the left. In this context, Labor's reluctance to negotiate on housing policy may be less about the specifics of the bill and more about maintaining its political position. By standing firm, Labor signals that it is still the party of *serious governance* (even if this governance has led to the housing market crumbling away), while painting the Greens as impractical and *radical ideologues* (even if they are proposing workable solutions)—this narrative has worked to Labor's advantage in the past but could be way past its use-by date.

What is clear is that this kind of political brinkmanship, while a familiar feature of Australian politics, can only last so long before it becomes self-defeating. The Housing Australia Future Fund, another policy area that saw an extended deadlock, was ultimately passed after extensive negotiations. This shows that standoffs in politics are sometimes necessary, but also that they can lead to better outcomes when both sides are willing to engage in good faith. The same could be true for housing policy if Labor and the Greens are willing to put aside what seem to be *personal* animosities (rather than *ideological* animosities) and focus on the common good.

A POLITICAL GAME THAT HAS NO WINNERS AND IS FAILING THOSE IN NEED OF REAL SOLUTIONS

As this extended housing debate continues, one thing is clear: the political machinations around housing policy during a time of crisis is not just frustrating: *it's unacceptable*. Housing shouldn't be a political football to be kicked around by parties vying for votes—it's a fundamental human need, one that affects personal security, wellbeing, and livelihoods. The longer the blame game between political parties persists, the more it becomes apparent that, for many politicians, maintaining power and appealing to their base takes precedence over real, substantive change.

The housing crisis is complex, and the solutions to it will necessarily be multifaceted and require more than just sloganeering or short-term political strategies. The collision of many factors—rising home prices, stagnant wages, limited housing supply, and the commodification of property—demands a coordinated, long-term response. But who's got time for that in a parliamentary term which only lasts three years?

Politicians, by their very nature, are inclined to *play politics*—they *are* politicians, after all: it's a part of the job, and in many cases, it's what gets results. But this current action is not getting the results. When the stakes are as high as they are in the current housing crisis, with so many Australians struggling to afford homes or even meet basic rental costs, this type of politicking becomes particularly unseemly and grotesque. For sure, the Labor Party and the Greens are ultimately chasing the same voters within the electorate, yet both parties ostensibly want the same outcome: a housing market that works for ordinary people. While it will take many years for the Build to Rent scheme to come to fruition, when taking into account funding, planning and construction considerations, time is critical, and the longer these negotiations drag on, the longer Australians will have to wait for relief.

But why stop at two small policy proposals? While all sides of politics seem to acknowledge the seriousness of the housing crisis to varying degrees, there is little appetite for the kind of sweeping reforms that would be necessary to address these systemic issues. Tax reforms, such as changes to negative gearing and capital gains, are politically difficult, and both major parties have shied away from them for fear of alienating certain voter blocs. But without these reforms, any policy aimed at making housing more affordable will be hampered by a market structure that incentivises speculation and hoarding rather than making homes available to those who need them. What is the point of small band-aid solutions such as Build to Rent and Help to Buy if the main causes of the housing crisis are neglected and remain in place?

The time for half-measures and political gamesmanship has passed. What is needed now is bold, decisive action. Governments must step in, not only to provide immediate relief through programs like Build to Rent and Help to Buy, but to address the underlying structural issues that have turned housing into a commodity rather than a basic right. This means revisiting tax policy, rethinking the role of government in housing supply, and developing a coordinated national strategy that prioritises people over profit.

What we need now is for politicians to stop treating housing as a battleground for political point-scoring and start treating it as the urgent national crisis that it is. The public doesn't care about who wins the rhetorical battle in Parliament—they primarily care about being able to afford a place to live.

In the end, the housing crisis is a test of whether our political system can rise to meet the challenges of the 21st century. If politicians continue to bicker while ordinary Australians struggle, they will have failed that test. But if they can put aside their differences, focus on the common good, and work toward real, lasting solutions, they may just prove that our democracy is capable of solving even the most complex and urgent problems.

***

ISRAEL'S ESCALATING WAR CRIMES IN LEBANON AND AUSTRALIA'S WEAK RESPONSE

28 September 2024

The expansion of Israel's war beyond the Gaza Strip into Lebanon marks another terrible chapter in the region's escalating violence, further entrenching the cycle of destruction that has already been inflicted upon Palestine for decades. Israel's bombardment of southern Lebanon, now stretching up to Beirut, echoes a familiar and devastating pattern of military aggression and war crimes, displacing up to a million people who have fled their homes in fear of further strikes, and killing thousands of civilians.

These attacks follow in the wake of previous tragedies, such as the pager-bomb explosions—suspected to be orchestrated by Mossad—that killed around 300 people and injured over 3,000 others in Lebanon. The scale and intensity of Israel's military operations in Lebanon are an extension of its ongoing campaign in Gaza, where evacuation orders for civilians often presage devastating strikes, disproportionately affecting women and children.

Israel's military operations, whether in Gaza or now in Lebanon, have repeatedly violated international law, defying United Nations resolutions and conventions designed to protect civilians. The bombardment in Lebanon, just like the massacres in Gaza, appears to have been premeditated and unrelated to the events in Israel from October the previous year, which were used as a justification for the mass killing of well over 40,000 Palestinians in Gaza. By extending its war beyond its borders, Israel is deepening the humanitarian crisis in Lebanon, and even more troubling are Prime Minister Benjamin

Netanyahu's threats to expand the war into Jordan, a nation with which Israel has a long-standing peace treaty. The international community is witnessing an escalation that threatens to destabilise the entire region, yet there is an alarming passivity in global responses.

In Australia, the government's weak stance on Israel's actions reflects a broader issue of political inertia in the face of blatant human rights abuses. Many Australians, along with political commentators, continue to question what their country *can actually* do in response to this conflict and have suggested that the Foreign Minister, Senator Penny Wong and the Australian government are being unfairly targeted for their inaction. Yet the reality is that there is a considerable range of diplomatic tools and practical actions that Australia could employ to signal its opposition to Israel's aggression and contribute meaningfully to international efforts to halt the violence.

For example, recalling its ambassador to Israel; expelling the Israeli ambassador in Canberra; imposing high-level trade sanctions; halting military exports to Israel, and reducing cultural and sporting ties are just a few of the options available to Australia. These are not unprecedented measures; Australia has a history of using such tactics to oppose apartheid in South Africa during the 1970s and 1980s. At that time, few people questioned whether such actions would make a difference: aside from people such as Margaret Thatcher in the U.K. and a young Tony Abbott in Australia, it was accepted that standing up to systemic human rights abuses and racial injustice was a moral imperative, and Australia played a significant role in that global effort. The same rationale should apply today in the case of Israel's ongoing war crimes in Palestine and Lebanon.

The Israeli government is on a dangerous path, and if it continues, it risks self-destruction, and hard diplomacy, sanctions, and international pressure are essential to stop Israel from perpetuating further violence and violating the rights of Palestinians and Lebanese civilians. The silence and inaction from the western countries, particularly from countries such as Australia that hold considerable diplomatic and economic influence, allow these atrocities to continue unchecked.

When nations fail to act, they become complicit in the violence they passively observe. If countries like Australia had taken decisive action when it became clear that Israel was committing war crimes and engaging in genocidal practices in Gaza, we might not now be witnessing the tragic extension of these actions into Lebanon and further afield. The unchecked military campaign Israel has launched across its borders further exposes the need for international intervention, not just to protect the lives of those caught in the conflict but to uphold the principles of international law and human rights that are supposed to govern relations between states.

AUSTRALIA'S COMPLICITY IN MIDDLE EAST INJUSTICE: FAILING MULTICULTURALISM, HUMAN RIGHTS, AND GLOBAL PEACE

Australia's consistent alignment with Israel in the Middle East, often at the expense of acknowledging the grievances of the Arab world, reflects a broader failure in its foreign policy. This approach not only undermines Australia's claim to being a global advocate for human rights and peace but also neglects its own multicultural values, which should inherently drive more balanced diplomatic stances.

Former prime minister Scott Morrison's decision to move Australia's embassy from Tel Aviv to Jerusalem in 2018 stands as an example of this, a move that pandered to a narrow ideological worldview, one rooted in apocalyptic and religious interpretations rather than rational, diplomatic considerations. This decision, deeply offensive to Palestinians and the wider Arab world, was largely ignored by the mainstream media in Australia, and this lack of critical discourse around such a significant diplomatic blunder revealed how deeply embedded the bias toward Israel is within Australian political and media establishments.

The question arises: why can't Australia implement a range of actions against the state of Israel, or even express solidarity with the Lebanese people, who are being devastated by Israeli bombs? Australia's Lebanese community has played a significant role in shaping the nation's modern identity, yet their voices are conspicuously absent in policy discussions concerning the Middle East. For a country that prides itself on multiculturalism, it is baffling that the federal government is unwilling to take a stand that reflects the values of its diverse population, particularly when it comes to condemning the illegal actions of a foreign government. The Labor Party, which touts itself as a champion of multiculturalism, has been disappointingly silent on this front.

Despite the United Nations condemning Israel for its continued illegal actions, Australia, along with the United States, the United Kingdom, and a few other nations, persists in shielding Israel from any meaningful consequences. Australia's foreign policy toward the Middle East also reflects a broader indifference to the suffering of innocent civilians, particularly in the Arab world. The government's refusal to condemn Israel's actions, while simultaneously turning a blind eye to the suffering of Lebanese and Palestinian civilians, is a profound moral and political failure. Surely, it is possible to condemn the actions of extremist groups and criminal factions on all sides without ignoring the reality that it is overwhelmingly innocent civilians who are caught in the crossfire. It is these civilians—whether they are Palestinians in Gaza, Lebanese in Beirut, or refugees fleeing the region—who deserve Australia's solidarity and protection.

A MORAL CRISIS AND THE LOOMING POLITICAL CONSEQUENCES

The weak and ambiguous response from the Australian government, exemplified by Senator Penny Wong's carefully worded statements, reflects a longstanding issue in Australia's foreign policy regarding Israel and the broader Middle East. The statements are familiar: *deeply concerned, gravely concerned*, and calls for *de-escalation* echo across the media but lack real conviction or specificity. The situation was even extended to Wong's meeting with Iran's Foreign Minister Seyed Abbas Araghchi, with firm discussions about pressing *Iran* for "regional de-escalation and restraint". Yet, there was no mention of "pressing" Israel, despite its efforts to destabilise the region and escalate tensions with Lebanon, Iran, Jordan and Egypt.

The omission of Israel's name, particularly in instances where it is directly responsible for military actions and civilian casualties, speaks volumes about the government's reluctance to challenge the narrative propagated by Israel and its allies. Even when the death of

Australian aid worker Zomi Frankcom, killed in a missile attack by the Israel Defense Forces, cannot prompt a direct acknowledgment of Israel's role, it is clear that Australia's political establishment is deeply entrenched in a policy of *both-side-ism* —careful not to offend Israel, and cautious to the point of cowardice.

The foreign minister's failure to explicitly condemn Israel in instances where its military actions have clearly crossed ethical and legal boundaries highlights an alarming reluctance to hold the state accountable. This failure is not born of ignorance; the Australian government knows full well the role Israel has played in escalating conflicts in Gaza, Lebanon, and beyond. The use of vague language and diplomatic equivocation allows the government to avoid any substantial policy shifts or criticisms, effectively continuing a status quo that props up a regime currently led by Netanyahu, a man whose political survival hinges on perpetuating conflict.

The ongoing support for Israel, particularly under the Netanyahu regime, raises questions about why Australia continues to follow this path. Of course, the answer lies in a combination of political influence, strategic alliances, and a deeply ingrained reluctance to deviate from U.S. foreign policy, which remains steadfastly pro-Israel. The influence of a powerful ultra-conservative Israel lobby within Australia, particularly in Sydney and Melbourne, also ensures that any significant political pushback against Israeli policies is stifled before it gains momentum.

The consequences of this approach are more than just moral; they have real political implications, especially within Australia's diverse and multicultural electorate. The Lebanese community in Australia, particularly in Western Sydney, is large and politically active. The community's roots in Lebanon, a country now under bombardment from Israeli forces, create a strong connection to the conflict that the government can no longer afford to ignore. While the Lebanese–Australian community is diverse, with various religious, political, and regional differences, the escalating violence in Lebanon could galvanise parts of the electorate that feel abandoned by the government's refusal to condemn Israel's actions.

While there is undoubtedly frustration within the Lebanese and broader Arab communities, it is difficult to predict whether this will be sufficient to influence voting patterns at the next federal election in a significant way. However, it would be a mistake for the Australian government to assume that foreign policy issues like Israel's aggression in Lebanon will have no bearing *at all* on domestic politics. The Lebanese community, along with other Arab and Muslim communities in Australia, is growing increasingly aware of the gap between Australia's professed values and its actions on the global stage. This disconnect could lead to a loss of support for the Labor government, particularly in key electorates in Western Sydney, where disillusionment with the party's failure to act is driving voters toward alternatives, such the independent candidates supported by Muslim Voice and the Australian Greens.

The political inertia that has characterised Australia's foreign policy toward Israel is unsustainable in the long term. As the conflict deepens and more innocent civilians are killed, the government's refusal to take a firm stand will become harder to justify to both the international community and the Australian electorate. The current approach, dictated by an unrepresentative Israel lobby and a fear of upsetting powerful allies, is fundamentally at odds with the values that Australia claims to represent.

Ultimately, the Australian government must decide whether it is willing to continue supporting a foreign policy that is driven by political expediency and alliances rather than principles. Certainly, the next federal election will not hinge on foreign policy, but it will be influenced by the broader sense of whether the government truly represents the values of the electorate. Whether or not the current government is willing to listen to community concerns remains to be seen—and so far, they haven't—but one thing is certain: the era of blind support for Israel without consequence is drawing to a close, and the political consequences for this delusion may arrive sooner than anticipated.

***

OCTOBER

AUSTRALIA'S UNQUESTIONING SUPPORT FOR ISRAEL AND A DEAFENING SILENCE

5 October 2024

The conflict in Lebanon, spurred by Israel's expansion of military action beyond Palestine, brings into sharp focus a long history of territorial aggression, misrepresentation in Western media, and cynical political games in countries like Australia. The escalation into Lebanon is not a new chapter but rather an extension of Israel's aggressive posturing, a strategy it has employed for decades with impunity.

Since the invasion of Lebanon, the Israeli Defense Forces have pushed forward with strikes that have caused considerable devastation. Iran's response, in the form of missile attacks, follows a predictable script of retaliation that gets highlighted and exaggerated by the global media, which in turn paints Lebanon and Iran as the primary antagonists. This media narrative—especially in Australia—glosses over the fundamental reality that Israel is the *main aggressor* in this scenario, continuing its campaign of occupation and violence.

Since the most recent eruption of conflict, with its beginnings on October 7 last year, the human cost has been staggering. By many estimates, at least 42,000 Palestinians have been killed—potentially rising to 200,000, according to the medical journal *Lancet*—and over 2,000 Lebanese lives, while, during this time, 1,700 Israelis have been killed.

These numbers are not presented to create a hierarchy of suffering but to highlight the asymmetry of the violence. Around 99 per cent of *all* deaths have been inflicted by Israeli forces and settler paramilitary groups in the West Bank, while 1 per cent can be attributed to Hamas, Hezbollah, and the state of Iran. This disparity makes it clear who the primary perpetrators of violence are yet, this critical perspective is conveniently absent from mainstream Australian discourse, where figures such as leader of the opposition Peter Dutton seek political capital in the conflict.

Dutton's exploitation of this conflict for domestic political gain is clearly evident. His remarks about the Australian government's response paint a picture of weakness, casting Prime Minister Anthony Albanese as 'failing in his leadership duties'. His criticism, however, conveniently ignores the broader historical and ethical context of Israel's actions, reducing a complex international crisis into an opportunity for political point-scoring and appealing to the Australian right-wing base, eager to see a more testosterone-fuelled response in alignment with the West's pro-Israel stance.

Senator Bridget McKenzie—not known for any expertise on Middle East affairs at all—also chimed in, selectively championing the United Nations' call for Hezbollah's removal from the northern border of Israel, conveniently ignoring Israel's continued violation of countless UN resolutions. Such one-sided rhetoric not only fuels Islamophobia and xenophobia but also contributes to the further alienation of Arab and Muslim communities in Australia.

This marginalisation was further exacerbated by statements from Home Affairs Minister Tony Burke and, as an MP representing a western Sydney seat, where 25 per cent of voters come from an Islamic background, he should know better. Burke linked claims of hate speech and symbols to the Islamic community, even threatening to revoke the visas of those displaying the Hezbollah flag or images of its recently assassinated leader, Hassan Nasrallah.

The political responses in Australia reveal the extent to which the conflict is being manipulated for ideological and political gain. The reflexive alignment Australian political parties with pro-Israel rhetoric, while casting any dissent or criticism as support for terrorism, reveals an intellectual and moral bankruptcy. These positions rely on a wilful ignorance of historical facts and a cynical exploitation of the fear and anxiety surrounding Middle Eastern conflicts. For politicians such as Dutton and McKenzie, it is easier to stoke division and fear than to engage in the complex realities of the conflict, where Israel's actions must be critically assessed against the backdrop of decades of occupation, violence, and expansionism.

The reduction of complex historical, cultural, and political issues into talking points meant to fuel ideological divisions only makes the conflict worse. It reduces the Australian public's understanding of a deeply nuanced issue to simplistic narratives of *good versus evil*, perpetuating the myth that Israel's actions are purely defensive. It also contributes to the larger global problem of how Western countries, including Australia, uncritically accept and support Israel's militaristic approach, further emboldening it to expand its aggression into countries like Lebanon and beyond.

HOW AUSTRALIA'S NATIONAL SECURITY RHETORIC FUELS ISLAMOPHOBIA

Ever since the late 1990s, when John Howard's Liberal–National Coalition government began to sharpen its focus on asylum seekers and border security, national security has been the Achilles' heel of the Labor Party. Key events such as the Tampa crisis in 2001 and the September 11 attacks in the U.S. dovetailed perfectly with these narratives, creating a political environment where security could easily be exploited to generate fear, division, and justify far-reaching, authoritarian policies. Over the years, these issues have grown to become a permanent fixture of Australian politics, linking internal policies with Middle Eastern geopolitics, particularly Palestine.

What is remarkable is how, more than two decades later, the Labor Party has still not devised an effective strategy to counter these conservative national security narratives. Rather than challenging the framing or interrogating the supposed links between domestic security and foreign conflicts, Labor often capitulates to the Liberal Party's agenda, whether they're in government or not. This reluctance to push back results in poor legislation that not only infringes on civil liberties but also disproportionately affects marginalised communities. The willingness of both major parties to prioritise "security" over human rights perpetuates harmful stereotypes, further marginalising communities that are already under immense social and political pressure.

In recent years, this tendency has intensified, particularly when it comes to Palestinian solidarity movements in Australia. Pro-Palestine events in cities like Sydney and Melbourne have drawn large crowds, reflecting the deep sense of hurt and suffering felt by many in the Arab and Muslim communities, especially in response to the violence in Gaza and the West Bank. Despite the peaceful nature of these gatherings, media narratives and political rhetoric often paint these protests as *dangerous* or *extremist*.

It is in these moments that national security rhetoric is deployed most cynically, conflating peaceful protest with terrorism, and using symbols like the Hezbollah flag to justify police crackdowns and oppressive legislation—the presence of a yellow flag is deemed by the establishment to be more threatening than the ongoing violence in the Middle East, where tens of thousands of people have been killed by Israeli forces. This rhetoric reveals how national security is used as a blunt tool to suppress expressions of solidarity with oppressed peoples, even when those expressions are peaceful and legal.

The escalating crackdown on Palestinian solidarity movements in Australia sets a dangerous precedent. It not only criminalises symbols of resistance but also reaffirms a broader pattern of equating national security with the suppression of dissent, particularly when that dissent is tied to Muslim or Arab communities. The focus on security becomes less about protecting the Australian public and more about reinforcing the dominance of a particular narrative—one that positions Israel as the victim only and any critique of its actions as inherently dangerous. This framing not only distorts the realities of the Middle East conflict but also stifles the political discourse necessary to hold both Israel and Australia's political establishment accountable.

By treating these solidarity movements as a national security threat, Australia is aligning itself with a broader global trend that seeks to criminalise criticism of Israel while bolstering support for its continued occupation of Palestinian land and beyond. This trend is not unique to Australia—but a very common trait of the settlercoloniser states of Britain, Canada and the United States, whose support for Israel has been most vociferous—where the government's commitment to security at all costs has consistently led to the erosion of civil liberties and the marginalisation of communities deemed *the other*.

HOW POLITICS AND MEDIA SILENCE PALESTINIAN AND ARAB VOICES

The Australian political class, along with the mainstream media, have long taken a one-sided approach when it comes to Israel and its ongoing occupation of Palestine, a position that is mirrored in the country's broader discourse on the Middle East—it paints Israel as a nation under siege, constantly threatened by an aggressive Arab world, while ignoring or minimising the suffering inflicted upon Palestinians, Lebanese, and other Middle Eastern communities. Even the illustrations and cartoons in mainstream media must reflect a pro-Israel bias, ensuring that everyone is aligned in promoting the cause.

A narrative that is rarely heard in Australia is that the Arab world, particularly the 57-member Arab and Muslim coalition, is ready to guarantee Israel's security in exchange for an end to the occupation and the creation of an independent Palestinian state. This is a narrative of peace, a plan for co-existence, but it is also a plan that the Israeli government continues to ignore. Instead, Israel perpetuates cycles of violence with no long-term vision for peace.

Australian politicians and media, aligned with Israel's narrative, fail to critically interrogate this lack of an endgame. They instead propagate the notion that Israel's security can only be guaranteed through military dominance and suppression of Palestinian resistance, ignoring decades of diplomatic efforts from the Arab world that have sought a two-state solution.

What remains bewildering is how little the Australian public knows about these alternatives, largely because the media and political elite focus on a singular, distorted narrative that portrays Israel as a beleaguered nation fending off existential threats and is the true partner for peace that is ignored by the Arab world. The reality, however, is far more complex, with Israel being a military powerhouse that has consistently pursued expansionist policies at the expense of Palestinian lives and land. And yet, discussing Israel's role as an aggressor is virtually taboo in Australian political discourse. Any deviation from the mainstream narrative, especially in defence of Palestine and now, Lebanon, is often framed as radicalism or extremism, once again marginalising voices that seek to highlight the brutal realities of occupation.

In Australia, mainstream political figures are entirely comfortable supporting Israeli policies that many human rights organisations have labelled as apartheid, while paying lip service to human rights in their rhetoric. The term *apartheid* itself, when applied to Israel, is met with accusations of anti-Semitism, even though it is a well-documented reality for Palestinians living under occupation, subjected to different laws, movement restrictions, and systemic violence. This complicity in maintaining Israel's oppressive regime is troubling, particularly given the increasing global recognition of Israel's violations of international law.

The Australian media also plays a significant role in perpetuating these distortions—media outlets regurgitate the same pro-Israel talking points, framing the conflict in binary terms: *Israel as a democracy defending itself against barbaric, radical forces*. The violence and suffering inflicted on Palestinians and Lebanese civilians, often framed as unfortunate collateral damage, rarely make the headlines in a way that captures the depth of the human tragedy.

In Australian politics, the Australian Greens have consistently raised concerns about these issues, but their voices are also marginalised. The broader political class, including the Labor government, tends to fall in line with the dominant narrative, perhaps out of fear of being branded anti-Israel or anti-Semitic. Yet, this silence does not only reflect a lack of political courage; it speaks to a deeper failure to represent the diversity of opinion within Australia itself.

The Arab and Muslim communities have contributed significantly to Australian society yet, they remain an easy target for demonisation, especially when tensions flare in the Middle East, and this is compounded by a simplistic understanding of those communities and Islam itself. Australian media and politicians often lump the diverse range of Islamic thought and practice into a monolithic category, focusing primarily on the most radical elements while ignoring the rich diversity of opinion within the faith.

The demonisation of Middle Eastern Muslims in particular mirrors broader Western tendencies to ignore the progressive and peaceful voices within Islam, an approach that is not only intellectually lazy but dangerous, as it fuels further Islamophobia and alienates Australian Muslims from the political process.

In contrast, Australia's political class demonstrates an unwavering commitment to conservative Zionism, conflating the interests of the Israeli state with those of the Jewish people. This conflation is not only inaccurate but harmful, as it silences critical voices within the Jewish community itself, many of whom oppose the Israeli government's policies. Figures such as Noam Chomsky and many other Jewish intellectuals have long critiqued Israel's expansionism, yet their voices are often ignored or sidelined in favour of maintaining a simplistic narrative that casts any criticism of Israel as inherently anti-Semitic. Newer local voices such as the Jewish Council of Australia are also frequently ignored, mainly because they also present an alternative progressive perspective to the prevailing conservative Zionist narrative.

Ultimately, what is needed is a more honest and open discussion about these issues, one that acknowledges the complexities of the Israel–Palestine conflict and allows for diverse perspectives within Australia. Politicians need to move beyond the tired and lazy security rhetoric that demonises the Arab world and Muslims, and instead, engage with the root causes of the conflict, including calling out Israel's ongoing occupation and systemic violence. Such a shift would not only help improve Australia's foreign policy but also foster a more inclusive and empathetic domestic discourse, where all communities are respected and their contributions to society are recognised.

***

THE POLITICS OF PROTEST: DOUBLE STANDARDS AND UNDERMINING FREE SPEECH

11 October 2024

The Premier of New South Wales, Chris Minns, has raised the controversial idea of shutting down the pro-Palestine protests that have become a regular occurrence in Sydney. Minns' primary justification revolves around the costs associated with policing these protests, suggesting that such financial burdens on the state are unsustainable. However, this rationale, presented as a pragmatic response to budgetary constraints, fails to address the broader implications for freedom of speech and protest in Australia. What we are witnessing is a deliberate attempt to suppress a significant political movement under the guise of fiscal responsibility.

The suggested costs associated with these protests, claimed to be upwards of $5.4 million over the past year, seem questionable. The pro-Palestine gatherings in Sydney, have been largely peaceful, where the attendees chant, wave signs, and give speeches—hardly the kind of activities that demand such a heavy police presence and each event, which typically lasts for about two hours, does not resemble the kind of disruptive or violent events that would justify an inflated price tag on law enforcement. The NSW police union has already dismissed the idea that patrolling these protests is preventing them from addressing crime elsewhere. This raises the question: what is the real motivation behind Minns' push to ban these protests?

At the core of his argument is a thinly veiled pandering to Sydney's influential pro-Israel lobby. It is a familiar tactic: drown out dissenting voices, particularly when they challenge entrenched interests. The pro-Palestine protests represent a growing public consciousness about the ongoing crisis in Gaza and the Middle East, and these protests serve as a legitimate expression of outrage at the actions of the Israeli government and the Israel Defense Forces. By attempting to silence these voices, Minns is not only undermining free speech but aligning himself with a particular political agenda that seeks to shield Israel from criticism in the public sphere.

This move also flies in the face of historical precedent in Australia, where the right to protest has long been regarded as a fundamental aspect of democratic engagement. Minns seems to have forgotten, or is wilfully ignoring, the labor movement's own historical roots in public protest and civil disobedience. The Labor Party, under whose banner Minns serves, was itself forged in the collective action and resistance against a government. To now attempt to limit or shut down peaceful protests against a foreign government's actions, as well as to protest against the inaction of the Australian government—especially when those actions and inactions are increasingly seen as unjust and oppressive—is a betrayal of the principles Minns should be defending.

The argument about cost ignores an obvious solution: scale back the unnecessary and excessive police presence at these events. The protests have consistently remained peaceful, and the several skirmishes that have occurred over the past year have been primarily caused by Zionist agitators. Many attendees bring their children; there are no signs of the violence or chaos that would justify lining the streets with police officers. Reducing the police force at these gatherings would not only cut costs significantly but also reflect the reality of the situation—the fact that these are *not* dangerous protests.

The leadership of Minns has been a disappointment for many who hoped for a progressive and dynamic direction since he became Premier in March 2023. Instead, he has come across as a continuation of the same policies and approaches seen under his Liberal Party predecessors, Dominic Perrottet and Gladys Berejiklian and his handling of the pro-Palestine protests is just one more example of this conservative, risk-averse approach. By framing the protests as a financial burden, Minns is diverting attention from the real issue at hand: the right of people to protest against what they can see is an ongoing genocide. In a world where political leaders are increasingly expected to take bold and principled stands, Minns seems content to sidestep controversy and cater to established power structures.

ALIENATING COMMUNITIES AND UNDERMINING LABOR VALUES

The commentary provided by Minns over the pro-Palestine protests—to the right-wing shockjock, Ben Fordham at Radio 2GB—not only signal a disconnect from Labor's historic values, but they also reveal a troubling pattern of double standards that risks alienating a significant portion of the NSW community, particularly the Islamic and pro-Palestine groups.

By focusing on the financial cost of these protests while simultaneously remaining silent on other, arguably more costly and disruptive protests, Minns is sending a clear message: the voices of some communities are more burdensome and less welcome than others. This is a dangerous road for any political leader, but especially for one leading a party that traditionally prides itself on inclusivity and justice, and seem to be designed to stoke division within the community.

Rather than engaging in meaningful dialogue with the pro-Palestine protesters, or addressing the legitimate concerns of the Islamic community, Minns has chosen to position these protests as a costly inconvenience. Yet, if the federal and NSW governments and political class had not been so steadfastly one-sided in their support of Israel, or if they had engaged in more balanced and open dialogue with these communities, such protests might not even be necessary. The protests themselves are a direct response to being systematically ignored, and Minns' attempts to shut them down without addressing the root cause will only exacerbate the issue.

There is also glaring inconsistency in the NSW Government's approach to protest. While the pro-Palestine gatherings are labelled as too costly and are viewed as disruptive, other protests, such as the anti-lockdown and anti-vaccine demonstrations that took place during the pandemic, went on for nearly two years without similar complaints from the government. Some of these protests were openly hostile, with participants openly calling for the execution of political leaders, yet there was no outcry over the police resources needed to manage them. Similarly, neo-Nazi rallies have been treated with far more leniency, with police presence often seen as more of an escort than a control measure. Where is the outrage over the costs of these events? Where is the call for them to be banned or scaled back?

Minns' failure to apply a consistent standard suggests that his actions are less about fiscal responsibility and more about political posturing. The fact that Minns would never dream of asking the Jewish community to refrain from public shows of support for Israel due to cost only highlights the double standard further. If he were to make such a suggestion, the backlash would be swift and severe, and rightly so. Yet, when it comes to the Islamic community, their right to peaceful protest is treated as expendable.

Even within his own party, Minns is facing backlash for this stance. Several Labor MPs have spoken out against his push to ban protests on the basis of cost, warning that such actions threaten civil liberties. This criticism highlights a growing concern that Minns is out of touch not only with the values of his own party but with the broader electorate as well. There is also a notable reluctance among many Labor MPs to openly support Palestine, fearing political retribution or alienation, and this reflects the broader atmosphere of suppression around the issue, where open support for Palestine is often stifled or discouraged, even within supposed progressive circles.

Ultimately, Minns' approach to these protests raises serious questions about his fitness to be a Labor Premier. His failure to engage with the concerns of the pro-Palestine community, coupled with his consistent appeasement of pro-Israel lobby groups, suggests he is a leader more interested in maintaining the status quo than in representing the diverse voices of his electorate. This behaviour might be more fitting for a leader on the conservative side of politics, but it has no place in a party that claims to champion the rights of the oppressed and marginalised.

The Labor Party, at its best, is a party of inclusion, social justice, and equality. Its leaders are expected to stand up for all communities, not just the ones with the most political capital or influence. Chris

Minns has not only failed in his leadership responsibilities but has alienated a significant part of the population he is meant to represent. If he continues down this path, he risks not only losing the trust of these communities but also jeopardising the very fabric of the multicultural society that Sydney prides itself on being.

***

ALBANESE AND THE MISTAKE OF ENDLESSLY APPEASING THE ISRAEL LOBBY

14 October 2024

The commemoration of the October 7 2023 Hamas attacks in Israel has become a flashpoint in Australian politics, showing the deeply polarised differences between Labor and the Liberal Party. When Prime Minister Anthony Albanese introduced a motion in parliament to mark the first anniversary of these tragic events—1139 deaths in Israel and the start of a genocide in Gaza—his words were measured, designed to strike a delicate balance, where he sought to acknowledge the pain felt by Israeli and Palestinian communities, to emphasise the sanctity of innocent life, and to reaffirm Australia's commitment to a two-state solution.

While critics have said that his actions have been meaningless gestures and called on the Australian government to do more to act against Israel, his remarks highlighted the Australian government's consistent call for a ceasefire, the protection of civilians, and a path toward peace that acknowledges both Israeli and Palestinian suffering.

Any statement on such a volatile issue would inevitably invite criticism from all sides. Yet, his approach reflected the need for bipartisanship, or at least the appearance of it, in handling such a sensitive international conflict. His speech demonstrated an effort to engage with multiple communities—Jewish, Palestinian, Lebanese—and to appeal to the broader Australian public, who, after witnessing a year of devastation in Gaza, are increasingly disillusioned with political and media narratives that minimise or obscure Palestinian suffering.

But whenever there is a need for political bipartisanship, the Leader of the Opposition Peter Dutton cannot be relied upon, whose response to the Prime Minister's motion was predictably combative and divisive. Dutton's objection—that Albanese's call for a ceasefire and peace efforts went beyond the scope of a commemoration—revealed his endless unwillingness to engage in constructive dialogue, where he portrayed Albanese's balanced stance as duplicitous, accusing the Prime Minister of political opportunism. Dutton's insistence that the motion should focus solely on the lives lost in Israel, while ignoring the broader humanitarian crisis in Gaza, speaks volumes about his political strategy: one of narrowing the conversation to suit his agenda while sidestepping the complex realities of the conflict.

Dutton's reaction is emblematic of a broader pattern in his leadership, where he thrives on division, seizing on moments of national or international significance to sow discord rather than fostering unity. In this instance, his refusal to engage with the humanitarian disaster in Gaza reveals a lack of empathy not just for Palestinians but for the broader Australian electorate, which increasingly recognises the importance of addressing the root causes of conflict.

This approach to leadership may have short-term political benefits for Dutton, especially in electorates that are predisposed to his hardline stance, however, it also carries significant risks. The Liberal Party, under Dutton's leadership, appears increasingly disconnected from the diverse, multicultural makeup of Australia and many immigrant communities, who might traditionally lean toward the Liberal Party for its economic policies, are finding themselves alienated by Dutton's divisive rhetoric on social and international issues.

His tactics—focused on driving wedges between communities rather than uniting them—are out of step with a growing desire among Australians for political leaders who can offer genuine solutions to global challenges. As the Australian political landscape continues to shift, the need for bipartisanship on international crises such as the Israeli–Palestinian conflict is becoming more urgent. But Dutton's divisive approach stands in the way of that possibility. Instead of offering a vision for peace and cohesion, he has chosen to exploit this tragedy for political gain, revealing once again how unfit he is to lead the country.

LABOR'S UNWAVERING SUPPORT FOR ISRAEL BACKFIRES

While Dutton has been busy sowing the seeds of division, the situation surrounding the Labor government's handling of the Israeli–Palestinian conflict over the past year illustrates a deeper problem: the pursuit of appeasement, especially toward pro-Israel lobby groups, with little regard for the Islamic community or traditional Labor supporters. This dynamic has unfolded as the government bends over backward to maintain a pro-Israel stance, hoping this will quell tensions domestically and secure political favour. However, despite their efforts, the government, Prime Minister and Foreign Minister Senator Penny Wong, are receiving no political reward, and instead, they find themselves criticised from all sides.

At the outset of the conflict following the October 7 attacks, it appears that the Albanese government calculated that expressing unequivocal support for Israel, while minimising criticism of Israeli military actions in Gaza, would be a pragmatic short-term choice, where historically, conflicts between Israel and Palestine since 1987 have often faded from the spotlight after a short period, allowing governments to weather the storm domestically without long-term consequences. This time, however, the situation has dragged on for over a year, with humanitarian crises and continued military actions forcing the issue to the forefront of political discourse in Australia and around the world.

What Albanese would not have anticipated is how entrenched and enduring this crisis would become. The political pressure on the Labor government has mounted, especially from progressive factions within the party and the broader Australian community, many of whom are appalled by the loss of life and destruction in Gaza. Labor's initial instinct was to support Israel and sideline the Palestinian cause, yet, despite this one-sided support for Israel, the government is still being lambasted by pro-Israel groups, as was shown by the hostile reception Albanese received during the commemorative event in Melbourne, where he was jeered while Peter Dutton was cheered.

This reflects a clear political reality: no matter how much the Labor government tries to appease the pro-Israel lobby, they will never satisfy their demands. Groups like Zionism Victoria have criticised the government for not being "steadfast" enough in their support of Israel, even though the Labor government has gone to great lengths to avoid harsh criticism of Israel's actions. As a result, the Labor government has alienated their traditional base without gaining any new support from the pro-Israel factions they sought to placate and, in any event, they were unlikely to receive any political support from these groups who are traditionally conservative, right-wing and hostile to the interests of the Labor Party.

This political conundrum has left the Labor government appearing weak and reactive. Instead of taking a principled stand from the beginning—one that recognised the complexity of the situation and the need to balance the rights and lives of both Israelis and Palestinians—they chose the path of least resistance and, in doing so, they underestimated the long-term consequences of their approach. Labor's reluctance to condemn Israel's military actions, coupled with its failure to offer meaningful support to Palestinian communities, has exposed a disconnect with the progressive values many of their supporters hold dear.

Their attempts to please the pro-Israel community have not only failed to garner support but have also given the opposition, particularly Peter Dutton, ample ammunition to criticise them. Dutton has seized upon this opportunity, using the government's wavering stance to paint Albanese as indecisive, while he positions himself as a staunch defender of Israel. This opportunistic strategy may resonate with parts of the Liberal Party's base, but it further polarises the political landscape and damages Australia's reputation as a neutral arbiter in global conflicts.

The Attorney-General Mark Dreyfus's attempt to label the term "Zionist" as an anti-Semitic slur reflects the broader challenges facing the Labor government. While it is crucial to combat anti-Semitism, conflating all criticism of Israel with anti-Jewish sentiment is a dangerous oversimplification, as it undermines legitimate political discourse and fails to recognise the diversity of views within the Jewish community itself, many of whom oppose Israel's actions in Gaza. By pushing this narrative, the government risks alienating those who seek a more nuanced understanding of the conflict and further distances itself from the Islamic community, which has long felt marginalised by Australia's foreign policy stance.

This capitulation to powerful lobby groups, rather than standing firm on principles of justice and human rights, only weakens the Labor government, as it always has. Australia's historical stance, particularly under leaders such as Gough Whitlam, was one of neutrality and fairness, recognising the need to avoid involvement in foreign conflicts and to condemn the loss of civilian lives wherever they occur. Today, however, the government appears beholden to a small but influential group, and this influence shapes policy decisions that fail to reflect the will of the broader Australian community.

COULD LABOR'S PRO-ISRAEL POSITION COST IT AT THE NEXT ELECTION?

The Labor government's one-sided support for Israel is setting the stage for a political fallout in the next federal election. The disconnect between Labor's foreign policy stance and the concerns of many of its supporters, particularly those aligned with progressive values and the Islamic community, is becoming increasingly difficult to ignore. As the crisis deepens and the death toll in Gaza, West Bank and Lebanon continues to rise, a growing number of Australians recognise the extent of the violence as genocide, and Labor's failure to address this head-on, risks alienating a crucial part of its voter base.

The Australian Greens, led by outspoken MPs such as Max Chandler-Mather, have been unwavering in their criticism of Israel's military actions and the Australian government's complicity. Chandler-Mather's pointed questions in parliament—demanding to know how many more atrocities must be committed before the government sanctions Israel—reflect the frustration of many Australians who feel that Labor has abandoned its moral compass. The Greens' position has exposed a fundamental weakness in Labor's strategy: their reluctance to condemn Israel's actions forcefully and to end military cooperation with a nation that is, by many accounts, inflicting widespread destruction on civilians in Gaza.

This unwillingness to act decisively is not without consequence. Labor may believe that it is striking a careful balance to avoid inflaming tensions with Israel's supporters in Australia, but this strategy has already proven to be a political miscalculation. Zionist organisations, such as the Zionist Federation of Australia, are now pressuring Labor government to preference the Australian Greens last on election ballots, a clear sign of how entrenched the influence of the Israel lobby has become in Australian politics.

This interference in electoral processes—where external organisations are seeking to dictate preference deals—demonstrates a troubling erosion of democratic integrity. Yet, the most significant political damage from Labor's position on Israel is likely to come from within its own ranks. By failing to stand up for Palestinian civilians and aggressively distancing itself from the Greens' more assertive stance, Labor risks bleeding votes to its left flank. The Greens, who have long positioned themselves as the true progressives on issues of social justice and foreign policy, can capitalise on this discontent, especially in urban and multicultural electorates where Labor's voters are increasingly frustrated by their party's complicity in what they see as a humanitarian catastrophe.

Albanese's categorical rejection of any coalition with the Greens seems like a defensive posture designed to maintain a fragile sense of party unity. However, the strategic calculus behind such a declaration may be shortsighted. If the Greens continue to gain ground, particularly in seats in inner-city parts of Brisbane, Melbourne and Sydney, Labor may find itself forced into some form of collaboration post-election. Albanese's reluctance to engage with the Greens on foreign policy issues such as Israel and Palestine could come back to haunt him if Labor loses critical seats to the Greens. For many voters, particularly younger Australians and those in immigrant communities, Labor's perceived indifference to Palestinian suffering may be a decisive factor in how they cast their ballots.

The next election will likely be fought on multiple issues, and while foreign policy may not always be the top priority for most voters, the situation in Gaza is unique. The scale of the devastation and the perception that a genocide is being carried out under the watch of complicit governments could galvanise voters in unexpected ways. Labor's failure to offer a more balanced approach—one that acknowledges the rights of both Israelis and Palestinians—could cost it dearly, particularly if the Greens continue to gain traction by positioning themselves as the party of principle.

In rejecting any formal alliance with the Greens—as has been suggested by their leader Adam Bandt—Albanese may be playing to the immediate political gallery, attempting to secure a majority government without reliance on minor parties. Yet, this strategy ignores the broader shifts happening within the electorate. Voters are increasingly savvy, and many are no longer willing to accept the kind of mealy-mouthed foreign policy that sidesteps the hard truths of international conflicts. For Labor, the risk is clear: if it continues to toe the pro-Israel line while ignoring the growing humanitarian outcry over Gaza and Lebanon, it could lose not just the next election, but the moral authority that has historically set it apart from the conservative parties.

***

NACC FAILS TO DELIVER, CORRUPTION WINS AGAIN

21 October 2024

The National Anti-Corruption Commission finds itself in the spotlight once again, this time over its determination that there was 'no corruption' in the notorious Paladin affair. This was a case in which the previous Liberal–National Coalition government paid $532 million to the Paladin security company to manage three refugee centres on Manus Island from 2017 onwards, and these payments occurred during the Turnbull and Morrison governments, and at a time when Peter Dutton was the Minister for Home Affairs.

Paladin was no ordinary security company. Initially known as High Risk Security—the name alone should have raised eyebrows—but instead, it was awarded a massive government contract despite glaring red flags. Paladin's headquarters was a beach shack on Kangaroo Island, and the company had no prior experience in managing immigration detention centres. Yet, inexplicably, it still ended up receiving over half a billion dollars in taxpayer funds. This affair didn't just raise suspicions due to the company's inexperience—there were allegations of money laundering, mismanagement, and claims of people being paid for work not being performed at all.

Adding to the intrigue, Paladin was the only company invited by the government to tender for these services, a process that typically involves competitive bids—this alone should raise questions about transparency and political favouritism.

Despite these glaring signs of misconduct, the NACC's investigation into the affair, dubbed Operation Bannister, concluded that there was no evidence of corrupt conduct, with the Commission's executive report delivered a short and unsatisfying statement, essentially declaring there was *nothing to see here*.

The Paladin case is not an isolated incident. It follows closely on the heels of the Robodebt scandal, another example of alleged misconduct where the NACC also failed to uncover any evidence of corruption. These failures suggest a deeper issue, that the Commission is not looking in the right places—or worse, is being deliberately steered away from those places by forces within the political establishment. The NACC's repeated inability to deliver meaningful findings in cases that seem riddled with corruption undermines its purpose and casts a long shadow over its credibility.

In the wake of Robodebt, it was shocking that another similarly suspicious operation such as the Paladin affair would be treated with such a light touch. The Australian public is owed more than just a flippant dismissal, they deserved a thorough and transparent explanation. How could a company operating out of a beach shack on Kangaroo Island, with no relevant experience, win contracts worth over half a billion dollars? How did the Coalition government find this Paladin company? And why *this* particular company? And how could there be no explanation for the apparent mismanagement of public money?

The Paladin affair highlights these shortcomings all too well. The result is not just a failure to root out corruption, but a failure to maintain public trust, and if the NACC cannot adequately investigate cases that seem so obviously suspicious, then it risks becoming irrelevant and just another toothless watchdog, unable to serve the very purpose for which it was created.

HOW THE NACC HAS FALLEN SHORT OF ITS PROMISE TO REFORM AUSTRALIAN POLITICS

When Labor won the 2022 federal election, part of the mandate they were given was to clean up corruption—through a functional anti-corruption watchdog, a watchdog that could stand up to entrenched power and expose the misuse of public funds.

The creation of the National Anti-Corruption Commission in August 2023 was hailed as a crucial reform in Australian politics, a long-awaited measure to weed out entrenched corruption within government. After years of scandals performed by the Liberal–National Coalition, public trust in government oversight had eroded to a dangerous low. According to the Corruption Perceptions Index published by Transparency International, Australia was ranked eighth in the world in 2013; by the end of the nine years of Coalition rule, Australia ranked 18th, a drop of 10 places.

The NACC was supposed to mark a new era of transparency and accountability, with promises of rigorous investigations and no tolerance for corrupt activities. Yet, in practice, it has fallen woefully short of those expectations.

The Paladin scandal was not a hidden secret, nor a marginal issue. It was a protracted and well-documented disaster, with years of media reports and audits flagging gross mismanagement, potential corruption, and glaring inconsistencies in government contracting. The Australian National Audit Office itself released a scathing report highlighting serious issues within the contracts awarded to Paladin, raising clear alarms about the propriety of the government's dealings with this inexperienced company. Yet, despite this wealth of public evidence, the NACC's response arrived at an underwhelming conclusion. How can such a stark disjunction between the appearance of malfeasance and the NACC's findings be justified?

Part of the problem lies at the top. Paul Brereton, the Commissioner of the NACC, has repeatedly found himself in compromised positions where he recuses himself from investigations or public announcements due to personal connections with individuals implicated in the very scandals he is tasked with investigating. It raises the question of whether the Commission can be truly independent when its leader's proximity to political elites creates the perception, and the reality, of bias.

Brereton's repeated recusals, combined with the Commission's seeming reluctance to confront obvious examples of corruption, suggest that systemic issues plague the NACC. While the Albanese government may not have directly interfered with the actual operations of the Commission, their choice of leadership was a miscalculation and, as a result, the NACC has become a source of growing frustration and disillusionment.

This failure of the NACC is not just a stain on the institution itself but a reflection of the broader disappointments with the Albanese government's first term. When Labor took office, the public's expectations were extraordinarily high, driven in large part by the sheer dysfunction and scandal of the preceding Coalition governments. Labor promised change—*real, substantive change*—in the areas of transparency but with each passing month, a sense of disappointment has crept in, exacerbated by failures like that of the NACC to deliver on its promise to clean up corruption.

The expectation that any new government could instantly rectify years of systemic problems might have been unrealistic. However, some disappointments are indeed justified and raises the question that NACC is operating in *exactly* the way the Labor government intended: give the appearance of addressing corruption without finding any. The government's response has been tepid at best—instead of taking immediate action to address the NACC's shortcomings, there has been a concerning silence. As a result, the public is left wondering why obvious cases of corruption continue to be brushed aside, and who, exactly, the NACC is protecting in the process.

The Albanese government may be hesitant to take drastic measures with the NACC before the next federal election—due before May 2025—and not wanting to introduce such a politically volatile issue into the campaign. But that does not change the fact that something must be done. If the government is serious about restoring public trust and addressing corruption, then significant reforms to the NACC will be necessary in the next term, should Labor remain in power.

There are models of anti-corruption bodies around the world that have proven successful, and Australia need only look to its own past to see what could be done differently. The original vision of the NSW Independent Commission Against Corruption was a shining example of what an anti-corruption body could achieve. While far from perfect, the ICAC did not shy away from confronting corrupt practices, regardless of the political affiliations of those involved. If Australia's federal anti-corruption efforts are to be salvaged, the NACC must embrace a similar ethos and supporting legislation, and it must be willing to pursue corruption wherever it leads, without fear or favour, and with a leadership that is free from the entanglements of political friendships.

HOW THE NACC HAS BECOME A SYMBOL OF POLITICAL WEAKNESS AND COMPROMISE

From the outset, it was clear that the NACC was arriving under considerable pressure. The previous Coalition government, led by Scott Morrison, spent years dragging its feet on anti-corruption measures, dismissing calls for meaningful reform. Public sentiment had grown increasingly hostile as scandal after scandal arose—yet, this version of the NACC that has been delivered is inadequate. Worse than no commission at all, it now seems like a watered-down body designed more to protect political elites than to expose corruption.

One of the key failures of the NACC is that it was conceived with bipartisan support in mind—a noble intention *in theory*, but in practice, it has resulted in a commission so weak that it is barely functional. Labor sought the backing of the Liberal Party, perhaps hoping for a smooth passage of the legislation or out of a misplaced desire for political unity. But seeking approval from a party that had been steeped in corruption for nearly a decade was a massive mistake. It is no surprise that the one piece of bipartisanship that the leader of the Liberal Party Peter Dutton has sought has been on the issue of the NACC. His motives were clear: a weakened NACC protects him and his colleagues from scrutiny for their actions from the time they were in government.

The Australian Greens and independent MPs have rightly criticised the Commission's limited powers, and are currently pushing for legislative improvements. But the problem runs deeper than just technical adjustments: the very foundations of the NACC were built on compromise, not strength. The Labor government had an opportunity to push through a robust anti-corruption body by negotiating with the Greens and independents, forces that would have supported a commission with real investigative powers. Instead, they chose to placate the very party responsible for much of the corruption they were supposed to be rooting out.

Many experts at the time, such as Anthony Whealy and Geoffrey Watson, warned that the structure of the NACC was flawed from the beginning, and now those warnings have been vindicated. It is not just that the NACC hasn't gone far enough—it is that it was designed *not* to go far enough. This is a failure that Labor will carry as a burden into the next election, a misstep that could have been avoided had they seized the moment to create real change.

After nine years of overt corruption under the Coalition, during which ministers seemed almost indifferent to public outrage, the Labor government had a chance to create a new chapter on public accountability. It could have drawn a clear red line under the past, pursued justice, and set a new standard for government integrity. But instead of punishing those responsible and securing a lasting legacy, Labor has allowed the NACC to become a political liability. It's not just a policy failure; it's a failure to capitalise on a political moment that could have cemented the government's place in history.

The NACC could have been this government's legacy. Instead, it is shaping up to be one of its biggest disappointments. There were also political benefits to be gained from doing the right thing—Labor didn't need to invent scandals or go after its political enemies with vengeance in the same way the Liberal Party has done with concocted Royal Commissions into trade unions and the insulation schemes; the corruption that occurred during the Coalition years was blatant and well-documented and by simply acting on the evidence in front of them, Labor could have garnered political capital and public trust. Instead, their decision to create a weakened Commission leaves them looking timid and indecisive. Worse, it allows the perception of corruption to linger, even if they have no direct involvement in the scandals of the previous government.

Ultimately, the NACC's failure is emblematic of a larger problem within the Labor government—it is a government with great potential but lacking in political skill. It's time for Labor to start governing with conviction and if they can't, they risk being remembered not for what they accomplished, but for what they failed to do at a critical point in Australia's political history.

***

FUCK THE COLONY: THE UNCOMFORTABLE TRUTHS ABOUT COLONISATION

25 October 2024

The recent royal visit to Australia was yet another reminder of the nation's ambiguous and often contradictory relationship with the British monarchy. In what has become a predictable spectacle, political leaders and mainstream media alike rolled out the red carpet for King Charles III and Queen Camilla, who were met with the usual fanfare, despite a weak public response.

The political and media establishment, once again, abandoned any semblance of critical faculties, indulging in obsequious behaviour that has come to define these visits. The tour was filled with the obligatory orchestrated public relations opportunities—photo-ops with community leaders, sheepdogs, parrots, alpacas, and brunches with recycled supermarket salads. However, the real significance of the visit only emerged when Senator Lidia Thorpe delivered a raw and unapologetic critique of the monarchy's legacy in Australia.

> "This is not your country. You committed genocide against our people.
> Give us our land back.
> Give us what you stole from us—our bones, our skulls, our babies, our people.
> You destroyed our land.
> Give us a treaty. We want a treaty in this country.
> You are a genocidalist.
> This is not your land. You are not my king. You are not our king.
> Fuck the colony!"

Senator Thorpe's fiery speech was a contrast to the carefully curated optics of the royal tour. She directly addressed King Charles, accusing him and his forebears of committing genocide against Indigenous Australians and demanded the return of stolen land, bones, and lives—direct, emotional, and unapologetic, a bold departure from the polite deference that usually surrounds royal visits, the Senator's outburst sparked outrage among conservative MPs and monarchists, with calls for her resignation.

However, what Thorpe said was historically correct: British colonisation in Australia did lead to the displacement, exploitation, and systemic eradication of Indigenous peoples. Yet, instead of confronting this uncomfortable truth, the political right focused its energy on condemning the messenger rather than addressing the message.

Her comments also reflected a broader reckoning with the monarchy's place in modern Australia. While King Charles has inherited the crown, the scars left by British colonialism are far from healed. The concept of *terra nullius*, which declared Australia an uninhabited land ripe for British settlement, legitimised the theft of Indigenous lands and cultures. There has never been a treaty between the Indigenous peoples and the British or Australian governments, leaving a significant gap in the nation's history and its attempts at reconciliation. If King Charles genuinely wanted to contribute to Australia, he could acknowledge this dark history and support a meaningful process toward reconciliation, including the negotiation of a treaty. Instead, the tour was little more than a ceremonial exercise, disconnected from the pressing realities of Indigenous justice.

The royal visit achieved little more than superficial pageantry. Prime Minister Anthony Albanese's interactions with the King, while diplomatically necessary, carried an air of discomfort—an awkward balancing act between respect for the head of state and the growing republican sentiment in the country. It was a far cry from the dignified yet clear republican stance that former leaders like Paul Keating and Bob Hawke managed to strike. King Charles' diminishing popularity, coupled with a lack of meaningful engagement with Australia's political and cultural challenges, left many questioning the necessity of the visit in the first place. While the media tried to paint a picture of royal success, the reality on the ground suggested otherwise: a monarchy increasingly out of touch with the modern Australian ethos.

Ultimately, Senator Thorpe's speech may have been the most memorable part of the royal tour—not so much for its shock value, but for the uncomfortable truths it laid bare. The British crown's historical and ongoing relationship with Indigenous Australia is fraught with injustice, and the royal family's unwillingness to acknowledge or address this legacy only deepens the divide. While the political and media establishment may continue to treat the monarchy with reverence, the public's growing disinterest, combined with the resurgence of republican debate, suggests that the royal family's days as Australia's head of state are numbered.

THE FOCUS ON POLITE DECORUM INSTEAD OF THE DAMAGE OF COLONISATION

Following Senator Thorpe's public outburst, a chorus of conservative MPs quickly brandished constitutional rhetoric to support their calls for her resignation from Parliament. Most notably, Senator Bridget McKenzie, infamous for her involvement in the sportsrorts affair, positioned herself as an authority on constitutional matters, claiming that Thorpe had breached her oath of allegiance and—delivered without any sense of irony—*she must therefore face consequences*.

This assertion was not only legally unsound but also revealed the shallow understanding many of these MPs have of Australia's Constitution. McKenzie's response, much like others from her conservative counterparts, centred on Thorpe's perceived breach of decorum, rather than addressing the substance of Thorpe's critique.

McKenzie's claim that Thorpe had violated her oath of allegiance by disavowing the King betrays a misunderstanding of constitutional principles. The oath of allegiance, which all parliamentarians swear upon taking office, binds them to serve the interests of the Crown according to the law, but it does not preclude them from criticising the institution or advocating for political change. In fact, the Constitution guarantees freedom of speech, even for parliamentarians expressing dissent against the monarchy. Thorpe's declaration that Charles is *not my king* may have been inflammatory to some, but it was well within her constitutional rights. The calls for her resignation reflected not a misunderstanding of law, but an ideological disagreement that conservative figures chose to frame as a constitutional crisis.

What was lost in this conservative uproar was the essence of Thorpe's message. Instead of engaging with these critical issues, conservative MPs such as McKenzie fixated on her tone and choice of words, and deflected from this reality by appealing to "respectability politics", choosing to attack Thorpe's "manners" rather than confront the brutal truth of colonisation.

The notion that the King has "earned our respect," as some conservatives argued, is also dubious at best. King Charles III's ascent to the throne was a matter of birthright, not merit. He has neither been a towering figure of moral authority nor a leader of significant social change. His refusal to meet with Senator Thorpe, an elected representative seeking dialogue on critical historical injustices, speaks volumes about the monarchy's disconnection from the issues that matter to many Australians. Thorpe's frustration, far from being an act of *bad manners*, was a reflection of the deep-seated anger and pain felt by Indigenous Australians who have been historically ignored and sidelined by the institutions of power.

A treaty has long been a critical issue for First Nations Australians, and it would represent not only a recognition of Indigenous sovereignty but also a step towards reconciliation and justice. The British Empire's legacy in Australia, marked by the theft of land, the destruction of cultures, and the systematic genocide of Indigenous peoples, remains a wound that has never fully healed.

In this context, the conservative backlash against Thorpe's speech was not just about protecting the monarchy—it was about *preserving the status quo*. The insistence on decorum over justice, on manners over truth, reveals a deeper discomfort with confronting the violent history of colonisation and the demands for accountability that come with it.

Radical voices in Australian politics, both on the left and the right, have long used provocative language to push their agendas. Pauline

Hanson, for example, has made a career out of inflammatory rhetoric, yet her place in Parliament has never been threatened by the same conservative voices now calling for Thorpe's removal. This double standard is telling—when a radical figure from the right engages in polarising speech, they are often defended as a representative of *free speech*. But when a Black Indigenous woman speaks truth to power, she is met with demands for her resignation.

In many ways, the outrage surrounding Thorpe's speech is less about her actual words and more about the discomfort they caused. Thorpe's refusal to adhere to the expected norms of civility in the presence of royalty may have offended conservative sensibilities, but it brought much-needed attention to the issues of colonisation, Indigenous justice, and the role of the monarchy in modern Australia.

A CALL FOR JUSTICE SILENCED BY AUSTRALIA'S POLITICAL AND MEDIA ELITE

With nearly a million Indigenous people in Australia, there is, of course, a diversity of opinions within the community about the path toward justice, recognition, and reconciliation. Not every Indigenous person will agree with Thorpe's methods or rhetoric, but her powerful outburst likely resonated with many who share her frustration at the slow pace of change.

Thorpe's speech, now being referred to as the *Not My King* moment, could well be seen as a modern counterpart to Paul Keating's historic Redfern Speech in 1992. While Keating's speech was delivered with measured statesmanship, Thorpe's was raw, unfiltered, and deeply personal. Yet, both speeches share a common theme: the urgent need for Australia to reckon with its colonial past and the ongoing oppression of its Indigenous peoples. Thorpe's speech, while brief, spoke to the heart of Australia's unresolved history of dispossession and genocide.

The backlash Thorpe faced, especially from white conservative figures, was both predictable and telling. Her critique of the monarchy and call for a treaty were met with the same dismissive reactions that have historically been used to silence Indigenous voices. As Thorpe herself noted, the colonial system in Australia has a long track record of shutting down Black women who dare to speak out against injustice. The immediate focus on her tone, rather than the substance of her critique, is emblematic of a broader pattern in Australian society—when Indigenous people speak out about their oppression, particularly in ways that challenge the comfort of white Australia, they are met with derision, hostility, or attempts to silence them altogether.

The recurring symbolism in Australian politics—telling Indigenous people to *sit down, shut up*, and accept whatever limited gestures of recognition are offered—has been a persistent barrier to progress. We saw it with Adam Goodes, a proud Indigenous footballer whose outspoken stance against racism was met with vicious booing and media condemnation. And we see it again with Thorpe, whose uncompromising stance has been met with calls for her to be silenced, removed from Parliament, and dismissed as a radical. It's a pattern that has played out time and time again: when Indigenous people speak out, particularly in ways that make white Australia uncomfortable, the response is to shout them down, not to engage with the substance of their critique.

The scene of King Charles and Prime Minister laughing together in the aftermath of Thorpe's outburst also reinforced this dynamic. To them, it may have been a momentary disturbance—an irritation to be smoothed over before returning to the pleasantries of royal protocol. But to many watching, it was a symbol of how the political and cultural establishment in Australia continues to dismiss Indigenous voices. As Prime Minister, Albanese could have used the moment to engage with the issue of a treaty, to ask the King what role the monarchy might play in addressing the injustices of colonisation. Instead, the moment passed in a smug exchange, with no acknowledgment of the real, painful history that underpins Thorpe's anger.

When Indigenous people express their views in ways that align with the expectations of white Australia—*calm, conciliatory, and deferential*—they are tolerated. But when they speak with passion, anger, and truth, as Thorpe did, they are vilified and shut down. This is not a new phenomenon; it has been the default response to Indigenous activism for decades. Yet, this unwillingness to engage with the harder truths of Australia's colonial past and present is precisely what holds the nation back from genuine reconciliation.

Thorpe's speech may have been *radical*, but it was *not wrong*. Her words reflected the frustration and anger of many Indigenous Australians who are tired of being told to wait, to compromise, and to accept symbolic gestures in place of real justice. As long as the establishment continues to silence those voices and avoid the difficult conversations, the wounds of Australia's colonial past will remain unhealed. The country will not move forward until it is willing *to listen* to Indigenous people—not just the ones who speak softly, but also the ones who, like Lidia Thorpe, refuse to be silenced.

***

WHEN WILL AUSTRALIA EMBRACE A REPUBLIC OF IDEAS?

28 October 2024

The royal visit to Australia by King Charles III and Queen Camilla is over—a cursory glimpse at the colonised subjects of the British Crown—but it has prompted a subdued, yet vital revival of the Republican movement in Australia, highlighting a paradox that's deeply ingrained in the country's political and cultural fabric.

Australia often prides itself on being the land of the "larrikin"—a place of easy-going individualists who challenge authority, a place where fairness and mateship supercede obedience to outdated institutions. However, in reality, Australia has proven to be anything but a nation of self-determined rebels when it comes to its relationship with the British monarch. Instead, the country often stands deferentially in line, reluctant to offend a foreign king or criticise the centuries-old institution he represents. This institution, steeped in colonialism, imperialism, and the legacies of genocide, remains politely accepted by a country that claims to reject such past atrocities.

This compliance extends well beyond attitudes toward the monarchy; it permeates the very governance and structures that uphold Australia's legal and social framework. The state increasingly resembles an enforcer of conformity, a warden, rather than a protector of public liberty. Australians watch, largely subdued, as voices are silenced and protests are swiftly subdued. Unions, once a backbone of resistance and workers' rights, have been made fragile by decades of institutional suppression. Protesters face arrest not for violent actions but for just daring to express dissent. The *larrikin ideal*, in many ways, is a distant myth that seems to crumble further each time Australia willingly bends to the grips of authority rather than standing tall against it.

Such a stance sharply contrasts with the vision of former Prime Minister Paul Keating, who, in 1992, had the boldness to challenge the monarchy and call for an Australian republic. At the time, Keating argued that nations could either passively respond to public sentiment or act as leaders, guiding people toward the future they deserve and he envisioned an Australian head of state who would embody the nation's contemporary values, a representative of its diversity, aspirations, and the evolving partnerships Australia fosters in the Asia–Pacific region. Keating's Republican initiative wasn't about nationalism or exclusion but rather about acknowledging the growth of Australian society, a mature, inclusive view that recognised the importance of constitutional reform as a means of solidifying Australia's independence and true sovereignty, and creating a clearer pathway for reconciliation with Indigenous people.

However, the challenge lies far beyond the symbolic head of state. Changing the figurehead is a comparatively easy task when considered alongside the monumental reforms required to make the Constitution, as well as the institution it represents, reflect modern Australian society. The connection between these institutions and the Australian public has been fractured for years. Constitutional reform should not stop at severing ties with the monarchy; it should go further, seeking to overhaul governance structures and reimagine democratic processes to prevent the abuses of power and lack of accountability seen in recent history.

Australia's previous attempt to move toward a republic, the 1999 referendum, floundered in part due to the narrow, minimalist and elitist framing of the debate. Political leaders and wealthy stakeholders dominated the discussion, creating an atmosphere that alienated the everyday Australians who would stand to benefit most from republican reform and this disconnect left the movement without the grassroots support needed to succeed. The referendum was also marred by internal discord among supporters and a lack of a cohesive vision for what an Australian republic could truly look like.

It was not a movement fueled by the people's interests but rather by the ambitions of a select few—a flaw that contributed to its downfall.

In this context, another referendum, especially after the recent failure of the Voice to Parliament, may feel like a distant prospect. Current Prime Minister Anthony Albanese, despite early support for a republic, is hesitant to tackle another divisive issue in the wake of that defeat, even going to the extent of removing the position of Assistant Minister for the Republic in July 2024. This delay is not only a political tactic but an indictment of a system that continually places critical decisions at the mercy of electoral cycles, where true reform risks taking a backseat to political expediency. The Republican movement, if it is to succeed, must find its footing beyond party lines and influential backers, connecting instead with the people it seeks to empower.

AN URGENT NEED FOR DEMOCRATIC RENEWAL

Australia's deeply ingrained *she'll-be-right-mate* attitude has created a culture of political inertia, stifling progress and hindering meaningful reform. This complacency, a comfort with the status quo, has allowed the nation to drift rather than actively shape its future, especially when it comes to constitutional reform and modernising democracy. Instead of fostering an engaged, adaptive political environment, Australia has become a 'lazy' democracy—one that not only resists change but also makes it actively difficult for citizens to engage. While the mechanisms of democracy are technically available, they are increasingly dominated by organised interest groups and corporations, overshadowing the voices of the general populace. This passive approach has ceded significant space to powerful, right-wing forces, whose influence grows as the political will to counterbalance them falters.

In this stagnant political climate, corporations have thrived, their influence strengthened by a government that operates more secretively and serves the interests of a select few. When citizens are not given an easy avenue to participate in or influence their democracy, they are effectively locked out of the decisions that shape their lives, leaving corporate interests to fill the vacuum. This secrecy and resistance to change have created a system that seems deliberately designed to favour those with power and wealth, while the majority remains politically disconnected and disempowered.

Attempts to disrupt this status quo are often met with fierce resistance. For example, when Keating declared in the 1990s that Australia should look to Asia for its future rather than Europe, his assertion ignited a nationwide backlash. The visceral reaction to this idea exposed an unwillingness to embrace Australia's geographic and cultural reality, showing a nation still clinging to outdated ties and hesitant to define a truly independent identity.

This reluctance to change—to even acknowledge the need for change—has kept Australia tethered to antiquated values and a hierarchical social order that perpetuates privilege. It's a mindset that discourages daring leadership, one where new ideas or bold directions are often seen as *threats* rather than *opportunities*. When leaders hint at change, the political rhetoric shifts toward fear: any shift from the status quo will allegedly compromise what citizens already have, creating a *politics of envy* that pits Australians against one another. Instead of fostering solidarity or collective vision, the narrative centres on loss, risk, and resentment, a formula that has reliably suppressed democratic enthusiasm and keeps people clinging to familiar patterns.

Australia's past as a penal colony may explain some of this conservatism, with an inherited tendency to comply rather than question. But perhaps it's more reflective of Donald Horne's famous observation in *The Lucky Country*: that Australia is a place blessed with abundant resources but often led by unimaginative, second-rate leaders who are more interested in preserving their own influence than in pursuing ambitious reforms. Over time, they have streamlined institutions that are self-serving, designed to maintain the comfortable positions of those in power while failing to serve the broader public effectively. This "second-rate" mentality has left Australia in a state of democratic atrophy, where public institutions are becoming increasingly hollowed out, offering little to those they were originally created to serve.

It's unlikely that Prime Minister Albanese will be the one to break this cycle, certainly not in the foreseeable future. But it will require more than symbolic gestures; it will demand a direct challenge to the complacency that has kept Australia from realising its potential as a fully independent nation. This challenge involves more than severing ties with the monarchy or altering constitutional language—it requires a fundamental transformation in how Australians engage with their democracy and a willingness to accept that real progress often comes with discomfort and uncertainty. Without this shift, Australia risks remaining a comfortable, yet stagnant, democracy—one where the only true beneficiaries are those already in power.

SEIZING THE MOMENT AND MOVING TOWARD AN INCLUSIVE REPUBLIC

Of course, Australia will always have the opportunity to reshape its democracy, fostering a more equitable relationship between the government and the electorate, and creating a genuinely representative system. However, it depends on the presence of *political will*, which at this stage, is nowhere in sight. Over the past four decades, the link between government and the electorate has been diluted by neoliberal policies, privatisation, and a shift in focus from serving the public to catering to corporations and vested interests. As essential services and utilities have gradually been sold off to private interests, the government's role has narrowed, becoming more about managing the demands of corporate stakeholders than fulfilling its duty to the people.

This shift means that while elected governments may change, the corporations controlling these vital services remain constant, wielding significant influence without the accountability mechanisms of a democratic process. The compact between government and the electorate, once stronger and more direct, has morphed into a partnership between government and private corporations, with citizens relegated to the role of passive observers rather than active participants in democracy.

To establish a true republic, Australia must re-evaluate and dismantle this arrangement, restoring government responsibility and accountability to the people it is meant to serve. The reforms required go beyond superficial constitutional adjustments; they demand a restructuring of how government operates, who it answers to, and how the interests of the electorate are prioritised over those of powerful corporations.

Achieving these changes is no easy task, especially in a country where reforms occur at a glacial pace, hindered by an elite political and corporate class that fiercely guards its privileges. A true republic for Australia cannot coexist with an elite that considers itself above accountability and resists being challenged on merit and Australia's institutions must represent the diversity of its population, not the narrow interests of a few who inherited power rather than earned it.

Privilege should not be an unchallenged entitlement passed through generations; rather, opportunity should be accessible to all, regardless of one's family background or educational pedigree—and any change should start at the very top: the removal of an inherited King who resides in a foreign country. The republic should stand as a model of inclusive governance, rewarding ability and commitment to public service over this inherited status.

At its core, this transformation requires a shift in values—from an Australia that clings to the lazy *lucky country* narrative, to one that envisions itself as a land of true equal opportunity and democratic integrity. Only then can Australia create a republic that genuinely represents its people, where government policies prioritise public wellbeing over corporate profits, and where the relationship between government and citizens is restored to one of trust and accountability.

***

NOVEMBER

A DARK NEW ERA FOR U.S. DEMOCRACY?

7 November 2024

The 2024 U.S. presidential election marks a deeply troubling chapter in American democracy, one that is more aligned with authoritarianism than any recent precedent. Donald Trump's victory highlights an unsettling shift in the political fabric of the United States, signaling the public's apparent tolerance, even preference, for a candidate whose actions and rhetoric challenge the very foundations of democratic governance.

This victory not only reinstates Trump, the disgraced former president, but also inaugurates a leader with an unparalleled sense of impunity—a man who openly disregards legal constraints, touts unbridled executive power, and is unfazed by criminal convictions or constitutional breaches. That he achieved such a commanding win, by more than four million votes and with 312 electoral votes, reveals a transformation in the American electorate and raises alarming questions about the future of American democracy.

This electoral outcome is not just a rejection of an alternative candidate; it is an endorsement of a style and substance that have compared to the authoritarian shifts in pre-war Germany and fascist Italy. Trump's campaign was marked by a relentless stream of divisive, inflammatory rhetoric that was grotesque: racist remarks, blatant falsehoods, personal attacks.

Yet, despite the constant flow of insults and fabrications, the American public *chose him*. It reveals a disturbing cultural shift—one in which the electorate has not only normalised but embraced for a second time, a brand of politics was once deemed unacceptable, and the implications of Trump's re-election extend far beyond the borders of the United States.

As the world's preeminent economic and military power, the character and direction of American governance have profound consequences for global stability. With Trump at the helm, America risks becoming a model of authoritarianism cloaked in democratic attire, a regime where the leader's words carry the force of law and opposition voices are drowned out by a chorus of loyalty and fear. This erosion of democratic norms—of accountability, transparency, and respect for institutional limits—will serve as a blueprint for other leaders seeking to consolidate power and erode democratic checks and balances worldwide.

The U.S. has weathered incompetent administrations and highly questionable governance before. Richard Nixon, for example. George W. Bush's presidency, though highly controversial, still operated within at least some of the perceived boundaries of democratic norms. But Trump's presidency is different: he doesn't just bend the rules; he flaunts his disdain for them, turning constitutional limits into punchlines in a performance that mocks the democratic ideal.

This version of Trump's America veers dangerously close to fascism—he openly fantasised about the violent punishment of his political opponents, notably Nancy Pelosi, and showed no remorse over the events of January 6, when a mob stormed the Capitol, many with the apparent intention of harming elected officials. The violence that accompanied his first administration has evolved, not diminished, with groups of armed supporters ready to defend their leader's vision at any cost.

The impending years threaten to see America not as a model of democracy but as a nation spiraling into internal decay, a decline that will inevitably have far-reaching effects. The Trump administration's anticipated targeting of journalists, political opponents, and social critics raises the spectre of a country where dissent is no longer a right but a dangerous gamble. Left-wing activists, progressive journalists, and anyone opposing Trump's policies may now be forced to weigh their words carefully, knowing that retaliation is not only possible but inevitable.

This marks a dark turning point, one where democracy is no longer taken as a given, where the ideals of freedom and equality are mocked by those who hold power. The coming years will challenge not only the resilience of American institutions but also the world's faith in the American democratic experiment itself. This election may well be remembered as the moment America opened the door to fascism—an open invitation to authoritarianism disguised with the fig leaf of democracy.

HOW AUTHENTICITY AND EMOTIONAL APPEAL IS REDEFINING POLITICS

The fact that Trump could win by such a decisive margin, garnering both a significant popular vote lead and overwhelming support in the Electoral College, speaks volumes about a changing dynamic in the American political psyche. Trump, with his bombastic and unapologetic persona, embodies a form of raw, radical and brash political authenticity—and this persona, more than policy or competence, appears to be a crucial factor in shaping contemporary voter behaviour.

Trump's tactics in 2024 were as blunt and polarising as they were in his first term, relying on familiar conservative tropes: painting America as overrun by immigrants, derailed by liberal agendas, and hamstrung by foreign competition. He offered simple, often drastic solutions—tariffs on Chinese goods, strict immigration policies—that resonate deeply with segments of the American population feeling increasingly alienated by globalisation and economic shifts. Trump's solutions won't be viable in the long run, potentially worsening the economic conditions they purport to fix, but they are easy to grasp. They offer immediate emotional comfort, a balm for the resentment and dislocation felt by many working-class voters who believe that mainstream politicians have ignored their struggles. This simplicity, however flawed, inadequate or accurate, is part of his appeal.

The Democrats, on the other hand, struggles to present a coherent, compelling message that resonates on an emotional level. Since 2016, the Democrats have attempted to define themselves as the *antithesis* of Trump, yet this approach has often translated into a form of elitism, reinforcing perceptions of the party as out of touch with the average American.

Despite policy achievements and economic improvements under Joe Biden, the Democrats seem unable to shake the perception that they are too much a part of the Washington elite or too influenced by the narratives that fit into the fiction of *West Wing*—steeped in institutional politics, mired in technocratic language, and uncomfortable with bold, populist rhetoric. This inability to connect at a visceral level has created a vacuum, one that Trump has filled with ease, however incendiary his approach might be.

The Democrats' continual attempts to appeal to both progressive ideals and centrist pragmatism have only diluted their message. Rather than embracing a clear, progressive vision, the party has often resorted to a "small target" strategy, attempting to be all things to all people. The party's reluctance to fully align with the working class has driven these voters to seek representation elsewhere, and they have found it in Trump's unabashed populism, which, however hollow, *feels* authentic to them.

This authenticity, ironically, is one of Trump's most potent weapons. In 2016, Trump was an outsider disrupting the political establishment, and many voters found his bluntness refreshing, even if unsettling. His 2024 campaign, though still chaotic, lacked the same novelty yet retained an air of unapologetic defiance. For his supporters, this isn't a flaw but a feature; Trump is simply *being Trump*. He makes no effort to polish his image, nor does he attempt to conform to traditional presidential decorum. This stands in contrast to the Democrats, who are perceived as carefully crafted and overly concerned about avoiding offence, and hide their true progressive nature, unwilling to risk authenticity for fear of alienating moderates. While Democrats might see this caution as necessary, many voters interpret it as a lack of conviction, as though the party itself is unsure of its own principles.

In this environment, the Democrats' alliances and strategies further complicated their standing with the electorate. By associating with figures like Liz Cheney—a conservative, yet vocal Trump opponent—they attempted to convey bipartisanship but instead came across as even more aligned with Washington's elite, reinforcing their out-of-touch image. Conservative media, particularly outlets such as Fox News, capitalised on this, focusing heavily on personal attacks on Kamala Harris and portraying the Democratic leadership as weak, out of step, and ineffective. Progressive voters were left frustrated by what they saw as a lack of genuine progressive vision, while centrists perceived the party's message as muddled and uninspiring.

Rather than acknowledging these votes as signs of disillusionment, the Democrats overlooked the underlying issue: the Democrats failed to offer a compelling reason for enough voters to support them.

Trump's victory, then, is a reminder that politics is as much about perception and emotion—if not *more*—as it is about policy. While his opponents may decry his incompetence or point to his cognitive decline, these criticisms miss the larger point. The electorate is not necessarily voting on the basis of expertise or coherence; they are voting for someone they feel understands and speaks to their frustrations. Trump's speech patterns, though disorganised and nonsensical, resonate on a personal level, as if he is addressing each individual rather than an abstract electorate and this form of connection is one of the reasons Trump remains a formidable political figure at this stage.

The Democrats now face a critical crossroads, one that extends beyond the U.S. and reverberates globally. Other left-leaning parties, from Australia's Labor Party to the British Labour Party, must take heed of these dynamics. These parties must confront the issue of authenticity and offer a vision that is not merely reactive but boldly addresses the economic and social discontent that drives voters to populist figures like Trump with fascist tendencies.

In this sense, the 2024 election is more than just a political loss for the Democrats; it is a call to re-evaluate their approach to connecting with the electorate. The rise of Trump is a shift toward authoritarianism, but it also reflects a vacuum in American politics—a vacuum left by a party unable or unwilling to fully commit to the principles it claims to represent. If the Democrats cannot evolve, if they cannot articulate a vision that feels both genuine and inclusive, they risk solidifying a political landscape where figures like Trump are not aberrations but the new standard.

A DIVIDED NATION: DEEP-ROOTED CHALLENGES IN AMERICAN POLITICS

This U.S. election has highlighted the deeply entrenched divisions within American society, yet these divides are nothing new. They are the product of more than half a century of conflict between the conservative, white-settler America and a progressive, multicultural America that is increasingly shaped by immigration and shifting demographics. This clash has defined American politics for decades, reflecting broader global patterns of left and right political tensions. While many point to Trump's re-election as evidence of an unprecedented polarisation, this is just an extension of a longstanding ideological divide—*this is America*, after all, it has always been like this. The more intense right-wing MAGA fringe that has emerged in recent years may add a new layer to this split, but the divide itself remains rooted in an age-old American narrative.

One of the more contentious debates around this election has been the Democrats' handling of specific issues, particularly those with a pronounced international dimension, such as the Palestinian cause. The party's stance to completely ignore the plight of Palestinians may have cost them support in certain areas, most notably in Michigan, where a significant Arab community resides. Although it's too early to draw definitive conclusions, such issues reveal how the Democrats' strategic choices, including international stances in Palestine and Ukraine, may have alienated potential supporters. Younger voters, too, may have felt disenfranchised by the Democrats' foreign policy positions or uninspired by a candidate they saw as representing more of the same.

The initial choice of Joe Biden as the Democratic nominee has also raised questions. Although Biden had once beaten Trump—and as the sitting president, he should have the right to seek a second nomination—his age and lack of vigour created a sense of instability within the party. If he had stepped aside much earlier, it may have provided Kamala Harris with the time and space to carve out her own identity and distance herself from the Biden administration. But Harris's messaging, often centred on continuity with Biden's policies, reinforced the sense that the Democrats were offering nothing new.

A fresh vision, even if imperfect, might have given her campaign the strength it needed to appeal to a broader base.

Yet beyond strategic missteps, this election also laid bare the enduring sexism that has plagued American politics, evident in the experiences of both Hillary Clinton and now, Kamala Harris. Each faced an opponent known for his sexism and documented history of misogynistic behaviour—Trump's rhetoric and conduct have been consistently degrading toward women, with statements and actions that many find abhorrent—yet this has not prevented him from twice defeating female candidates in presidential races. In both 2016 and 2024, the U.S. had the chance to elect a strong, competent woman, yet the electorate chose instead to support a man who promotes violence against women, shows disregard for democratic norms, and openly derides women.

While there might be a case to put forward that both Clinton and Harris were flawed candidates, these critiques fail to acknowledge the fundamental bias they faced: the unwillingness of a significant portion of the American electorate to embrace the idea of a female leader, especially one running against a hyper-masculine figure like Trump. Clinton was widely viewed as highly capable and prepared in 2016, yet her qualifications were overshadowed by Trump's populist appeal. Now, despite Harris's qualifications, her gender—and the pervasive sexism still at play in American politics—also played a role in her defeat.

The broader implications of this sexism reach beyond these two candidacies. The choice to favour an overtly misogynistic candidate over qualified women sends a powerful message about the state of gender equality in U.S. politics. It suggests that, for many voters, a brash and unapologetic man—even one with a history of behaviour that would disqualify others—is preferable to a woman in the Oval Office. This attitude raises troubling questions about the future of American democracy and the inclusivity of its highest office.

As Trump embarks on his second term, he does so with a greater sense of validation than in 2016. This time, he won both the popular vote and a significant Electoral College majority, bolstering his mandate and potentially empowering him to pursue more extreme policies. The dangers of this cannot be overstated. His rhetoric during the campaign hinted at severe crackdowns on dissenting voices, especially journalists, activists, and leftist commentators, and some independent and progressive media outlets have already expressed concerns about censorship or legal repercussions, fearing that they may be silenced or curtailed under an emboldened Trump administration.

There is always a risk of viewing these developments as overly catastrophic, but the U.S. has reached a point where worst-case scenarios can no longer be dismissed, and the potential for serious erosions of civil liberties, judicial integrity, and press freedom is *very real*. Trump's promises to restore "law and order" may soon translate into more aggressive policing, judicial appointments that skew further to the right, and legislation that stifles dissent and these policies could reshape the U.S. into a version of itself that is almost unrecognisable to those who once saw it as a bastion of democracy and freedom.

Ultimately, Trump's victory serves as both a caution and a call to action for the Democrats and other left-leaning parties globally. The loss was not just about strategy or individual flaws; it was a consequence of failing to recognise and address the deeper cultural currents that influence voter behaviour. Authenticity, clear messaging, and the ability to connect with a disillusioned working class are more important now than ever. Without these, the Democrats risk continuing down a path where the party's disconnect with voters grows, and figures like Trump become not outliers but the norm.

Whether this is the beginning of a lasting authoritarian shift or a wake-up call for the political establishment remains to be seen. What is certain, however, is that the American political landscape has been reshaped in ways that will have profound consequences for years to come. Trump's second term is the mark of the decline of a certain ideal of America, one that valued equality, liberty, and inclusion, and the rise of a new political order where power, rather than principle, reigns supreme. The challenge for the Democrats—and for all who value democracy—is to respond to this reality with the clarity, conviction, and courage required to reclaim those ideals before they are lost for good.

***

THE UNMASKING OF THE WEST REVEALS AN UGLY FACE

16 November 2024

In recent years, the narrative surrounding the behaviour of Israel has become a mixture of political rhetoric, selective outrage, and, at on many occasions, *blatant distortion*. The recent football match in Amsterdam, where Maccabi Tel Aviv supporters turned a sporting event into a festival of violence, highlights the power that mainstream media and political figures wield in shaping public perception in favour of the state of Israel—often to align with a particular political agenda. For those who witnessed or later learned of the events as they truly unfolded, the gap between media reports and reality was glaring and unsettling, raising pressing questions about the manipulation of truth in service of political allegiances.

At the heart of this incident were Israeli supporters who arrived in Amsterdam to watch their team play Ajax in the Europa League (yes, *Israel* plays in a *European* league), ostensibly to support their team but quickly transformed the city into an arena for provocations, aggression, and racism where bystanders and residents were not simply caught in crossfire but were specifically targeted. Eyewitness accounts and independent media revealed that Maccabi Tel Aviv fans shouted racist slurs directed towards Palestine, harassed and physically assaulted people they perceived as 'Middle Eastern', and tore down Palestinian flags in brazen acts of provocation.

In an even more disturbing event, they disrupted a moment of silence meant to honour victims of recent floods in Spain, turning a display of respect into yet another arena for their anti-Palestinian vitriol. The next day saw more aggression on the city streets, ultimately leading to inevitable confrontations between the Israeli hooligans and Dutch locals, who retaliated in defence against the repeated provocations.

Yet, in the media, the narrative that reached international audiences was drastically different. Rather than highlighting the Maccabi fans' violence and bigotry, reports widely focused on the backlash from the Dutch public, depicting it as an outburst of anti-Semitic violence against innocent Israeli fans. Mainstream outlets drew dramatic parallels, likening the incidents to the *Kristallnacht* from 1938, casting the Dutch response as an attack on Jewish identity itself, rather than a defensive reaction to aggression. This shift in focus, this reinterpretation of events, served to shield the instigators and reframe the incident within a context that evoked collective Western guilt and sympathy, minimising the violent role the Israeli supporters played.

Australian politicians were also quick to adopt this skewed narrative, with Foreign Minister Senator Penny Wong condemning what she described as "anti-Semitic attacks" on the Israeli fans. There was no acknowledgment in her statement of the cause of these tensions—and certainly no recognition of the actions of Maccabi supporters that led to the confrontation—and it demonstrated an unwillingness, either out of convenience or political strategy, to question the origins of the conflict. Instead, Wong's statement reinforced a long-standing pattern in Western politics: denouncing anti-Semitism while remaining silent on provocations and violence perpetrated by Israeli supporters and Zionist sympathisers.

While anti-Semitism must be confronted—*as we must always point out*—and violence unequivocally condemned, this one-sided response contributed to a narrative that holds one group immune from accountability. This is not a new pattern in matters related to Israel and Palestine, where narratives are often shaped to protect or justify Israeli actions while minimising or vilifying Palestinian responses. This selective outrage has, over time, solidified a concerning pattern in Western foreign policy and media coverage, where Israeli actions are never held to the same standards. For politicians such as Senator

Wong, the optics of appearing 'neutral' or 'aligned with allies' often come at the cost of truth.

SHIELDING ISRAELI AGGRESSION FROM ACCOUNTABILITY

This was just a game, but the tolerance shown towards Israel's actions extends far beyond football violence. Israel has long enjoyed vast financial and military support from the United States, despite persistent human rights abuses in Palestine since 1946, and accelerated since October 2023. Billions of U.S. dollars are funneled to Israel each year, supporting military operations that result in significant Palestinian casualties, destruction of homes, and widespread displacement. Meanwhile, countless Americans struggle with economic hardship, job insecurity, and rising living costs. Although there isn't a direct correlation between U.S. domestic policies and its unwavering support of Israel, the vast sums allocated to Israel reveal a priority in U.S. foreign policy that many American citizens are beginning to question, especially when they themselves lack adequate social support.

This disconnect between the public's interests and the priorities of political leaders was one factor in the Democrats' recent defeat in the U.S. elections. Despite widespread calls for a foreign policy shift that emphasises human rights and equitable treatment of all nations, President Joe Biden continues to authorise funding for Israel's military, supporting its airstrikes and operations in Palestinian territories. This disparity in treatment—both in terms of resources and diplomatic immunity—sends a clear message: Israel, despite its actions of genocide and ethnic cleansing, remains a protected ally.

This immunity raises questions about the underlying factors that influence Western leaders' responses to Israel. The influence of intelligence and information-gathering agencies, such as Mossad, has long been speculated as a force shaping global attitudes toward Israel. While these claims are difficult to substantiate, the pattern of unwavering support, even in the face of clear misconduct, suggests that many political leaders feel compelled to maintain favourable relations with Israel, irrespective of how repulsive, repugnant and violent its behaviour is, fearing potential political backlash or fallout.

HOW AGGRESSION ABROAD REFLECTS PRACTICES IN PALESTINE

The behaviour of the Maccabi Tel Aviv hooligans in Amsterdam also mirrors the broader dynamics of Israeli conduct in the occupied Palestinian territories. Their aggression, racially charged provocations, and disregard for local norms were more than just instances of football hooliganism; they were symptomatic of a larger pattern of behaviour rooted in entitlement, impunity, and a pervasive disregard by Israel for accountability. Just as these fans acted as though they were beyond reproach in Amsterdam, Israel's actions in Gaza and the West Bank similarly proceed unchecked, unchallenged by the same Western leaders and media who regularly demand human rights and accountability from other nations.

Many observers, including governments worldwide, now openly call Israel's actions in Gaza a genocide. Ireland—a European country with similar political values to many Western democracies, including Australia, recently passed a resolution condemning Israel's actions as genocidal, highlighting that it's not just a radical viewpoint but a global concern recognised by many governments.

Meanwhile, Western media and political leaders seem not only reluctant to confront these realities but actively complicit in perpetuating a narrative that excuses Israel's actions, often resorting to what can only be described as propaganda to shift blame onto Palestinians. The deliberate and systemic targeting of Palestinian homes, the near-daily bombings, the destruction of essential infrastructure, and the enforced famine are all documented in independent media and widely condemned by human rights organisations. However, Western politicians, such as Senator Wong, continue to offer only hollow expressions of "deep concern" while stopping short of real condemnation or action. How can they continue to deny and ignore the actions that everyone else can see with their own eyes?

The events in Amsterdam exemplify this pattern. The international media portrayed the Israeli supporters as *victims* rather than *aggressors*, just as it often frames Palestinians as the instigators of violence in their own territories, rather than resisters to an occupying force. Politicians who should be speaking out against such flagrant behaviour instead default to condemning anti-Semitism, a stance that overlooks the racist, violent actions directed toward Arabs and Palestinians. This selective condemnation reveals a troubling hypocrisy that extends beyond political alignment to reflect a deeply ingrained bias in how Western media and political institutions view and report on the Israeli–Palestinian conflict. It is a bias that allows Israel to act with impunity, assured that the media will obscure its actions and redirect blame to the Palestinians, who are framed as perpetually at fault, regardless of the evidence.

The United States plays a central role in this double standard. Despite Israel's escalations, from daily bombings to a planned annexation of the West Bank, the U.S. government continues to stand by Israel unequivocally, dismissing the grave human rights violations occurring under its watch. American leaders have issued ultimatums to Israel, cautioning against further violence or expansionist measures, but these warnings have never been enforced. It is a cycle of empty threats and inaction, enabling Israel to continue its policies without fear of repercussion. The result is a situation where U.S. politicians condemn violence in principle but fail to hold the region's most aggressive actors accountable.

For many—not all, but a substantial number—this is the "mask-is-off" moment, revealing the true nature of Western political and media complicity in Israel's actions. Politicians who proclaim to be defenders of human rights reveal their selective application of these values, as they ignore or justify the violence inflicted on Palestinians. This selective blindness exposes a deep-seated bias that elevates Israeli interests over Palestinian lives, allowing a campaign of dispossession and oppression to continue unchecked. Zionism, in its most extreme manifestations, presents itself as an ideology that sees no limit to Israel's expansion and control over Palestinian land. This belief system fuels the violence in Gaza and the West Bank, and it is precisely this worldview that played out on the streets of Amsterdam, where Maccabi supporters felt entitled to act as they pleased, assured that they would face no consequences.

In this double standard, we can see the *ugly face* of the West—a face that prioritises political alliances over justice, that condones and accepts racism when it comes from a preferred ally, and that perpetuates a system where Palestinian suffering is either ignored or justified. The events in Amsterdam may seem minor in the global scope of Israeli–Palestinian relations, but they are a microcosm of the larger narrative that plays out daily in Gaza, the West Bank, and Western media.

It's a selective empathy, a refusal to confront reality, and perpetuates an environment where the violence against Palestinians is normalised, while any form of Palestinian resistance is condemned. But it's the actions and inactions of Western leaders and their supporters in the media, that has to be condemned—whether it's on the football field or in occupied territories.

***

THE SOCIAL MEDIA BAN IS JUST ANOTHER POLITICAL SMOKESCREEN

20 November 2024

The federal government's proposal to ban social media for children under 16 is more of a political tactic rather than a solution to the issues it claims to address, and this type of policy-making usually results from a desire to shift public focus, drawing attention away from other pressing matters. It's a tactic both sides of the political spectrum adopt—it's more commonly used by conservatives but the Labor government has shown that it's a tactic that it's more than happy to borrow.

With this proposed ban, we see the same formula: create a moral panic, ignite public outrage, and turn what could be nuanced issues into black-and-white talking points. But it raises the question: what's actually behind this proposal, and how much does it genuinely engage with the complexities of social media and youth?

To begin with, this policy is tailored more for the *parents* of the children affected than the children themselves, who lack the power to vote and remain outside the immediate political equation. This narrative speaks to a different audience—parents who may feel overwhelmed by the challenges of raising children in the digital age, and now see the consequences in terms of screen dependency and exposure to a relentless online world, and taps into the underlying anxieties of parenting in the digital era, offering a symbolic solution rather than one grounded in practical realities.

The government's reasoning behind such a drastic measure seems oblivious to real-world dynamics and suggests a disconnect with how young people interact with media and digital spaces. Banning social media for this age group not only misunderstands its purpose but overlooks the value it holds for many children and teenagers. Social media, for young people today, can be far more than a digital distraction: it's a place of connection, a cultural and social language, a virtual space for discourse, camaraderie, and identity formation.

The government's proposal ignores the reality that digital interaction is the predominant means by which youth communicate and build relationships, particularly in an age marked by digital transformation.

Even in practical terms, the proposal falls at the first steps: it's unclear how this ban would be enforced or even defined. There's also ambiguity surrounding what platforms qualify as "social media." For instance, including YouTube in the ban reflects a lack of nuance regarding the platform's multifaceted role, particularly in education. YouTube is more than a social platform: it's a resource for learning that enables access to a world of knowledge. Its limitation would disrupt the availability of digital learning resources, particularly for schools and educators who rely on its content for enhancing educational engagement and broadening student access to knowledge.

What further complicates the government's stance is the inconsistency in its approach to media consumption and social issues for young people. While the government expresses concern over the dangers of social media, it allows gambling advertising on free-to-air television, which is arguably as impactful, if not more, on young minds than the content they might encounter on YouTube or TikTok. This selective morality—acting harshly against social media while ignoring other equally significant issues—highlights a deeply problematic approach to policymaking that prioritises optics over coherent, thoughtful strategies for youth welfare.

APPEASING NEWS CORP RATHER THAN PROTECTING CHILDREN

The proposed ban also reveals another dimension: a desire to appease powerful media conglomerates and vested interests, particularly News Corporation. This isn't solely about protecting children; rather, it reflects the influence wielded by legacy media over political decisions. In this case, the *Daily Telegraph*'s aggressive "Let Them Be Kids" campaign isn't so much about safeguarding young Australians as it is about advancing the News Corporation agenda and consolidating their influence over both government policy and public opinion.

News Corporation's track record when it comes to the welfare of children is woeful. The company has consistently shown it has little interest in protecting young people, having been embroiled in scandals involving phone hacking and invasive behaviour that exploited and harmed children and families. The company routinely manufactures crises in public schools, distorting incidents, railing against *woke* and creating moral panics to manipulate public perception. Yet here, it claims to be acting in the interest of child welfare—a stance that is not only hypocritical but also obviously self-serving.

The government's alignment with News Corporation is a strategic choice that goes beyond a desire to address social media's effects on children, and Prime Minister Anthony Albanese's effusive public praise for the "Let Them Be Kids" campaign further demonstrates this appeasement. It's typical of a broader political strategy, one that seeks to placate conservative factions and demonstrate an affinity with "traditional" values—values often defined and amplified by the platforms of News Corporation.

This approach also highlights a troubling dynamic within Australian politics: the selective willingness to challenge vested interests based on where they're located. Local entities, particularly media giants like News Corporation and gambling firms, receive kid-glove treatment, while overseas-based tech entities, such as Google and Meta, are easier targets for government scrutiny—they lack the local leverage and are easier to criticise without fear of local media backlash. By targeting social media companies, the government can posture as proactive on child safety, even as it sidesteps confronting powerful domestic interests with arguably greater societal impact. The government has decided that it's easier to condemn Mark Zuckerberg's algorithms in California than to hold accountable Australian media or gambling companies that directly profit from children and families.

THE GOVERNMENT'S FOCUS ON SOCIAL MEDIA IGNORES THE PROBLEMS IN LEGACY MEDIA

This proposal reflects a trend where the political establishment, and particularly legacy media, is waging an ongoing battle against social media and its influence. This dynamic speaks to a deeper struggle between old and new media, a clash of traditional top-down information control versus a modern, bottom-up approach that social media has enabled.

Social media has empowered individuals, given voices to movements from the Arab Spring in the early 2010s to #MeToo, and highlighted global injustices in real time, circumventing the slow or biased coverage of legacy outlets. Social media, despite its flaws, offers a platform for ordinary people to report, discuss, and engage with issues independently of large media conglomerates, which is why the establishment views it as such a threat.

This ability to democratise information flows is something the mainstream media often mocks or diminishes, dismissing social media as *chaotic*, *unreliable*, or *dangerous*. It is true that platforms like Twitter/X and Facebook harbour their share of toxic content and misinformation. However, the value social media provides—empowering people to communicate and mobilise without relying on traditional media—is profound.

In an era when media giants are often beholden to political or commercial interests, social media represents a rare avenue for independent, grassroots expression. The establishment's disdain for this is no surprise—social media is harder to regulate and control, and for governments accustomed to controlling narratives through traditional media channels, it represents a challenge to their influence.

Albanese's government, however, seems oblivious to this, choosing instead to align with legacy media and direct its energy towards policies aimed at regulating or restricting social media rather than addressing the many issues entrenched in the traditional press. The federal government currently has legislative control over legacy media, as it has for many decades. There are long-standing calls for a Royal Commission into media ownership, especially into Murdoch's near-monopoly, and for inquiries into misinformation and disinformation propagated by these outlets. Yet the government has ignored these calls, shying away from meaningful action that could curb legacy media's political influence and improve media diversity in Australia. This lack of initiative is a missed opportunity to address the ways in which traditional media, rather than social media, have historically influenced elections (although social media's influence *is* increasing), manipulated public opinion, and prioritised corporate interests over accurate reporting.

The government's blind spot with social media also ignores the sophistication of the current generation—younger people today have grown up with social media and possess a level of media literacy that previous generations did not. They navigate platforms, sift through content, and bypass traditional media with an ease that seems to baffle older politicians and journalists. They're not beholden to any one platform; if one social media site is restricted, they'll simply migrate to another or find ways to circumvent restrictions. Whether it's through Reddit, Discord, or other upcoming future platforms, this generation will continue to engage with social media in ways that legislation is unlikely to prevent. This adaptability also suggests the futility of an age verification policy that can easily be bypassed with a VPN or an alternate IP address, rendering the government's proposed restrictions nearly unenforceable.

Yet, the government seems set on pushing this unwieldy policy forward, even though it presents numerous logistical and ethical issues. Suggestions have surfaced that the proposal will introduce an identity card by stealth, requiring people of all ages to verify their identity to access social media—how *else* could it be done?—this idea raises significant privacy concerns and evokes memories of the poorly executed initiatives of previous governments, such as the 2016 census data debacle. Forcing Australians to prove their age before accessing social media platforms could mirror these past failures, creating yet another poorly designed data system that's vulnerable to privacy issues, corruption, misuse, or outright failure.

The irony here is that this policy, similar to other rushed digital restrictions, treats social media use as inherently *negative* without considering ways it could be integrated productively. The mobile phone bans enacted in New South Wales and South Australia schools are recent examples: rather than implementing measures that encourage responsible use, these policies issued blanket bans, ignoring the role phones play in daily life and education. Rather than encouraging students to learn phone etiquette—turning off devices in class as they would in a cinema or public setting—the government opted for an absolute prohibition, failing to acknowledge the ubiquity and utility of mobile devices in today's world. A similar oversight is evident in this proposed social media ban; instead of working with digital tools, the government's instinct is simply to ban them outright.

This reactionary approach reveals an outdated perspective on both media and technology. A blanket ban on social media access for under-16s doesn't just fail to address the root issues of online safety and media literacy—it does nothing to engage or educate young people on responsible online behaviour.

Rather than expending resources on a proposal that's impractical and likely unenforceable, the government would be better off to focus on policies that address the real issues in Australian media—especially legacy media, which remains firmly within their control. This social media ban is little more than a political diversion, a show of force against the uncontrollable tide of digital platforms, while ignoring the longstanding influence and issues of traditional media. It fails to engage with the realities of the modern world, where the focus should be on integration and education, not restriction and suppression.

***

DEMOCRACY FOR SALE: DONATIONS REFORMS WILL PROTECT THE POWERFUL

25 November 2024

The federal government's proposed reforms to donation laws aim to reshape the financial landscape of Australian politics, but a closer examination reveals significant shortcomings. While the changes *might* appear progressive on the surface—lowering individual donation thresholds, tightening disclosure timelines, and raising public funding for primary votes—they fall short of delivering the transformative overhaul the political funding system desperately needs. These reforms, at best, represent a cosmetic adjustment to a deeply entrenched problem and, at worst, serve to entrench the dominance of major political parties while marginalising smaller parties and independent candidates.

The most publicised element of the reform package is the reduction in donation thresholds. Under the proposed laws, donations exceeding $1,000 must be disclosed monthly, a dramatic reduction from the current $16,900 threshold with annual reporting. In principle, this change is excellent. Greater transparency in campaign financing is essential to curbing undue influence, and lowering the threshold makes it harder for large donors to obscure their contributions through incremental payments. Yet the reform stops short of real-time disclosure—a glaring omission in an age where digital tools can facilitate instant accountability. Monthly reporting, while an improvement, still allows for strategic manipulation of the rules, such as clustering donations shortly before election day, leaving voters none the wiser until after the polls close.

The legislation also imposes a $20,000 annual donation cap per individual or entity for each candidate and a $600,000 overall limit across the board. Similarly, spending caps of $800,000 per candidate and $90 million per political party will be introduced. These limits seem designed to curb the outsized influence of mega-donors and the arms race of political advertising. However, the scale of these caps still overwhelmingly favours the established major parties, which can command millions in public funding and attract broader networks of smaller contributors. Smaller parties and independents, which already struggle to compete on a national stage, will find these caps suffocating rather than liberating.

The legislation also introduces an increase in public funding, raising it from $3.31 to $5 per primary vote. While this move supposedly reduces dependence on private donations, it still disproportionately benefits larger parties, which can count on a significant share of the vote. This funding model perpetuates the vicious cycle: major parties enjoy greater resources to campaign effectively, securing more votes and more public funding, while smaller players and newcomers remain on the periphery, unable to break through the established duopoly.

The process through which these reforms are being advanced raises other concerns: the bill spans over 220 pages (*yes, 220!*). The short timeline for its passage leaves little room for thorough scrutiny or debate, and independent and minor party Senators have rightly criticised the government for providing inadequate time to digest the dense legislation. The absence of any resistance at all from Leader of the Opposition Peter Dutton—known for his staunch opposition to government initiatives and reputation for just saying "no" to everything—confirms suspicions that this bill is yet another bipartisan step to cement the dominance of major parties. This rushed process not only undermines democratic accountability but also suggests that hidden clauses within the legislation may contain provisions which are detrimental to smaller players.

If the proposed laws provide a disincentive to political newcomers and constrain the ability of smaller campaigns to fundraise effectively, they contradict the broader objective of fostering a diverse and competitive political ecosystem. A strong and healthy democracy depends on *pluralism*, not consolidation: the major parties, far from fearing the rise of independents, should recognise that being held to account by diverse perspectives ultimately strengthens governance and *makes them better* too.

By prioritising the interests of entrenched power structures, the proposed legislation risks exacerbating the very problems it claims to address. The path to meaningful reform requires not just tinkering at the edges but a bold reimagining of how money flows through the political system, ensuring that all voices—*not just the loudest*—are heard.

HOW THE PROPOSALS ENTRENCH POWER AND STIFLE DIVERSITY

The legislation's focus on donation caps and spending limits supposedly aims to level the playing field, but in practice, it will exacerbate existing disparities. The major parties—Labor, Liberal and Nationals—have extensive, entrenched donor networks and access to substantial public funding streams, ensuring they can campaign effectively even with tighter limits. Independent candidates and smaller parties, however, rely heavily on larger, one-off donations or grassroots fundraising drives. By capping individual donations and introducing cumbersome compliance measures, these reforms place additional financial and administrative strain on the very groups that already struggle to compete.

The timing and opacity of the legislative process only heighten these concerns. As the independent member for Warringah Zali Steggall suggested, the lack of an exposure draft and the rushed timeline for parliamentary debate suggests an intentional effort to curtail meaningful scrutiny. The implications are great: Senators and MPs are being denied the opportunity to identify and address the loopholes and unintended consequences of this far-reaching reform. For example, the allowance for donations to reset after each election and the treatment of state branches as separate entities enable parties to effectively bypass caps, preserving their fundraising advantages. These loopholes are not just oversights—they are systemic flaws that disproportionately benefit the two major parties.

The legislation's delayed implementation, set for 2026, also removes any urgency for such an expedited process, so why is there such a big rush? By rushing this through Parliament without adequate examination, the government—and the opposition—is hoping that the legislation is enshrined before the broader electorate can fully grasp its implications. The delay also conveniently shifts the focus away from immediate accountability, kicking the can down the road while entrenching structural advantages for the next electoral cycle.

The reforms also reveal a broader strategy to stymie political movements that have recently gained traction. High-profile independent campaigns and groups such as Climate 200, which challenge the status quo through their support of the teal independents movement, represent a growing appetite among voters for alternatives to the major parties. Similarly, figures such as Clive Palmer, whose massive outlays of over $200 million to the United Australia Party over the past two federal elections have reshaped campaign dynamics, are clear targets of these changes. Yet while Palmer's influence may be curtailed, the same restrictions apply to grassroots-funded independents, further consolidating the power of the entrenched two-party system.

While it might be politically unpalatable *at this stage*, a more equitable solution would involve fully publicly funded elections, where campaigns are financed through capped public funding rather than private donations. Such a system would eliminate the undue influence of wealthy individuals and organisations, ensuring that political campaigns focus on ideas rather than fundraising abilities. While the major parties may argue that these reforms are a step toward fairness, their unwillingness to embrace full publicly funded elections reveals their true priorities: preserving their financial and structural dominance at the expense of democratic diversity.

THE MISSED OPPORTUNITY IN REAL-TIME TRANSPARENCY

The disclosure component of the proposed reforms, while a marginal improvement over the current system, remains deeply disappointing. Transparency in political donations is a central component of democratic accountability, yet the proposed changes fail to deliver the level of immediacy and clarity necessary for the public to trust that private money is not unduly influencing legislation and electoral outcomes. While moving from annual to monthly disclosure with a 21-day delay is a step forward, it is still a long way from the real-time transparency that modern technology makes entirely feasible.

Real-time donation disclosure is not a utopian ideal; it is a practical necessity in an age of instantaneous communication and digital record-keeping. This ensures that voters can see who is funding candidates and political campaigns, as critical legislative debates and election cycles unfold. Australia lags behind in this area, choosing instead to embrace half-measures that allow significant delays in public knowledge. This creates a vacuum of accountability during the moments it is most needed—when major legislation is being debated or when voters are heading to the polls.

The failure to implement real-time disclosure is particularly glaring given the resources and time available to the government. With nearly three years to prepare this legislation, there was ample opportunity to design and test a centralised online clearinghouse for donations. Such a system could easily log and publish donations in real-time or within a day of receipt. Instead, the government chose to release this legislation in the shadows of this parliamentary term, leaving minimal time for debate or refinement. This lack of urgency and openness raises serious questions about the government's commitment to genuine reform and suggests a deliberate effort to minimise scrutiny.

The major parties face mounting pressure from independents and smaller parties, particularly in traditionally safe seats: there is no question about this, as shown by the consistent drop in the primary vote for major parties since 1983. Independents have already proven to be formidable challengers in Liberal strongholds, and there is no reason they could not make inroads into Labor's territory as well. Rather than addressing the legitimate grievances of voters seeking alternatives, the major parties have crafted reforms that insulate their dominance while imposing new hurdles for those attempting to break through.

The Australian Greens also face challenges under this framework. Despite a growing share of the vote, their support is often spread thin across multiple electorates, making it difficult to translate votes into seats. Like independents, they rely on donations to remain competitive, and while their support base is growing, they lack the institutional backers that the major parties enjoy. Labor's ties to unions, the Liberals' connections to big business, and the Nationals' close relationship with the mining sector, provide them with a steady stream of financial support that smaller players simply cannot match. By failing to create a genuinely level playing field, these reforms entrench existing power dynamics and limit the ability of alternative voices to gain traction.

If the Labor government was serious about electoral funding reform, it would be best to reconsider this legislation. Rather than rushing it through an impossible timeframe, the government should delay its implementation until after the next federal election. Delaying the legislation would not only improve its quality but also demonstrate a genuine commitment to democratic accountability rather than the weak optics of reform.

By prioritising expediency over thoroughness, the government is squandering an opportunity to implement meaningful change. If it truly wishes to position itself as a champion of electoral reform, it should resist the temptation to push through flawed legislation and engage in the hard, collaborative work of crafting a system that is fair, transparent, and inclusive. Anything less will serve only to reinforce the perception that the political system is rigged in favour of those already in power.

***

LABOR'S IMMIGRATION RETREAT: PANDERING TO FEAR AND LOATHING

27 November 2024

The federal Government's recent changes to immigration laws, particularly the cap on international students and the lowering of the yearly intake of migrants, are indicative of a broader political strategy that exposes the Albanese government's inability to dominate a fraught and politically charged policy area. Instead of crafting policies based on evidence and long-term national benefit, the government has allowed itself to be drawn into the Coalition's well-worn territory of immigration as a proxy for societal anxieties, including housing affordability, labour competition, and cultural identity. This is not simply a case of poor policy; it reflects an ongoing failure of political strategy and a willingness to cede ground to xenophobic narratives promoted by sections of the conservative media and extremists within the electorate.

The decision to restrict international student numbers is particularly perplexing: international education is one of Australia's largest export sectors, contributing significantly to the economy and fostering cultural and intellectual exchanges that benefit Australian society. These students do not exist in a vacuum; they contribute to the vibrancy and diversity of local communities, participate in the workforce, and often stay on as skilled migrants, filling crucial gaps in sectors ranging from healthcare to engineering. Yet, instead of embracing these values, the Labor government has chosen to frame its policy in a way that panders to populist concerns about "excessive" immigration.

This is the context that has brought the higher education sector to this point: universities, under successive governments, have become dependent on international students as a revenue stream, due to chronic underfunding of domestic higher education. This structural reliance was evident at the start of the Covid pandemic in early 2020, when border closures and international travel restrictions decimated the income of many institutions, leading to staff layoffs and program closures, along with the Coalition government's refusal to place university casual staff under Jobkeeper support. If any reform of international student numbers was warranted, it should have occurred years ago, based on the need for sustainable university funding models and a balanced approach to education as an export. Instead, the current government's approach appears reactionary and devoid of coherent long-term planning.

The decision is also undermined by its disingenuous justification. Linking international student numbers to housing affordability or labour shortages ignores the complexity of these issues and provides a false narrative. Housing affordability in Australia is driven by factors such as stagnant wages, restrictive zoning laws, speculative investment, and insufficient government intervention in social and affordable housing. Targeting immigration, whether through student visas or other mechanisms as a solution, is a cynical ploy to deflect from these systemic failures. It is a strategy that plays into the Coalition's rhetoric, which simplistically positions immigration as a root cause of all societal pressures, despite evidence to the contrary.

Politically, the Coalition's rejection of the proposed legislation reveals the futility of Labor's attempt to align itself with conservative positions on immigration. In seeking bipartisan support, the Albanese government has alienated its progressive base while gaining nothing from the Opposition. The Coalition's rejection was predictable; it allows them to claim that Labor is ineffective in managing immigration while continuing to stoke fears about population growth and cultural displacement. This is a game the Coalition has long played, and by engaging on these terms, Labor has handed them a platform to dominate this debate yet again.

A FAILURE OF LEADERSHIP AND VISION

The Labor government's reliance on seeking approval from the Liberal Party—instead of the crossbench—demonstrates an inability to break free from old patterns of political games, at a time when the electoral has become sick and tired of this traditional hyperpartisanship and immature horseplay.

Rather than pursuing meaningful reform or focusing on long-term benefits to the Australian community, the government appears intent on negotiating with an Opposition that has no intention of providing constructive support. This approach not only undermines Labor's ability to govern effectively but also allows damaging and simplistic narratives around immigration to dominate public discourse.

The proposed cap of 270,000 international students—a reduction of 53,000 from the previous year—highlights the reactive and politically cautious nature of Labor's policy-making. This figure is only marginally lower than pre-pandemic levels, yet it has drawn predictable condemnation from Peter Dutton and the Coalition. Dutton's suggestion to lower the cap even further to 160,000, paired with his inflammatory comparison of international students to "modern versions of boat arrivals," highlights the futility of engaging with the Opposition on this issue. It's not a matter of finding a compromise; it's a strategy to paint Labor as weak, ineffective, and complicit in the so-called immigration crisis.

Labor's persistence in negotiating with the obstructionist Dutton borders on self-sabotage, and appears to forget that his political currency lies in opposing for opposition's sake. Whether the cap was set at 270,000, 160,000—or even 50,000—Dutton's response would have remained the same: rejection and escalation of rhetoric.

Instead of pandering to a party that thrives on 'no', the Albanese government has a viable alternative: the crossbench, which has always offered a potential pathway to implement policies without the need for Liberal Party approval, and engaging in substantive discussions and negotiations, crafting legislation that aligns with the progressive and evidence-based priorities of these parties. Labor could bypass the Opposition entirely, diminishing its relevance in the debate and re-focusing attention on solutions rather than political point-scoring.

The treatment of international students further exposes the structural flaws in Labor's policy and its approach to governance. Successive governments have allowed universities to treat international students as financial lifelines, extracting exorbitant fees without providing the necessary support for their academic and social integration. Stories of students struggling with advanced academic English requirements, facing inadequate support services, and being left to navigate complex systems with minimal assistance are all too common. Despite the significant revenue international students generate, they are often treated as second-class participants in the education system, with the burden of their challenges falling on overstretched lecturers and tutors.

Capping student numbers without addressing the underlying funding structures of higher education only perpetuates this cycle of instability and exploitation. Targeting international students as scapegoats to these and other problems in society does nothing to address these root causes; it merely diverts attention and reinforces xenophobic sentiments.

A RACE TO THE BOTTOM IN CRUELTY AND POLITICAL EXPEDIENCY

The Albanese government's introduction of draconian asylum seeker policies, including the deportation and surveillance conditions in the Migration Amendment bill, signals a distressing escalation in Australia's already hardline approach to refugees. This legislation, which allows the government to designate any nation as an offshore detention site, strip legal protections from asylum seekers, and revoke permanent protection visas, is a betrayal of the principles Australia claims to uphold under the United Nations 1951 Refugee Convention. By enabling the forced deportation of vulnerable individuals to countries where their safety cannot be guaranteed, the bill is indicative of the race to the bottom in Australian politics on asylum seeker issues—a race where cruelty has become the defining metric of success.

The bill is part of a broader pattern in which successive Australian governments, both the Coalition and Labor, have treated asylum seekers not as human beings but as political liabilities. For decades, policies have been crafted not to address humanitarian concerns or to manage migration effectively but to placate a xenophobic minority within the electorate and to put pressure on political opponents. Labor's willingness to introduce legislation even more punitive than that envisioned by the Coalition demonstrates how deeply entrenched this approach has become. In seeking to avoid accusations of being "soft on refugees," Labor has not only adopted quite a large section from Coalition's playbook but is writing new chapters of its own.

Australia's asylum seeker policies over the past quarter-century have reflected a profound moral failure, rooted in political expediency. From the Howard-era Pacific Solution to the offshore processing arrangements in Papua New Guinea and Nauru, and now to the deportation powers bill, the common thread has been a willingness to dehumanise those fleeing persecution. The arguments used to justify these measures—that Australia faces a potential influx of "millions" of asylum seekers if it relaxes its policies—are based on fearmongering rather than evidence. The geographical realities of reaching Australia make such scenarios impossible, and the relatively small number of asylum seekers who do arrive should be well within the capacity of a wealthy, G20 nation to manage humanely.

Instead, Australian governments have consistently opted for policies that are cruel because cruelty is perceived as an effective deterrent. This reasoning, however, ignores the desperation that drives people to seek refuge in the first place. The journey to Australia, often fraught with danger, is not undertaken lightly. For someone fleeing war, persecution, or systemic injustice, the decision to risk everything is a last resort. To meet such courage and desperation with policies designed to strip away dignity and hope is an indictment of Australia's political class and its failure to lead with compassion.

Labor's approach to asylum seekers, like its immigration and international student policies, reflects a deeper malaise: the inability to resist the gravitational pull of political games and posturing. By framing asylum seekers as threats and imposing ever more punitive policies, Labor not only legitimises the Coalition's narrative but also ensures that future governments—remembering that the Coalition will return to office at some point—will take these measures to even greater extremes. The result is a vicious cycle in which bipartisan cruelty becomes the norm, and genuine reform becomes increasingly unthinkable.

The media has also played a significant role in shaping and sustaining this dynamic. Many sections of the mainstream media have long favoured simplistic narratives that equate toughness with competence and humanitarianism with weakness. These outlets thrive on the portrayal of asylum seekers as invaders, cultural disruptors, or economic burdens, reducing complex human stories to inflammatory headlines. In this environment, governments find it easier to craft policies that appeal to fear and prejudice than to challenge the narrative with facts and empathy.

Australia's hardline stance on asylum seekers is particularly egregious given the scale of the global refugee crisis. Countries with far fewer resources and far greater internal challenges, such as Lebanon, Jordan, and Bangladesh, host millions of refugees. In contrast, Australia's contributions, both in terms of resettlement and financial aid, are minimal. The argument that Australia cannot afford to take in more refugees is not only disingenuous but also an affront to the values of fairness and egalitarianism that the nation purports to hold dear.

The deportation and surveillance powers bill is a symptom of a broader political pathology: the prioritisation of short-term political gains over long-term ethical governance. Labor's retreat into the politics of fear and division not only betrays its progressive base but also erodes public trust in the possibility of a more humane and just Australia. At its core, the failure to treat asylum seekers with dignity reflects a deeper societal malaise—the triumph of the easy, cruel solutions over the hard, courageous decisions that improve the lives of all.

This is a forlorn hope but Labor should have the courage to lead with principles, to challenge the media narratives that reduce asylum seekers to political pawns, and to articulate a vision of Australia as a nation that upholds the fair go for everyone, regardless of where they come from. Anything less is a betrayal not only of the refugees who seek Australia's protection but also of the country Labor claims to represent.

**

DECEMBER

NETANYAHU ARREST WARRANT COULD SEE A RAPID CHANGE IN PALESTINE

3 December 2024

The arrest warrant issued by the International Criminal Court for Israeli Prime Minister Benjamin Netanyahu over alleged war crimes in Gaza has cast a spotlight on international justice and the geopolitical issues that arise when principles of law collide with political alliances. This decision by the ICC has prompted a debate in Australia which, of course, has fallen along predictable party lines.

Foreign Minister Senator Penny Wong has emphasised Australia's respect for the ICC's independence and its role in upholding international law and pointed to the principle that adherence to international law is not only a *moral* obligation but also serves Australia's strategic interests. This stance aligns with the broader framework of ensuring accountability for war crimes and maintaining Australia's credibility as a nation committed to international norms.

The Liberal Party Senator Michaelia Cash, has fiercely criticised the ICC's decision—her response is based on two key points: alignment with the United States' unequivocal rejection of the arrest warrant and an assertion that there is no moral equivalence between the actions of Israeli leaders and those of Hamas. Cash also raised the possibility of Australia re-evaluating its membership in the ICC, suggesting the court's actions as 'overreach' that jeopardises key international alliances. This reaction not only mirrors the stance of the United States but also reveals a deeper discomfort within certain conservative circles about the ICC's *perceived* bias and its focus on allies of the West.

However, such arguments sidestep Australia's historical commitment to the ICC, a commitment that began under the conservative Howard government in 2002. The court's role in prosecuting war criminals from regions such as the former Yugoslavia, Rwanda, and Sudan highlights its importance in delivering justice for atrocities and crimes against humanity. Calls to abandon the ICC now, when its focus shifts to leaders such as Netanyahu, just for the reasons of political convenience, risk undermining the credibility of a system designed to be impartial and universal.

This tension also exposes a deeper inconsistency in the Liberal Party's rhetoric. By selectively opposing ICC actions, critics appear to condone a double standard: one set of rules for Western-aligned states and another for less powerful nations. This selective application of justice parallels historical attitudes where marginalised groups and weaker states are subjected to the full force of law, while powerful nations or their allies are shielded from scrutiny.

In the unlikely event that Australia did withdraw from the ICC, it risks diminishing its influence in shaping global norms of justice and accountability. Such a withdrawal would align Australia with nations that reject the ICC's authority, often for reasons rooted in their own leaders' potential culpability for crimes against humanity.

Netanyahu's position as Israel's leader is itself precarious. The ICC's warrant adds to the mounting pressures he faces domestically and internationally. His political survival increasingly hinges on maintaining power, as stepping down could expose him to a wide range of legal consequences. This fragility reflects a broader crisis for Israel as a state dealing with its atrocious policies toward Palestinians, its strained relationships with neighbouring countries, and its dependence on diminishing American support.

NETANYAHU'S TIRED OLD TROPE OF ANTI-SEMITISM

Netanyahu's framing of the ICC's arrest warrant as an 'anti-Semitic' conspiracy follows a well-trodden path of deflection and politicisation. His claim that the court's actions constitute a "modern Dreyfus trial" not only misrepresents the principles of international law but also weaponises historical anti-Semitism to shield himself from accountability, a narrative which exploits the legitimate sensitivities surrounding Jewish history and identity while ignoring the substantive legal basis of the charges against him.

At its core, the ICC's decision is not about Israel's identity as a Jewish state but about the actions of its leadership, particularly Netanyahu's alleged role in policies and military operations that have led to widespread civilian deaths and suffering in Gaza. Over 45,000 Palestinians, two-thirds of them women and children, have lost their lives in conflicts where Israeli military strategies have been criticised—and documented—for their disproportionality, the targeting of civilian infrastructure, and the enforcement of a blockade that amounts to collective punishment. These actions are not protected under international law, nor are they beyond scrutiny simply because they are carried out by a allied nation-state.

Netanyahu's characterisation of the ICC as biased or 'rogue' fails when examined alongside the court's broader record. The ICC has a history of prosecuting leaders and military figures from diverse backgrounds, including those from African nations and the former Yugoslavia. These cases were not dismissed as discriminatory by the international community; they were widely seen as necessary steps in holding individuals accountable for crimes against humanity. The same standard *must* apply to Netanyahu, whose actions as a head of state do not grant him immunity from international law.

Netanyahu's refusal to engage with the ICC also shows his lack of confidence in his own defence: if he *truly* believes in his innocence, as he has repeatedly asserted, the appropriate course of action would be to appear before the court, present evidence, and allow an impartial legal process to determine the truth. The fact that he has chosen to attack the court's legitimacy suggests *guilt* rather than *innocence*, and it also speaks to the overwhelming evidence that has been documented, not only by independent investigations but also by members of the Israeli Defense Forces themselves, whose actions have been recorded and disseminated globally.

The argument that the ICC has suddenly become biased is particularly disingenuous given its previous broad acceptance. There were no significant objections when the court pursued cases against African leaders or officials in former Yugoslavia—Slobodan Milosević, Ratko Mladić and Radovan Karadžić—nor when it issued arrest warrants for Russian figures such as Vladimir Putin. The principle of universal accountability is the foundation of the ICC's legitimacy, and to abandon this principle now, in the face of highly credible allegations against Netanyahu, is to render that legitimacy meaningless.

GLOBAL PRESSURE WILL LEAD TO A RAPID TRANSFORMATION IN PALESTINE

The trajectory of Israel–Palestine relations, long characterised by stagnation and regression—while it might not seem evident at this stage—now appears poised on the edge of transformative change. While the situation in Palestine has been marked by decades of entrenched oppression, there is reason to believe that the international and economic pressures bearing down on Israel may finally bring about a long-overdue and positive change.

This arrest warrant for Netanyahu is emblematic of this growing pressure. It signals a shift in global attitudes and a willingness to hold Israel accountable for its actions, actions that have increasingly defined it as a pariah state. The comparison to apartheid-era South Africa is not hyperbolic; Israel's policies in the Occupied Palestinian Territories—ranging from blockades and forced displacements to a system of *de facto* segregation—mirror the systemic injustices that South Africa once institutionalised. The parallels are not lost on the global community, which is beginning to coalesce around the necessity of change.

This momentum has been bolstered by diplomatic shifts, such as Australia's recent vote at the United Nations to demand an end to Israel's unlawful presence in the Occupied Territories. For the first time in over two decades, Australia has aligned itself with 156 other countries in supporting a resolution that unequivocally calls for justice and peace. This is a significant departure from its historically cautious stance, particularly given the influence of Israel's staunchest ally, the United States, and reflects a growing recognition that Australia has a responsibility to support international efforts toward ending the cycle of violence and advancing the two-state solution, efforts which have, so far, been lacking and highly supportive of the actions of Israel.

Economic factors further amplify these pressures. Just like apartheid South Africa and the Eastern Bloc, Israel faces mounting economic vulnerabilities exacerbated by its prolonged occupation and military aggressions. While it does seem that the state of Israel has an endless supply of military and financial support from the United States, the financial toll of maintaining such policies, coupled with increasing isolation from significant segments of the international community, threatens to undermine its economic stability. As history has shown, economic collapse often serves as a catalyst for political change, forcing regimes to confront their untenable positions.

Netanyahu himself symbolises the fragility of Israel's current trajectory. His political survival hinges on maintaining power, not merely to enforce his hardline policies but to evade the legal consequences that await him. His indictment by the ICC serves as both a personal and political crisis, further destabilising a leadership already on precarious ground, and a leadership that is not worth supporting. As with other historical figures whose tenure ended in ignominy, Netanyahu's eventual departure will become a turning point for Israel, paving the way for a more just and equitable future.

However, the path to resolution remains fraught with challenges. Ceasefires, such as the one recently established between Israel and Lebanon, offer a temporary reprieve but fail to address the deeper, systemic injustices that fuel the conflict. The situation in Palestine, where millions endure daily violations of their human rights, remains the most pressing and unresolved issue. While international consensus is increasingly aligned against Israel's policies, meaningful change will require sustained pressure, coordinated diplomacy, and a genuine commitment to justice.

Australia's renewed engagement at the United Nations on Palestine—although we're yet to understand how long this will continue for—highlights the importance of collective action. While Australia alone cannot significantly influence the Middle East, its willingness to vote for resolutions that contribute to peace reflects a shift in priorities and an acknowledgment of the broader moral and political stakes.

History teaches us that when change does come, it is often swift and unexpected, although in hindsight, it always appeared inevitable. The end of apartheid in South Africa, once considered improbable, came rapidly after decades of international isolation and internal resistance. The fall of the Berlin Wall in 1989 and the collapse of communism in Eastern Europe were similarly unforeseen, yet they reshaped the world in profound ways. Israel and Palestine, though mired in decades of conflict, could likewise experience a dramatic and positive transformation. This is not naïve idealism or foolish speculation: when that moment arrives, it will be the result of years of sustained pressure, growing international condemnation, and the undeniable reality that the current status quo is unsustainable.

The mechanisms for change—economic instability, legal accountability, and international moral clarity—are already in motion. While the timeline remains uncertain, the inevitability of change is clear. For Israel to survive as a legitimate and democratic state, and for Palestine to achieve its rightful independence, autonomy and justice, the world must continue to press forward, united in purpose and unwavering in the pursuit of peace and justice.

***

LABOR'S LEGISLATIVE INERTIA COULD COST IT AT THE NEXT ELECTION

2 December 2024

The final week of Parliament for the year unfolded in a way that was both disappointing and symbolic of a government struggling to balance ambition with delivery. One absence from the legislative slate in this final week was the withdrawal of the Misinformation and Disinformation Bill. Initially heralded as a critical step in curbing the spread of harmful falsehoods online, its withdrawal reflects deeper issues with the Labor government's legislative strategy, priorities, and political will.

The Minister for Communications, Michelle Rowland, had spoken emphatically about the bill's necessity just a few weeks before, citing strong public support for action against misinformation. According to the Australian Media Literacy Alliance, 80 per cent of Australians want this issue addressed, yet despite such a compelling public mandate and the declared urgency of the problem, the government was unable to gather enough support from either the opposition or the crossbench. The decision to pull the legislation highlights a pattern: promises and proposals without the necessary follow-through to ensure they become law.

This specific event encapsulates a broader problem within the Albanese government. Faced with resistance, they appear willing to let significant reforms falter rather than fight for their passage. The withdrawal of the Misinformation and Disinformation Bill mirrors the stalled progress on truth-in-political-advertising legislation, another high-profile promise seemingly relegated to the "too hard" basket. In both cases, the government has opted to blame external factors—whether it be the opposition, crossbenchers, or minor parties—rather than taking responsibility for crafting and advocating for stronger, more viable proposals.

Such moves may point to a deliberate tactic: introducing bills designed to fail as a way of signaling intent without risking political capital. When the legislation inevitably falls short, the government can claim to have tried its best while conveniently shifting blame. But this approach undermines the public's trust in their commitment to meaningful reform and suggests a government more interested in managing appearances than in delivering substantive outcomes for the electorate.

The government's approach to closing out the year seems particularly perplexing given the proximity of a federal election within the next six months. Conventional wisdom would suggest using the final legislative sitting of the year to demonstrate boldness and resolve, passing laws that resonate with the public and reinforce the government's agenda. Instead, the withdrawal of key legislation has sent a muddled message about Labor's priorities and political competence. Certainly, key housing legislation was passed in this final week—after long, protracted and hostile negotiations with the Australian Greens—but the smaller number of these decisive legislative victories makes it harder to set a compelling narrative for re-election, leaving the government vulnerable to critiques that it is more invested in political games than in addressing critical issues.

While Labor can point to a record of achievement in its first term, with successes in economic management and managing inflation, incremental reforms, and improved employment figures—and perhaps these are the *main* issues that really matter to the electorate – these gains are overshadowed by continuing challenges such as the cost-of-living crisis. Inflation, while trending downward, has not translated into perceptible relief for struggling households. The Reserve Bank's interest rate policies may bear much of the blame, but the public inevitably vents their frustration at the government, further complicating its task of promoting the obvious achievements it has made.

LABOR'S RELUCTANCE TO TACKLE THE TOUGH ISSUES

The government's approach to governing in these final stages of the parliamentary term also reflects a calculated effort to avoid controversy and minimise political risk. While this is understandable, governance is not just about surviving the electoral cycle; it is about making decisions that serve the public interest, even when those decisions are difficult. The choices that the government has made in recent weeks highlight a troubling dynamic: an administration that seems more intent on sidestepping contentious issues than on addressing the systemic problems it was elected to resolve.

Aside from the withdrawal of the Misinformation and Disinformation Bill, other legislative developments provide examples of this trend. The withdrawal of proposals such as the superannuation tax concession reform is emblematic of a government reluctant to challenge powerful vested interests, even when the proposed changes would have minimal impact on the broader electorate. Taxing superannuation balances over $3 million was a modest measure, targeting only the wealthiest 1 per cent of Australians who often use these accounts as tax shelters. Yet Labor abandoned this policy, citing fears of a backlash reminiscent of the ill-fated franking credits reform in 2019. In doing so, they not only ceded the moral high ground but also signaled that their commitment to equity and fiscal responsibility is negotiable when electoral consequences loom, real or imagined.

This pattern of capitulation extends beyond tax policy. Recent legislation that could have meaningfully reformed political donations—a key driver of public cynicism about politics—was designed in a way that secures bipartisan support by entrenching advantages for the major parties. The haste with which the opposition endorsed these changes highlights how the reforms protect entrenched political power rather than addressing the systemic imbalances that erode public trust.

Similarly, the passage of draconian immigration and asylum seeker policies caters to the xenophobic undercurrents in Australian politics, a tactic long employed by both major parties to placate reactionary segments of the electorate. These policies—which ultimately benefit the major parties politically—fail to reflect the compassion and fairness that voters might reasonably expect from a Labor government; instead, show a fear of changing the status quo and pander to the racist elements in the community.

What emerges is a disheartening portrait of a government preoccupied with neutralising risks rather than embracing the challenges of leadership. Instead of advancing bold reforms that address inequality, climate change, or democratic integrity, Labor appears to be prioritising short-term political calculations over long-term progress. Certainly, this is in the shadows of an upcoming federal election campaign where caution is to be expected but governments do have three years to prepare and implement their agenda, and most of this could have been addressed much earlier in this parliamentary term.

It's also a strategy rooted in the belief that being "better than the opposition" will be enough, an assumption that severely underestimates the electorate's demand for substantive change, as was discovered in the recent U.S. election, which saw the return of Donald Trump to the presidency.

Simply suggesting that a government will be better than its opponents, or that Peter Dutton and the Liberal Party are terrible and woeful, isn't good enough in contemporary politics: Australians deserve better than a government that governs through omission or promotes itself as the least-worst option. While it is true that no government can please everyone, effective leadership means delivering policies that, even if contentious, are implemented competently and with a clear sense of purpose. The superannuation reform, for example, could have been a defining moment for Labor—a demonstration of their commitment to fairness and fiscal discipline. Instead, its abandonment has left voters questioning whether Labor can be trusted to uphold even the mildest of progressive principles.

Governance requires more than just avoiding missteps; it demands the courage to stand for something, even at the risk of alienating a segment of the electorate. The current approach not only erodes trust but also creates fertile ground for opposition narratives that paint Labor as indecisive or beholden to elite interests. Worse, it deepens public disillusionment with politics as a whole, reinforcing the view that governments, regardless of their promises, ultimately prioritise their own survival over the public good.

WILL ALBANESE REGRET THE HOSTILITY TOWARDS THE GREENS AND INDEPENDENTS?

The marginalisation of independents and the antagonistic approach towards both the Greens and the teal independents highlights a misstep in the Albanese government's strategy: a failure to recognise or accept the shifting dynamics of Australian politics. This oversight not only jeopardises the immediate legislative effectiveness of the government but also risks eroding its long-term viability in an era where minority governments and coalition-building are likely to become the norm.

The hostility shown toward the crossbench, particularly the teal independents, has been evident since the early days of the Albanese administration. The decision in 2022 to reduce their staffing and resources sent a clear message: independents, no matter their mandate or the scale of public support behind them, would not be afforded the tools to effectively engage with the legislative process. For a Prime Minister who campaigned on promises of transparency, collaboration, and a new approach to politics, this move felt not only contradictory but also petty.

Similarly, Albanese's long-standing antagonism toward the Greens—which seems to be that of a belligerent old man—has shaped the government's approach to key legislation. While some tension between Labor and the Greens is to be expected—particularly given the Greens' tendency to push for policies that Labor may see as electorally risky—the outright rejection of the demands from the Greens reflects a failure to adapt to the political realities of a more pluralistic parliament. On issues like housing, climate policy, and social equity, collaboration with the Greens could have bolstered the government's reform agenda and delivered stronger outcomes for the public: that's the nature of *smart* politics. Instead, Labor has often opted for a more combative stance, alienating a critical partner in the process.

This is shortsighted, especially given the likelihood of a minority government after the next election. Labor's narrow victory in 2022 was hardly a resounding endorsement of the party's agenda—also, the first election victory for a new government is usually its high-water mark—and it's unlikely to retain its majority in a political environment increasingly characterised by dissatisfaction with the major parties. The rise of the independents and the Greens reflects a broader shift in the electorate—one that demands more nuanced and contemporary responses to the challenges of the 21st century.

At the heart of this shift is the growing irrelevance of the traditional two-party system. Both Labor and the Liberal–National coalition remain mired in ideological battles and economic frameworks that no longer resonate with a public grappling with issues like climate change, housing affordability, and economic inequality. Labor's internal factionalism and its inability to move beyond the Hawke–Keating economic model further highlight this disconnect. While different figures such as Kevin Rudd, Wayne Swan, and Jim Chalmers have attempted to modernise the party's economic approach, their efforts have been stymied by resistance from an entrenched old guard. The Liberal Party, meanwhile, remains wedded to a Thatcherite worldview that has little relevance in today's economic landscape.

The failure of both major parties to evolve has created fertile ground for independents who are unburdened by the ideological baggage of the past and better positioned to address contemporary concerns. These independents, representing constituencies that demand action on issues like climate change, political transparency, and gender equity, have already begun reshaping the political landscape.

The government's refusal to meaningfully engage with the crossbench not only alienates potential allies but also undermines its own ability to govern effectively. The stalled gambling advertising legislation, for example, shows how the interests of powerful donors and lobbyists can take precedence over the public good. This kind of inaction, driven by fear of backlash or loss of financial support, reinforces the perception that Labor—and the entire two-party system—is more interested in self-preservation than in delivering real change.

If Labor continues to overlook the independents and alienate potential partners like the Australian Greens, it risks more than just losing the next election. It risks becoming irrelevant in a political landscape that increasingly values collaboration, adaptability, and innovation: *new* politics, rather than *old* politics. By refusing to embrace the changing nature of Australian politics, the government is not only neglecting the public interest but also jeopardising its own survival in a system that is evolving far beyond the confines of the past.

***

EPILOGUE

December 2024

The final year of this Labor term, led by Prime Minister Anthony Albanese, revealed a government seemingly searching for purpose. Despite his earlier claims of being someone who "fights Tories," Albanese worked closely with the Liberal Party to pass legislation deemed advantageous to both parties. Yet on almost every other issue, Leader of the Opposition Peter Dutton refused to compromise. To his supporters, this obstinacy signified strength; to others, it seemed petty and obstructive.

Viewed from the vantage point of 2024, Australian politics appears to be undergoing profound shifts, perhaps as part of a broader global zeitgeist affecting Western democracies. While these changes are complex, several overarching themes have emerged throughout the year.

THE DECLINE OF THE TWO-PARTY SYSTEM

The Australian Labor Party, founded in 1891 to champion the rights and interests of the union movement, has evolved significantly over time. However, the party now seems trapped in a 1980s paradigm, shaped by its embrace of neoliberalism under Bill Hayden in 1977. This framework has kept free-market principles at the forefront of policy. While Kevin Rudd and Wayne Swan's neo-Keynesian strategies successfully navigated the 2008 global financial crisis, subsequent governments have largely adhered to free-market orthodoxy. Efforts by Treasurer Jim Chalmers to modernise this 45-year-old philosophy face resistance from those who have benefited from the status quo. Even if he succeeds, critics will likely remain unconvinced.

The Labor Party's factional system—arcane and confusing to outsiders—further complicates its cohesion. Often state-based as much as ideologically driven, these factions have fueled speculation of a rift between Albanese and Tanya Plibersek, despite both belonging to the NSW left faction. If such rumours hold merit, they may indicate a fracturing unity within the party.

The Liberal Party's decline into electoral irrelevance mirrors Labor's struggles but is more conspicuous. Its blend of 1980s Thatcherism, Howard-era conservatism, and Trumpist populism, built on culture wars and manufactured outrage, has failed to resonate with voters. The party is hemorrhaging support among women and voters born after 1980, raising existential questions about its future. Without substantial youth membership, its prospects appear grim.

Meanwhile, the Australian Greens under Adam Bandt face a different challenge. As Australia's most diverse and ideologically broad party, they represent a wide range of demographics and classes. This breadth produces mixed outcomes, such as increased primary votes but fewer seats, as seen in Queensland's state election. Whether their strong youth support consolidates into a cohesive electoral force or fragments due to their diverse base remains uncertain.

The National Party, historically stable since its formation in 1920, holds its small but secure base of around 13 seats. However, its future is threatened by the declining quality of its members, exemplified by figures like Barnaby Joyce. Local independents may begin to chip away at its support, particularly as stronger challengers emerge. While irrelevant outside the eastern mainland states, the National Party's influence remains entrenched in regions like northern Queensland.

THE DECLINE OF MAINSTREAM MEDIA

The mainstream media's decline continued in 2024, adding to the decline from 2023 and preceding years. As the government and opposition stumble toward an election neither seems poised to win outright, the media landscape reflects a similar malaise. Annual newspaper readership has dwindled, while online platforms dominate news consumption. With profits falling, resources for quality journalism have been slashed. Even institutions such as the ABC have replaced quality programming with cheaper options such as repeats and cooking shows. Programs that remain, such as *Insiders*, have showcased right-wing journalists, turning them into echo chambers that alienate potential audiences.

Australian media ownership remains one of the most concentrated in the world, with News Corporation dominating the landscape. This concentration contrasts sharply with the media's declining influence; audiences increasingly tune out when the media's views do not align with their own. This dynamic has contributed to a drop in the quality of journalism across most outlets. While independent media offers some balance, these platforms are typically small and under-resourced.

One of the Albanese government's missed opportunities has been its failure to launch a Royal Commission into media ownership and the conduct of major players such News Corporation and the Murdoch family. A *prima facie* case exists to question whether the owners of major outlets meet the legislative standards to run media companies in Australia. A Royal Commission could provide clarity and accountability.

A GROWING MISTRUST OF INSTITUTIONS AND VOTER DISENGAGEMENT

Compulsory voting theoretically ensures public engagement in politics, but declining trust in institutions undermines this ideal. Scandals such as Robodebt, which resulted in destroyed lives, suicides, and widespread harm, have left deep scars on the Australian psyche. Despite its establishment as a watchdog, the National Anti-Corruption Commission has disappointed, with its chair, Paul Brereton, declining to investigate Robodebt. Allegations of conflicts of interest and procedural failings have further eroded public confidence in the NACC.

The Commonwealth public service, though composed largely of hardworking individuals, is demoralised, underfunded, and directionless. The great Labor governments of the past expanded the public service in ways that delivered lasting benefits. In contrast, the current government's timidity has hindered the sweeping reforms many expected. While much of the dysfunction stems from the previous Liberal government's mismanagement, reform is slow, and voters are not known for their patience.

A CHANGING WORLD

On the global stage, 2024 has been a tumultuous year. The re-election of Donald Trump in the United States has ushered in a period of incompetence, corruption, and chaos. Questions about the legitimacy of his election linger, but his leadership's disastrous implications are undeniable. Internationally, the blind support for Israel, despite its government's crimes against humanity, remains a stain on Western governments' records, even as public sentiment begins to shift.

In Australia, 2024 felt like a year of contraction. While the public yearned for bold solutions to pressing problems, they were met with dithering, small-scale politics, and pervasive disappointment. The 2025 election will likely chart a new course for the nation. Whether that course will be one Australia desires—or needs—remains to be seen.

***

INDEX OF PEOPLE

A
Tony Abbott 11, 33, 35, 36, 77, 113, 115, 234, 244, 246, 266, 293, 307
Yassmin Abdel-Magied 154
Lord Acton 126
Anthony Albanese 6–7, 11–12, 15, 19, 30, 45, 54, 67, 73, 75, 85, 87–89, 94, 109–110, 115–116, 118, 120, 126–129, 132, 137, 142–143, 155, 157, 159, 171, 176, 179, 189–190, 192, 199, 201–202, 207, 210, 214–215, 220, 222, 224, 243, 246, 264, 265—272, 292, 300, 313, 324–327, 329, 333–334, 338, 342, 346, 348, 366, 367, 376–379, 388, 392, 395–397, 399, 403
Emma Alberici 154
Waleed Aly 204
David Anderson 61
Seyed Abbas Araghchi 309
Clare Armstrong 11
Julian Assange 147, 150, 171, 189
Stella Assange 147, 149

B
Adam Bandt 330, 396
Kim Beazley 200
Jodie Belyea 44
Gladys Berejiklian 173, 241, 320
Jo Biden 21, 69, 86, 128, 147, 218, 219, 220, 221, 232, 257, 353, 355, 360
Senator Simon Birmingham 143
Joh Bjelke-Petersen 260
Antony Blinken 17
Jair Bolsonaro 234
Andrew Bolt 203
Richard Boyle 8, 140, 193
Paul Brereton 173, 239, 240, 333, 397
Mike Burgess 243
Tony Burke 71, 146, 212, 313
George H. Bush 221
Ita Buttrose 59, 61
Diana Butu 144

C
Jim Cairns 200
Olivia Caisley 12
Senator Michaelia Cash 382
Nicolae Ceaușescu 274
Jim Chalmers 90, 113, 114, 115, 130, 132, 160, 270, 286, 287, 393, 395
Max Chandler-Mather 299, 300, 328
Liz Cheney 353
Ben Chifley 159
Noam Chomsky 318
George Christensen 192
Jason Clare 110, 127, 212
Manning Clark 8
Melissa Clarke 12
Bill Clinton 115, 190, 221, 356
Hilary Clinton 221
Matt Comyn 280
Phillip Coorey 11
David Crowe 11
John Curtin 159

D
Alfred Deakin 205
Delia Donovan 119
Mark Dreyfus 8, 76, 148, 194, 327
Dan Duggan 171
Michael Dukakis 221
Peter Dutton 8, 13, 15–16, 23–30, 31, 35–36, 38, 46, 47, 50, 54, 76, 93–94, 109–111, 116, 133–134, 143, 151, 158, 175–180, 182–183, 186, 201, 203, 206, 207, 258–264, 266, 270, 271, 287, 288–289, 293, 300, 313, 314, 325–327, 331, 335, 371, 378, 391, 395

E
Sophie Ellsworth 151
Craig Emerson 91
Gareth Evans 71

F
Senator Mehreen Faruqi 262
Ben Fordham 321
Andrew Forrest 51, 81, 276
Zomi Frankcom 85, 310
Malcolm Fraser 33
Josh Frydenberg 126, 127, 162, 163, 164, 165, 166, 176
Gail Furness 174

G

Senator Katy Gallagher 160, 300
Merrick Garland 149
Julia Gillard 159, 189, 292
Jonathan Glazer 72
Adam Goodes 342
Al Gore 221
Stan Grant 154, 204
Michelle Grattan 11
Nick Greiner 172

H

Amelia Hamer 166
Senator Pauline Hanson 234, 340
Brian Harradine 291
Kamala Harris 221, 222, 232, 235, 354, 355, 356
Simon Harris 145
Gerry Harvey 276
Bob Hawke 70, 131, 292, 338
Bill Hayden 395
Brittany Higgins 102, 105
Eric Hobsbawm 6
Simon Holmes à Court 80, 83, 187
Donald Horne 347
John Howard 11, 33, 35, 63, 76, 77, 110, 132, 205, 213, 243, 244, 265, 291, 314, 380, 383, 396
Billy Hughes 244
Senator Jane Hume 144
David Hurley 139
Vincent Hurley 122
Ed Husic 19, 71, 146

I

Fauziah Ibrahim 204

J

Boris Johnson 234, 257

K

Radovan Karadžić 385
Bob Katter 158
Paul Keating 70, 112, 131, 133, 159, 265, 292, 338, 341, 345, 347, 393
Joe Kelly 12
Khaled Khayat 245
Mahmoud Khayat 245
King Charles 337, 338, 340, 342, 344
Koch brothers 82

L

Justice Michael Lee 102
Bruce Lehrmann 102, 103, 104, 105
Sussan Ley 47
David Littleproud 13, 37, 175, 185

M

Richard Madeley 88
Ramona Manglona 191
Chelsea Manning 149, 189
Sharri Markson 163
David McBride 8, 136, 137, 138, 140, 148, 149, 171, 193, 194
John McCain 219
Senator Bridget McKenzie 36, 313, 339
Warwick McKibbin 131
Senator Nick McKim 25
Craig McLachlan 105
Jonathan Mead 255
Robert Menzies 35, 162, 163, 244
Steven Miles 160
Slobodan Milošević 385
Chris Minns 122, 319, 320, 321, 322, 323
Ratko Mladić 385
Scott Morrison 25, 31, 33, 36, 38, 73, 75, 77, 113, 115, 137, 139, 210, 234, 238, 246, 257, 264, 266, 308, 331, 335, 403
Rupert Murdoch 56, 176, 186, 208, 250, 274
Peta Murphy 45
Murugappan family 259

N

Benjamin Netanyahu 21, 108, 109, 127, 142, 143, 144, 307, 310, 382, 383, 384, 385, 386

O

Kerry O'Brien 59
Alexandria Ocasio-Cortez 192
Clare O'Neil 25, 71
Senator Deborah O'Neill 24
Viktor Orbán 234

P

Sarah Palin 219
Clive Palmer 80, 234, 373
Senator James Paterson 71
Nancy Pelosi 351
Dominic Perrottet 320

John Pesutto 47
Tanya Plibersek 396
Christian Porter 105
Anthony Pratt 54
Vladimir Putin 385
Christopher Pyne 297

Q
Queen Camilla 337, 344

R
Hind Rajab 42, 43
Ayn Rand 276
Ronald Reagan 217
Senator Linda Reynolds 105
Chris Richardson 130
Gina Rinehart 54, 186, 273, 274, 276, 284
Ben Roberts-Smith 105
Nick Ross 154
Michelle Rowland 155, 388
Kevin Rudd 81, 131, 132, 133, 192, 210, 292, 393, 395
Monique Ryan 162, 166

S
Sarah Schwartz 214
Paul Scully 98
Jillian Segal 214
Senator David Shoebridge 255, 256
Bill Shorten 171, 248, 249, 252
Mark Speakman 98
Zali Steggall 211, 258, 372
Justin Stevens 153
Kerry Stokes 104, 176, 208, 250, 274
Rishi Sunak 86
Wayne Swan 112, 131, 393, 395

T
Angus Taylor 134, 289
Marjorie Taylor Greene 192
Ian Temby 240
Margaret Thatcher 108, 307
Senator Lidia Thorpe 337, 338, 339, 340, 341, 342, 343
Laura Tingle 151, 153, 154, 155
Donald Trump 8, 217, 218, 219, 220, 221, 222, 223, 232, 233, 234, 235, 236, 274, 350, 351, 352, 353, 354, 355, 356, 357, 391, 398
Malcolm Turnbull 25, 113, 115, 164, 170, 198, 246, 250, 288, 331

U
Tom Uren 200

V
JD Vance 219
Yanis Varoufakis 66

W
Geoffrey Watson 335
Jay Weatherill 164
Anthony Whealy 335
Gough Whitlam 33, 159, 267, 292, 328
Andrew Wilkie 137
Kim Williams 59, 60, 151
Roger Williams 78
Josh Wilson 19
Senator Fatima Payman 19, 71, 146, 195, 196, 197, 198, 199, 200, 201, 202, 203, 204
Senator Penny Wong 19, 21, 67, 85, 107, 109, 125, 198, 224, 225, 227, 307, 309, 326, 359, 360, 361, 382
Graeme Wood 83

Z
Mark Zuckerberg 366

**ALSO BY
EDDY JOKOVICH +
DAVID LEWIS**

FIXING AUSTRALIAN POLITICS
HOW TO CHANGE THE SYSTEM OF GOVERNMENT

Australia's political landscape stands on the precipice of transformation. The need for reform is palpable, driven by evolving societal values, demands for greater transparency, and a push towards inclusivity. *Fixing Australian Politics: How to change the system of government* outlines a multifaceted strategy to reshape Australian politics across various fronts—electoral systems, campaign finance, governance, media, the Constitution, and diversity in representation. These reforms are critical for the rejuvenation of the nation's political framework and the restoration of public faith in the democratic process.

Available in paperback and ebook.

Fixing Australian Politics: How to change the system of government
ISBN (paperback):   978-1-7635701-0-8
ISBN (Amazon):   979-8-3249179-2-0
208 pages

RISING PHOENIX, FALLING SHADOWS
THE YEAR IN AUSTRALIAN POLITICS

This exploration of Australia's political landscape in 2023 uncovers a year that began with high hopes, yet was marred by a series of unmet expectations and enduring challenges: the Voice to Parliament referendum and its subsequent defeat, the persistent housing crisis, cost of living and environmental concerns, AUKUS and Palestine—guiding the reader through the intricate web of political and social dynamics that define contemporary Australia. *Rising Phoenix, Falling Shadows* is a compelling read for anyone interested in understanding the multifaceted nature of governance and public policy in Australia.

Available in paperback and ebook.

Rising Phoenix, Falling Shadows: The year in Australian politics
ISBN (paperback):   978-0-6456392-9-2
ISBN (Amazon):   979-8-8720426-0-0
446 pages

DIARY OF AN ELECTION VICTORY
LABOR'S RISE TO POWER

POLITICS, PROTEST, PANDEMIC
THE YEAR THAT CHANGED AUSTRALIA

In early 2020 at the onset of the coronavirus pandemic, Morrison held record high electoral ratings and Albanese was told to not worry about the next election: it was already out of reach and best to focus on the 2025 election and beyond. In 2022, Labor saw an opportunity: Morrison had made promises he ultimately couldn't deliver and it unravelled quickly. *Diary of An Election Victory* explores the key political moments of the 2022 election year, Morrison's demise, and Albanese's ascendancy and victory against the odds. It's a must-read analysis of one of the most dynamic and unusual election results ever in Australia's political history.

Available in paperback and ebook.

Diary of an Election Victory:
ISBN (paperback):   978-0-6456392-1-6
ISBN (hardback):   978-0-6456392-2-3
ISBN (Amazon):   979-8-3681569-7-2
304 pages

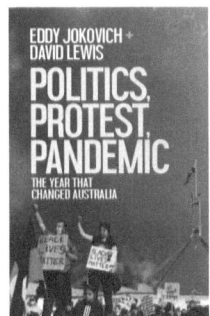

2020 was one of the most dramatic years in human history, shaped by the coronavirus pandemic that influenced society in so many different ways, combining health, politics, economics, business and education into the one sphere—and that proved to be difficult for many governments around the world to manage. *Politics, Protest, Pandemic: The year that changed Australia* is the story of the year in Australian federal politics, told through a collection of extended political essays from the New Politics Australia podcast series.
This is a must-read analysis of one of the most dynamic years ever in Australian political history.

Available in paperback and ebook.

Politics, Protest, Pandemic: The year that changed Australia
ISBN: 978-0-6481644-8-7
ISBN (Amazon): 979-8-7372030-8-5
414 pages

**ALSO BY
EDDY JOKOVICH +
DAVID LEWIS**

DIVIDED OPINIONS

THE NEW POLITICS ANALYSIS OF THE 2019 YEAR IN AUSTRALIAN POLITICS

As the mainstream media struggles to retain audiences and survive under new business models and shrinking revenue streams, independents are filling in the gaps left behind by the older mastheads. New Politics is one of the more important voices appearing in this new landscape, and *Divided Opinions* presents some of the best work from the monthly podcast, and a selection of articles published during 2019. Guaranteed to make you think; aggravate, or inform and enlighten—and maybe all at once—this is a must-read analysis of one of the most dynamic years ever in Australian politics.

Available in paperback and ebook.

Divided Opinions: The New Politics analysis of the 2019 year in Australian politics
ISBN: 978-0-6481644-5-6
ISBN (Amazon): 978-1-6611355-7-7
338 pages

www.ingramcontent.com/pod-product-compliance
Lightning Source LLC
Chambersburg PA
CBHW030225100526
44585CB00012BA/219